MW00678826

GREECE

Publisher: Aileen Lau
Editors: Emma Tan
Catherine Khoo
Design/DTP: Sares Kanapathy
Sarina Afandie
Illustrations: Shirley Eu-Wong
Cover Artwork: Susan Harmer
Maps: Hong Li

Published in the United States by
PRENTICE HALL GENERAL REFERENCE
15 Columbus Circle
New York, New York, 10023

ISBN 0-671-87902-2

Titles in the series:
Alaska - American Southwest - Australia - Bali - California - Canada - Caribbean - China - England - Florida - France - Germany - Greece - Hawaii - India - Indonesia - Italy - Ireland - Japan - Kenya - Malaysia - Mexico - Nepal - New England - New York - Pacific Northwest USA - Singapore - Spain - Thailand - Turkey - Vietnam

USA MAINLAND SPECIAL SALES
Bulk purchases (10+copies) of the Travel Bugs series are available at special discounts for corporate use. The publishers can produce custom publications for corporate clients to be used as premiums or for sales promotion. Copies can be produced with custom cover imprints. For more information write to Special Sales, Prentice Hall Travel, Paramount Communications Building, 15th floor, 15 Columbus Circle, New York, NY 10023.

Printed in Singapore

GREECE

Text by David Bellingham

With contributions from:
Morten Strange

Editors
Emma Tan
Catherine Khoo

Prentice Hall Travel

New York London Toronto Sydney Tokyo Singapore

C O N T E N T S

INTRODUCTION

HISTORY, GOVERNMENT & ECONOMY

PHYSICAL PROFILE

MEET THE PEOPLE

C O N T E N T S

C O N T E N T S

C O N T E N T S

and people mingle, where

A country where gods

ology and reality

were to have merged.

frescoes, sculpture

Relics of mosaics,

ntings and architecture of 2,000 years' of history fascinate visitors today

Greece's pure-blue waters

tempted many

an ancient nymph and leisure seekers of today.

The mystery of ancient

civilizations beckon...

Introduction

I first arrived in Greece on a boat from Italy as the sun was rising. "Rosy-fingered Dawn" was how Homer described it; and that feeling that I was entering a magical land of gods and poets has never left me. The contrast between the modern style and speediness of Italian life and lying back sipping an *ouzo* (licorice-flavoured aperitif) in a quiet Athens *taverna* (bar) or lazing around in a sun-kissed island harbour, was bliss. Greece is a wonderfully relaxed and laid-back country and the Greek people are so friendly to tourists, even in the crowded beach resorts. They will love you even more if you venture to address them in the exotic Greek language; *kalimera* (good-morning).

Land of Contrasts

Greece is a land of extreme contrasts. Firmly attached to the European continent, the mainland peninsula reaches like an outstretched hand into the "wine-dark" waters of the eastern Mediterranean. The mainland is fringed with a green belt of

Greek Orthodox priest – an influential voice in the community.

Beauties in traditional costume.

coastal plains, brimming with vineyards and olive groves. Behind the coastlands, formidable mountains rise up and seem to touch the heavens – no wonder the ancient Greeks believed that their gods dwelt therein.

The inland mountains form the bulk of mainland Greece, sometimes broken by river valleys. Within an hour by plane from the modern metropolis of Athens and the mainland, you can find yourself on one of a myriad of islands, scattered like stepping-stones around all three sides of the Greek peninsula. Within half an hour's walk from the excitement and bustle of the town or harbour, you can find yourself in the idyllic Greek countryside with only the sounds of goat-bells and the smell of thyme as companions. The rural Greeks are equally hospitable and it is not uncommon to be offered a quick drink back at the farmhouse, before continuing on your way.

Political Beginnings

Greece has the feeling of a country newly born. Two and a half thousand years ago the small city-state of Athene expelled the tyrants which ruled it and replaced them with a political system which promised a vote for every male citizen: the new system was labled "democracy", meaning "rule of the people". It established a role-model for the political systems of the free world. After the fall of Constantinople in 1451, Greece was under Turkish rule for some 400 years, and it is a tribute to the pride and courage of its people that both its language and cultural identity were never wiped out during this "dark age".

As Greece slowly emerged as an independent state during the struggles against foreign rule and intervention in the nineteenth century, it began to rediscover its Classical past, whilst at the same time keeping an eye on the modern world. Everywhere in Greece you will find broken temple columns, their white marble or golden limestone gleaming in the blazing summer sun, or ghostly and romantic under the rising moon. Everywhere you will also see the Greek flag flying; a symbol of the pride of a rediscovered democracy, its blue back-

Classic whitewashed churches dot the countryside.

ground signifying the classical heavens and the ever-present sea.

Greeks & "Barbarians"

The mountains and the sea have always acted as barriers between Greek communities. Each mainland town and each island has its own local traditions and individual identity. What makes this scattered country a unified nation is its language: in antiquity, anyone who did not speak Greek was called *barbaros* (barbarian), perhaps because they appeared to say "bah-bah-bah" when they spoke! The Greek civilization was defined as being different in every way from the barbarians: they were orientals, dark-skinned and wore baggy breeches and jewellery.

This xenophobia (from the Greek word *xenophobos* (fear of strangers)) is to some extent still present in modern Greece. There is a constant fear of new invasions from the east and the Greeks continue to maintain a difference between themselves and the Turks – the troubled past is still too recent to abandon entirely. In the northern mainland, Macedonia is currently pushing for its independence from Greek control. Greece, now a member of the European Community, suffers some isolation since it has no land frontier with any other member of the EEC.

This feeling of comparative political isolation does however have its ben-

Greek's beaches promise the best of sun, fun and sea.

Fast Facts

Total land area (including islands): 131,944 sq km. 169 inhabited islands: 24,909 sq km. Approximately 2,000 uninhabited islets: 257 sq km.
Population: Approximately 10 million (1981 census: 9.71 million).
Capital city: Athens (population approximately 3 million).
Political structure: European republican democracy.
Currency: drachma.
Religion: Greek Orthodox Christian Church (95%); Muslim (1%); Catholic (.05%).
National flag: Four horizontal white stripes and white cross in top left corner on blue background.
Maximum distance from sea: 100 km.
Coastal length (including islands): 15,020 km.
Mountainous land area: Approximately 80%.
Highest mountains: Olympos (2,917m); Parnassos (2,457m); Taygettus (2,407 m); Athos (2,033m).
Navigable rivers: none.
Major sea-ports: Piraeus (Athens); Thessaloniki; Patras; Volos; Igoumenitsa; Kavala; Irakleion (Crete).
Major airports: Athens, Thessaloniki.
Bordering nations: Albania; Serbo-Croatia; Bulgaria; Turkey.
Nearest EEC neighbour: Italy.

Natural Resources and Industry

Minerals: bauxite; lignite; iron; clay; gypsum; marble.
Agricultural land area: 40% pasture; 25% arable; 20% forest; 10% uncultivated.
Crops: wheat; cotton; tobacco; raisins and currants; grapes; olives; citrus fruits.
Manufacturing: steel; foods; chemicals; aluminium; handicrafts; textiles; shipbuilding.
Others: Tourism; fishing.

Wildlife

Common wild plants: oleander; bay; oak; olive; juniper; pine; plane; poplar; chestnut; crocuses; tulips; irises; poppies.
Wild animals: brown bear; roe deer; wildcat; wild boar; wolf; lynx; tortoise; porcupine; wild goat; martin; jackal.

efits, especially since it endows Greece with a uniqueness that any visitor to Greece cannot fail to fall in love with, and the Greek people respond warmly to such love.

Colors of Eternity

Colors are vivid in Greece. Whether approaching the islands by air like the ancient messenger of the gods, Hermes, or like Poseidon across the sea, you will surely notice the jewel-like qualities of the white limestone rock and emerald-green foliage, glistening in the sun amidst the gorgeous blues of sea and sky. The harbour-towns rise like marble temples from the lapping deep-blue waters; the buildings are invariably freshly whitewashed and the whole dramatic effect is like a Cubist painting.

When you step ashore, these gleaming white walls provide the perfect back drop for shop-keepers to display their wares: the browns of polished leather hats to keep the midday sun at bay; the beautiful earth-colors and blood reds of shoulder-bags, rugs and other textiles; the subtle reds, blues, greens and floral yellows of modern folk pottery; the classic blacks and reds of imitated ancient vases. Although Greece has its share of "international" shops, you will definitely always be able to find local goods for sale.

The mainland cities of Athens and Thessaloniki have their share of color too. There is no more impressive sight in the world than watching the sun setting on the white limestone rock of the Acropolis at Athens, its ancient marble columns glowing a warm gold or a host of other colors, depending on the light and the time of the day. The Athenians have a cafe/bar on the top of the Lykabettos hill from which you can view this timeless scene. The Plaka area on the northern slopes of the Acropolis has a maze of narrow streets and alleys lined with colorful shops selling handmade goods and crafts. Here are also some of the best places to eat and drink, whilst enjoying the wonderful spectacle of Greek musicians and dancers.

Spirits of the Land

Greek cuisine, like Greece itself, is a blend of the familiar and the exotic. Centuries of Turkish rule have bequeathed exotic spices and sweets; the infamous Retsina wine tastes peculiar at first, but many grow to love it and, served chilled drawn from the barrel, it is one of the most refreshing alcholic drinks I know. The traditional Greek *taverna* (bar) will offer you a huge wooden tray of different small dishes, from which you can pick and choose. There is no better way of spending a relaxing evening after the exhilarating climb to visit the Acropolis ruins or a hot afternoon in the dusty flea-market below the Plaka.

The music of Greece is another treat. No one can fail to be enchanted by its peculiarly "Greek" melodies and rhythms. Walking through the streets of the old town at night, you will be enticed into *tavernas* by the siren-like sounds evincing from aromatic, lamp-lit lemon-gardens. A group of musicians will entertain you as you share a bottle of wine or eat a meal. They will make you laugh with their satirical songs, touch your heart with their passionate love-songs, and make you cry with their sad songs of the revolution – no matter that you cannot understand the words - Greek musicians communicate soul to soul.

If you feel in a boisterous mood, watch the dancers. Dressed immaculately in national costume, the male dancers perform the most incredible athletic leaps to the rhythms of drums and bouzouki melodies.

Local island dances can be more informal; you might find yourself pulled in to dance the hypnotic weaving hands-on-shoulder dance made famous in Nikos Kazantzakis' ***Zorba the Greek***. A cliché? Not when you are there and doing it!

Long, cool evenings and seaside tavernas.

"Its All Greek to Me!"

Greek language adds yet another exotic element to your experience of this magical country. Do not worry – street-names and many other public signs in the curious alphabet (the word "alphabet" is derived from the first two letters of the Greek alphabet, *alpha, beta*) are usually accompanied by the more familiar Latin letters! It can be fun to try to learn the letters for yourself; the tourist booklets on beginners' Greek are perfectly adequate for familiarizing yourself with the alphabet; and learning how to say "hello, how are you?" and "cheers" in Greek, more than repays your hard work, when you see the smiling responses.

What makes Greece such an experience is this unique feeling of being "at home" and relaxed in a friendly and familiar "modern" country – whilst at the same time seeing, hearing and scenting the unfamiliar, the ancient, the exotic. You can spend the morning on the beach, and the afternoon in the cool of a Byzantine church, golden mosaics glittering from the shadows. You can walk to the high mountain peaks, just a bus-ride away from the center of Athens, and in the evening end up dancing on the slopes of the Acropolis. You can spend a romantic hour wandering around the ancient sites in the moonlight and take a midnight dip in the sea. Culture and pleasure are perfect partners in this ancient and modern land.

History

In Petralona cave, some 60 km from Thessaloniki, a Neanderthal human skull was discovered. It is 500,000 years old and we know from other evidence in the cave that this prehistoric human being had the use of fire. In Greek mythology, the Titan Prometheus stole fire from the Olympian gods and brought it to mankind hidden in the hollow stem of a fennel plant. The gods had withheld it from to stop mankind/them becoming civilized and ultimately challenging their power. Prometheus' gift of fire enabled man to cook, keep warm, make pottery, metal tools and weapons. Some believe that the Petralona people were the earliest human inhabitants of the European continent. If this is so, then the frequently used maxim that "Greece is the mother of western civilization", can be said to be of some truth.

Fertility goddess carved in white marble.

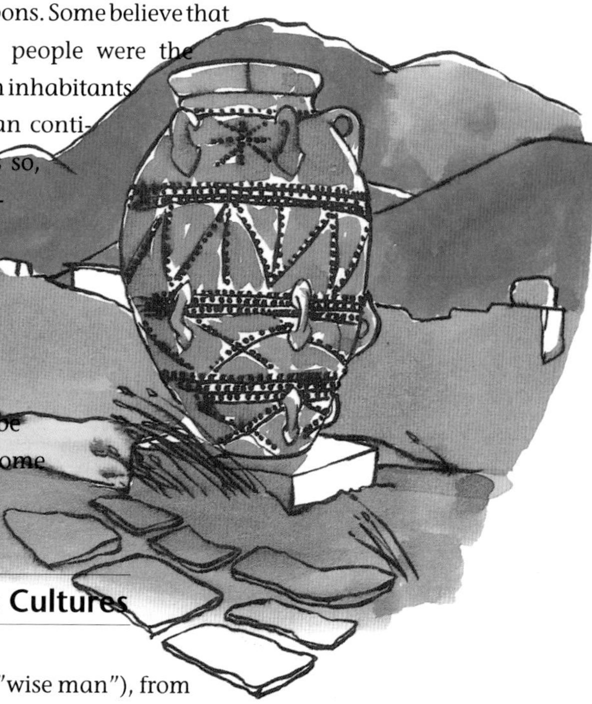

Prehistoric Cultures

Homo sapiens ("wise man"), from

The headless statues of Delos date from the late Hellenistic era.

whom twentieth century man is directly descended, appears to have arrived in Greece from Africa some 40,000 years ago. For many millennia, the Stone Age pre-Greeks remained unsettled, hunting wild animals with stone weapons. In the seventh millennium BC they learnt the secrets of farming from Anatolia (modern Turkey), and settled in the fertile valleys of Thessaly and Macedonia. These New Stone Age (neolithic) farmers did not discover writing, but they have left us evidence of their religious beliefs: using stone and clay they styl-

Scenes of everyday life decorate the walls of the Palace of Knossos.

zed figurines of naked women, their bellies and breasts exaggerated representing fertility goddesses, these offerings were designed to bring rich harvests and children to the settled communities.

Prehistoric art was also produced in the Cycladic Islands. The islands of Paros and Naxos are rich in beautiful white marble, which the sophisticated islanders of the third millenium carved into splendid angular figures of both women and men. The Cycladic culture flourished in the third millenium BC at a time when the eastern Mediterranean was becoming a center of sea trade. They dwelt in small citadels near the sea, their defensive walls suggesting piracy and the possibilities of invasion. The eastern Mediterranean had already learnt to produce metal objects by mixing copper and tin into bronze; the islanders were ready learners and Greece quickly entered into the Bronze Age.

Minoan Civilization on the Islands

It is no surprise to find that the large island of Crete, lying to the south of the Greek mainland and the Cyclades, began to dominate the eastern Mediterranean trade routes and to develop large and wealthy communities. Palaces are the most spectacular archaeological sites here, especially those at Knossos and Phaistos, which date from around 2000-

With over 2,000 islands, the ancient Greeks obviously loved the sea!

1500 BC. These buildings appear to have been the main social centers of Crete, with all levels of society living around the rooms of the presiding monarch. The Minoan culture gets its name from Minos, the legendary King of Knossos.

The Minoans were not just skilled builders and metal-workers, like their bronze age contemporaries elsewhere, they could also read and write using letters – now called Linear A – which can be classified as between Egyptian symbolic hieroglyphs and the alphabet. Their surviving writings appear to list the contents of the storage rooms, but Linear A has yet to be deciphered.

The palaces had no defensive walls which perhaps signifies a peace-loving culture; however, some scholars have suggested that the Minoan Empire, like that of the later Athenian, ruled the seas with its navy, and that no land defences were necessary. Minoan palaces are built on a number of levels and consist of a maze of rooms arranged around a central courtyard. The British archaeologist Arthur Evans excavated Knossos from 1900 onwards and discovered "civilized" features such as bathrooms and sewers, workshops for tools as well as art objects, and storage rooms filled with huge pots to preserve corn and olive oil. The most spectacular discoveries were the colourful frescoes decorating the walls with scenes from the Minoan world such as dolphins, plants and human figures. This wonderful civilization had its darker side: recently the remains of human sacrifice have been found in a religious shrine at Arkhanes, and even more sinisterly at a private house near the Knossos palace – could this be evidence that this "golden race" as Arthur Evans perceived the Minoans, had been indulging in cannibalism?

Barbarianism & the Minotaur

The Greek myths also suggest a barbaric side to the Minoans. The master craftsman Daedalus and his son Icarus were held captive by King Minos and Queen Pasiphaë. The queen lusted after a handsome bull which grazed in the fields around the palace. She tried unsuccessfully to make love to the bull and called in Daedalus, who constructed a hollow wooden cow for her. Inside the cow she had better luck, but became pregnant and gave birth to the Minotaur – half-man and half-bull.

The embarrassed parents had Daedalus construct the "labyrinth", a maze beneath the palace, where their son was imprisoned. Every year the Athenians were forced to send seven boys and seven girls to feed the Minotaur. The Athenian prince-hero, Théseus, took the place of one of the boys and killed the Minotaur. Ariadne, princess of Knossos, fell in love with Théseus and helped him to retrace his footsteps through the labyrinth using a ball of string. The two lovers escaped from Crete by boat, whilst Daedalus and Icarus flew away with wings made of feathers and glued with wax: Icarus flew too near the sun, the wax melted and he dropped to the sea and drowned.

The Demise of an Empire

How did the Minoan Empire fall? All evidence points to a sudden cultural debacle. The answer might lie on the island of Thera (Santorini), where a massive volcanic eruption is now known to have occured around 1500 BC, coinciding with the estimated time of the Minoan collapse. The blast was greater than that of Krakatoa in 1883 and volcanolgists have suggested that the resulting huge tidal waves might well have destroyed the palaces and people of Crete (only 100 km south of Santorini).This solution is not without its drawbacks, especially since the Cretans built new palaces which appear to have also been destroyed around 1450 BC. However the end of Minoan civilization came, it is clear that by 1500 BC, power had shifted from the islands to the mainland.

Mainland Mycenaean Civilization

"Golden Mycenae", as the poet Homer called it, was a fortified citadel built on the rising ground overlooking a fertile river plain in the northeast Peloponnese. It was the home of the legendary leader of the Greeks, King Agamemnon

Death mask of King Agamemnon.

when he invaded Troy. The city of Mycenae has given its name to a civilization which grew up on mainland Greece and took control of the eastern Mediterranean from the Minoans around 1500 BC. The Mycenaean culture spread from the many walled citadels of southern and northern Greece across the sea to Crete, where there is evidence of Mycenaeans moving into the old Minoan palaces. The Mycenaeans, like the Minoans, kept written accounts of their stores beneath the palaces. Unlike the unreadable Linear A script of the Minoans, however, the mysteries of Mycenaean Linear B were unravelled in 1952 by Michael Ventris. Although the subject-matter – long lists of merchandise – is a little dull, the exciting discovery was that this was an early form of Greek.

The best-preserved Mycenaean site is Pylos in the southwestern Peloponnese. Written records discovered at Pylos inform us about the political set-up Each administrative area of Greece ha a king who lived within the citadel itsel surrounded by his courtiers. Outside th walls, farmers worked the land accord ing to a feudal system: records sugges that this was highly organized, wit each farmer contributing a proportio of his produce to the royal court. I return, the king and his "knights" woul fight on behalf of the whole commu nity, increasing its wealth and influ ence.

Peasants, of course, could not a ford such protection and therefore spare themselves the risk of being part of th kings' army, this however also mean that they did not have the capital t rebel, they were therefore forced int

Homer alluded to the gold treasures of Mycenae.

The Rediscovery of Ancient Greece By the Romantics

Lord Byron's Journey

"Yet to the remnants of thy splendour past
Shall pilgrims, pensive, but unwearied, throng"

Lord Byron's words from ***Childe Harold's Pilgrimage*** were prophetic. Travellers in the nineteenth century were attracted, not to the islands and beaches, but to the Classical ruins of ancient Greece. Byron's attitude was typical of European Romantic intellectuals. He himself was to die in the land that he wished to see freed from Turkish rule.

This Romantic love of Greece was given a boost when the Elgin Marbles were put on public display in London. The Parthenon sculptures were considered great masterpieces from the height of ancient civilization. Soon Greece had become a "must" in every Grand Tour of civilization: it would be assumed that every cultured lady and gentleman had visited the Acropolis at Athens, and the other famous Greek classical sites. Byron's poetry tells us how they viewed the ruins:

"...When wandering slow by Delphi's sacred side,
Or gazing o'er the plains where Greek and Persian died".

A far cry from the speedy visits of modern coach tours!

Passionate Philhellenes

The Romantics' fascination with early Greek civilization was rooted in their education which placed the ancient Greek and Latin languages at the top of the curriculum. Their reading of the great Classical writers inspired them to travel to see the places where their heroes had performed brave and mighty deeds, or where the Greeks had valiantly defeated the barbarian Persians in battle. Writers such as Byron would express their rapture in poetic responses, whilst painters returned home laden with watercolor views of shepherds amid the broken columns. Even the composers found their muse in ancient Greece: Berlioz's opera ***The Trojans*** is a Romantic musical rendering of Homer's epic tale.

The best example of this Romantic impulse in action can be seen in the archaeology of the German *Philhellene* (lover of Greece), Heinrich Schliemann, who even as a schoolboy yearned to "make my beloved Greece live again". Serious excavations did not begin until later in the nineteenth century: Olympia, the famous home of the eponymous games, was excavated in the 1860s. Schliemann himself excavated Mycenae and Troy (in modern Turkey) in the 1870s.

Schliemann's aim was to follow Homer's ***The Iliad*** in trying to uncover the Pre-Classical age of the Greek heroes. "I have gazed on the face of Agamemnon" were his famous words when he uncovered the golden face-mask in one of the royal tombs at Mycenae. Schliemann's excavations have more recently been criticised for their lack of careful, scientific methodology.

The modern visitor to Troy can see the rashness of Schliemans'approach; a great trench was dug through the center of the site in the search for dramatic finds and treasure. This technique destroyed as much as it found, but such was his impulsive desire to rediscover the ancient Greeks. His wife Sophie even wore the ancient jewellery discovered in her husband's excavations: such was the desire to return to the "Golden Age" of the Greek past. Berlioz summed up the nostalgic attitude of the Philhellenes when he referred to his reading of the Homeric tales: "I have lived my life with this race of demigods; I know them so well that I feel they must have known me".

submission.

The wealth of this militaristic culture came from conquest of cities across the sea. The Mycenaean kings and queens built massive beehive-shaped tombs (housing possessions of great ostentation and value) outside the palace walls to signify of their continuing wealth and power after death. These were looted in antiquity, but the earlier kings were buried in shaft graves topped by small tombstones. The man most associated with the 19th-century excavations at Mycenae is the Romantic archaeologist Heinrich Schliemann: "I have looked on the face of Agamemnon" were his words when he uncovered the famous gold "Mask of King Agamemnon" in one of the shaft graves; unfortunately the mask is from a pre-Agamemnon period. Finds of gold and silver from Mycenae do confirm Homer's description of "Mycenae rich in gold".

Troy in Legend & Archaeology

Schliemann, romantically tracing the footsteps of Homer's ***The Iliad,*** the poetic account of the Mycenaean war against Troy, rediscovered the site of Troy across the Dardanelles in north-west Turkey. The legendary war would now appear to be partly based on fact. Archaeologists have uncovered many layers of occupation one of which, "Troy 6", was particularly rich but was devastated in a great fire.

The traditional Greek date for the Fall of Troy is around 1300-1200 BC and the pottery and other dating of Troy 6 suggests a similar date. It is highly probable that there was an actual invasion of Troy by a confederacy of mainland

Greeks led by a King Agamemnon of Mycenae, and that the heroes of Homer's poem, such as Achilles, Hector, Ajax and Paris actually existed. It was not unknown for ancient cities to go to war over the abduction of their women.

In the story, Helen of Sparta, wife of Agamemnon's brother Menelaus, was promised as wife to Paris of Troy by the

The passage of time measured by a water-clock dating from the Roman era.

oddess of sexual love Aphrodite. She ad bribed him with this promise for udging her as the most beautiful of the lympic goddesses. After taking her way, Menelaus and Agamemnon ailed across the Aegean Sea to Troy vhere, aided by other Greek leaders such as Achilles, they finally won a siege after nine years of fighting. The stalemate was broken by the Greeks entering the city inside a hollow wooden horse, which the Trojans believed to be a sacred gift: "Beware of Greeks bringing gifts" was the famous unheeded warning of a Trojan priest.

Pottery and other artifacts discovered at Troy, suggest that the city was a typical "Mycenaean" city, with its own wealthy royal citadel and feudal farming community. Like the mainland Greek citadels, it too imported and exported goods from as far away as Egypt. The Mycenaean culture finally collapsed soon after the fall of Troy in the 12th century BC. The palaces at home and abroad were burned and mass emigration followed.

Contemporary Egyptian writings talk of mass invasion of the eastern Mediterranean by the "Sea Peoples", whoever they were. But it is still not clear what caused the downfall of such a powerful civilization. It has recently even been suggested that a series of devastating earthquakes destroyed the citadels. The cultural collapse is clear if you look in the museums at the pottery of 1200 to about 1050 BC. Fine, confident shapes with bold decoration had evolved to small, slipshod forms carelessly decorated. This 150 year period was a "dark age" in cultural terms.

The Great Age of Athens

The "Dark Age" of prehistoric Greec ended when a new Greek-speaking cul ture, called the Dorians, invaded main land Greece from the north. The ol Mycenaeans probably emigrated acros the Aegean Sea to settle on the wes coast of Asia Minor (modern Turkey where they spoke a dialect called Io nian. The Dorians and Ionians were t become the two main cultural strands o Archaic and Classical Greece, rivallin one another in commerce and war, ar chitecture and language. Each had it Greek dialect – the Athenians calle theirs Attic – as well as its own style o architecture, the Doric and Ionic.

Athens was the first of the main land communities to slowly move out o the dark age into a more stable an economically confident community This head-start has kept Athens in th forefront of Greek politics to this day Attic pottery from about 1,000 BC on wards is noticeable for it eggshell thi

The ruins of ancient Athens.

clay, thrown on a fast-spinning wheel as well as its taut shape and precise geometric decoration. Greek culture of the next 300 years is named "Geometric" after the pottery, which is nearly all the evidence we have, since it was not until around 750 BC that a proper alphabet was adopted by the Greeks. Once again, this cultural innovation comes from the east, this time from Phoenicia.

The introduction of writing coincides with a sudden upturn in the Greek economy. During the Archaic Period (c 700-500 BC) there was a population boom; Greek colonies were established from Spain to the Black Sea; commercial competition became heated; complex urban societies developed. It is important to realize that Archaic Greek cities were "city-states" or autonomous urban centres, each controlling their own territories as the Mycenaean kings had once done. This meant that there was never political unity in Greece, except in the case of barbarian (or non-Greek) invasion. Every *polis* (city-state) spoke Greek and worshipped Greek gods; but each *polis* was also proud of its own local traditions and jealous of its neighbours. This political rivalry was the dynamic factor in ancient Greek politics and economics.

If you look at the map of Greece you will see that the habitable coastlands and river plains are separated from one another by high mountains, whilst the islands are obviously set apart in the sea. This encouraged the individual de-

Engraving of Temple of Victory, dedicated to Theseus who slayed the Minotaur.

velopment of the city-state. The old royal monarchies of the Mycenaean age collapsed with their palaces and aristocracies ("rule of the nobility") took over. In the seventh century BC individual tyrants took control of the city-states. Unlike more recent tyrants it seems that they had the support of the people because they promised to curb the abuse of power by the aristocracy.

During the Archaic Period, several city-states vied with one another to control the trade routes. Corinth had the largest port and exported perfumed oils in "black-figure" pots to all areas of the Mediterranean. Sparta's economy was based on state military control of the surrounding peoples of the southern Peloponnese; this also meant that it always had a professional and highly motivated army to fight other Greeks and barbarian invaders. The other great naval power was Athens, who during the sixth century overtook the Corinthians in Mediterranean trade.

Athens Protectorate & Peloponnesian War

Towards the end of the Archaic Period the Athenian tyranny collapsed and was replaced by a democracy ("rule of the people"). This allowed an equal vote to every mature male citizen within a certain wealth bracket: it was by no means a total democracy. Athenian wealth was based on slave labour and

Ancient Greece – A Thriving Society

In the absence of any written evidence, our knowledge of prehistoric Greek culture is highly dependent on art and archaeology, but what this can reveal is indeed considerable, as the following examples show.

From settlement remains along the fertile river plains, we can learn of farming communities dating back as far back as 6000 BC, the earliest being in Macedonia and Thessaly in Northern Greece. Artefacts from these sights suggest links with Anatolia (central Turkey) and the near east. At the settlement of Sesklo in Thessaly (c 5000 BC), the presence of imported obsidian from the Aegean island of Melos, is evidence for maritime trade; the absence of defensive walls suggests a relatively peaceful community; their pottery survives well, household utensils are well decorated with painted designs and then polished to a shiny finish.

By contrast the people of nearby Dhimini (c 3500 BC) surrounded their hill-top village with defensive rings around a palatial residence; this suggests a ruling monarchy and a more war-like culture. Figurines of what are probably fertility goddesses are evidence of religion.

The Art of Simplicity

Around 3000 BC the New Stone Age (Neolithic) peoples learnt metalwork crafts from the east and began to produce more efficient tools and weapons from bronze. The most striking art objects of the early Bronze Age are the white marble figurines created in the central Aegean Cycladic Islands.

The Cycladic culture lived close to the sea in walled settlements, with outlying farmland. The figurines, which range in height from a few centimeters to life-size, are highly stylized. This is partly due to the limitations of the artists' tools: copper is too brittle to use with confidence on stone; therefore they used emery blades, which produced the unnaturalistic, angular human forms.

The naked women hold their arms folded beneath their breasts and above their abdomens, again pointing to their child-bearing capabilities; now glowing white, originally they were coated in bright red paint. The men sit and strum the lyre or stand and play the *aulos* (Greek flute), perhaps these are representations of the travelling poets of the day.

The "abstract" qualities of the Cycladic figurines have provided inspiration for a number of twentieth century sculptors and painters such as Epstein, Brancusi and Modigliani. Henry Moore admired Cycladic sculpture for its "great elemental simplicity".

Minoan & Mycenaean Civilizations

The Minoan culture (c. 2000-1450 BC) was based on Crete and was organized into palace communities with monarchic leadership. Their interior decoration included frescoes with brightly coloured representations of everyday life and nature.

The famous bull-leaping scenes depict young men and women athletically leaping over the horns of large bulls – a possible precursor of the modern bullfight. Their pottery is decorated with flowing curvilinear designs, unsymmetrically arranged around the vessel: subjects include sea-creatures (the octopus is a favourite), flowers and grasses.

The Mycenaeans (c 2000-1150 BC) were apparently more warlike than the Minoans, and this is reflected not only in their heavily defended citadels, but also in the style and subject-matter of their art objects. The Mycenaean pots have similar subjects to the Minoans, but the style is much stiffer and symmetrical: where a Minoan octopus will wrap its tentacles freely around a vessel, the Mycenaean appears with its head in the center of the pot, tentacles neatly arranged in mirror-image on either side. Bronze daggers found at Mycenae depict battles and lion-hunts, the two main activities of royal warrior cultures. The Mycenaeans valued gold and silver objects highly; not only did they use golden goblets with beaten images on their sides, they also placed golden masks on the faces of their royal dead, signifying their hoped-for immortality.

Athenian women were expected to remain at home behind closed doors. At this time the Kingdom of Persia invaded Greece and was repelled by the Athenians at Marathon in 490 BC. The famous victory endorsed Athens as the leader of Greece. Ten years later the Persians invaded a second time under King Xerxes. This time the barbarians landed successfully and their advance towards Athens was mitigated – this time by the bravery of the "300 Spartans" who died delaying the Persian army at the pass of Thermopylai in 480 BC.

The Persians however, marched on Athens and destroyed the Archaic temples on the Acropolis. The Athenians meanwhile had fled to the island of Salamis where later that year they won a resounding naval victory against the Persian navy. The Persian army went home to recuperate, but a large force was left behind to winter in Thessaly. In 479 the Greeks, this time led by the Spartan army, finally defeated the Persians at Plataia in Boiotia. The Greek *hoplites* (foot-soldiers armed with javelins and swords) and the Athenian navy had proven their invincibility.

The victory over the common barbarian enemy allowed Athens to assume the role of protector of the Greeks. A league of city-states was formed on the island of Delos. Members of the Delian League paid annual contributions to maintain the Athenian navy as a defence against any further Persian attacks.

It was not long, however, before the League turned into an Athenian Empire, Athens commencing military action against those who refused to pay.

Under the military leadership of General Perikles, Athens exploited her position by using surplus League funds to subsidize the rebuilding of the temples on the Acropolis. In 431 BC, war broke out between Athens and Sparta and their respective allied city-states: the Peloponnesian War lasted until the final defeat of Athens in 404 BC. The defeat was due to the loss of many Athenian ships and *hoplites* in the disastrous Sicilian expedition of 415 BC as well as to the patience and discipline of the Spartan army.

Alexander The Great – "The New Achilles"

The Spartans failed to exploit their victory. A succession of complex wars between new groupings of Greeks around Sparta, Athens and Thebes diverted mainland Greece's attentions away from a new and unexpected enemy. In northern Greece the Macedonian monarchy was preparing to expand its territory into the south with a huge mercenary army.

In Athens, the orator Demos thenes made a series of public speeches warning his people of the new threat from Philip II of Macedon. His warnings went unheeded and in 338 BC Philip defeated the new Greek alliance at Khaironeia in Boiotia. The king's son led the Macedo-

Statue of Alexander The Great.

ian cavalry into battle: his name was Alexander the Great.

In 336 BC Philip was assassinated and the twenty-year-old Alexander became king. Alexander had received an Athenian education from the great philosopher Aristotle. He was therefore cultured as well as a good fighter. He kept Homer's ***The Iliad*** under his pillow and saw himself as a new Achilles, son of a god, whose destiny was to impose classical Greek language and culture upon the old enemy, the Persians in Asia Minor. In 337 BC he crossed the *Hellespont* ("Bridge to Greece"– the modern Dardanelles) into Asia and began a military campaign which lasted just ten years and set up new Greek colonies as far away as the Indus valley in the east and Egypt in the south.

Alexander's global vision was of a Greco-Persian empire and he expressed his dynastic aspirations by marrying the Persian princess Roxane. In 323 BC whilst holding court at Babylon, Alexander died of a fever. He was just 33, and his early death confirmed to future Greek and Roman generals that he was indeed "a new Achilles".

Roman Hellenism

Alexander's sudden death left the Greek world in turmoil. There was infighting between his generals for control of the empire, but not one of them had Alexander's vision and none were able to gain the upper hand. During the next 150 years the eastern Mediterranean was divided into "Hellenistic" kingdoms, each with its own royal monarchy and mixture of local and dominant Greek culture. The arts flourished as kingdoms vied with one another to become the new center of culture. Great libraries were built at Alexandria in Egypt and Pergamon (in modern Turkey). But Athens, deprived of its former political power, retained its intellectual prestige in its University of Greece.

In 146 BC the Romans, already in control of the western Mediterranean, destroyed Corinth (saving its temples), and the Hellenistic kingdoms fell one after another to the new Roman rulers. One of the last dynasties to fall was that of the Ptolemies in Egypt, whose Queen

A hero from Greek mythology.

Cleopatra and her Roman lover, the celebrated general, Mark Antony, were defeated by the first Roman Emperor Augustus in 31 BC. Greece was now under Roman governorship.

The first few centuries of Roman rule brought peace to the eastern Mediterranean. The Greeks were permitted to keep their gods as well as their language; Athens was even allowed to retain a local democracy. The Romans saw the Greeks as more cultured than themselves: "When captive Greece took Rome captive" was how the poet Horace described it. The Roman emperors Nero and Hadrian were passionate Philhellenes, but took advantage of their power; Nero, not surprisingly, won every event at the Olympic Games! In Athens Emperor Hadrian built a beautiful library and arched entrance to the "Cit of Theseus"; and completed the grea Temple of Olympian Zeus. The first tw centuries AD were a period of settle prosperity. This all ended however i 267 when the barbarian Goths sacke Athens; meanwhile the Roman Empir in the west began to crumble.

Byzantine Greece

In AD 284 the emperor Diocletian divided the Roman Empire into two parts east and west. An emperor and the on in line to be his successor, were to gover each half. Diocletian's successor Galeriu ruled the eastern empire from Thessaloniki, where several of his monument have survived.

In 324, after civil war between riva emperors, Constantine set himself up a the new single Christian Emperor wit his base at Constantinople (now Turkish Istanbul). Greece had by now entered its Middle Ages, known as th Byzantine period, named after the ear lier Greek name for Constantinople Byzantium.

Greece was once more at peace fo most of the next three centuries. Close t the new center of the Empire it profite from both military protection and imperial patronage. The splendidly preserved early Christian basilicas a Thessaloniki bear witness to this. During the fifth century AD Theodosius I ordered all surviving pagan classica

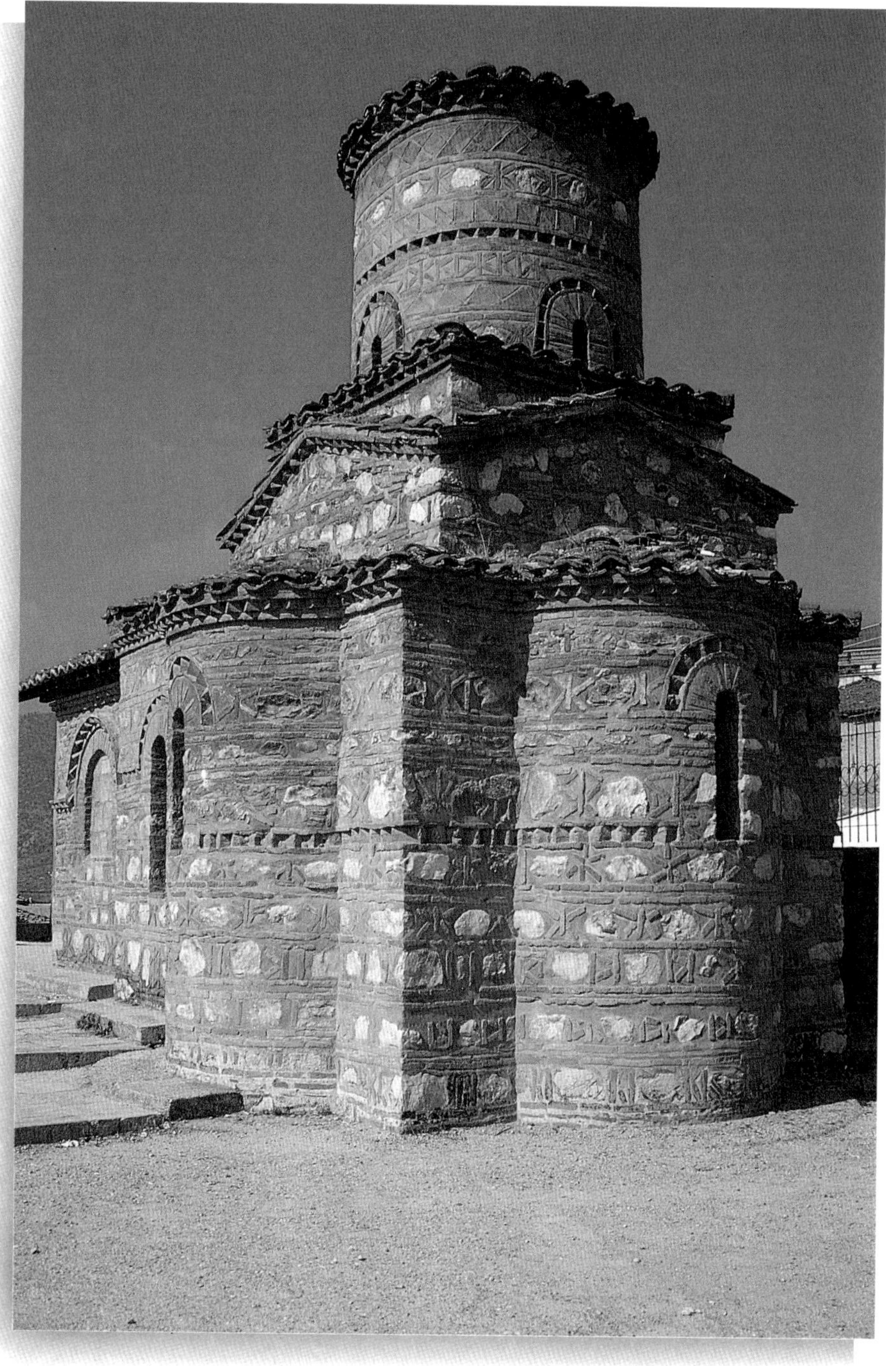

An ornate work of art: a building in Kastoria pays silent tribute to the craftsmen of ancient Greece.

The Creation Myth

Hesiod, a contemporary of Homer in the eighth century BC, lived in central Greece on the slopes of Mount Helicon – one of the homes of the Muses. One day, when he was out tending his sheep, the Olympian Muses, daughters of Zeus and Memory, awarded Hesiod with a staff as token of the poet's craft. Hesiod was instructed to sing the story of how the immortal gods came into being, and how Zeus and the Olympians became all-powerful. The poem, called the ***Theogony*** ("Birth of Gods"), has survived to be our fullest version of the Greek creation myth. I say "version" because other writers produced their own differing accounts of Creation. Modern scholars have pointed out the similarity of Hesiod's creation myth to oriental versions. This is not surprising: Hesiod was an immigrant from eastern Greece (now the west coast of Turkey).

Introducing the Gods

To the Greeks, there was no one individual from whom the cosmos emerged. Hesiod tells us that the feminine "broad-breasted" Gaia (the Earth Mother) appeared in the Void, as the future home of both mortals and immortals. Beneath Gaia was a dark, hellish region called Tartarus, the future destination of rebels and sinners. The young god of physical love Eros also appeared and under his influence Gaia gave birth to her own husband, the starry-cloaked Uranus (heaven). From their union, the seas and mountains were created. The Greeks believed these natural elements to be living Giants or Titans.

Uranus feared that one of his children would one day destroy him, so he pushed them back into Gaia's womb. Her son Kronos (Time), came to her aid by cutting off his father's genitals and flinging them into the sea. The action of the waves on Uranus' dismembered phallus, caused foam to appear out of which Aphrodite, the Goddess of Physical Love was born.

"Ungodly" Relationships

Meanwhile Nyx (Night) made love to Erebus (the Underworld) and from them were born personifications of Death, Misery, Sleep and Dreams, Argument and Strife – the early Greeks had a god for every strong emotion or natural phenomenon. Into this increasingly troubled world came the new, patriarchal gods.

After destroying his father, Kronos made love to his sister Rhea: their children included Hera and Zeus, who eventually married and

temples to be converted into churches. This explains a number of temples have survived for over two thousand years: the Parthenon and the Temple of Hephaistos in Athens were both preserved by their conversion into churches.

In the sixth century Slav immigrants entered Greece from eastern Europe and many settled permanently, in spite of Emperor Justinian's attempts to keep them out. It is still a question how much of Greece became Slav, but in the tenth century, these "barbarians" were forcefully converted to Christianity. Other immigrants from the north moved into Greece during this period, including the Vlachs and Bulgars: all three groups still exist in the nations which border northern Greece.

In the seventh century, the growth of Islam in the eastern Mediterranean led to Arab conquest of North Africa. The next few centuries saw the Arabs taking Crete whilst the Byzantines were busy protecting the northern borders. At the same time the Normans arrived

uled the cosmos. Positions were then delgated to their brothers and sisters; Poseidon ecame god of the sea and earthquakes; Hades, ne unseen god of the Underworld; and the arvest goddess, Demeter. Kronos had been varned by mother Gaia that the same fate was n store for him as had happened to his father Jranus; therefore Kronos swallowed his chilren as Rhea gave birth to them. When Zeus vas due, Rhea replaced the baby with a stone vrapped in cloth, and handed Zeus to the ymphs on Crete for safe-keeping.

Zeus & the Olympian Citadel

eus grew into a strong youth and took his evenge on his father by slipping an emetic into is wine. Kronos immediately threw up the wallowed brothers and sisters of Zeus. Zeus led hem all to Mount Olympus, which became heir citadel. Kronos stormed Olympus with an rmy of Titans, but they were defeated by Zeus nd his fraternity and are now in eternal torment imprisoned beneath the earth as volcanoes and other destructive natural phenomena. he Classical Greeks identified with Zeus and he patriarchal Olympian gods – the Titans were ssociated with foreign barbarians.

rom western Europe and occupied Corfu and parts of mainland Greece. By this ime Greece had become provincial, with he capital Athens now little more than a village.

Venetians, Franks & Turks

n the twelfth century, Byzantium became increasingly overwhelmed by the pread of Islam in the east and the Norman threat from the west. Byzantium turned to the powerful Italian naval power of Venice for help: the Venetians agreed to assist them in return for access to Byzantine trade routes.

However, the Venetians exploited the agreement and soon became an enemy of Byzantium. In 1199 the Venetian navy "assisted" the French and western European crusaders on their way to the Arab-occupied Holy Land: this consisted of a shameless attack on Christian Constantinople rather than on the Arabs. The Venetians saw this as their opportunity to completely dominate the eastern Mediterranean: antique treasures from Constantinople can still be seen in Venetian art collections!

Following this "crusade", the Venetians took control of the Aegean Islands. Although the Turks expelled them after the fall of Constantinople in the sixteenth century, their cultural influence remains: some of the few remaining Roman Catholic churches survive on the ex-Venetian islands.

From the thirteenth to the fifteenth century, mainland Greece was subjected to various western "Latin" invasions. Athens, for example, was consecutively ruled by Franks, Catalans and Florentines. The Greek east fought back and by the early fifteenth century the Peloponnese had returned to Byzantine rule: the wonderfully preserved late Byzantine town of Mistra near Sparta dates from this period. Their success was shortlived: on 29 May 1453, the Ottoman Turks destroyed Constantinople and a new era began for Greece.

ΑΚΛΙΝΗΚΕΝΗΦΕ
ΤΑΙΕΣΤΡΩΜΕΝΗ
ΝΑΦΑΝΩΝ
ΜΑΣ
Α
ΡΟΝ
ΛΑΠΑΚΙ

Government

The story of the evolution of modern Greece is born out of the Turkish occupation, when the rule of repression shaped a people's desire to re-establish their own nation. This was an almighty task, especially given the glorious past of Greek civilization, to which the Greek people and many romantic Europeans aspired. The reality was a bitter struggle utilizing ancient and modern methods of governance towards the birth of a new Greece, with the auspices of the old.

entries guarding the Tomb of the Unknown Soldier.

The Great Leviathan

After the fall of Constantinople, Greece no longer had the protection of the Byzantine army and found herself occupied and ruled by an alien culture. The Ottoman Turkish Empire, moreover, was constantly at war with the Venetian Republic over the control of Mediterranean sea-lanes. For two and a half centuries the Greeks could only stand well back and watch as the two sides

Parliament Building with the Tomb of the Unknown Soldier in the forecourt.

battled over their strategic ports. The war was all the more bitter because of religious differences. The Christian Venetians held many of the important islands, such as Crete, Cyprus and Corfu, but by 1505 the Muslim Turks held Lepanto on the northern shore of the Gulf of Corinth, and quickly gaine control over the Peloponnese.

In 1571 Cyprus fell to the Turks wh were now in a position to invade Eı rope. The Pope assembled Rome, Spai and Venice into a Christian Leagu which sailed out to engage the Turkis

navy in the Gulf of Corinth. The great naval battle of Lepanto was the last ever to be fought with oar-powered galleys. The Turks had previously sacked Corfu and captured 14,000 Greeks to man their ships. On 7 October 1571 the Turkish fleet closed in on the Christian ships, which included an odd mixture of western idealists and opportunists: the English were represented by the three pirate galleys of the bastard son of Henry VIII, Sir Thomas Stukely.

Turkish naval strategy was to try to engage the enemy by boarding their ships with foot-soldiers. At Lepanto they were unable to get close enough: the western forces had equipped their ships with cannon and guns. Soon the Turk-

Lord Byron – the Romantic poet who died for love of Greece.

Airing his views.

sh fleet was sinking and the Greek galey-slaves broke their chains and swam o dry land; 25,000 Turks were killed and 180 ships were sunk; just 7,000 Christians and 12 of their galleys were ost. The tide of Turkish expansion was halted, and the battle of Lepanto was mythologized in the paintings of Titian and the poetry of G.K Chesterton.

Venetian & Turk Rivalry in Greece

During the 17th century the Venetians and Turks continued to fight over the Greek islands. In 1667, Crete fell to the Turks and was to remain Turkish until he 20th century. However, Turkish attempts to attack Europe by land failed, and this allowed the Venetians to push the Turks out of the Peloponnese. By 1686 the Venetians had reached Athens where the Turks were camped on the Acropolis.

An infamous Venetian cannonball hit the Turkish gunpowder stores and the Parthenon temple was badly damaged: not that anyone seemed to care at the time; Athens was a mere village under Turkish rule and the Parthenon was just a collection of pre-Christian columns.

In the 18th century the Turks, once more exploiting Greek ship-building skills, built up their fleet and took control of the Peloponnese. However, after an unsuccessful siege of Corfu, the Turks decided to limit their power in Greece to the mainland and the eastern islands: this situation was to last until their final expulsion.

Meanwhile the native Greeks were exploited by the Sultan who used them to fuel his military campaigns. Greeks were forced to pay high taxes, provide agricultural produce and build ships for their Turkish overlords. However, as under Roman rule, they were allowed to maintain their own religious and social customs.

The Islamic Turks encouraged the activities of the Greek Orthodox Church, seeing it as a useful alternative to the western Latin Church of Venetians and Romans. Greek language and literature once honoured by the Romans, was thus ironically kept alive by Turkish imperialist policy. In the remote monasteries of the mainland and islands,the priests nurtured their Greek identity, waiting for the day when it could once more be exposed to the world.

The Brewing of Discontent

Although Greek adults were not converted to Islam nor were they made to fight for the Sultan, promising Greek children were selected every four years to be trained for the civil service or even the *Janissaries* (the Sultan's elite army). This was one custom which fuelled Gree resentment against the Turks in th growing tide of European Nationalisr of the late 18th century. The Turkis aristocracy despised trade and com merce, and in Greece, this vacuum wa filled by wealthy Greek merchants wh soon controlled the trade-routes wit their merchant navy based on island such as Hydra. This new middle-clas strove to re-establish their Greek ider tity: they sponsored schools, co lected libraries of Greek literatur and met secretly to discuss th possibilities of rebellion.

The Wars of Independence

By the early 19th cer tury, Venetian powe had dwindled and th French hero, Napoleo Bonaparte, had briefl taken control of the Gree territories. After Napoleon' defeat in 1814, the Britis established themselves o Corfu and other wester Greek islands.Various local uprising and conspiracies combined to begin th War of Independence (1821-32). Gree patriotic tradition dates the start of th Greek uprising to 25 March 1821, whe Germanos, bishop of Patras in the north west Peloponnese, raised the Greek fla in Ayia Lavra monastery near Kalavritc today you can still see the flag and littl

The Working of Ancient Athenian Democracy

The ancient Athenians developed the idea of *demokratia* (rule of the people) towards the end of the sixth century BC. After a series of increasingly cruel tyrannies which became intolerable to the Athenian people, it was ironically, Athens' great rival Sparta, which helped the Athenians to expel the tyrant Hippias and his family. The aristocracy (noble rulers) remained in power, but according to Herodotus, one of them Cleisthenes, broke the deadlock by "enroling the *demos* (people) as his followers". Democracy was born.

The Athenians were extremely proud and protective of their new political system. In the fifth century, they were able to expand their own political influence by offering democracy as a "political freedom" package to other Greek city states, who might otherwise have become allies of the oligarchic Spartans. Statues and paintings were set up and displayed in prominent public spaces to propagate the democratic ideology. The most famous were the bronze "tyrant-slayers" who stood heroically in the *agora* (marketplace).

The Democratic Assembly

Athenian democracy was limited: eligible voters were restricted to male citizens of a certain wealth bracket. It has been calculated that about 50,000 had the franchise in 431 BC out of a total population (including foreigners, lower class men, women, slaves and children) of about 300,000. All voters had the right to speak in the *Ekklesia* (Assembly), and all could be selected by lot (i.e. not election) to be one of the 500 members of the *boule* (deliberative council), or even one of the ten leading *archons* (magistrates). Not surprisingly the *strategoi* (military generals) were the only elected officials.

The Assembly met on the Pnyx Hill – the open space and speaker's platform is now used for sound-and-light shows – whilst the Council met in the *Bouleutrion Agora* (Council House). Another new feature of the democracy was the trial-by-jury legal system.

The equipment of the courts can be seen in the Agora Museum: exhibits include a water-clock for limiting length of speeches; named bronze ballots for recording votes; and an incredible allotment machine, used like a modern bingo-ball machine, to make random jury selections.

Democratic Devices

Among other exhibits in the Agora Museum, are *ostraka* (potsherds) with the names of unpopular politicians scratched on them. The system of ostracism allowed the Athenians to exile possible new tyrants. Every citizen would name his most-feared fellow on one of the potsherds and the man whose name appeared most was exiled for ten years: a system which would probably prove popular in some modern democracies!

church where Greek independence was proclaimed.

Forty thousand Turks were immediately driven from the Peloponnese and half of them were killed. The merchant sea-captains of Hydra, Spetsae and Psara transformed their ships into men-of-war and threatened Turkish naval dominion. The uprising had its share of atrocities; the British consul reported that after the siege of Tripolitsa "The prisoners were taken out of the town, and above 12,000 men, women and children were put to death by their inhuman conquerors. Some were hanged, others impaled, many roasted by large fires...200 Jews, who were inhabitants of the city, were put to death, some of them by crucifixion". In retaliation the Sultan publicly hanged the

Greek Patriarch of Constantinople and handed the corpse over to the Jews whotriumphantly dragged it through the streets.

The Philhellenes

As is usual in revolution "Free Greece", as it was now called by European intellectuals, became divided into various political factions. There was always a danger, as there had been since antiquity, that they would end up fighting one another, rather than the common enemy. In the meantime, the Sultan offered Crete and the Peloponnese to the Pasha of Egypt in return for help in quelling the Greek rebellion.

By 1826 the Egyptians controlled the Peloponnese and Missalonghi was captured by Turkish troops. The European powers were hesitant about offering aid to Greece; many saw the Greek Nationalist movement as creating a potential trouble spot in the eastern Mediterranean and preferred the stability of the Turkish Ottoman Empire. The struggle for independence only continued because of the constant pressures put on governments by European liberal intellectuals who called themselves *Philhellenes* (lovers of Greece).

Many Philhellenes volunteered to fight in Greece, imagining that they were defending the intellectual world of the classical past – many of them returned home immediately, disillusioned by the harsh realities of guerilla warfare. The most famous of the Philhellenes was the English poet Lord Byron, who arrived in Greece in 1824 with a retinue of servants, his own doctor and a trunk load of splendid uniforms. He died of a fever within three months, but his death in Free Greek territory made him a symbolic martyr for the European Romantic Movement, who continued to press their governments to assist the Greek cause. In 1827 the British, French and Russians sent a fleet and defeated the Turks at the Battle of Navarino.

Imperial Greece

Victory came at a price for Greece, as the Europeans took charge, deciding to impose the institution of a royal monarchy. In 1832, the 17-year-old Prince Otho of Bavaria, became the new King of Greece – a far cry from the Romantic Philhellenic idea of restoring the classical democracy. The War of Independence had left Greece poor and politically unstable. In 1843, the threat of revolution compelled Otho, to produce a constitution of an elected parliament with limited franchise.

Nationalist ideas were fostered under Otho. Greece began to make claims on land which had belonged to it in antiquity, and Greek children were brought up to believe that they were the direct descendants of the Classical heroes who had once repelled the barbarian Persians, a belief which persists among many Greeks to this day. The classical grid-plan of modern Athens and its many neo-classical buildings are surviving examples of this attitude.

In 1862, further rebellions forced Otho to leave Greece and a new King, George I, took his place. George, "King of the Hellenes", made popular political moves by widening the franchise of the parliament and abolishing the upper chamber.

The Greeks referred to the new constitution as a "Crowned Democracy". However, real economic progress was slow: for example, Greece had only 36,000 factory workers in 1917. To balance its poor industrial base, the Greek merchant navy, boosted by the opening of the Corinth Canal in 1893, became one of the world's greatest.

Expansionism & World War I

In the early 20th century, the radical, liberal Prime Minister, Venizelos, managed to double the population from 2.75 to 4.75 million by an expansionist policy combining diplomacy and force, called the "Great Idea". Macedonia, Epirus and Thrace were annexed from the Bulgarians in the two Balkan Wars, whilst Crete was wrested from the Turks.

In 1913, George I was assassinated and Constantine I took his place as King. Greece remained neutral during World War I, in spite of Venizelos' efforts to join the allies (Britain, France and Russia) in the hope of gaining further territory for Greece. King Constantine refused to agree to Greece joining the war and Venizelos was ordered to resign.

Backed by the allies, Venizelos began a revolution against the king, who conceded immediately and went into exile. In 1917 Greece entered the war by fighting the pro-German Bulgarians. The Bulgarians retreated and the Greeks tried to march on towards Turkish Constantinople; they were thwarted by the signing of an armistice between the Turks and the British.

After World War I, Venizelos successfully negotiated with the allies for Turkish territory on the coast of Asia Minor. However, the Turks resisted, and the Greek army lost a number of battles before finally being forced out of Asia Minor by the end of 1922. Constantine I had returned and Venizelos had fallen from power. By 1929 Venizelos was back and trying to boost the home economy: the time was wrong, as the Great Depression had begun. This desperate political situation for Greece at home and abroad led to the dictatorship of George Metaxas. In 1936 Venizelos died in exile, in the same year Constantine appointed Metaxas as Prime Minister. There had been no election and the parliament was dissolved, never to meet again until after the Second World War.

Metaxas & the Communists

Opposition to the unconstitutional rule

The Elgin Marbles : Treasures in Exile

The history of the Parthenon since it was built in 447-432 BC is ambivalent. It owes its preservation as well as its partial destruction to its conversion into a Byzantine church and later a Turkish mosque. These activities led to the destruction of a number of the sculptures which once adorned the exterior of the building: others were deliberately defaced as pagan tokens.

"Cultural Booty" & Symbols of Democracy

Western European interest in the antiquities of Classical Greece dates back to the 17th century, when in 1674 the French painter Jacques Carrey, made his famous drawings of the pedimental sculptures from the great Parthenon temple on the Athenian Acropolis. Thirteen years later, a Venetian missile struck the Parthenon, which apparently housed Turkish ammunitions: the north and south (i.e. the long) sides were blown apart, and several of the sculptures present in Carrey's drawings, were obliterated.

The man responsible for the Venetian bombardment, Morosini, decided to carry some of the sculptures back to Venice "to add to the splendour of the Republic". He tried to remove some of the eastern pediment, but was thwarted by a sudden fall of building-blocks, which nearly killed his workers. Morosini eventually made do with a few marble lions, one of which still stands before the Arsenal in Venice.

Since the time of Morosini, the sculptures from the Acropolis in general and the Parthenon in particular, have taken on a new political significance. Whilst the Greeks see them as symbols of their lost and found democracy, other Europeans have desired them as "cultural booty" to be displayed in their own museums. There have been exceptions: Carrey preferred to record rather than remove the marbles; whilst the British artists James Stuart and Nicholas Revett made paintings and drawings in 1751-54 which were published as ***The Antiquities of Athens.***

Any justification for the removal of the marbles was to come from arguments about their

Lord Elgin's Marbles.

deteriorating condition if they were left *in situ* Stuart and Revett stated "unless exact drawings from them be speedily made, all her beauteous fabrics, her temples, her theatres, her palaces will drop into oblivion, and Posterity will have to reproach us".

Lord Elgin & The Turks

Before Lord Elgin left Britain for Istanbul in 1799, he had already made plans to obtain

Preserved for antiquity.

ermission from the Turkish occupiers to re-
nove examples of Classical architecture and culpture from Athens. His primary purpose, owever, was not to save them for posterity but export them from Greece where they would e "beneficial to the progress of the Fine Arts in reat Britain".

In 1801, after protracted negotiations, the urkish commander of the garrison which then xisted on the Acropolis, took a payment of five uineas per day in return for the removal of the narbles. The work was then held up by the efusal of the commander to allow scaffolding be erected on the Parthenon, which would nable the workmen to observe the women in ne garden of his harem! Elgin eventually obained an imperial decree from the Sultan.

Over the next ten years, Elgin supervised the emoval of most of the Parthenon frieze, the emnants of the pedimental sculptures and fteen *metope* (rectangular panels at the roof of ne columns) sculptures from the south side; he lso took part of the frieze from the Temple of thena Nike, as well as an Ionic column and one f the beautiful Caryatids from the Erechtheum. hese continue to form the climax of a visit to ne British Museum. Lord Byron was politically nd romantically disgusted by Elgin's activities:

> "Let such approach this consecrated land,
> And pass in peace along the magicwaste;
> But spare its relics - let no busy hand
> Deface the scenes, already how defaced!"
>
> (***Childe Harold's Pilgrimage***)

The Argument

nce the subsequent liberation of Greece from ne Turks there have been calls from Greece as ell as other European countries for the return f the marbles to their home in Athens. The gument for their retention in London is: (a) nat they were taken with permission, albeit om an occupying power – an Act of Parliament necessary to reverse that action; (b) other ountries during the nineteenth century have

One of the treasures saved from destruction.

also removed art objects "illegally" from Greece as well as other disadvantaged nations – why are they not willing to return these to their rightful homes?; (c) The British have preserved the marbles from deterioration – surely they have a right to keep them?

Political Activists

In the early 1980s, the socialist Minister of Culture (and famous Greek actress) Melina Mercouri, spearheaded new demands for the return of the marbles to Greece, by linking their ancient meaning as symbols of the victory of democratic civilization against barbarism (seen for example in the metope depictions of Greeks fighting Centaurs) with their significance for modern Greek democratic ideals.

She made a series of scathing attacks on the legacy of British Imperialism and during a visit to London, she obtained a promise from the British Labour Party leader, Neil Kinnock, that if Labour came to power they would return the marbles to Greece. Since then both Mercouri and Kinnock have fallen from power, and the question remains unresolved. In the meantime, a new museum has been built in an old army barracks to the south of the Acropolis. Space has been left for the marbles, should they ever be returned.

An emerging voice in local politics.

of king and dictator first came from the Greek Communist Party (KKE).

The KKE was founded in 1918 and tended to recruit its members from a number of refugees in Asia Minor; however, the due to the lack of industrial workers (to whom Communism appealed), the numbers of their party were kept small.

In 1929, during the Depression, Venizelos had pushed the Communists underground, with a law forbidding "attempts to undermine the social order". This however only served to gain the KKE an increasing amount of public sympathy, particularly when the unpopular Metaxas came to power.

In the 1930s the Communists organised strikes, including a mass demonstration by the tobacco workers Thessaloniki, in 1936. Constantine I wa terrified of the consequences of the grow ing Communist threat; obviously h own position as monarch was in dan ger. This gave Metaxas an excuse fo repressive action: the KKE was declare illegal; strikes and demonstrations we banned; political enemies were exile to the islands; the press was censore Metaxas imitated the fascists of Ge many and Italy by founding a Yout Movement and propagating a return the racial purity and national pride Classical and Byzantine Greec Metaxas' dream of a "Third Greek Civ lization" was never fulfilled: World W II led to further problems for Greece an emerging nation.

World War II

: was the geography of Greece and its .aval importance which once more ıade it difficult to remain neutral. The ıreat came, not from the Allies or Ger- ıany, but from the Italians under Mus- əlini, who in 1940 accused Greece of ȷnoring the Albanian border and in- aded. The Greeks rallied to the nation- list cause and defeated the Italians in .lbania. Metaxas continued to pursue neutral policy in the war, but he died ı 1941, and the British were allowed to se Greece as a base against Hitler.

On 6 April 1941, Hitler invaded ugoslavia and Greece, the attack was ıccessful: by 21 April the Greek army ad suffered a number of brave defeats nd the British Commonwealth army ·treated to the Peloponnese and then › Crete. Hitler swiftly launched air at- ıcks on Crete and after heroic resist- nce from the poorly armed Greek vil- ıgers (several hundred German para- ıutists were killed), on 25 May his ttack proved successful.

Hitler divided occupied Greece into erman, Italian and Bulgarian portions. ny resistance from the Greeks was se- erely dealt with. Two hundred Cretan illagers were shot in revenge for the erman losses; 1,400 Greeks were mas- ıcred in 1943 near Kalavryta. Entire ·wish communities – a feature of Greek ›wns since the Middle Ages – were xported to concentration camps. The reeks, prompted by the KKE communists, organized themselves into Resistance groups. By 1941 the National Liberation Front and the National Popular Liberation Army had been founded.

The KKE hoped to exploit the political situation once the war was over and they were soon fighting right-wing groups who had the same idea. Winston Churchill, hoping for the return of the monarchy in Greece, sought to overthrow any Communist elements. Churchill and Stalin signed an agreement allowing Britain to influence the future political system of Greece.

Churchill's "Terror" & the Civil War

In 1944 a new government was created with George Papandreou as Prime Minister. The liberal Papandreou was anticommunist and supported the monarchy: it seemed that Churchill had achieved his aims for Greece. Many Greeks were annoyed by foreign intervention in their affairs and the KKE mobilized demonstrations in Athens which were broken up in violent confrontations with police and troops. A telegram from Churchill to the British General Scobie stated: "We have to hold and dominate Athens...without bloodshed if possible but also with bloodshed if necessary". In the next few years there was a purge against anyone associated with the Left. An estimated 80,000 fled from what became known as the Terror, and civil war broke out between government forces and the "Democratic Army". The British abandoned their "protectorate" role in 1947, and the Americans took over, supplying the government with arms and military advice to curb the revolutionary threat. By 1949, after several defeats, the Democratic Army had ceased its activities; half a million people had died during the civil war.

In 1951 Greece joined NATO and its political future was headed by the new Greek Rally party under Field Marshal Papagos. Greek Rally believed in a free market within the western alliance; there were social problems which they failed to address, but worse was the Cypriot question. Since 1878 Cyprus had been under British annexation; in the 1950s the Greek Cypriots called for union with Greece but the British refused, leading to armed uprisings. In 1955 Constantine Karamanlis became the Greek Prime Minister, with his right-wing National Radical Union party. In 1959, after negotiations between Karamanlis and the British, Cyprus became an independent republic with legal rights for both Greeks and the Turkish minority.

The Fiasco of Democracy & the Colonels

In 1961 George Papandreou formed a Centre Union Party, whose aim was to win the votes of those who had become disillusioned with the Left and the Right. The post-war right-wing governments had boosted the Greek economy: average incomes had doubled; tourism an other industries had flourished; but gros wealth inequalities existed, and th move from a farming to an industria ised economy produced social problem in the cities. The Left still had a grea deal of popular support because of it spearheading of the Resistance durin the war.

Karamanlis managed to win th 1961 election, but Papandreou refuse to accept the outcome, saying that th voting had been rigged. In 196 Karamanlis resigned and Papandreo was successfully elected. By 1965 Gree politics had become a fiasco; after series of political intrigues Papandreo resigned and the young Kin Constantine II refused to allow elec tions. In 1967 there was a successfu military coup by a group of hithert unknown army officers, now known a the infamous "Colonels".

George Papadopoulos and the othe Colonels ushered in a new nationalis anti-communist state in which eve Papandreou was seen as a subversiv enemy of Greece. Western tourists t Greece were shocked to find that the fashionable 1960s long hair and min skirts were frowned upon by the ne regime. Any criticism of the Colone was swiftly dealt with by the securit police and George Papadopoulc emerged as a dictator. In 196 Constantine II went into exile after a abortive attempt to depose the new sy tem. In 1973 Papadopoulos responde by abolishing the monarchy and ma ng himself president of the Greek Republic. Six months later the security police chief Ioannides pushed Papadopoulos out and the Colonels moved on Cyprus to bolster popular support for the dictatorship. They failed to assassinate the "left-wing" Cypriot Greek Archbishop Makarios and the Turks themselves responded with a massive invasion of the island. The Colonels failed to counter the Turks and Karamanlis was called back from exile to become the new "saviour of democracy".

Karamanalis & the New Democracy

In the ensuing elections, Karamanlis's right-wing conservative party, New Democracy won 54 per cent of the vote. Significantly, the Communists were allowed to participate in the "free" elections and Andreas Papandreou (son of George) campaigned with his new Socialist party PASOK (Panhellenic Socialist Union). Cyprus was now divided, and relations with Turkey were obviously hostile. Karamanlis decided that the future of Greece lay in Europe and entered the European Community in 1979. The Socialist Papandreou criticized this move as being in the interests of big business; at the same time PASOK called for the closure of American bases in Greece and withdrawal from NATO. Papandreou exploited popular feelings of resentment against America and the western powers: many felt that the west had connived in the Turkish victories in Cyprus.

In 1981, PASOK won its first elections under the banner of "Change". The promised "changes" of withdrawal from the EEC and NATO have yet to be fulfilled; the Cypriot problem remains unsolved; Turkish relations remain bitter. To many Greeks, PASOK has proved a deep disappointment. Support for the party dwindled in the 1980s, and the situation was not helped by various scandals, including charges of corruption.

Greece Today

In 1990 the right-wing New Democracy won a narrow victory in the elections. They polled 47 per cent, with the defeated center/left PASOK with 39 per cent and the far left parties gaining 10 per cent. The government faces not only severe social and economic problems with growing unemployment at home, it also has to deal with an increasingly complex foreign policy situation: the Cypriot question will not go away and Turkey appears as menacing as ever after its involvement in the Gulf War. Most crucial at the present time is the Balkan problem which has returned, with fragmentation of what was Yugoslavia, causing ethnic problems on Greece's Albanian border; Macedonia is also making noise as it persists in demanding its autonomy from Greece. The evolution goes on.

Economy

Since antiquity, Greece has been at the center of important trade networks between the western and eastern Mediterranean, as well as Africa and northern Europe. The nature of the land with its islands and coastal settlements, has meant that for hundreds of years, Greece has been inspired to produce ships and sailors of the highest calibre. Shipping has always been the most efficient means of transportation, and merchant shipping will always play an important role in the Greek economy.

Fishing will always remain a way of life.

The Greek merchant navy has grown rapidly since World War II, from about two to over 50 million tons of Greek-owned ships: it now accounts for more than 16 per cent of world merchant shipping and enjoys a good international reputation. This is more than other "naval" countries such as Great Britain and Japan, and is particularly surprising consider-

Greece is a world player in merchant shipping.

ing that Greece does not have its own national trade to support such a fleet. Both men and women find employment at sea, and in spite of the current recession, there is still a demand for more sea-persons. Greece's full entry into the European Economic Community (EEC) in January 1981 boosted the EEC merchant navy from 20 per cent to 30 per cent of the world's shipping – this is the major Greek contribution to European trade.

Fruits of Land & Sea

The lack of good fertile land in Greece has always been a major problem. In antiquity, this led to the Greek colonisation of other Mediterranean lands. I the 20th century the reverse has hap pened, with 150,000 Greek refugee fam lies being settled on the land after ex pulsion from Turkey in the 1920s. In th same decade, land reclamation mo than doubled the cultivated area, b the average farm was still just ten acre The other economic problem caused b the large numbers of farmers was th only 15 per cent of the population we available for industrial jobs: within 20th century context, this lack of a stron industrial base has inevitably led to weak economy. Within the context the EEC, these small-holdings have b come increasingly unprofitable.

The introduction of modern farm machinery and chemical fertilisers i ne 1960s led to larger farms and a ramatic decrease in manpower. Although Greek agriculture is becoming ncreasingly efficient, many families who once lived off their small farms ave now moved to the towns, increasing urban unemployment.

Greece's geographical position gives the advantage of an early harvest eason in relation to other EEC members nd much of its agricultural export omes from these early products, in addition to high quality fruits and vegetales. Water supplies and irrigation techiques are being improved to combat he dry summers.

Agriculture provides about 20 per ent of the GNP and 35 per cent of its xports. Although it is self-sufficient in erms of wheat and vegetables, meat as to be imported at high prices: the EC is trying to encourage Greek meatroduction by selling it high-productivty animal feeds.

The Mediterranean Sea is low in utrients and fish populations are relaively low. Ironically, the greatest numers of fish in the Gulf of Athens are ound within five to ten km of the main ewage outlet at Keratsini, where the ea becomes "enriched".

There are about 30,000 full-time ishermen, whose productivity is roughly ust a quarter of their North Sea counterarts: about 25 per cent of the 120,000 ons of fish caught every year are from ong-distance Atlantic catches, or from nland waters and hatcheries. As a reult, Greece has to import five times as much fish as it exports: this is the reason for the relatively expensive prices in the fish restaurants.

Natural Resources

There is a shortage of oil in Greece, eight million tons of oil have to be imported every year, at a huge cost, which neutralizes any money made through tourism, for example. There have been some bitter disputes with Turkey, over oilfield ownership in the Aegean, which have yet to be settled.

The largest oil refinery is at Aspropyrgos (five-million ton capacity), with a smaller one at Thessaloniki (two million tons). Lignite deposits provide Greece with most of its energy, but these are likely to run out soon. There are some hydroelectric power stations, and these are likely to increase in importance, although seasonal rainfall patterns can create problems. Nuclear power is present, though only in small quantities. A tiny amount of natural gas is drawn from the small Cycladic island of Melos.

Mineral ores account for about five per cent of the GNP and 15 per cent of Greek exports. Over three million tons of bauxite are mined every year in central Greece, to be used prodigiously in the production of aluminium. Bauxite contributes by far the largest amount of mineral production; the 30,000 miners also find jobs in magnesite and nickel mines.

Coping With Tourism

Local wares make colourful souvenirs.

Greece is a very attractive destination for the many different types of tourists. On the one hand there are the 169 inhabited islands which, together with the mainland, produce a coastline equal in length to that of less sunny France. The proximity of these resorts by air encourages the beach-lover of every social class: there are exclusive and expensive villa holidays, as well as very cheap package deals. On the other hand, there are the classical and Byzantine archaeological sites, which attract the culture-vulture, as well as a surprising number of interested beach people on day trips.

The popularity of the cultural tour can be seen in the increasing number of package travel agencies who now run coach tours around the ancient mainland and the island of Crete. Yachting around the islands is also a growth industry, and has the benefit of taking pressure off hotel accomodation, whilst bringing money to local shops and restaurants. There is also a small but significant rise in the number of nature-lovers and mountain walkers visiting Greece, reflected by the increasing number of Greek wildlife and mountain-trail books currently available.

Who Are the Tourists?

In the 1970s the former Yugoslavians accounted for the largest number of non-Greek tourists: this source has been devastated by the current civil war. Germans now form the largest tourist group (greatly boosted by the recent unification), followed by the British, French and Scandinavians. American visitors have recently been put off by the weak dollar, as well as b international terrorism which emerged in Ath ens, during the Gulf War. By way of compens tion, the Japanese, Asian and Australasian tou ist is on the increase.

Economy & Ecology

About eight million people visit Greece eve year, a figure which many Greeks consider have reached saturation point but one whic makes tourism one of the biggest sources income for the Greeks. Tourists spend in cas about $2,000 million a year and this influx foreign money is largely responsible for th general increase in the standard of living e joyed by Greeks today.

The adverse affects of tourism are visible all but the most insensitive tourist: the scarci of water and often antiquated sewage systen ave led to pollution problems on both the nainlands and the islands; the island environ- nent in particular has suffered from the huge ncrease in package tours over the last twenty ears. Hotels have been built, often too rapidly, n previously unpopulated coastlines and the umber of unspoilt islands has dwindled to rtually zero. The problem is made worse by ne lack of sandy beaches on the otherwise ngthy coastline: as a result, resorts tend to be ver-crowded. At the same time, those Greek estaurateurs and craftsmen who have been nable or unwilling to compromise to the "in- ernational" tastes of foreign tourists, have gone nder.

Associated service industries include hotels, estaurants and transportation. The EOT (Greek ourist Organization) is the policy-maker. About 00,000 people are employed in tourism, hough jobs are mostly seasonal. Numbers of otels and restaurants have boomed every- where, providing employment for all levels of ociety. The island ferries are still run by a umber of different competitive companies. A rge number of tourists choose to go island- opping, greatly boosting the ferry business hich used to cater only to native Greeks visit- ng relatives or transporting goats or vegetables o neighbouring islands.

Diversification

he Greek tourist industry needs more tourists o visit the less frequented islands: for example the Ionian group – Zakynthos, Lefkas and ephallonia rather than neighbouring Corfu. or this reason, international runways have been uilt at Zakynthos and Cephallonia. The disad- antage of this diversification policy are that nore locations will become spoilt. Tourists are so being encouraged to visit all year round: kiing and mountaineering holidays are on the ncrease, as are cut-price package tours to the esorts in the early and late seasons. All-year mployment from tourism would be of great enefit to the Greek economy but of severe etriment to the environment and perhaps in ne long run to the ancient sites.

Boom Industries

Manufacturing industries were virtually non-existent at the start of the 20th century and only began to develop properly in the 1960s, when industrial production doubled. Now 35 per cent of the GNP and 50 per cent of its total exports come from industry.

The textile industry is particularly large, accounting for 30 per cent of industrial exports. This is followed by the chemical industry and metal-processing. However, these industries provide relatively few jobs compared to shipbuilding and textile firms. Many Greek workers have emigrated to Australia or western Europe where wages and job prospects are higher.

The Civil Service & Taxation

The civil service and public corporations provide jobs for thousands of school and college leavers every year. The educated country child becomes socially mobile within these white-collar jobs and some move on into the private sector, which is on the increase due to right-wing policies.

Greek bureaucracy was learnt from old France, and its complexity is a hindrance to modern requirements. However, those employed in the bureaucratic and government systems are rewarded with secure jobs and guaranteed pensions.

Ancient Greek architecture has boosted the tourist industry.

The taxation system is relatively weak: most tax is indirectly collected from sales of consumer goods, but Greece continues to have a sizeable "black economy" based on tax evasion. Various steps have been taken to curb this, including the publication of everybody's tax returns for all to see: the tax lists became a best-seller!

Agricultural income, unless exceptionally high is exempt from taxation, because of the problems of collecting it from the remote mountain districts. The absence of a tax on bank interest is due to the need of the government to encourage people to save, in order to pay off their own budget deficits.

As usual in the European economies, it is the wage-earner who suffers from heavy taxation. High taxes and threats of unemployment push many white-collar workers into "moonlighting": the schoolteacher offers extra lessons; the industrial mechanic mends cars. The government has tended to turn a blind eye towards these activities: after all it means that people have more money to spend on taxable goods.

Tourism & the Recession

Tourism is controlled by the EOT (Greek Tourist Organisation) which employs some 100,000 persons, although this is mostly a part-time seasonal figure. Over five million tourists visit Greece every year, and now bring in an annual income of $2,000 million: this is about

Fruits of the land.

half as much as Greece's total exports and twice that made by the merchant navy.

Woman-Power

The role of women in the Greek economy is ever more prevalent, many women finding employment alongside men in traditionally male preserves. About half of Greek women now work away from home, whereas in the past there were many "cottage industries". Until recently, it was the law that a woman had to bring a dowry with her when she married; today's Greek woman can provide for herself.

The civil service and government-owned businesses offer the best job op portunities to women, but the fact tha the work-day finishes at 2:30 pm mean that women are still under pressure t get home early enough to look after th house and cook the family meals. Mos would agree that working women i Greece are, as in most other Europea countries, still judged higher on thei family and household success than o their careers, but they are making in roads into traditional ideas.

In the rural regions, traditions lin ger and here you will see that wome contribute a large proportion of labou – wives and daughters bend to thei work in the fields, whilst their me lounge around the cafés. "May you hav male children and female sheep", re

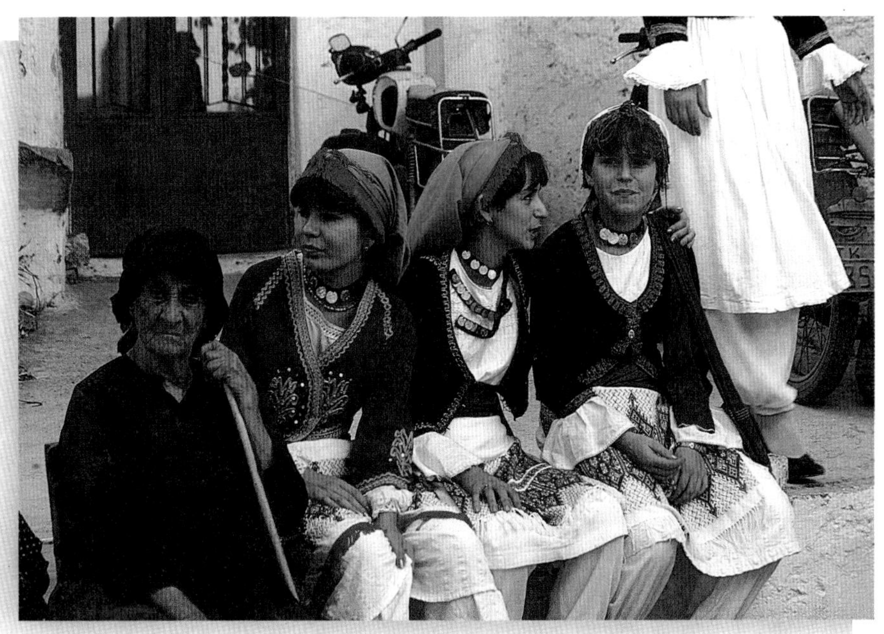

The old and the young in traditional costumes.

ɿains a common saying in Greece.

Welfare & the EEC

ɾreece has been badly hit by the reces- on, and has one of the worst inflation ɿtes in Europe. There are social services nd health care schemes, and these ɜem to run reasonably efficiently. hough it would be an exaggeration to ɔeak of a "welfare state" in the mature ɜnse of Britain or Denmark, social wel- ɿre systems have developed quite rap- lly over the last 25 years.

Greece now compares favourably ith countries such as the United States r West Germany. National insurance ow provides, at least theoretically, an umbrella for all. Whilst 20 years ago only urban workers had access to social welfare, today every Greek has a right to health care and an old-age pension.

There are still problems: new hospitals are badly needed to cope with the expanded health service; unemployment benefit is limited to the short term and entitlement is restrictive.

It remains to be seen whether Greece can produce a stronger industrial base, maintain and build on the potentials of its merchant shipping and cope well with its relations in the EEC. An indication that Greece, although hard-hit by unemployment, is coping with modern economic problems, is evident in the relatively low numbers of young beggars on the streets.

Geography & Climate

The Greek peninsula and its associated islands first appeared in its present form when a barrier stopping debris on the Strait of Gibraltar gave way, causing the Atlantic to spilled over into the Mediterranean basin, leaving the high mountains exposed above water. The mountain ranges of the mainland remained as an extension of the Dinaric Alps of Albania and Serbo-Croatia, with the Alpine spur of Rhodopi forming the border with Bulgaria. If someone pulled the plug on the Mediterranean, you would be able to walk a ridge of mountains from Albania, through mainland Greece and the Peloponnese, across to Crete (the highest of the islands) and on to the Turkish Tauros Mountains.

Most of Greece is no more than 100 km from the sea.

Geologically, Greece consists mainly of limestone or schist mountains, with sandstone and sedimentary rocks in the alluvial river plains. The limestone is very porous, producing many subterranean waterways and caves on both the mainland and the is-

The rugged splendour of the mainland.

lands. No land in Greece is further than 100 km from the sea, and Greece is very much a maritime land.

Geographical Area

Greece covers an area of 132,500 sq km – two to three times the size of England. One sixth of this territory is in the form of islands, most of which are small, although Crete, a little smaller than Cyprus, covers 8,378 sq km. The large island of Euboea, off the east coast of Attica, is separated from the mainland by a narrow strait – the bridge at Halkidha spans just 70m.

Technically speaking, the Peloponnese – the Greek means "Island of Pelops" (the ancient hero) – has also become an island since the breaking of the isthmus of Corinth crossing, by the 'orinth Canal in 1893.

Greece is geographically a fragiented land, which means that disances from one part of Greek territory) another can be further than you might xpect. The eastern island of Rhodes, for xample, is 830 km from its western ister Corfu. The small Greek island of 'astellorizo lies 70 km east of Rhodes nd north-east Greece is 750 km from ne south coast of Crete.

Mountainous Greece

Aost tourists think of Greece s a land of sandy beaches nd rocky coastline, but t its core is a wild and often esolate region of mounains. In fact over hree-quarters of he Greek mainand consists of nountain territory. The nainland covers the iorth-east Mediterranean coastline nd is bounded to the north by frontiers vith, (west to east) Albania, Serbo-Croatia, Bulgaria and Turkey. These iorthern boundaries push Greece away rom the European continent and out nto the Ionian Sea to the west and the Aegean Sea to the east. Thus mainland Greece forms a peninsula which reaches out longingly towards its island chilren.

The islands surrounding its rugged oast are scattered across the Mediterranean like knucklebones thrown from the hand of the mainland towards the coasts of Turkey, to the east and Egypt and Libya, to the south; to the west projects the Italian peninsula.

The islands are in reality the peaks of former mountains whose foothills were submerged long ago when the Mediterranean bowl was flooded with sea-water. So when you swim you are diving from the top of a mountain and when you go walking you are climbing its peak! There are no active volcanoes in Greece, but some of the islands – most notably Thera (Santorini) – are known to have once been volcanoes.

The highest and, since antiquity, most renowned Greek mountain, stands at the north-east corner of the peninsula, commanding views of the plains of Thessaly. This is Mount Olympus and it rises majestically to a height of 2,917 m. To its west is a central spinal column of mountain ridges known as the Pindos Mountains, whose peaks average over 2,000m and whose higher slopes wear an evergreen mantle of pines and firs. A criss-cross effect is caused by lesser ranges running from east to west.

It is to the mountains and higher valleys that the urban Greek retires for

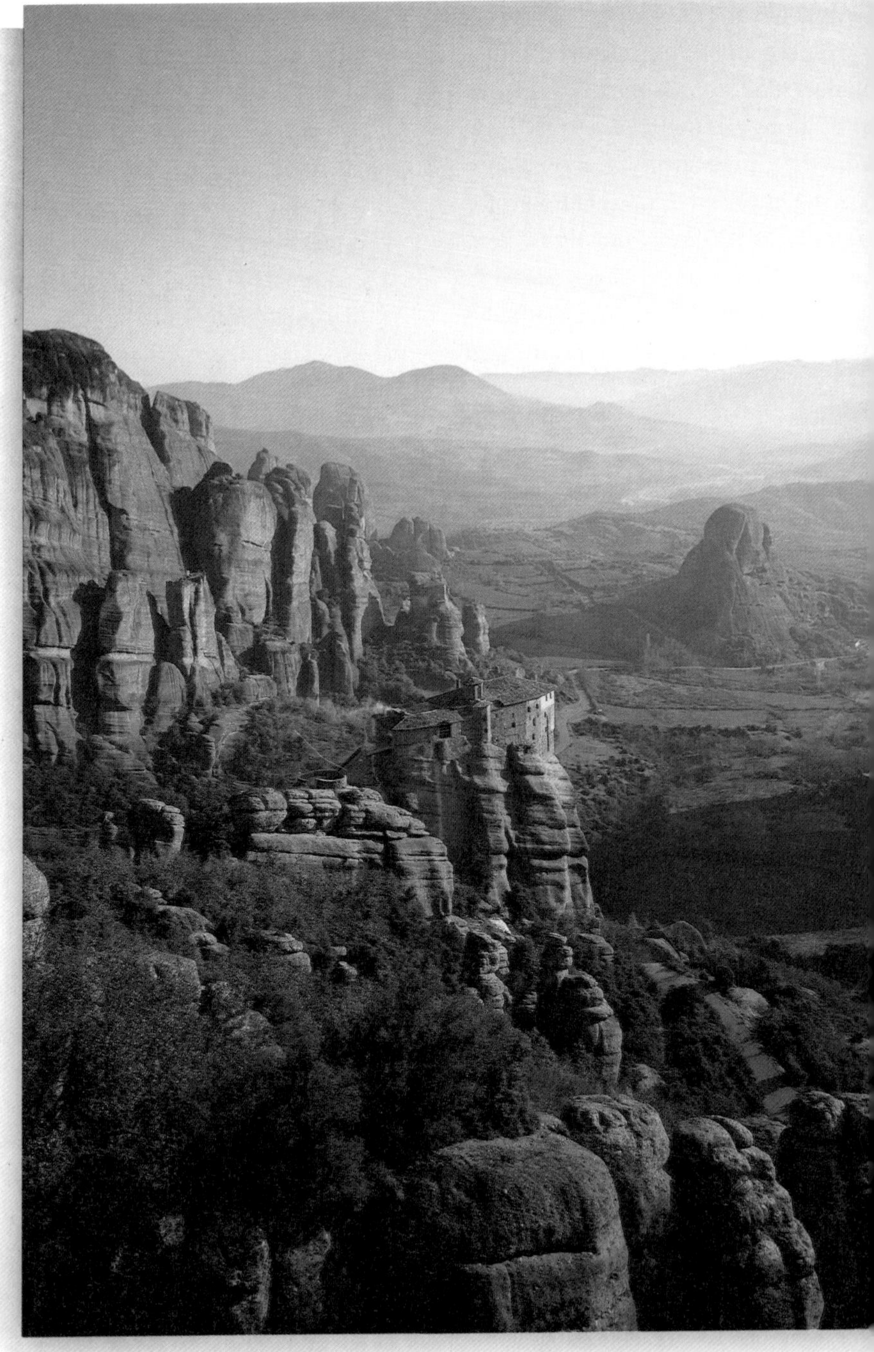

Spectacular views atop craggy landscapes.

coolness in summer: the Pindos peaks often retain their snow caps well into June. The climate of this mountain region is quite different from that of the mainland coasts and islands. Even in the hot, dry months of July and August, the higher slopes remain comfortable for the walker. September is a variable month in the northern mountains: walkers have woken up to find their water frozen even at 2,000m. As in any mountain climate, the visitor must take care of occasional volatile conditions: in summer, heavy and spectacular thunderstorms can blow up without much warning. The temperature drops dramatically at night, even in the warmer months.

In the winter, the mountain slopes are generally under snow from November to April and skiing is becoming popular with the development of resorts in proximity to Athens.

Rivers & Valleys

The criss-crossing of north-south and east-west mountain ranges divides Greek territory into a grid-pattern, with small valleys in the intervening spaces. In the north-east lie the valleys of Thrace framed to the west by the river Nestos and Macedonia, and to the east by Turkey and the Evros delta.

Rivers rather than mountains have divided the territories here since antiquity, and in Thrace they are relatively broad and fast-flowing, though none of

Greek Beaches

Had you been travelling in Greece thirty years ago, the chances are you would not have been going for a beach holiday. Certainly if you had chosen to take such an "eccentric" vacation, the facilities would not have been there for you to enjoy a beach holiday in the modern sense: walking straight onto a stretch of sand from a hotel with international cuisine and en suite bedrooms, and being transported reluctantly back to the airport by coach after seven, ten or fourteen days. The facilities were not there because travellers went for the antiquities, not the sun.

Times and fashions have changed: the Classics and the related interest in Greek archaeological sites are no longer at the core of western education, meanwhile travel companies have exploited the desire of an increasingly wealthy northern European working population, to escape the unpredictable weather back home and soak up some sun in an exotic but comfortable destination, only a few hours air-travel away. The Greeks have been fast to cash in on this.

Which beach for you?

Some tourists will prefer the more crowded beach resorts, with their concrete and glass backdrops giving a fairly accurate impression that you are back home in the municipal swimming pool. Others will prefer a backdrop of shade provided by overhanging pine trees, with hardly another tourist in sight. The more peaceful beach is obviously not easy to find, particu
larly on the mainland; but such beaches exis
everywhere, if you are only prepared to use
little effort and imagination.

I have found my favourite Greek beache
simply by walking out of the resort or harbou
town and along the coastline. You will often fin
that the coast road is worth taking when search
ing for your ideal beach. There are often nc
very promising-looking steep paths or track
leading through the olive groves on the sea
ward side of the road, down to hidden coves
often these locations have pebbles rather tha
sand, but you may feel that this is a small pric
to pay for solitude and excellent snorkelling, i
crystal clear water.

In many resorts you will find it possible t
pay a local fisherman to take you out in his boa
on a trip along the coast: generally such trip
include the added temptation of landing at
deserted, sandy beach, inaccessible from th
inland roads. There are even whole day outing
which include a barbecue. These kinds of trip
are unlikely to be organized on a mass touris
level – that would defeat the object – and yo
should scout around the harbour looking fo
small bill-boards.

Watersports

The more vigorous beach activities include any
thing from the humble pedalo to waterskiing
parasailing, and of course, windsurfing. Th

the Greek rivers are navigable.

The wonderful valley and mountain scenery of Greece is best seen from the railway, which winds along on a scenic route beneath the Rodhopi Mountains. This area of Greece is covered with trees and rolling hills – it feels more north European than the rest of Greece.

In Attica and the Peloponnese, the coastal plains often encroach into the
mountains, forming habitable territo
ries. Athens is a typically large squar
area of fairly flat land, surrounded b
the sea on one side and mountains o
the other three: its dramatic limeston
outcrops, such as the Acropolis itself
are also common in otherwise flat area
of Greece. The rivers which run throug
Athens are hardly noticeable and ofte
canalized: Greece has no equivalent o

harges are very modest compared to other Mediterranean resorts, with US$8 per hour being the approximate going rate for an hour's windsurfing. These facilities, including good lessons for beginners, can be found in all the major resorts, and many of the minor ones. Scuba-divers, however, will find themselves restricted to a smaller number of centres, owing to government attempts to combat antiquity hunters. Recognized centres include; Mikonos, Rhodes and Corfu, with the Halkidhiki peninsula on the mainland. The main resort beaches are sandy and shallow, but good snorkelling can usually be found just along the coast, by looking for rocky terrain.

Sun Nymphs

Activities for the less vigorous, include sitting under the shade of a beach *taverna* umbrella, sipping a drink, and watching the rest of the world at play. Sun bathing is of course popular with many tourists, but beware to protect yourself – those beautiful clear-blue skies, make for high quantities of ultraviolet rays.

Beach attire is always something to look out for while enjoying a lazy sun-kissed afternoon, or is it? Today's fashion or naturalist statement – depending on your opinion – tends towards scantiness. The bikini as a beach garment has not only become commonplace, but many women are now opting for the even more revealing monokini. It will surely not be long before the daring Germans pave the way to mass acceptance of the *pankat* (Greek for "nothing above, nothing below").

Apollo, certainly has many thousands of devotees in the Greek resorts!

Beach Resorts

The principal large resorts with good, sandy beaches, running clockwise around the coastline (nearest main towns, if there are any, in brackets) are at:

Mainland: Vouliagmeni (near Athens); Tolon (Navplion); Methoni and Stoupa (Kalamata/Pilos); Loutra Kaiafa (Olympia).

Crete: Mallia (east of Heraklion); Matala and Paleohora (south coast); Rethymnon (west of Heraklion).

Cyclades: Andros (Batsi); Ios; Naxos; Santorini (Kamari and Perissa); Seriphos; Siphnos (Kamares Bay).

Dodecanese: Karpathos; Kos (main town and Kardhamaina); Rhodes (east coast particularly good resorts).

Ionian Islands: Cephalonia (Skala); Corfu (Kavos, Ayios Gordis, Glifadha, Ayaios Stefanos West, Sidari); Kithira (Kapsali); Zante/Zakinthos (Alikes, Lagana).

North-east Aegean: Lesbos (Eressos, Sigri); Lemnos.

Saronic Gulf: Aegina (Ayia Marina).

Sporades: Skyros.

the Thames or Seine.

In the Peloponnese is found another typically Greek landscape pattern: Sparta, for example, like many of the Peloponnese as well as northern Greek settlements, lies well inland commanding the broad and fertile valley of the Eurotas: like Athens it is also protected by mountain ranges to the west, north and east.

Coastlines

The coastlines of both the mainland and the islands are rugged: even on a map you will see how indented they are with bays and inlets.

The smaller island landscapes are generally rocky, with the main towns, as on the mainland, fairly close to or at

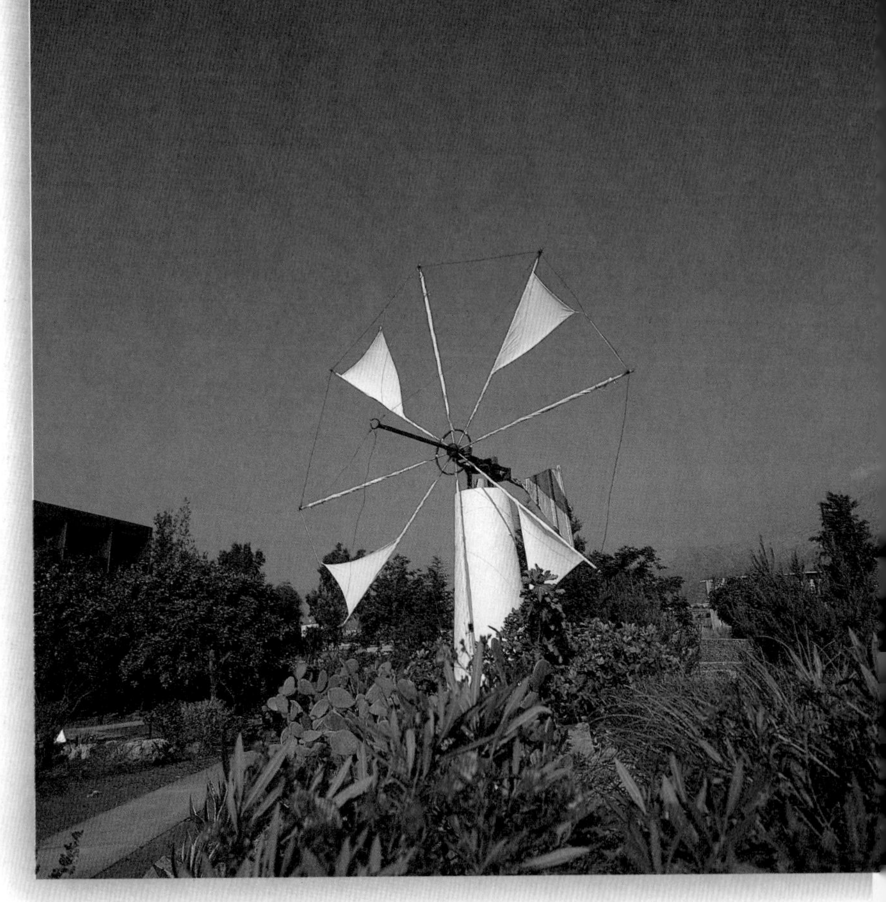

Greece is blessed with fertile and lush valleys.

sea-level.

Walking around the coast of a Greek island, you will feel that you are getting nowhere at times, so crenellated is the coastline. You will come across the odd deserted sandy beach, and then be up on the cliffs again. The centers of the islands, like the mainland, are generally higher and more rugged than the coast and alive with evergreen trees and springs.

Visions of Blue

The low humidity of the air in Greec makes for the famously intense blu skies and clear views, that is when th weather is fine and you are not in th polluted city. The south-east is the drie region: average annual rainfall aroun Athens, the Peloponnese and th Cycladic Islands is around 400 mm. It

Mount Olympus

ısing abruptly from the north-eastern corner of ıe Greek Peninsula, Mount Olympus looms at height of 2,917m, making it the highest ıountain in Greece. Although they lacked al-meters, the ancient Greeks appreciated that his was a high and sacred place. In Greek ıythology this is the home and citadel of Zeus nd the other Olympian gods.

The mountain is located virtually beside the ea; a gentle slope rises from the coastal area on ıe eastern side of the Thermaic Gulf for some 5 km, before rising rapidly to its peak. Homer escribes a god's-eye view of the mountain as pproached from this direction: "The immortal ods returned together to Mount Olympus vith Zeus at their head; the sea-goddess Thetis, emembering what Achilles her son had re-uested, rose out of the waves at first light and oared into the heights of the sky to Olympus. he found Zeus of the great eye-brows, son of ronos, sitting away from the lesser gods, on he uppermost peak of craggy Olympus".

The ancient Greeks believed that thunder-torms were created by Zeus, who hurled light-ning-bolts from Olympus to destroy his mortal nd immortal enemies. Zeus was often called he "cloud-gatherer", and it is easy to see why: he topmost peaks of Olympus are invariably hrouded in cloud. When Zeus nodded his ssent to mortal or immortal prayers, Olympus vould shake and thunder: perhaps a reference ıot only to the storms but also to earthquakes ı the Greek mainland. Whether or not you elieve the ancient stories, Olympus is still an we-inspiring place.

The Cult of Zeus

rchaeologists have investigated the peaks and he surrounding slopes. At 2,800m a ruined emple to Zeus was recently discovered. Incred-bly this was not just a token building to the god: excavations revealed that animals were brought all the way up here for sacrifice; stone slabs inscribed with prayers to the gods were also found, along with coins.

This signified a highly revered spot, and further investigations demonstrated that a sacred track led from the shrine down to the ancient city of Dion, which lies to the north-east, between the sea and the mountain. The name Dion is a variant of Zeus, which suggests that this was the cult center for the worship of the Olympians looming above the city.

Some ancient writers have suggested that Dion was the original home of the Olympic Games, which were transferred to Olympia in the Peloponnesese in the eighth century BC. The most recent excavations at Dion have revealed a wealthy town, with well-planned streets and houses and a theatre. There were several expensive temples dedicated to the various Olympians, but interestingly, there were also temples to non-Olympian deities such as Isis and Dionysos – Dionysos, the god of wine, was a son of Zeus, but was only accepted by the other Olympians when he grew up.

Natural Beauty

The wild flowers of Mount Olympus are unparalleled in Greece, but the area is a national park, and it is forbidden to pick them. The best base for walkers is the village of Litohoro to the east (six km west from a sandy beach, where you can swim after your climb), where there are also a number of campsites.

You can obtain booklets in the main square of the village, which detail the various routes up the mountain. The climb is not particularly strenuous or dangerous in clear weather, but it can turn bad quickly, and the mountain should be treated, as the ancients treated it, with great respect.

ı hot, dry country in summer. In ex-reme winters snow has fallen as far outh as Athens – during Christmas 1992, the international press displayed photographs of the columns of the Parthenon whitened during a blizzard.

The northern lowlands are generally dry and warm, though the closer

Lush valleys and vegetation against a winter backdrop in the mountains.

you get to the sea, the greater likelihood of rain: Thessaloniki has an average rainfall of 477 mm. The western islands and lowlands are relatively wet due to cloud formations arriving from the western Mediterranean. Whilst the eastern Aegean islands enjoy a good balance of sun and rain; you will notice more greenery the further east you island-hop. The further into the mountains you go, the cooler and wetter you can expect it to be though generally the rain will come in short, sharp bursts.

Average daily temperatures in Ath

ens range from 6°-11°C in January, to 22°-32°C in July; whilst Thessaloniki, some 300 km to the north, ranges between 2°C and 10°C in January and between 21°C and 32°C in July. The islands are on average a few degrees cooler in both summer and winter than these mainland cities, whilst island rainfall is not significantly different from Athens, except in May, when Athens has a higher than average rainfall.

When to Travel

So when is it best to visit Greece? The answer depends on what you are going for. If you want beaches and very hot sun and do not mind how hot and crowded it is, then late June to late August is a good time. If you want to miss the really crowded months, but still catch up on some solar worship, late May/early June and September can be superb. If you are lucky, October can be a beautiful month: it is often still warm enough to swim and the resorts are uncrowded.

The traveller searching for lowland flowers and antiquities is best suited by March to May. There is a greater chance of rain at this time, but it is not too hot for sight-seeing or searching for rare orchids. The mountain walker will be safest in the hottest months of July, August and September; earlier than this and you will still encounter snow on the peaks.

In October, though the autumn colours are magnificent, the weather can become cold and wet. November to March is generally cold and wet, though you can be lucky and have clear, crisp, sunny days, perfect for walking the ancient sites and picnicking out. The problems of finding reliable transportation and accommodation increase through the winter months.

Flora & Fauna

The wide variety of climate and geology in Greece produces a very broad range of flowers, trees and wildlife, as yet mainly undamaged by modern farming techniques. The ancient sites have a dual attraction in the spring, when the ruins are strewn with flowers. Unfortunately, many have recently suffered from weedkiller treatment due to the state archaeological departments' concern that the profusion of wild plants and their root-systems might damage the remains. It is to be hoped that a compromise can be reached, as the floral colours are a bonus to the spring visitor. In spite of this, the visitor will still, however, see carpets of wild flowers in the lowlands and along the coastline in the spring. In summer these areas will be somewhat barren – with the exception of 20 per cent of Greece, which is wooded – the early flowers dry up and go to seed to reappear the following spring. In high summer you can find a wonderful alternative flora, in the bracken

Pistachios – a popular nut to snack on.

of the high mountains.

The plants of Greece are rooted not only in modern soil, but in Greek history and mythology. Ancient and modern poets and singers allude to trees and flowers, to imbibe their texts with a pastoral or an exotic flavour. Hippocrates (460-370 BC), the father of medicine, lived on the island of Kos, where he studied the local flora, in his writings he describes the healing powers of various plants. Classical architects and painters regularly used stylized floral designs as decorative frames on their temples and pots.

The Flowering of Antiquity

Greece has over 6,000 species of wild flowers and ferns (nearly three times as many as in Great Britain), and of the Mediterranean countries only Spain boasts a greater number. There are about 750 species which are unique to Greece, as well as a number not otherwise found west of Asia. You will see the spring varieties the moment you travel out of the towns. There is no particularly special location to look for them: just stop the car and you will find interesting flowers by the roadside. As in every country there are, however, a number of famous Greek floral landscapes. Near Athens is Mount Hymettos, its slopes famed for their spring colours since antiquity. The Roman poet Ovid (43 BC to AD 14), described the scene which remains unchanged to this day:

Flowering beauty.

"Near where his purple head Hymettus shows
And flow'ring hills, a sacred fountain flows,
With soft and verdant turf the soil is spread,
And sweetly-smelling shrubs the ground o'ershade.
There rosemary and bays their odours join,
And with the fragrant scent combine.
There tamarisks with thick-leav'd box are found,
And cytisus and garden pines abound
While through the boughs, soft winds of Zephyr pass,
Tremble the leaves and tender tops of grass".

(Translation William Congreve, 167(1729).

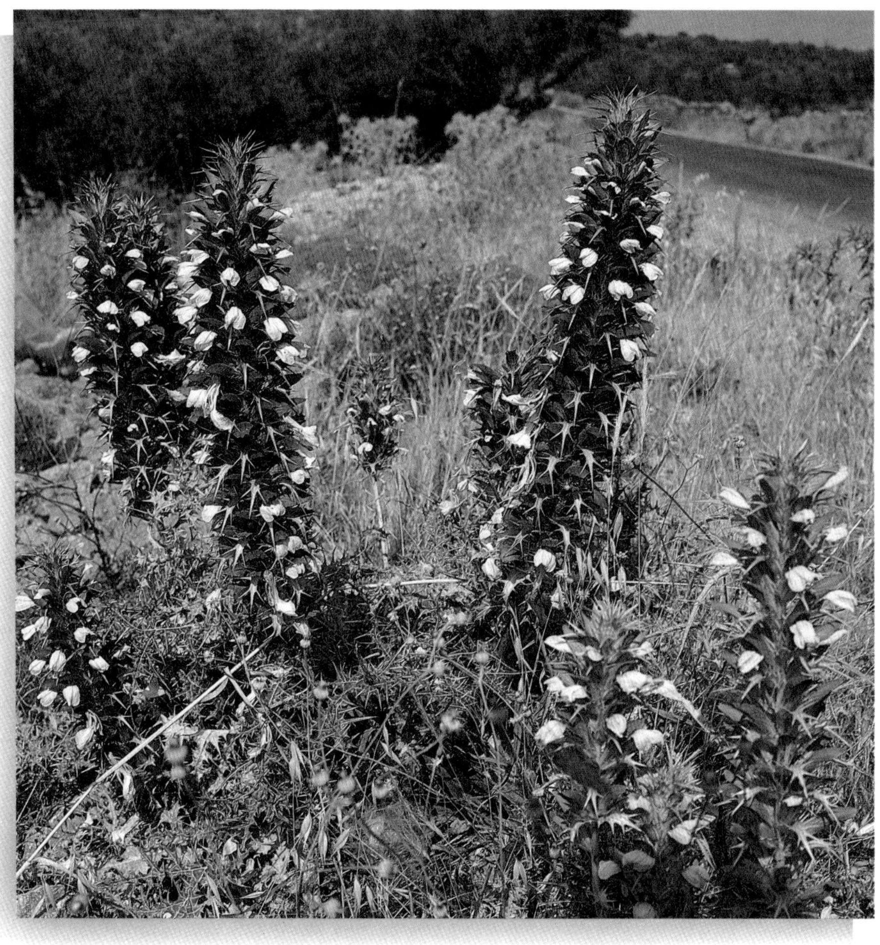

Over 6,000 species of wild flowers and ferns are found in Greece.

Island Illumination

The above excerpt was worth quoting in full, because it provides an accurate image of what the modern visitor can hope to experience, anywhere in the spring lowlands. The Greek islands are all renowned for their spring flora, but the greatest of all has to be Crete. Crete has over 2,000 species – to put this figure in perspective, Great Britain has a similar number, but Crete is only three per cent of its size. Rare plant hunters will find island-hopping a profitable activity. Whilst on the mainland, they will have to climb the highest peaks for their rewards.

However, such treks can often be combined with sight-seeing: Mount Athos with its Christian monastery; Mount Olympus with its more pagan gods; whilst the Peloponnese offers Mount Taygetos, near classical Sparta and medieval Mistra.

Obviously the exact time of flowering varies from year to year. In the drier soils by the sea you will see plants growing in winter and flowering as early as February. Early March is a good time for the higher and more south-facing parts of Crete.

In most lowland areas, however, the best month is undoubtedly April, when the majority of the spring flowers are open. As you retreat to the foothills, May becomes the best month and so on into the mountains, where you will find the highest number of summer varieties in July. August is a low month, but there is a floral renaissance in September, with cyclamens and crocuses reappearing in the mountains.

Flower Species

Among the most conspicuous spring flowers are anenomes, rockroses and orchids. The *anenome coronaria* (Crown Anenome) is a widespread and beautiful plant with a 20cm stem and a single, large flower. Colours vary from lavender to poppy reds and bright purples. *Cistus* (Rockrose), is a small bush which as its name suggests, likes rocky terrain. Like the anenome, the *cistus'* colours vary from delicate pinks to pastel crimsons and whites: all have yellow centres. In the mid-day sun, you might see a dark and fragrant resin oozing from the rockrose: this is "labdanum", which i antiquity was combed by herdsmen fron the beards of their feeding goats an sold as a constituent of perfumes an plasters. Monks collected it with a spe cial leather rake.

In early summer the lowlands ar spread with fields of Corn Marigold and Crown Daisies. Their golden flow ers reflect the colours of the summe sun: hence their well-known scientifi name *chrysanthemum* ("golden flower") Yellows predominate in June and Jul with large shrubs such as broom (Ovid' "cytisus") growing in abundance – glorious break to the monotony of thos long hot coach journeys along the coast

On the higher ground in autumn the smaller white, lilac and purple flow ers of the crocus family appear, includ ing the Saffron Crocus, whose flower produce yellow saffron dye: the drie orange stigmas are the ones we use t colour and flavour food. Delicate rose pink cyclamens also flower in the au tumn.

If you travel by the sea in the au tumn, you may see the magnificen white sweet-scented crowns of th *pancratium maritimum* (Sea Daffodil) growing alongside crocuses behind th beach. These appear in Minoan frescoe and decorate a Mycenaean sword, prov ing their continued existence in Greec over the last 4,000 years. Earlier in th year, rose or lilac flower clusters of Vir ginian Stock appear, as well as the smal bright pink *silene colorata* (campion) usually sprouting in the rocky ground

The prickly pear cactus has adapted well to the mountains.

n the way to the beach.

Flowers for Fertility

he ancient Greek word *orchis* meant testicle" and described the shapes of e double orchid roots. It was believed folklore that the larger root should be ten by men to have sons, whilst the naller should be eaten by women, if daughters were required. You can only wonder what the effect of eating both would have! The sweet-scented Italian Orchid can be found in April and May, sometimes covering fields, but more often at their edges. It is quite tall and handsome with pastel pink flowers at its top, each looking on closer view, like little people wearing purple stripes. It is no surprise that such orchids have always been considered magical.

Greek Flowers in Mythology

To the ancient Greeks, all natural phenomena were controlled by various gods. This extended to the world of animals, trees and flowers: some of the best-known stories concern the mythical origins of flowers. Many Greek flowers also have religious associations.

The Narcissus – Poignant Beauty

Perhaps the most famous tale of all is that of the aptly named *Narcissus poeticus*. Narcissus, son of the river Cephisus and the forest nymph Liriope, was a handsome young man, who spent his days hunting on the slopes of Mount Helicon in Boeotia. Other boys as well as the woodland nymphs themselves, lusted after his magnificent body, but Narcissus rejected them: he considered that none of them even remotely matched his own beauty.

In frustration over his unrequited attentions, one boy prayed to the Greek goddess of retribution, Nemesis, who punished Narcissus for his arrogance. One day, resting by a pool during the hunt, Narcissus saw his own reflection in the still waters. He immediately fell in love with his own image, and after many attemps to grasp the elusive beauty in the pool, he pined away and was transformed into the gold-centred, white-petalled flower. In Greece, you might still see the Narcissus drooping over a stream.

A separate Narcissus myth, connected to religious ritual, tells how the Underworld god Hades, took a fancy to Persephone, daughter of the goddess Demeter, and asked Gaia (Mother

The Narcissus – celebrated in legend.

Earth) to help him seduce her into his death realm. For this purpose Gaia created the Narc sus and gave it its sweet fragrance. The ancie custom of placing Narcissi on corpses and grav has continued into the 20th century.

The soporific juice of the *Papaver somniferu* ("sleep inducing", also known as the Red Popp was drunk by Demeter to help her forget h grief when Persephone was carried off in

Forestation

For native Greek trees, you must go to the northern valleys, mountains and islands. The southern areas, such as the Peloponnese and Crete, are very sparsely wooded. Greece has less forested land than any other European country (8 per cent of the land is treeless). There no apparent natural reason for thi and botanists combine with archaeol gists in suggesting that the deforest tion occurred at the end of the Neolith period (c 3000 BC), when the earlie farmers expanded their grazing lar

ades. The flowers cover the Greek landscape i spring and in mythology were thought to be gns of Demeter's gift of fertility to the land.

Blooms of Death

he striking red anemones were believed by the ncient Greeks to have been formed from the lood of the youth Adonis, who was so handome that he was even loved by Aphrodite. One ay the goddess discovered Adonis, goured nd killed by a wild boar. The tears she wept ecame *Rosa canina* (white dog roses), whilst ach drop of his blood became an anemome. he anemone are among the earliest spring owers, and for the Greeks, this signifies the remature death of Adonis. The Greek word *nenome* means "wind" and from this comes e popular English name "Windflowers", which sometimes given to them.

The Mediterranean *Delphinium ajacis* (larkour) gets its ancient name "Ajax's delphinium" om the story of the warrior hero Ajax. During e seige of Troy, Ajax's companion Achilles was lled and Ajax quarrelled with Odysseus for wnership of Achilles' armour. Divine interventon allocated them to Odysseus, whereupon jax committed suicide by falling on his own vord. From his blood sprang the blue larkspur. you look carefully at the flower, you will be ble to pick out the letter A with an I on each de: these are the first two letters of the dead ero's name (in Greek "Aias"), and they also oell "Ai" which was the Greek cry when in ourning or trouble.

nto the mountain regions by cutting own trees, which have never grown gain.

Forest fires and new housing estates n the edges of towns are the modern ontribution to the destruction of forstation. However, there are now ecoogical action groups who are encouraging the planting of trees on the lower mountain slopes, for example on Mount Hymettos near Athens.

Most of the highland Greek forest trees are conifers, though you will see plenty of beeches and chestnuts. As with the flowers there are a number of trees unique to Greece, such as the *abies cephalonica* (Greek Fir), which grows to heights of up to 30m and presents long slim cones in the Autumn. The *abies pectinata* (Silver Fir), pushes its pyramidal top up to 40m. Fir trees were often planted in ancient buildings, but the Silver Fir was sacred to the Greek moon goddess Artemis, who also watched over childbirth: until recently the tree symbolized birth.

There are several varieties of pines; the *pinus halepensis* (Aleppo Pine), is the most common in the southern mainland and islands – from its bark is taken the resin used to flavour retsina wine. You might well see tins hanging on the trunks for this purpose. The aptly named *pinus pinea* (Umbrella Pine) is found on lower land, sometimes besides the sea on the Peloponnese and the Aegean Islands: the white pine-kernels have been used in Greek cooking, since the classical period.

Of the deciduous trees, the Sweet Chestnut is common at moderate altitudes from Crete to Macedonia. Greek furniture-makers favour its wood, whilst the chippings are used by gardeners for humus. There are also the usual European varieties of oak, cypress, beech and juniper.

A common tree in both the wild lowlands, towns and parks (where it is planted in rows along the avenues), is the Judas Tree, which grows up to 10m in height and is unmistakable when in flower: according to folklore, the tree owes its striking rosy mauve colour to the stain of the blood of Judas Iscariot, who, legend has it, hanged himself from it, after betraying Christ.

Birdwatching

Besides enjoying the beauty of its flowers, Greece is also a good place to indulge in birdwatching; preferably combining this activity with visiting the ancient ruins. It is fortunate for tourists

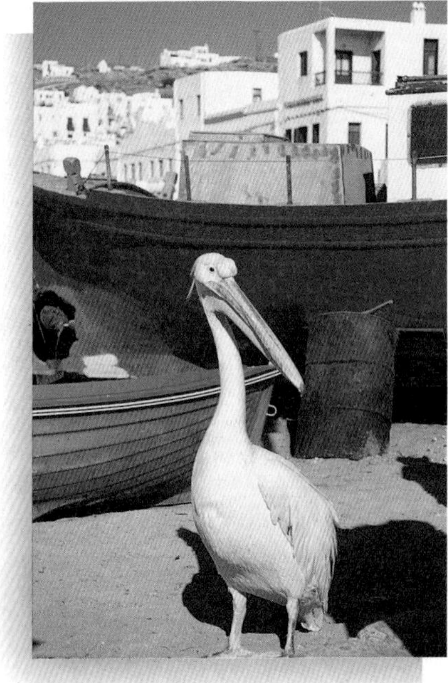

The pelican – wonderfully gregarious!

Birding in Greece

No visit to Greece is complete unless you go t Delphi. It is a spectacular terrain with rollin hills, endless olive groves and of course th Temple of Apollo and other sights from th ancient Greek civilization. It so happens tha Delphi is also one of the best locations i Greece, for land birds. When you walk aroun the ruins keep an eye out for the many sylvi warblers hopping about in the bushes. Yo may have to get out your guidebook to pick ou the different species like **Sardinian, Orphean Olivetree** and **Subalpine Warblers**; all Mediterranean specialists that you will not find i northern Europe. The same goes for man members of the bunting family Fringillide, loo out for **Black-headed, Girl**, and **Rock Buntings. Black-eared Wheatear** and **Stonecha** should be other sure sightings in this terrain.

Delphi Environs

Near Delphi the mountain of Parnassos is popular with birders, follow the signs towards th Athens' Ski Club and go to the end. The hill have some coniferous forest cover where yo can see **Firecrest, Short-toed Creeper** an **Black Woodpecker** and **Chough**, higher up Raptors, include the **Griffon Vulture** and th rare **Lammergeier**. Look out for the **Rock Nuthatch** which occurs here and in a few othe places in Europe. Make a point of scrutinizin the swifts flying by here; **Pallid Swift** and **Alpine Swift**, occur and might be new to you.

As is the case with many Greek towns it i worthwhile checking the local garbage dump This is often the hang-out for the native rapto population – in most places you can see th Black **Vulture, Egyptian Vulture** and several o the majestic **eagles** in the *Aquila* genus.

Montane Sightings in Meteora

Further inland, the montane country of Meteora is a popular stop over. From the gigantic clif formations you can watch many raptors lik **eagles** and **vultures** and especially many fal

Stone Chat

Red-footed falcon

Pratincole, found on Lake Koronia's shores.

ons, such as the **Lanner Falcon**, **Peregrine alcon** and the rare and endangered **Lesser estrel**.

The captivating beauty of the countryside in is part of Greece, is actually partly due to enturies of human exploitation – overuse by azing, soil erosion and general ecological egradation! The rich and fertile forests that ed to cover these parts of Europe are long one and the hills are left dry, windswept and arren. Check out the patches of deciduous rests that are left, they provide a habitat for editerranean birds like the **Sombre Tit**, **Syrn Woodpecker**, **Scops Owl** and the **Redoted Falcon**.

Wetlands

nywhere in the world there are always two abitat types sure to produce a good variety of rds; the forests and the wetlands! In Greece e Mesolongion Lagoons at the Gulf of Corth, on the west coast, have taken on special nportance recently, as work is intensifying to survey and protect this important refuge for resident waterbirds and passage migrants. You can stay at the field station if you are willing to help out as a volunteer with the work there. For more information, write to: Photis Pergantis, Wetland Research, Monitoring & Consultancy, 30400 Aitolikon, Greece.

Other important wetlands include some of the inland lakes such as Lake Ioannina west of Meteora, where there are huge congregations of migrant waders and terns and resident southern Europe specialists like the **Squacco Heron** and **Glossy Ibis**. The surrounding woodlands and hills are also good for land birds.

In the eastern part of the country, Lake Koronia is a well-known birding destination where there are, **Pygmy Cormorant**, **Pratincoles** and **pelicans** – all difficult species to see elsewhere in Europe. Watch out for the pelicans, both **White Pelikans** and **Dalmatian Pelikans** occur and they are pretty difficult to tell apart! The surrounding countryside holds **Hoopoe**, **Calandar Lark**, **Rufous Warbler** and other good, southern birds.

To the very east along the Turkish border, the Evros Delta is another important birding site. The wetlands have **Spur-winged Plover**, **Black-winged Stilt**, **Flamingo** and **Mediterranean Gull**. The nearby open country has **Beeeater**, **Masked Shrike**, **Turtle Dove** and **Shorttoed Eagle**. But generally the density of more common birds is also good and the whole area around Alexandroupolis is well worth a drive-

...Birding in Greece

Turtle-dove.

around, it holds some of the best birding opportunities in Greece.

The Aegean Islands

The Aegean Islands, great for sunbathing, swimming, yachting, island-hopping and generally having a good time, are from a birding point of view, pretty dull! The landscape is dry and barren and now also heavily built up with tourist facilities.

When sailing between the islands however, look out for some Mediterranean specialities that can be spotted here; **Cory's Shearwater** and **Audouin's Gull**. On the many smaller islands, **Ruppell's Warbler** and **Cretzschmar's Bunting breed**, can be sighted – these birds are difficult to see in other places in Europe. Another specialist is the wonderful **Eleonora Falcon** which occurs here in fair numbers.

While most of the islands in the Aegean Sea are too small to hold habitat and bird populatior of any size, Crete is the exemption to the rul Apart from several vultures there are goo chances of seeing **Bonelli's Eagle** and there a many **Chukars** in the mountains – this colourf pheasant species is difficult to see on the mai land. This part of Greece lies in a migrato funnel and there are always more birds to watc during spring and especially during autumn around September the migrants move sout wards after the breeding season finishes an birds suddenly appear everywhere on the i lands.

More Information

In few places are birds so well studied an documented as they are in Europe and the re of the Western Palearctic region. There a numerous high quality handbooks and fiel guides covering the area, including Greece. Th ***New Generation Guide to Birds of Britain an Europe***, by C. Perrins, Collins 1987, is current one of the most useful in the English languag with this book you will be able to identify all th birds you meet.

For detailed information on the best plac to find the birds in Greece, check out Joh Gooders's series on ***Where to Watch Birds ..*** published by Andre Deutsh. The most up-t date local information, can be obtained fro the Hellenic Ornithological Society, P.O. B 640 52, GR-157 01, Zographos, Greece; a interesting bird observations that you mig make during your visit should also be submitt to this contact.

that birds often feed amongst or even nest in, the broken columns; I have seen a stork's nest on top of a standing column! The islands are on the migratory route from Africa to Europe, and most of their birds can also be seen on the mainland. Towns turn into countryside very rapidly in Greece, and you will often se quite exotic birds in town parklands resting on telephone wires.

The medium-sized shrike can be see waiting to pounce on its prey of small birds and mammals: it is easily reco nised by its bandit-like black mask acro e eyes. In olive-groves you should look ut for the hoopoe, unmissable with its ack and white wing bars and brown nd black-tipped crest.

The classical Greeks had quite an terest in birdlife: Aristophanes' fifth-ntury BC Athenian comedy ***The Birds,*** scribes how hoopoes and other birds cided that human-beings should be oycotted and decided to set up a bird-ily republic called Cloud-Cuckoo-ind. In the play the chorus of birds reaten the human judges with drop-ngs unless they vote Aristophanes as p playwright!

For wetland birds you should go to e two massive lakes to the east of hessaloniki: ikes Koronia nd Volvi. ere you will e large wad-s such as pelicans, erons and egrets, as ell as the smaller avocets. In the moun-ins you might well see some of the rger birds of prey, including the rare olden Eagle; however, this is more kely to be the similar looking Griffon ılture, which soars like a hang-glider the thermal air-currents with its 2-3m ngspan.

Memorable Mammals

so in the mountains the larger wild ammals of Greece, can be found. Tor-ises can be seen quite regularly on the mountains close to Athens: if you see one on its back, turn it over or it will die. Badgers are sometimes seen in the wood-lands, but in the high northern moun-tain ranges, you might be lucky (or unlucky as the case may be!) and spot a brown bear, lynx or even a wolf. The large mountain sheepdogs can easily be mistaken for wolves and should be treated with the same caution. If walk-ing in Crete, look out for the Cretan *kri-kri* (wild goat). This beautiful silver-grey animal is about one meter in length and has a black band along its spine and around its neck. Its handsome double horns sweep back from its head in a great curve. Wild boars can also be sighted in the mountains.

By the sea, there are rare sightings of the dark chocolate monk seal, which breeds in remote sea-caves: it is threatened with extinction by pollution as well as hu-man hunters.

When island-hopping you might see various sea-mammals and fish breaking the surface: the dolphin and porpoise are quite common; the dol-phin is larger than the north European variety (up to two and a half meters long) and has a longer snout. Both leap playfully alongside boats, as does the rarer and magnificent Pilot Whale, a larger cousin of the dolphin, which grows up to eight meters in length.

People

In appearance the Greeks are generally quite different from what might be expected by those whose ideas are built on ancient Greek sculptures. The average Greek man does not look anything like the Athenian heroes riding on the Parthenon frieze: these have perfect "Grecian profiles" and symmetrical features, whilst their bodies are at the peak of physical fitness – added paint would almost certainly have depicted them with a healthy suntan.

...warm smile of welcome.

Likewise, Classical images of Greek women offer complimentary facial forms, though their bodies are covered unless they are Aphrodite, goddess of physical love and beauty. The nude Aphrodites are perhaps closer to the recent ideal of Mediterranean womanhood; fleshy, with smallish breasts and broad, childbearing hips. Female images differed from the sun-tanned men in being left in the white of the marble, to signify that their place was in the home. We are of course dealing with artistic stereotypes from over two thousand years ago. What are the ideals and realities of modern Greeks?

Ancient Heroes: Herakles & Theseus

Hero-worship was as essential to ancient Greek culture as it is to our own. Heroes such as Herakles (Hercules is his Roman name) and Theseus, even had their own temples. No one can say for sure whether they ever existed in reality, but their myths survived in the stories told by parents to their children, or through sagas sung by bards in the royal courts.

In the Archaic and Classical perids, the myths were also the favourite subjects for sculptors and painters. Look out for these art pieces in the museums; they are easily recognisable, the mature and macho Herakles with his lion-skin cloak and club, long shaggy hair and beard; the youthful and cool Theseus wears contemporary armour so that his Athenian descendants can identify with him. In contrast to Herakles, Theseus is clean-shaven and wears his hair short or in a trendy pony-tail, like a teenage aristocrat.

Propaganda & the Myths

The heroes were used for propaganda purposes by different city-states or political movements. The tyrants of Archaic Athens traced their ancestry back to Herakles and portrayed his labours and eventual deification, in temple sculptures and paintings to suggest their own fighting power and social status. When the tyranr was overthrown at the end of the sixth centu BC, Theseus took over from Herakles as a sym bol of the emerging democracy. His bone were recovered from Skyros and placed in shrine in the *agora* (marketplace). Although th legendary Theseus was himself a prince an eventual king of early Athens, the democra remembered his popular acts, such as freein ordinary Athenian children from being fed t the Minotaur, on the isle of Crete.

The Heroic Acts of Herakles

Herakles' mother was the mortal Alcmene, bu his father was none other than the god Zeu who by pretending to be Amphitry, gaine permission from Alcmene's husband, to slee with her in order to produce a son stron enough to restore the city of Tiryns t Amphitryon's family, who had been exiled b his cousins.

Even as a baby Herakles exhibited superhu man qualities: the goddess Hera, angry with he husband for his affair with Alcmene, sent tw snakes to Herakles' cot to kill him; little Herakle strangled them, but Hera continued to seek he revenge.

Keeping up Appearances

The modern visitor to Greece will be disappointed if he/she is expecting Classical features. The expected Classical physical type is tall and leggy with blond hair (the marbles have lost their painted hair!). The modern Greek is typically dark-haired, short and squat, whilst the straight-nosed profile and divine brow are nowhere to be seen. The olive skin (now missing in the lost paint of the ancient marbles or the originally gleaming bronzes) is equally visible in today Greek woman – unlike her ancient coun terpart she can enjoy the light of day

Behind the physical appearanc however, you will soon discover the sam inward characteristics which made th ancient Greeks portray themselves c gods and heroes. The men have th same sense of wit and cunning, th same spirit of adventure, the same nos for a good opportunity, as Odysseu There are still too many Penelopes, wai ing at home for their men to return, bu many more of today's women can b

Later in life Hera had Herakles kill his wife and ıildren in a fit of madness. In order to be ɔsolved from his crime, the oracle at Delphi ·dered him to perform a number of labours for s enemy, King Eurystheus of Tiryns. Eurystheus anted Herakles' death to retain the throne and ıose the most dangerous tasks imaginable. erakles had to fight monstrous animals, clean ut royal stables and fetch the many-headed uard-dog Cerberus back from Hades. His sucɜss led to his real father Zeus welcoming him to Olympus as a demi-god.

Theseus – the Civilized Hero

ıeseus grew up admiring the older Herakles. e imitated him by performing his own "Laɔurs". Theseus differed from Herakles in beaving in a more civilized fashion: he continued rid the world of monsters and cheats, but restled and fenced with his adversaries acɔrding to the proper rules and regulations. He ecame King of Athens and met his death by cidentally falling off a cliff on the island of cyros. Unlike Herakles he did not become a ɔd, but remained a model of the youthful hero r many generations of Greeks.

ound behind a computer.

The handsome Achilles and the ɜautiful Helen are still glimpsed by mantic visitors in the more remote llages and islands, where there has ɜen less foreign intrusion, but most odern Greeks are a physical mixture waves of invaders: you will find yourlf saying "Doesn't she look Italian?...He oks quite Turkish, or even French..." ıke care that you keep such comments yourself – the modern Greek, still nerging from centuries of Turkish rule ıd foreign interference is understandably sensitive about matters of racial purity.

Characteristics

In spite of inevitable racial mixing, the Greek character remains, with its ability to live life to the full. You will sense Greek enthusiasm in every situation: at the *taverna* the head-waiter will tell you of the great times he had when working abroad; the guide on the Acropolis will lay into the damage caused by Turks and Elgin with remarkable venom, but the next moment he will be running across the ruins to retrieve your windblown sun-hat! Sometimes you will moan that the Greeks are rude and obstreperous with every tourist they meet; then round the next corner, that ageless, heart-warming smile will unsettle you.

Like the land and the climate, the Greeks are creatures of extremes. They have suffered many blows in their history, but have lived through them with characteristic resilience. Their ancient sense of tragedy and comedy comes through in every aspect of family life, and like the ancient dramatic mask, they watch the joy and sadness of everyday life without burying their emotions.

Peoples & Patriotism

The Greeks are a very patriotic people. There has been so much struggle for

Greeks are by nature hospitable.

proper political representation since the country gained its independence that politics continues to play an important part in everyday conversation. Greeks are not embarrassed about politics, if you want to hear political opinions, you will hear them. The Greek people are extremely proud of their cultural heritage; the author Pericles Giannopoulos said, "Even if the Greeks are wiped out and only one is left, that one Greek will teach the invaders Greek and turn them into Greeks. The very earth, the stones and mountains are Greek and will always make Greeks".

You will see few signs of immigration in the main towns of Greece, though recently there have been increasing numbers of Albanians (often of Greek origin) entering the country across th mountains, owing to the general sta of unrest in the Balkans. There was a influx of Russians into Greece after th 1917 revolution – there are religious ti with Russia owing to the Orthodo Church – but they seem to have becom integrated with the local populatio There are some Greek-Turkish comm nities remaining from the centuries Turkish Ottoman occupation, but the account for less than one per cent of th population.

Ethnic Groups

However, there are a number of ethn minorities whom you will not see unle ou travel into the hinterland.

The Slavs came from the northern alkans as raiders of the declining Byzntine Empire between the seventh and ≀nth centuries AD. These have been ssimilated into Greek communities om the mainland down to the Pelooonnese: some Slavic place-names surive as historical reminders.

The Vlachs followed the Slavs into orthern Greece from Romania (the ord "Vlach" is derived from a former ame for Romania), but tended to settle ı their own ethnic communities. Being oth foreigners and nomads, the word Vlach" has always been used as an ısult by Greeks – implying "country umpkin" – and the Vlachs prefer to be alled Romanians. The Vlach language still spoken by some 0.5 per cent of the opulation, concentrated in the mainınd area of the Pindus mountains. ome have second winter homes in hessaly and western Macedonia. The lachs tend to mix Romanian and Greek ı their everyday talk, and there are ttempts to keep the Romanian lanuage alive by teaching it at school.

Another ethnic minority dwelling ı Epirus is the "Sarakatsani" tribe: these re Greek-speaking mountain nomads, ho are believed to be aboriginal. The reek government has forced them to ıke permanent addresses in their winr homes, but they continue to return to ıe mountains for summer pasturage of ıeir herds. If you go walking in the ndus mountains, you are very likely see them.

Let's have a chat!

Gypsies will be encountered in all areas of Greece, even while island-hopping, but like the Vlachs they tend to concentrate in the northern part of the mainland. You will rarely see them with traditional horse-and-carts – these have usually been traded in for motor trucks which they use to transport fruit to market. They are often Muslim in their religion.

Religious Groups

Catholics are found mainly in Athens and on the islands of Thera and Tinos. Their Italianate surnames remind us that they came into Greece with the Venetians during the Crusades. There

A festive occasion is always cause for celebration.

were already Jewish communities in the Greek towns of Ioannina, Larissa and Rhodes during the Roman period. The Jews of Thessaloniki were brought in by the Sultan in 1492 after they had been expelled from Spain and Portugal. The Jews in Athens came from Bavaria with the advent of first Greek King Otto i the1830s. Sadly, these communities we all but demolished by the Nazis in 194 45, when some 80 per cent were take off to concentration camps: now onl about 5,000 remain.

These ethnic minorities account f

Convivial family spirit.

ess than seven per cent of the total Greek population, but they are an interesting reflection of Greece's past history. Greece also has a long history of emigration, which has increased since it joined the EEC, allowing citizens easier access to often better-paid jobs in other member countries. It is however highly unlikely that a Greek will willingly settle abroad. The Greeks have a special word: *xenitia*, for the feeling of loss when outside their home-country and a famous saying which reflects this: "The most heart-rending feelings a Greek can experience are to be an orphan, to be alone, to be in love, and to be away from Greece – and the last is the worst of all".

Town & Country

There is a sharp divide between the town and the country in Greece. Most country-dwellers are farmers and spend most of their time in the home; the village community is extremely close-knit and hard for outsiders to penetrate. This does not imply unfriendliness: coun-

Seeing double?

try Greeks, following ancient traditions, are renowned for their hospitality to strangers, and you should not feel apprehensive about accepting a little food and drink if it is offered – you will probably be shown the livestock into the bargain! Most rural families live in houses, thse tend to be small in siz though there are likely to be three ch dren plus grandparents, occupying The children are generally expected help on the farm when they return hon from school.

In the cities, homes are smaller ar

fe is lived at a comparatively hectic ace. The housing problem caused by assive movement of Greeks from the ountry to the town led, in the 1960s, to e building of blocks of flats. Many thenian professional people live in ese flats and travel into the center of thens from the suburbs. The conse-uent traffic congestion has recently led laws which attempt to reduce the aily traffic by half: if your number-late is odd, you travel one day, if it is ven, you travel the next. Many Greeks omplain that this simply favours those ho can afford two cars!

For those who live on the islands, fe is particularly quiet in the winter onths when the hoards of summer ourists have gone home, and the wea-ner is not good enough for fishing. For nis reason, there is some seasonal emi-ration from the islands to the main-and during the cold months, such that number of island dwellers have two omes.

Family Life

amily life is still of great importance to he Greeks, and it will be interesting to ee whether the growing temptation for oung people to travel to Europe to seek vork, will lead to them being influenced y the ideas of the less family-orien-ated, northern Europeans. Employment as also led many young people to nove from the islands or country vil-ages to the cities, thus distancing them from their family members.

Wherever they are, all members of the family are expected to return home for holidays and celebrations: the family unit includes the extended family – grandparents, aunts, uncles and cousins – therefore such reunions are crowded and noisy affairs. The city family tends to live in a two-bedroomed flat, with the children (usually two) sharing a room.

It is also increasingly common for several generations to live together in the one house: where both parents are working, the retired grandparents look after the children, but there are also low-cost nurseries subsidized by the government. Often, the urban family will own a second home in the mountains, to which they return during the hot summer months.

Personality Traits

The Greeks are not only hospitable by nature, they are also curious. You will often find that, soon after meeting, you are asked what to you are highly personal questions; these vary from how much you earn, to how often you visit your mother, or even how often you make love! You will be surprised by how most Greeks think they are right and everyone else is wrong, and they will tell you this in no uncertain terms. Paradoxically, this big-headedness is accompanied by a warm sense of humour, which among the Greeks themselves, is often used cuttingly to bring someone

The Greek Language & Alphabet

Believe it or not, despite that well known phrase of incomprehension "its all Greek to me", the Greek alphabet, which seems so alien and creates an insurmountable linguistic barrier to most visitors to Greece, is really quite easy to learn. Once the alphabet is learnt, Greek sounds are all easily imitated by the English-speaker, and you should not have problems making yourself understood when asking for one-word items such as food, drink and bus destinations. The only remaining problem once the alphabet is mastered (and you can do this on the plane to Greece!) is that the right part of the word must be stressed.

Evolution

The Latin language of the ancient Romans which branched off into the Romance languages of French, Italian and Spanish, itself fell to extinction with the empire's demise. Ancient Greek produced no such branches but it did survive, although the language spoken in Athens today would be difficult to understand in Classical Athens, owing to natural evolution. In the same way the English of the poet Chaucer can only be half understood by English speakers some six hundred years later.

Greek was first written down when the Greeks learnt the 24-letter alphabet from eastern Mediterranean Phoenician traders in the eight cen tury BC. The same alphabet is still in use toda but the language and its grammar have unde gone many changes. The Greek spoken by th Athenians who built the Parthenon in the fift century BC, was of a different dialect to th language of Homer's epics of three hundre years before. After Alexander the Great's con quests, the eastern Mediterranean spoke a sim plified form of Greek called *koine*, the languag of the New Testament.

The Politics of Language

During the centuries of Turkish rule, the writte language was kept alive by the church, whil locally Greek developed into a popular spoke form, known as "demotic". After indepenc ence, some Greek academics decided to try t codify the language and return it to its ancier Athenian dialect. The *katharevousa* (cleansed c purified) form, as it became known, was force on students in schools and colleges, but clashe with the demotic which remained the people symbol of free Greece.

The two forms of the Greek language hav clashed since the nineteenth century, some times with violent results. In 1903 the ancier Greek tragedy ***Oresteia*** by Aeschylus was pe formed in demotic rather than in the origin.

with ideas above their station down to size – the ancient Greeks gave this job to their gods.

The smile in Greece is ambivalent: a Greek will smile when she is angry as well as happy. The ancient hero Achilles inspired terror in the Trojans when he appeared "smiling beneath his menacing brows". Greeks have an immense sense of pride which can be very damaging, although this will rarely be turned on you as a stranger. They share with the other northern Mediterranean cul tures a quick temper, which if provokec can lead to violence.

Chit-Chats

The Greeks love to get together for chat at all times of the day and night. Every where you go you will see the tell-tal gesticulating arms and hear the high pitched voices signifying that yet an

assical Greek, and this led to street fights! The ctatorial regime of the Colonels (1967-74) ed to enforce the use of *katharevousa* Greek in hools – they even used it in comics and on veet wrappers! In 1976 largely in a reaction gainst the Colonels, demotic became the offi-al language for use in schools as well as overnment, and is used everywhere today, ccept in the extreme right-wing (the right-ing are traditionally upholders of *katharevousa*) ewspapers, the Church and the Law.

Communication Style

though Greeks will love it if you make an effort speak a little of their language, you should nd few problems communicating; English is arnt in schools and ranks above German as a cond language.

Most hotels and restaurants use both Greek nd English for tariffs and menus, and off the eaten track, Greeks will be happy to explain shes by taking you into the kitchen and letting ou choose. When spoken communication eaks down completely, sign language and genious drawings are used. In a tiny hotel in atras, I was once asked whether I required a ngle or double room by means of a pair of atchboxes!

ther politician or workmate is being ubbished. If you know them well and ney are not including you in their gos-p, then you have cause to worry!

Greeks seem to find it hard to con-entrate for very long on their work, and vill look out for every opportunity to scape for a coffee and conversation. ike their Classical forebearers, Athe-ian intellectuals, politicians and busi-essmen can be seen at the sidewalk ables of fashionable restaurants near Constitution Square, engaged in lively discussion.

In the islands and villages you will see the local peer groups doing the same thing. What is refreshing, and very different from equivalent groups in foreign urban societies, is that the conversation rarely turns around a business or political deal, but rather focuses on ideals – philosophy, art and life in general.

General Roles

Women's roles have changed dramatically over the past 20 years. Laws have been passed in their favour; abortion is now legal, maiden names may be kept after marriage and women can instigate divorce procedures, dowries also are no longer needed to accompany women to their husbands' homes. However, Greek women are still behind their European neighbours in terms of real equality. There is still a sense of male pride which discourages the wife from taking work; the increasing number of women who do work still tend to say that it is only to keep them occupied, "as a hobby". Women in social gatherings will be seen providing for their men before themselves, and the two sexes tend to congregate in separate groups.

Generally speaking, of the two sexes, Greek men have it easy, but they do have a great sense of reponsibility for their relatives and will place the family group above everything else during a crisis. Within the family the father tends

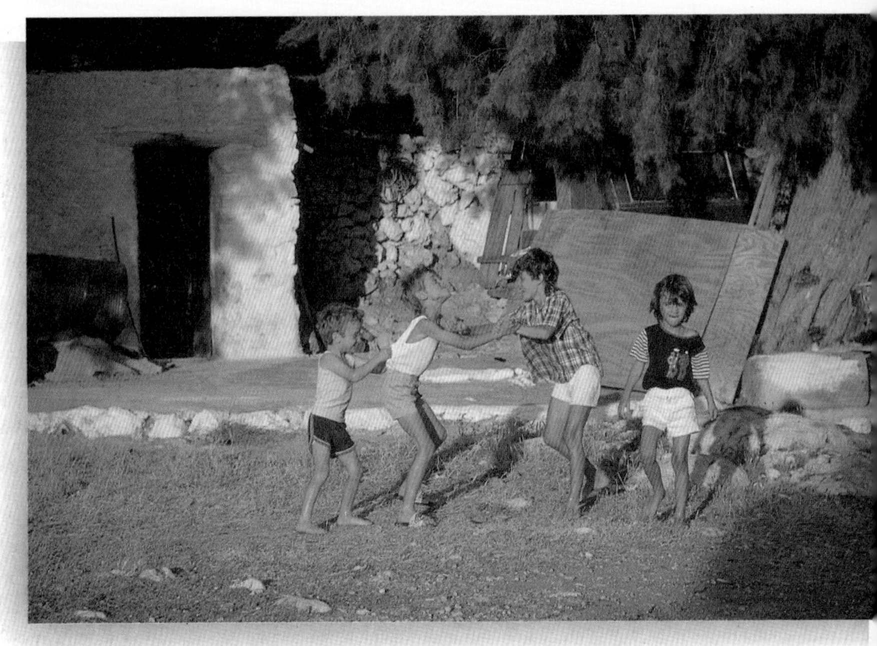

The joys of growing up.

to administer the discipline whilst the mother does everything else. As in Italy and Spain, Greek children are usually immaculately turned out in public, however poor the parents, they are also brought up to be polite and well-behaved, calling their elders by their formal titles, rather than their Christian names.

Hospitality

If you visit a Greek home you will be warmly welcomed with an embrace and cheek-kisses, which you should return without hesitation. In most cases the man will stay in the room where he receives you, and the woman will be in and out of the kitchen, bringing yo drinks and all sorts of nuts and sweet Traditionally the serving of these delicc cies will open with a glass of iced wate and a special tray – usually a treasure heirloom – bearing fruit jams. Each gues is provided with a spoon, and the elde goes first: you take a spoonful of th jam, raise your glass and wish goo health to your hosts by crying *Yiasa* (Cheers).

After this you will be offered some thing stronger, such as a glass of *ouzc* the Greek aniseed digestif. The intro ductory session generally ends with cup of strong Greek coffee. After this yo might well be asked to stay for a mea and it is not unknown to be offered room for the night. You should be gen

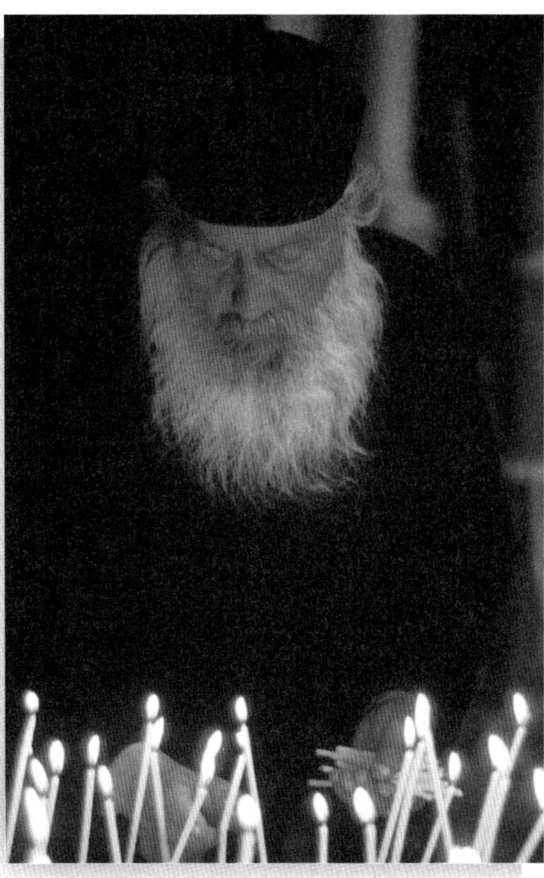

Priest celebrating Mass.

:ous with your compliments bout the interior decor, as the oman will have spent hours dying up for you; but beware f taking an interest in a sepa- ate object – the hospitable ireek will insist on you taking away! If there are babies and hildren present, and there sually are, you should com- liment their good looks and lothes, and give them some noney before you leave: this vill not offend your hosts, as it s the time-honoured way of raising children in Greece.

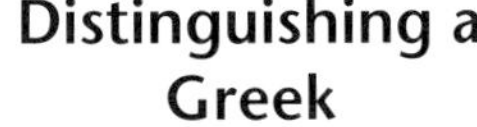

Distinguishing a Greek

:egional differences in the Greek peo- le are not obvious to the visitor. Vhereas they used to refer to the people f the next village or island as virtually eing of another tribe, today the strong- st demarkation is between town and ountry. Greeks tend to refer to Atheni- ns as a different race: more modern, nore sophisticated, more stressed. Wher- ver you go in Greece, however, you will eel that all Greeks share the same pride nd passion for weaving their own indi- idual threads into the richly coloured abric of the local community. Dismiss-ing the philosophy of solitude, they gather with groups of friends in the city squares or village *tavernas* where they argue intensely about politics or the price of olives.

The Greeks are warmly benevolent and hospitable to strangers, they are voluble and find it hard to stay quiet even in the solemn ambience of a Church! Gregarious, argumentative, hostile and friendly, with a genuine joy for living life to the full, the Greeks reflect the extremes of their landscape and climate and above all its beauty and warmth.

Religion

The ancient Greek religion developed from a primitive belief that there are divine causes behind every natural phenomenon and human emotion. These divine causes they attributed to various gods who were fickle in their affections for both state and individual and needed to be frequently appeased. If the state failed to sacrifice the right animal on the right day, the gods would punish it with plague or withdrawal of support during wars. These sacrifices took place in front of the open doors of temples, the earthly dwellings of the Olympians. The statue of the deity could thus enjoy watching proceedings as a bull or heifer was slaughtered to him or her. The inedible parts were burnt as offerings upon the altar, whilst the congregation shared the cooked meat.

Mosiac at Monastery of St. John, Patmos.

Sacrifices to the gods

In Greek mythology this sharing of the divine meal between mortals and immortals was the result of a crime. When Zeus saw that men were cooking meat, he demanded a share for himself and his fellow Olympians.

Prometheus (Forethought) – the craftiest of the Titans – made up two portions: one was wrapped in juicy fat, the other in unappetising animal hide. Zeus chose the succulent portion only to discover too late (he had sworn an oath to abide by his own decision) that within the fat was bone and gristle, whilst within the hide was edible flesh.

In his anger Zeus withdrew the benefits of fire from mankind in order to subjugate them. Whereupon rebellious Prometheus stole a spark of flame from Olympus and carried it to earth hidden in a fennel stalk. As a punishment for this, Prometheus was chained to a rock in the Underworld, where a vulture pecked at his liver continuously; whilst the first woman, Pandora ("gift of the gods") was created to bring misery to men. This was a smart gift, Pandora looked attractive on the outside, but her beauty masked her feminine wiles – an equivalent of the sacrificial hoax played by Prometheus. The story tells us a lot about how the Greeks viewed the gods, as well as how they understood the beauty of women!

Festivals & the Oracles of the gods

State sacrifices were usually just or part of a festival in honour of a go Like a modern music festival, pe ple came from miles aroun to enjoy the holiday ente tainments. There were ofte athletic and dramatic compet tions – the whole occasion inspire the Greek public sense of comp tition. For the rest of the year, th gods were attended by priests c priestesses, who were generall from the upper social classe this was one way that the cit zen's wife could escape confine ment in the home.

Although th Greek gods were wo shipped in man places, there were som sanctuaries whic were considered th most important cu centers of individu deities.

At Olympia, the fa mous games were hel every four years as the main part of th festival to Zeus – there was a universa armistice for the duration of the Game whatever the state of war. At Delph Apollo was also worshipped every fou years, there was a great emphasis o

Festivals attract people from miles around.

poetic competitions since Apollo was God of High Culture. At Athens, a four-yearly festival was held in honour of Athena, the city's patron deity.

Divination was an important part of ancient Greek religion. The seer's duty was to interpret natural signs such as the flight of birds or the entrails of sacrificed animals. His interpretations were considered signs of the divine will, and Greeks took them very seriously indeed – no Greek state in its right mind would go to war if the omen were against them.

Saint Paul in Greece

If you have space, pack a copy of the Bible's New Testament in with your holiday reading: tracing Paul's travels in Greece, and reading his provocative speeches *in situ*, brings the ancient places back to life in a way that no modern guide can. Here one can visualize the angry crowds of tradesmen, sailors and whores as they listened to the damning tirades of the Jew from Tarsus; a man who had once condoned the persecution of Christians, but whose dramatic conversion on the road to Damascus, transformed him into Christianity's greatest evangelist and eventual martyr for the faith.

The Greek Response

Saint Paul the *apostolos* (missionary), made two missions through Greece within a generation of Christ's death. In so doing, he opened up the central Mediterranean and the non-Jewish world to the new religion. The Greeks had always been attracted to such "mystery" religions, which promised – unlike the official State religion which kow-towed to primitive elemental gods – rebirth and life after death. To many Greeks, Paul's creed was just another new brand of the old religion – old wine in new bottles: to others it was something entirely different, preaching as it did, of a personal rather than detached god.

Paul's Missionary Journeys

One reason for Paul's astounding number of converts may have been his exceptional educ tional background. He had studied the Jewi religion in Jerusalem, but his home town Tarsus had given him a typical Greek educatic with its emphasis on public-speaking: use provisions for his teaching profession. In abo AD 49 Paul broke away on his own evangelizi mission, after a dispute with the church Jerusalem (which consisted mainly of the fi apostles) in which he upheld the conversion Gentiles without Judaizing (i.e. circumcisin them.

Paul's missionary journeys took him gre distances from his fellow Christians in Syria; trekked westwards overland through Turk before hopping along the Greek coast sprea ing the word in the rich trading centers Philippi, Thessalonika, Athens, Corinth, Ephes and Kos, in the first mission (*Acts* 16-18.2 Troy, Lesbos, Chios, Samos and Rhodes we added in the second (*Acts* 18.22-22.15). In final mission he called in at Crete on his way Rome, where tradition maintains that he w martyred by order of the Emperor Nero – had covered over 10,000 miles.

The New Testament Letters

Paul's New Testament letters (to the Corinthia Galatians, Ephesians, Thessalonians, Philippia and the church at Rome) suggest that Pa would roughly plan his itinerary in advan staying whenever possible with existing Chr

Top of the divination league was the Oracle at Delphi. The Oracle's mouthpiece was the Priestess of Apollo who, in a drug-inspired state of ecstacy would answer those consulting her with riddles. To misinterpret these utterances could lead to disaster, while to interpret them correctly could lead to the fulfilment of many an ambition.

One of the more successful inte pretations was that offered by the Ath nian general Themistocles, who whe the Delphic Oracle pronounced th Athens would be protected from th invading Persians by a wooden wa correctly stated that this meant the Ath

ıns and boosting the congregations whilst he as there.

He stayed in Corinth at least three times and rote encouraging letters to Corinthians, such Titus and Timothy, when he was elsewhere. was common in the ancient world to treat the tter as a serious literary form, which would be eserved through publication.

The Church in Corinth, Thessaloniki & Philippi

Philippi and Thessaloniki, Paul made a number new converts among the Greek population. ter he had left, he wrote his first letter (**I *essalonians***) to boost morale in his absence. e returned several times and the church at ilippi provided him with financial support. He opped briefly at Athens on his way from acedonia to Corinth where he stayed for a few onths in AD 50.

Corinth was the commercial center of Greece der the Romans and the city's courtesans ploited the presence of sailors ashore from all er the Mediterranean. There were over 1,000 the Temple of Aphrodite on the hill of rocorinth above the port. Paul's Letters to the orinthians (**Corinthians I & II**), castigate them r their incest and fornication – which had come notorious in the entire Roman world – dding them to maintain the life they had lived en they first became Christians. Paul was th an apostle and a mentor, he remains in story, Christianity's greatest evangelist.

an Navy. That year (480 BC), the rsian fleet was destroyed by the Athe-an triremes at the Battle of Salamis.

Greek Orthodox Church

uring the Roman period, Greek gods continued to be worshipped alongside some Roman additions, which included the Emperor himself; a temple dedicated to Rome and Augustus (the first Emperor) was built in front of the Parthenon in Athens. In the fourth century AD, the center of power shifted eastwards to Constantinople (Greek Byzantium) and Christianity became the official Roman religion. During this Byzantine era hundreds of churches were constructed in the Byzantine fashion, whilst many of the old pagan temples were converted to be used for the Christian liturgy.

The Byzantine tradition of worship developed into the Greek Orthodox Church. This Eastern Church became estranged from the Western Roman Catholicism in 1054, when the Roman Pope excommunicated the Patriarch of Constantinople, and the Patriarch then excommunicated the Pope! Since then the Greek Orthodox Church has maintained a very similar doctrine to Roman Catholicism, but has been described as closer to Protestantism in feeling.

Greek Orthodoxy officially accounts for some 95 per cent of the Greek population today. The Muslims come a remote second with just one per cent of worshippers, whilst Catholics account for just 0.05 per cent, about the same figure as the Jews. As with the rest of Europe, the number of "no religion" answers in the census has risen over the last forty years and the number of "nominal" orthodox members is also on the increase.

Greek Easter

Procession on Good Friday.

Greek Easter is by far the most important festival in Greece, and is one of the world's great religious events. It is a wonderful time to visit the country: it falls in the last two weeks of April or in early May, at a time when the weather is also good for sight-seeing and spring flowers. However, if you are going primarily for the archaeology and do not care too much for the religious activities, you will be frustrated by the closure of museums and sites over the Easter weekend.

To witness the Easter festivities, then you should book your accomodation well in advance and visit the island of Hydra, where the great number of churches and monasteries (estimated at 360) make for a particularly Demetrius on high concentration of ritual and processions. In Athens, the Church of Saint George at the top of Lykabettus (Lykavittos) has a magnificently sombre Good Friday procession and service around midnigh whilst the place to be at mi night on Easter Saturday is tl Church of St Demetrius c Philopappos Hill. If you can n be in these places, you will st find colourful local services even the smallest village.

Easter Eggs

Greeks "fast" during Lent, beginning on **Ro (or Clean) Monday**, which is also a publ holiday. The most devout "fast" for the full for days, whilst most keep to the first and la weeks. During this time, the rich tastes of me dishes and olive oil are avoided, and pickle vegetables and other special Lenten dishes a eaten instead.

In the week before Easter, on Maundy Thur day, the women sit and colour hard-boiled eg with red dye: the first to be painted is a gift f the Virgin Mary, whilst the others will be eat later in the week. When dry, they are polishe to a shiny finish with olive oil. The red eg symbolize the new life (the egg) of Christ ov death (red being the colour of blood). On tl

Importance of Ritual

"Orthodox" is Greek for "correct believing", and Orthodox priests have maintained a conservative tradition of behaviour and ritual from the earliest days; the Byzantine liturgy is still in use, this is attributed to John Chrysostom Antioch, Patriarch of Constantinop from AD 398-403.

In many ways the Orthodox atte tion to minute ritualistic detail is a co tinuation of the pagan tradition – Roman religion, you have to start religious ritual all over again if ar

ame day, lambs are killed and hung up – not a retty sight for vegetarians. The traditional Maundy Thursday evening meal is lentil soup.

Mourning & Fasting

ood Friday is the most solemn day of the aster season, and a total fast is observed. In the te evening, services commence in all the hurches of the land and last into the night; ıese celebrate the *Epitaphios* (the laying of hrist's body in the tomb) and are incredibly ıoving to observe. At dusk the *Epitaphion*, epresenting Christ's funeral bier, is carried from ıe church where it has been lying throughout oly Week, bedecked with flowers. It is paraded ırough the streets and a procession of local eople carrying candles form behind it. On the ame day the *lambropsomo* (Easter loaf) is baked: ıis consists of a sweetened bread twisted into raids, with red eggs placed on top.

Rituals & Rejoicing

n **Holy Saturday** (the eve of Easter Day), local ıen gather at communal roasting pits to roast ıeir family's lamb on gigantic spits – much *tsina* is drunk to lighten the task. In the meanme, the entrails are handed to the women who corporate them into the traditional Easter oup called *mayeritsa*; Easter sausages called *koretsi* are also prepared.

That night, everyone goes to church armed ith a red egg and an unlighted candle: the buildings are usually too small for the entire community and most congregate outside in front of the doors.

At midnight, all lights are put out to symbolize the total darkness of Christ's death. The priest then appears from behind the altar screen holding a long lighted taper and repeating *Christos anesti* ("Christ is risen").

If you are standing outside you will see an increasing glow as the priest lights the nearest candles of the congregation chanting "This is the light of the world...come take the light" (the light signifies the risen Christ). The priest then appears at the doors to repeat his chants to the waiting crowd. Each person lights their candle from their neighbour's until the whole congregation becomes a mass of flickering lights.

This is a highly emotional moment, the bells start ringing and fireworks often explode in the sky. The eggs are cracked and eaten to break the fast, and everyone walks back to their beds, shielding their candles in an effort to keep them alight. It is considered lucky to reach home with a lighted candle, and the sign of the cross is made with the flame on the lintel, leaving a sooty mark visible until the following Easter. Back home the *mayeritsa* soup is served, after beating lemon and egg into it just before serving.

On Easter **Sunday** the house is decorated with lilac and the paschal lamb is roasted for lunch, heavily seasoned with oregano and stuffed with garlic cloves. The rejoicing often continues well into the night, with plenty of music and dancing.

ıistake was made – the Orthodox priest as a special prayer to accompany every estment as he puts it on. Within ıurches candles stand in front of icons epresenting many different saints – the irgin Mary is held in great esteem and ıe majority of painted icons depict her s the Mother of Christ.

During the service, the congregation maintain their silence, with heads bowed in prayer. The priest and his chanters make all the prayers, and there are a great deal of them in Chrysostom's Liturgy – Orthodox services, particularly those on important feast-days can last for hours.

Feast of the Assumption of the Virgin Mary.

Whether or not you are a believer, the Orthodox ceremonies are wonderful to participate in or to observe at a distance. There is a great deal of colour, incense and an air of mystical activity which can not fail to move the viewer; in the larger churches beautiful choirs are employed.

Church services take place every Sunday wherever there is a reasonable community of Greeks. Upon entering the building the worshipper immediately makes the sign of the cross, makes a donation of money and lights a candle in front of an icon.

Before the service begins, the worshipper must also kiss the main icon, which is painted on a screen dividing the church into congregation and priest; only the priest may go behind the scree to the altar – again, an echo of th pagan ritual, where the congregatio had to keep their distance from th altar beneath a covered portico or *sto*

The Orthodox Liturgy emphasise that forgiveness must be sought fo worldly sins for our souls to receiv divine salvation. The educational dut of the priest is to explain Bible reading as part of his sermon, generally by refe ring to examples from everyday mod ern life.

The priest's bible is written in th ancient Greek language used by th original apostles. At the heart of th ritual is the Mystery of the Holy Eucha rist, in which the congregation receiv Communion of bread and wine.

Youthful fervour and devotion.

Coping with Change

ıe Church today has less influence on e community than it did earlier this ntury. Since the break with Roman Ca- olicism Greek priests have been allowed marry, but bishops and patriarchs must main celibate. Orthodox priests still wear eir traditional dress of black ankle-length ıssock and pillbox hat; their hair and ards remain uncut.

The Church plays an educational role r children whose parents wish to bring em up in the Orthodox tradition. There e "Sunday Schools" where children are ught the Church version of Greek his- ry; "fun" activities include learning tra- tional Greek dancing and singing.

Baptism and marriage remain important events in Greek popular culture, with parents and family dressing up for the occasion. These rituals, along with Christmas and Easter, are very similar to those performed in other Christian churches, and these major festivals still draw the crowds – most observers, however, will admit that there are few more colourful occasions to witness in the Greek festive calendar.

However, outside of these more important religious festivals, it has to be said that, over the last thirty years, fewer people attend church every Sunday, and the congregations are becoming increasingly elderly.

Spirit of the Land

There are, however, certain religious traditions which are so deep-rooted that one feels they will persist as part of the Greek landscape. Everywhere you travel, you will see way-side shrines, often at accident spots on winding mountain roads. Each shrine contains an icon in front of which flowers and candles are placed as thank-offerings for services rendered. In the churches, you will notice a similar emphasis on the personal votive offering; as in antiquity, models in wax or metal of part of the anatomy are hung before icons as tokens for the sick and diseased to be healed.

Festivals

Festivals have always been at the very heart of Greek public and private life. Family rites of passage – baptisms, marriages, deaths – are marked by elaborate rituals and family reunions. The progress of the religious year is punctuated with colourful festivals at Christmas and Easter, and the major political events of past history are remembered in public holidays.

Dancing and feasting are all part of Easter festivities.

Ancient Public Holidays

In ancient as in modern Greece, religious festivals lasted for several days, but there were far more of them owing to the great number of gods who had to be honoured. These ancient festivals were similar to the modern celebration of the Saint's day, but they differed in including a much wider range of public activities: most ancient festivals included theatrical performances of tragedy and comedy, together with athletic competitions in honour of the god. During the major state festi-

The Temple of Athena, which was the scene of many a festival in ancient Greece.

vals, everyone was given time off work and was expected to participate in one way or another. Athens in the fifth-century BC, had on average, a festival every other day, and all members of society; men, women, children and slaves, were expected to attend the more important ones. Sacrifices of animals to the gods came at the climax of the festival and the meat was shared out amongst the congregation.

Processions played an important part in ancient festivals, their purpose is to wind their way around the city streets collecting more and more people and finishing up at the relevant sanctuary. Sacred objects, such as gold baskets of grain and silver trays of cakes and honeycombs to be offered to the god, were carried in the procession; the priest o priestess marched at the front beneatl canopies carried by attendants. Durin the spring festivals in honour c Dionysus, God of agriculture and win large phallic images were carried a fertility symbols, along with wine-skin and special loaves of bread. A woode statue of the god was paraded throug the streets and finally placed in hi temple by the theatre; plays were the performed in his honour.

Competitions also took place i honour of the god, these were usuall elaborate and required lengthy prepa rations on the part of the state. The were athletic competitions at the Olym pic Games at Delphi, in honour of Zeu the Pythian Games in honour of Apoll

Each town has its own patron saint.

cluded both athletic and music consts. Many festivals included competiions between choirs or between playrights and actors. The most famous ama festival was held in Athens durg the spring festivities in honour of ionysus.

Christianity & Paganism

nce Christianity had become the offial religion of the late Roman world in e fourth century AD, the old pagan ast-days were abolished but the idea public festivals was too deep-rooted Greek society to do away with it together – in the countryside in parcular, many of the new Christian feast days were virtually superficial replacements of pagan equivalents. Today, as in antiquity, you will find a mixture of major religious festivals such as Saints' days, Christmas and Easter, impregnated with pagan traditions. Secular festivals include celebrations of music and theatre, there are also wine festivals, which echo the pagan worship of Dionysus.

In many ways the annual multiplicity of Saints' days can be seen as a Christian substitute for the many gods worshipped in antiquity. As in ancient Greece, each town had its own patron god or goddess, who would receive special days of worship and festivity, so in modern Greece each island or village community celebrates the Feast Day of

The Festival of Athena

A major festival was no doubt considered to be the best way that the ancient Greek city-state could win divine affection and patronage. Each city had its own patron deity, as every modern Greek island or district nowadays has its own patron saint. These gods would be attended continuously by priests if male, priestesses if female, who lived within the sanctuary environment, and saw to the day-to-day running of the cult. Some communities would have annual festivals, but the more powerful cities, such as Athens, tended to have an extra special festival every four years. At Athens, the annual festival was called the Panathenaia, and the four-yearly one was called the Great Panathenaia which was "for all Athenians". The festival, which lasted several days, was seen as both a civic and sacred event, propagating the traditional values of the society in a community display of wealth and power.

Athena, patron saint of Athens.

Hard-earned Blessings

The Panathenaic Festival took place after the first moon of the Athenian year had waned. The Athenian civic year began in the month called *Hekatombaion* which ran from June to July, when the sun is at its height. The festival, in honour of the patron deity of Athens, the goddess Athena, became a major organized event during the rule of the tyrant Peisistratus; ancient historians state that the first one was held in 566 BC.

The festival included a mixture of exciting and colourful events, including athletic and poetry contests, banquets and processions. The focus of these events was in the Agora, at the point where the sacred road, the Panathenaic Way, ran through on its way from the Dipylon Gate by the Kerameikos up the north side of the Acropolis, to the sanctuary Athena.

Where the road passed through the Ago it was cordoned off and the space was th used for sprints, long-jumps, boxing, wrestlin discus and javelin throwing; there was ever race for men in full hoplite armour, to mainta and exhibit the fitness of the Athenian Arm

It is hard for us to understand how impo tant it was to win these competitive events: n only were you thought to be favoured Athena herself, but the material rewards we also high. We know that a typical prize co

its own individual pagan saint. They are noisy, vibrant and fascinating to watch, and no doubt you will find yourself pulled in to the more "pagan" activities of dancing and feasting.

The ancient religious spirit of co test still survives in some local mode Greek festivals. In the village Arachova, on the way to Delphi, **T Feast of St George** (23 April), who is t

ısted of 105 *amphoras* (terracotta storage jars) olive oil pressed from the sacred olive groves Athena. Many of these Panathenaic *amphos* have survived; in the museums you will cognise them by the image of Athena on one de, whilst on the other the particular athletic vent is portrayed – they are always in the black-gure style even long after red-figure became shionable for other types of pot. It has been lculated that each jar contained 35 litres of oil, nd that the prize of 105 *amphoras* would have n equivalent value today of about £25,000! ne *rhapsodes* (poets) competed with new poems that were meant to vie with the great poet omer.

Processions & Presentations

ne climax of the festival was the Panathenaic ocession which consisted of young warriors, arioteers, priestesses, magistrates and sacrifial attendants carrying water, oil and leading eifers for sacrifice to Athena. The warriors ongregated by the Dipylon Gate on the north-est of the ancient city at the Kerameikos metery. They then proceeded to the Agora ong the Panathenaic Way, and attended by hers, wound their way up on to the Acropolis.

The revered archaic wooden statue of Athena olias (made in the days before marble or onze statues) which had been saved from the ersian sack of 480 BC was placed in the ectheum (rather than the Parthenon). During e Great Panathenaia, a new robe, woven by nmarried girls, was placed on the statue. A crifice of cows (one sent from every ally of hens) was then made on the altar in front of e main temples. The event is portrayed on the rthenon Frieze, where the gods witness the ents from their Olympian thrones.

atron of shepherds, is marked by a race etween the old men of the village. As in e ancient festivals, there is dressing up nd dancing and plenty of feasting: olourful traditional folk costumes are worn.

Name Days are more important family festivals than birthdays. The Christian name given to a Greek Orthodox person is celebrated on the name day of the relevant Saint – for example if your name was George, your Name Day would be on the 23 April, the Feast of St George. Active Christians visit the church on their Name Day and take part in a special Communion service for family and friends. They also take offerings of bread, boiled wheat, candles, olive oil and wine. The candles are lit and handed to everyone present, and the food is eaten in celebration after the service.

Rituals & Feast Days

New Year's Day marks the ***Ayios Vassilios*** (Feast of Saint Basil) – a similar figure to the western Saint Nicholas (Santa Claus). There are special church services on this day and families traditionally bake a ritual loaf called *Vassilopitta* (Saint Basil's loaf): like the British Christmas pudding and its counterpart in other European countries, a coin is baked inside the loaf, which brings good luck for the next year to whoever finds it when the loaf is cut and shared. The New Year greeting is *Kali Hronia* which echoes the pagan festival of the primitive god Kronos (time) at this time of the year.

On January 6 the festival of **Epiphany** is celebrated as the ritual

Dressing up is part of the fun.

packing off to the underworld of the pagan *kalikantzari* (hobgoblins) who are believed to stalk the country during the twelve days of Christmas. For the religious this festival not only commemorates the baptism of Jesus but purification ceremonies designed to rid the country of evil spirits are conducted wherever there is a large or sacred body of water, such as the sea, a lake or a baptismal fount. After blessing a lake, the priest throws a crucifix into the depths and local youths dive in to retrieve it – the competitive spirit that pervades is somewhat reminiscent of the pagan competitions in honour of the gods.

Pre-Lenten Carnivals

During the three weeks before Lent, carnivals take place throughout Greece. At Patras in the north-west Peloponnese, the carnival is a huge event: there are parades of chariots with people in fanc dress and traditional costume. Simil festivities take place in Macedonia wit masked revels, as well as in the island Skiros boasts a pagan "goat dance".

The Athenians give vent to the energies by smashing each another wit plastic hammers in the pre-Lenten fe tivities of their city.

National & Religious Holidays

Independence Day, March 25th, is bot a political as well as religious feast da

Folk-dancing during Easter celebrations in Patmos.

olitically it marks the revolt against e Turks which began on that day in 321 – cannons are fired from Mount ycabettus in Athens as the sun rises, hile all over Greece the Greek flag proudly raised. For the religious is day is also **Annunciation Day**, hich commemorates the visit of e Angel Gabriel to the Virgin ary to announce at she was to ecame Christ's other. There e church serv- es everywhere onouring the ent, with special stivals on the is- nds of Hydra and Tinos. Generally speaking, the historical and religious festivities have merged on this special day: both events being cause for rejoicing.

The month of April is taken up with preparations for the most important celebrations in the Greek year – those of **Easter** (see box story on page 98). The exact date of Easter Sunday, and therefore of other key Easter dates, varies from year to year according to the

Festivals of Culture

The Athens Festival takes place between late-June and September and consists of performances of ancient dramas, opera and ballet. These take place in the magnificent setting of the Roman Odeon ("place of song") of Herodus Atticus. This is an open-air theatre with an auditorium built into the south-west slope of the Acropolis, with a free-standing arcaded stage-building for the performers.

There are few better ways of getting a feeling for Greek culture, ancient and modern, than being in the audience on a warm summer's evening, watching music or drama performed near the place where it received some of its earliest manifestations.

To your left, just along the slopes of the Acropolis is the ancient Theatre of Dionysus, where the great plays of Aeschylus, Euripides and Sophocles were given their premiers. Behind you is the Parthenon, and to your right the Pnyx hill, where the Athenian citizens met to listen to political speeches. In front of you is Philopappos Hill, or the Hill of the Muses, with its commemorative monument to Philopappos, a Roman consul and benefactor of Athens.

Performances take place throughout the week, but are popular and need to be booked in advance. So if you are planning to be in Athens during this period, it is well worth obtaining information and tickets in advance. Write to or call in at: The Festivals Box Office, 4 Stadiou Street, Athens (Tel: 322-1459 or 322-3111, ext. 240). You can also buy tickets here for other cultural festivals.

Athens Alternatives

Sound and light performances are held on the Pnyx Hill at Athens throughout the Summer. These are a bit "touristy" but are nevertheless spectacular, with the Acropolis temples lit up during the show, with a range of coloured spotlights. There are similar events at the Old Venetian Castle on Corfu, and the Palace of the Knights on Rhodes.

Athens also has a winter festival, held in the *Lyriki Skini* (Lyric theatre) in the Odeon of Herodus Atticus. Indoor symphony concerts take place at the Athens Concert Hall, Va
Sofoas Avenue 11521.

From May to September you can see trad
tional Greek folk dancing at the open air theatr
on the west slope of Philopappos Hill, pe
formed by the Dora Stratou Song and Ball
Group (Tel: 324-4395).

Classical Drama Festivals

In the weekends between mid-June and Se
tember, those with a taste for ancient maske
drama should make the effort to travel
Epidavros, where the Classical tragedies ar
comedies are annually revived. There is r
better place than this to watch the ancie
dramas unfold; the theatre is the oldest (four
century) and best-preserved Greek theatre. Yo
will have to listen to the plays in ancient
modern Greek, but the spectacle and music a
usually enough to keep you on the edge of yo
seats.

Ten years ago the National Theatre of Gre
Britain performed their English version
Aeschylus' ***Oresteia*** trilogy here. Directed
Peter Hall, translated by Tony Harrison wi
music by Harrison Birtwistle, it was performe
as in ancient Greece, by an all-male cast wearir
masks. With Greek dignitaries such as Meli
Mercouri, actress and formerly Minister of Cu
ture, in the audience, it succeeded in producir
a standing ovation at the end of four hours
theatre.

Cultural Centres

Finally, there is the increasingly popular Eur
pean Cultural Centre at Delphi which sponso
a summer festival of music, theatre and the ar
This takes place in the Stadium at the top of t
ancient sacred site, and must be one of t
world's most inspired and beautiful settin
under the watchful eye of Apollo, god of Hi
Culture.

Putting her best foot forward.

rthodox calendar, and you will usu- ly find that it differs from that of estern Europe. As a social festival, ıster is taken more seriously in Greece an anywhere else in Europe, and akes up for a less commercialized nristmas. The Greek national radio ıd television networks take Easter seri- ısly with most broadcasts during Holy 'eek devoted to the relevant religious ıbject matter.

On **May Day**, the urban Greeks ead for the countryside to gather flow- s which are woven into wreaths and ıng on doors and balconies: on Mid- ımmer's Eve, they are burnt. The day is so celebrated as "Worker's Day" with ›litical demonstrations and festivals ganized by left-wing parties.

August 15th is The **Assumption of the Blessed Virgin Mary** when Greeks traditionally return to their family homes from wherever they happen to be.

For Athenians this often entails going back to the village from the city. On September 8th the **Birth of the Virgin Mary** is celebrated especially on the island of Spetses: this was also the date of a local sea battle against the Turks in 1822. The battle is re-enacted in the harbour, with feasting and fireworks in the evening.

October 28th is **Ohi Day**: *Ohi* means "No!" and celebrates the response of Metaxas to Mussolini's famous ultimatium in 1940 – the day is marked by national parades and festivities.

Festive Calendar

Greek sacred and secular festivals take place during all seasons of the year. The following calendar gives the main ones, and warns you of public holidays (PH), when most sites and museums will be closed. On all these days you will find celebrations everywhere; particularly special local celebrations which are mentioned below.

Sacred, Greek Orthodox festivals fall on the same days as in the western Church, with the notable exception of Lent/Easter, which can be up to three weeks earlier or later. The exact time of Lent is calculated by the date of Good Friday which is the first Friday after the first full moon after the Spring Equinox. There are also over 330 local Saints' Name Days, which celebrate the patron saint of the village/island church. The major Saints' Name Days listed below are also the more popular Greek Christian names, and you will therefore find many family celebrations on these days.

January 1 (PH): **Saint Basil's Day.**
January 6 (PH): **Epiphany** (Baptism of Christ).
March 25 (PH): **Independence Day**; Feast of the Annunciation.

Pre-Lenten Carnivals: Lasting three weeks, culminating in the seventh weekend before Easter.
Major mainland events: Patras; Thebes; Macedonia (various locations).
Islands: Skiros; Cephallonia; Crete (Heraklion)

Variable Easter Feasts (all below are PH, i cluding Easter weekend from Good Friday).
1994: Lent Monday (March 14 Easter Sunday (May 1); Wh Monday (June 20).
1995: Lent Monday (March 6); East Sunday (April 23); Whit Mo day (June 12).
1996: Lent Monday (February 2 Easter Sunday (April 17); Wh Monday (June 3).

Holidays & Celebrations

April 23: **Saint George's Day** (Mai land Arachova and Skir island hold special celebr tions.)
May 1 (PH): **May Day.**
May 21: **Saint Constantine's a Saint Helen's Day** (the fi Byzantine Orthodox r ers).
June 29: **Saint Peter's and Sai Paul's Day.**
June 30: **The Holy Apostles' Day**
July 17: **Saint Marina's Day** (Chr tian protector of crops).
July 18-19: **The Prophet Elijah's D** celebrated at his hill-to shrines.

Christmas & New Year

Christmas (December 25th) is less important as a traditional festival to the Greeks than is Easter, but it is gradually becoming westernised with Christmas trees and decorations. The Greeks celebrate Christmas less lavishly than Easter in terms of food and drink but some special foods are made; families and guests are treated to *Kourabied* (shortbread cookies) and speci *Christopsomo* (Christmas Bread) decorated with a dough cross, sesame seed and walnuts.

On **New Year's Eve** children sin carols door-to-door and St Basil's loaf shared out just before midnight, whic reminds us that the festive celebration in Greece take place the night before th actual feast day.

gust 6:	**Feast of the Transfiguration.**
gust 15 (PH):	**Assumption of the Blessed Virgin Mary** includes pilgrimage to islands of Tinos and Paros.
ptember 8:	**Birth of the Virgin Mary.** Double celebrations on Spetses island to commemorate the Battle of the Straits (naval defeat of Turks, 1822).
ptember 14:	**Exaltation of the Cross.**
:tober 26:	**Saint Demetrius's Day.** Special in Thessaloniki (patron saint).
:tober 28 (PH):	**Ohi Day** celebrates Metaxas' "No!" (Ohi) to Mussolini's invasion ultimatum in 1940.
›vember 8:	**The Holy Day of Archangels Michael and Gabriel.**
›vember 30:	**Saint Andrew's Day.**
›cember 6:	**Saint Nicholas's Day** – patron saint of seafarers.
›cember 25 (PH):	**Christmas**: birth of Jesus Christ.
›cember 26 (PH):	**Meeting of the Virgin's and her Attendants.**
›cember 31:	**New Year's Eve.**

Cultural Festivals

. Greece, the main cultural events take ace, as they did in the ancient world, ıring festivals. The largest of these is ıe **Athens Festival** which is held annuly from mid-June to mid-September: ıcient plays are resurrected and performed in the ruined theatres; classical usic, opera and ballet rub shoulders with jazz and rock. International stars are invited from all over the world in this modern equivalent of the ancient Panathenaic Festival.

There are also local festivals of the arts which are published in advance by the Greek Tourist Organization (EOT) in a leaflet called "Greek Festivals". The most important include the island music festivals on Thira in late August to October. Crete celebrates the arts in early August, whilst the Ionian island of Lefkadha has a lively **Festival of International Dance** during August. On the mainland outside of Athens, there are festivals in Patras from mid-June to August, whilst Thessaloniki boasts two major festivals: the **Dhimitria arts festival** in October, and an **International Film Festival** in November.

As a tourist you will be welcome as spectators at all types of festials; whether you will be invited to participate depends on the individual occasion.

Traditions of the Spirit

Throughout mainland Greece and the islands, the ancient spirit of sacred and secular festivities remains alive and well. The Greek festivals are as colourful and competitive as they have ever been, with locals vying to wear the best traditional costumes or perform the best poems or dances. It is in these festivals that the heart-beat quickens, embracing traditions and the spirit – be it pagan or religious – of what it is to be Greek.

Culture

The poets, playwrights, philosophers, orators and historians of ancient Greece, have provided the world with a magnificent cultural heritage. This heritage has been most influential over the western world, but it has recently been demonstrated that in its development, Greek culture was itself influenced by oriental and African societies. This influence, is being recognized by non-western cultures today.

Dedicated to the Gods.

Poetic Classics

Long before the Greeks learnt to write, their poets travelled around the royal courts of the Mediterranean, singing songs of warriors and heroes. These epic poems were recorded when the Phoenician alphabet was adopted in the eighth century BC; few have survived, but we are lucky to have ***The Iliad*** and ***The Odyssey***, of Homer, which tell of the siege of Troy and the magical adventures of the hero Odysseus, on his

The Theatre of Dionusus could accommodate 17,000 people in its time.

journey home to Ithaka. Homer's epic metre and use of literary similes, have influenced writers of epic from antiquity to the present day. The opening to Book 19 describes the Goddess of dawn, Aurora, bringing light to both gods and mortals, whilst the Greek hero Achilles' divine mother Thetis brings a new set armour to her son:

"Soon as Aurora heaved her orient Head
Above the Waves that blushed with early Red,
(With new-born Day to gladden mortal

Sight,
And gild the Courts of Heaven with sacred Light)
The immortal Arms the Goddess-Mother bears
Swift to her Son: Her Son she finds in Tears..."
Iomer, ***The Iliad***; Translation: Alexander Pope)

The Greeks also developed a more private and down-to-earth form of poetry called "Lyric" – thus called because it was accompanied by the lyre. Lyric poems were sung at *symposia* (drinking parties), and were short pieces set to varied metre and music. Their subject-matter often reflected the atmosphere of the symposium: erotic (and often homosexual), religious and political: The most famous of the lyric poets was the female Sappho:

"What is the most beautiful sight on this black earth?
Some will answer cavalry, or infantry, or warships;
But the woman I most love
Is lovelier than all these".

(Sappho of Lesbos; sixth century BC; translation: D. Bellingham)

The Great Playwrights

In the fifth century BC the first dramas were produced for performance at the Theatre of Dionysos, Athens. The plays were part of an annual spring festival in honour of the wine and fertility god, Dionysos. The dramatists competed for prizes and it was the greatest civic honour to win.

The dramas included a chorus which tended to comment on the action, plus three or four actors who played the main roles. They wore face-masks and these, together with their costumes, signified gender and social status. Only male actors were allowed on the stage.

The Ancient Greek Theatre

Ancient theatre differed from what we are used to, in several ways. It was nearly always performed as an integral part of a religious festival, and the choruses of the tragedies in particular, reflect the sacred aspect with their hymns of praise to the gods. Both tragedies and comedies conformed to a highly formalized structure, and were a mixture of music, dance, acted dialogues between individual characters, and sung solo speeches and choruses.

Unfortunately hardly any of the music has survived, but we are fortunate to still have texts of plays by the great fifth century BC Athenian tragic playwrights, Aeschylus, Sophocles and Euripides, as well as several comedies by their contemporary Aristophanes. From the fourth century BC onwards, tragedy declined as a dramatic form, but comedy continued to thrive in the so-called New Comedy, of the poet Menander (341-291 BC).

Stage Set

The theatres themselves were not built of durable materials until the fourth century BC. For example, during the fifth century BC, the Theatre of Dionysus in Athens consisted of wooden benches for the audience, set into the natural hollow of the southern Acropolis, whilst the circular "orchestra" between the auditorium and the stage, on which the chorus sung and danced was beaten earth and the *proskeni*
(stage) and *skene* (stage-building), were of woo
Only at the time of Alexander the Great wa
permanent stone theatre built.

We know from ancient writers that scene
was painted on wooden panels which we
placed against the stage-building, behind t
stage. Tragedies were usually set in front o
royal palace, and Greek theatres had a lar
central doorway in the stage-building for ex
and entrances. New Comedy plots tended
involve squabbles between next-door neig
bours, and smaller doors were inserted eith
side of the "palace" door for this purpose. T
chorus entered along *parodoi* (side passage
between the stage and the auditorium.

Stage props included a crane for hoisti
characters on and off the stage as if in flight a
a kind of trolley on which the dead bodies
tragic victims could be wheeled onto the sta
for the audience to see (killings always to
place off stage).

The Athens Arts Scene

Theatre first developed in Athens in the la
sixth century BC when, during choral singing
certain Thespis, stepped aside and began
sing his own lines, so becoming the first ev
actor (hence our word "thespian"). By the fif
century, tragedies were being performed

Playwrights used Greek myths and legends for their themes, but they would often incorporated contemporary ideas into the dramas.

The works of three writers of tragedy have survived from the fifth century. Aeschylus is the earliest (born 525 BC) and was called old-fashioned by his younger contemporaries. However, his plays (for e.g. the ***Oresteia*** trilogy), were critical of political tyrants and celebrated the birth of the democratic ideals of la
and freedom. Sophocles (496-406 BC
who like Aeschylus acted in his ow
plays, developed the psychological fe
tures of his characters and was noted f
his use of irony. Euripides (born c 48
BC) was the most *avant garde* of th
three. His plays were often critical of th
gods and of heroic warrior behavio
and his female characters have bee
interpreted as early feminists:

ramatic competitions during the great Dionysia pring Festival at Athens, in honour of Dionysus, ut it is still not certain whether women and hildren were allowed in.

The tragedies were written for a chorus and hree or four main actors, who often took sev-ral roles. Masks and costumes helped the audi-nce to identify different characters. Dramas sted the whole day, often with three con-ected tragedies telling the story of, for exam-le, Prometheus or Oedipus. The evening ended vith a hilarious "satyr play", in which the chorus nd the actors dressed as woolly satyrs and cted out a comic version of one of the myths.

Genres

ragedies were designed as "tear-jerkers" to nake audiences weep in pity and fear for the agic hero or heroine. Aristophanes' comedies, n the other hand, were bizarre mixtures of ntasy and contemporary worlds. Living politi-ans, philosophers and other playwrights and oets were all openly ridiculed – we must re-ember that they would all have been sitting in ne audience with the other citizens!

Menander's later comedies were similar to ur "situation comedies", with next-door neigh-ours arguing in a realistic manner about trivial veryday affairs.

"Of every living creature we women ave the worst lot. First we have to ttract a husband with our father's oney, and then we find that he turns ut to be a bully; but worst of all, if we on't like him, we can't get rid of him, ecause it's not considered proper for a oman to divorce a man...we can't get way from him when we're upset; yet ır husbands can go out drinking with s friends whenever he chooses...They

Socrates, the great philosopher.

say that we sit at home whilst they do the fighting; but I would rather fight in the frontline several times than suffer the pain of giving birth to one baby". (Euripides, ***Medea***; translation: D. Bellingham)

Ancient Comics

Tragedies were balanced by comedies, but only one comic playwright, Aristophanes (c 450-385 BC) has survived history. His comedies are set in the real world of Athens, but incorporate fantastical elements. They ridicule and attack contemporary politicians, philosophers, poets as well as the tragic playwrights.

The Ancient Greek Drinking Party

The ancient Greeks held special drinking parties called *symposia* (singular, *symposium*). The *symposium* was a mainly aristocratic institution in which friends were invited to the host's house, where a special room called the *andron* (men's room) was often constructed for the purpose of such gatherings. These rooms were arranged so that the participants could recline on wooden couches placed around the edges of the room. Wooden tables were placed in ready-made slots in front of each couch to carry plates of food and drinking-cups. These rooms have also been found in state and religious contexts for political and sacred dinners.

Only male guests were invited – their wives were excluded from the *symposium*, but often female *hetairai* ("companions") were hired for the evening, to entertain the men with dancing, music and sex. All of these activities can be observed on the many sympotic scenes which decorate Athenian drinking vessels.

Apart from drinking-songs and sexual pleasures, there were also drinking-games. The favourite among many was *kottabos,* in which you flicked the, dregs of your wine at a target your neighbours cup or sometimes a disc place on a stand.

Measures of Indulgence

The evening began with dinner, which appea to have consisted of small, varied dishes of fis bread, olives, cheese, eggs and vegetables very similar to the mixed dishes often served a modern *taverna*. The dessert might have bee honey-cake or figs. After eating, slave bo would enter to wash the hands of the partic pants. The diners were each given perfum and floral wreaths to wear on their heads for th drinking party – violets were popular.

A libation of wine was then poured and th *potos* (drinking part) of the evening bega Activities varied from a relatively restraine evening of philosophical or political convers tion, helped along by moderate amounts wine, to full-blown orgies.

A "master of ceremonies" was elected, who

Later Hellenistic Greek poets continued to write epic and lyric, but, like Euripides, they preferred to place their heroes in a more realistic context:

"...Theseus threw off his soaking clothes
And putting on a ragged tunic that the old woman had laid out on the bed
Made himself at home on her humble couch...
She served him hand-picked olives swimming in brine
And from an earthenware tub she gave him bread,
And while Theseus ate the ploughman's lunch,
Hecale told him her life-story and how she had
Once come from a wealthy family..."

(Callimachos (c 320-285 BC), ***Heca*** translation: D. Bellingham)

Of the later Greek playwrights, on a few survive in fragments; the exce tion is the comic Menander (342-2 BC), who was the leading writer of Ne Comedy (Aristophanes was Old Co edy). Unlike Aristophanes, his pla avoid fantasy situations – Aristophan had a chorus of kitchen pots and pans his ***Wasps*** – and are more like our "s coms". The scene is usually set in Athenian street, with two next-doo neighbours bickering about who is sponsible for the daughter's baby, similar "everyday" themes. Much use

uty it was to say how much water was to be ıixed with the wine – only barbarians drank it nmixed – and how much was to be drunk. The reeks were fully aware of the effects of alcohol: a play by Eubulus, the god of wine Dionysus, ays that "Three bowls are sufficient for the emperate – one is for good health, one is for ve and enjoyment, and the last is for sleep. If ou drink a fourth you will become violent; a fth will lead to uproar; the sixth to drunken evel; the seventh to black eyes; the eighth calls the police; the ninth is for vomiting and the nth leads to madness and a throwing of rniture".

Classical Drinkers & Maudlin Sayings

ot all *symposia* were like this! The philosopher ato wrote a dramatic dialogue, called ***The ymposium*** which describes an evening's philoophical discussion about the nature of Love. Although the drink is flowing, this encourages the guests to be open and sincere their attitudes on love.

The comic playwright Aristophanes, gives a hilarious account of true love: we all used to be two people joined at the navel, we therefore had four arms and four legs and used to get around by cart-wheeling. Zeus became worried that we might eventually take over Mount Olympus through our double power and manoeuvrability. He therefore had us bisected, and the navel part was tied up in a knot. This is the reason that we are all looking for our "other half" or soul-mate.

Socrates, Plato's teacher, is reputed to have stayed up until daybreak talking about philosophy. The wine-cup is still being passed around by the group from left to right, as the cock crows.

Finally, all except Socrates nod off to sleep and he makes his way back home. Socrates was renowned for being able to drink as much as anybody else, without the effects of drunkeness.

ıade of mistaken identity which influnced the "comedy of manners" in later uropean literature.

History in the Making

erodotus (c 484-420 B.C.) has been ılled "the Father of History", but only ecause he was the first ever writer of story: the modern reader finds his riting more entertaining than historiıl. He was born at Halicarnassus odrum in modern Turkey), but spent uch time in Athens and travelled ound the Greek islands gathering marial from all kinds of sources – poets, traveller's tales and anything which made for a good story – for the writing of his histories. Like the poets, he would hold public readings of his writings, apparently at a rate of 10 talents per session, which is about 15 year's wages to a Greek soldier!

Herodotus' anecdotes about foreign lands are bizarre and often hilarious: we are told of Arabian sheep whose tails are so long that the shepherds attach tiny wooden carts to their hind-quarters to carry them. The racist Greek attitude towards barbarians is evident throughout his work: "the Indians copulate in the open like cattle; their semen is not white like other peoples, but black like their own skins – the same peculiarity is to be found in the Ethiopians".

Thucydides (c 455-400 BC), was in a different league from Herodotus. He fought as a general in the Peloponnesian War between Athens and Sparta and their respective allies. Although an Athenian, his history shows little bias against the Spartans, and is often highly critical of Athenian imperialism. Like the modern historian, Thucydides was cautious with his source material and discussed the causes of the war as well as its events. Referring to his methodology against the more racy style of his contemporary Herodotus, he says:

"Either I was there myself at the incidents which I have described or else I heard them from eye-witnesses whose accounts I have checked with as much thoroughness as possible...it may well be that my history will seem a less entertaining read because of the absence in it of a romantic element".

(Thucydides, ***History of the Peloponnesian War***)

The Philosophical Tradition

Greek philosophers did not always record their thoughts in writing: the work of the most influential *philosophos* (lover of wisdom), Socrates, is only know through the surviving literature of h pupil Plato.

The first philosopher to write a pros treatise was Anaximander (c 610-54 BC). Like many early Greek thinke and poets he came, not from mainlan Greece, but from the eastern Mediterr nean (Miletus on the western coast modern Turkey). He believed that go was infinit and agele and that th cosmos co sisted of opp sites which we always in a pro ess of balancir one another. Tw and a half thousar years befo Darwi he cr ated a theory of the evol tion of animals and human beings. H was also interested in astronomy ar drew the first map of earth.

Perhaps the most profound of th early pre-Socratic philosphers Heraclitus.

Like Anaximander, he came fro the eastern Mediterranean. He record his thoughts in about 500 BC and d posited them in the Temple of Arten in his birthplace at Ephesus for sa keeping. The temple was later burn down by the barbarian Persians and h writings now survive only when quot by other authors. These quotations a ıemorable and even in use in the modern world: "God is both day and night, ımmer and winter, war and peace, bundance and famine".

Heraclitus' dualism, like Zen Budhism, refused to accept that only Good an exist. Enlightenment, according to eraclitus, could not be found in learnıg about the physics of the cosmos, but ı losing oneself in an awareness of a ommon world order.

The Search for Truth; Socrates & Plato

ocrates (469-399 BC) was condemned death by his fellow Athenians on a ıarge of introducing alien gods and orrupting the youth. In fifth-century thens, there were many *sophists* (wise en), who taught young men to make peeches in the law-courts and the poical assembly. Their teaching openly dmitted that lying was an acceptable art of public-speaking so long as you on your case.

Socrates attacked the *sophists* and gued that young men are better off ırsuing Truth through discourse with ıe another. A hint of why he might ave been prosecuted by the Athenian emocracy, can be found in the writings his pupil Plato (c 429-347 BC). Plato's ***epublic***, poured scorn on democracy a political principle, arguing that the norant masses can be controlled by lf-seeking demagogues. He preferred state governed by a limited number of philosophers who have discovered "The Good".

Knowledge of the "Good" could only be acquired through a search for "ideal forms" which do not exist in the world we perceive, because our senses are corrupted by falsehood. Therefore, Plato argued that in his ideal state (the Republic), artists would be controlled so that only poems representing the Good could be performed.

Plato admired Egyptian art for its lack of innovation: "If you go and look at their art, you will find that ten thousand years ago (and I'm not exaggerating: I mean literally ten thousand), paintings and reliefs were created that are no different to those of today, because the same artistic rules were applied in making them...whereas the desire for new pleasures and avoidance of monotony lead our artists in a never-ending search for novelty – it is this which corrupts". (***The Laws***).

Plato set up a school at Athens called the "Academy". One of its pupils was Aristotle (384-322 BC), who continued Plato's research into the Good, but tended to be more down-to-earth and realistic in his political theories. He believed that the middle-class was the most stable element in society, and that they should therefore be its rulers.

Philosophies of Reality & Enjoyment

Two rival schools of philosophy emerged

Theodorakis & Contemporary Greek Music

Modern Greek composers of music are much closer to the average Greek's experience of life and much more obviously integrated into broad cultural ideas than many of their contemporaries in other countries. Music of all genres is rooted in the melodies and rhythms of both "low" and "high" culture; in folk songs from all regions of Greece, in the *rebetika* "blues" of the urban environment, as well as in the long, unchanging tradition of Byzantine church music. Greek music definitely has an eastern flavour, in both its instrumentation and in the manner in which it is sung: a good deal of intense emotion and even oriental "wailing" is put into the vocal line.

The top composers are popular in the sense that their music is heard and known everywhere in Greece, and also because they have written musical scores for well-known films: Mikis Theodorakis for *Z* and *Zorba the Greek*, and Manis Hadjidakis for *Never on Sunday.*

Theodorakis – Poignancy & Politics

Mikis Theodorakis emerged from the *Neo Kima* (New Wave) music which developed in Athenian clubs in the 1960s. He himself was not member of this young, politically radical mov ment, but he identified with its left-wing po tics. Theodorakis, now a right-wing New D mocracy minister, was once an active memb of the Greek Communist Party and warm supported its desire to create a musical for with the power to change society from th grass-roots. His haunting melodies and trad tional rhythms have produced wonderful m sical renditions of the work of contempora poets, including the Nobel Laureate Odysse Elytis and the poet Nikos Gatsos, whose lyri have also been set to music by another popul composer, Stavros Xarhakos.

Hadjidakis – Romantic Reality

Manos Hadjidakis is less overtly political, ar has encouraged the work of less well-knov musicians with his own record label. His inspir tion comes from the grim urban experiences gypsies and the young, often focusing on trag tales of love. His poetry lies in the drean romanticism which he is able to instil into seemingly mundane environment.

in Athens, during the Hellenistic period: Stoicism and Epicureanism. The founder of Stoicism was Zeno (335-263 BC), who set up his school in the *Stoa Poikile* (Painted Stoa), a colonnaded public hall in the Athenian Agora. The Stoics believed that wisdom can only be achieved by knowledge of reality and reason (as opposed to the abstract thinking of the Academics).

Epicurus (341-270 BC) founded a school called "The Garden" outside of Athens because Epicureans believed that pleasure was to be found in the natur world of the countryside: the city broug only ambition, material wealth ar attendant stress. Truth lay in the pursu of pleasures, but only pleasures whic do not end in pain: to Epicureans heav drinking was right out!

Musical Interludes

The ancient Greeks regarded mus highly and incorporated it into mo

In Hadjidakis' song *Dream of Urban Children*, slow, lilting and yearning opening section is llowed by a fast, bouncing passage reminis- nt of the traditional slow *syrto* and fast *pedecto* nces."Every garden has a bird's nest, every reet has a heart for the children. But you, girl, hy do keep talking with the dawn, and why e you always looking at falling stars?"

Rock & Pop

reece has its international rock and opera stars o. The mezzo-soprano Agnes Baltsa, follow- g in the footsteps of her heroine Maria Callas, w sings the major roles at Covent Garden and e Met, making it big with her darkly tragic, d very Greek, rendition of Carmen, opposite se Carreras' Don Jose. She has also recorded eodorakis, Hadjidakis and Xarhakos songs for major international record label.

At the opposite end of the muscial spectrum the Bruce Springsteen of Greece, George laras, who sings heart-rending Greek songs all kinds to massive Greek audiences in foot- ll stadiums. Recently he has collaborated with e flamenco guitarist Paco de Lucia. Like Agnes ltsa, he is helping to spread the best of Greek odern culture to the international scene.

pects of their culture. The poets sang eir poems, and accompanied them- lves on a stringed instrument such as e lyre. Religious choral singers were so joined by *aulos* (flute) players: The eek flute can be seen being played by th men and women in vase-paint- gs, it consisted of a double flute with a ed mouthpiece and holes which could finger-stopped to produce different tes, probably sounding more like our oe than a flute. "Flute-girls" were tually high-class *hetairai* (prostitutes) who entertained men at the aristocratic drinking parties with their music. Unfortuately very little of ancient Greek music has survived, but there have been several recent attempts to reconstruct the original instruments from depictions in the vase-paintings, and a recording has been made of the music fragments. It sounds very oriental, reminding us that much of ancient Greek culture was derived from the eastern Mediterranean.

The Spirit of *Kefi*

Dance was also an integral part of the ancient culture, forming like music, an essential aspect of Greek education as well as being incorporated into the theatre: the choruses danced as they sang, and the ancient dramas must have been very like grand operas, with singing, musical accompaniment and occasional dance sequencies.

Research into ancient dance has manifested that the dances performed in Greece today, secular and religious, are remarkably similar to dances performed up to 4,000 years ago. The purpose of these ancient dances was to praise the gods through complex and beautiful body movements and gestures: dance even had its divine Muse, Terpsichore. Until very recently, girls used to perform pagan fertility dances on the fields of Epirus.

The modern Greek dances out of an urge to show the world his sense of joy.

Celebrations often culminate in dance performances.

.e Greeks have a word for this elusive irit – *kefi*. When sitting enjoying a eal with friends and the drink is flow-), the special sense of shared *joie de re*, brims over into the desire to dance d sing. Look on the walls of Greek *ernas* and you will often see musical truments hanging there, waiting for ose special, but unpredictable, occa- ns of *kefi*.

Dance today provides an opportu- y for social gatherings. In the villages etings between boys and girls are still ainly at such events, where the dance ables the men to exhibit their virility d athleticism and the women to dis- ay their grace and beauty. In tradi- nal dance, women are not allowed to rform the fast dances. There are hun- eds of different Greek dances and the rious regions of Greece have their n traditional dances: recently these ve become more widely known ough the formation of professional ncing troupes. You can see the fa- ous *Dora Stratou troupe* in an open-air eatre on the slopes of the Philopappos l, Athens.

Traditional Dance

ere are two main types of traditional nce in Greece: *syrto* is danced at a slow npo, the feet are dragged and the ps are shuffled in complex move- nts; *pedecto* entails a faster tempo d more dynamic movements, includ- springing steps punctuated by vigorous leaps. Both types are performed by several dancers, who might move anti-clockwise in a twisting line or a circle. The "leader" improvises whilst the rest conform to strict foot movements. If you are watching this dance, you will almost certainly find yourself invited to join in: you should not refuse as the guest is expected to see this as an honour. It does not matter if you can not dance properly: the Greeks love those who try, and only the "natural" will be expected to perform improvisations!

Popular Dances

There are four or five really popular dances, and you might be able to identify them from their different speeds, steps and moves. The *Zeibekiko*, was made famous by Anthony Quinn's dancing of it in the film ***Zorba the Greek***. If you saw the film you will remember two men circling one another slowly, arms outstretched, giving the dance its alternative name of "Dance of the Eagle". It is usually danced by men in *tavernas*, though women are beginning to dance it, and some of the other "male" dances, more frequently.

There are no set movements, the whole dance depending on individual interpretation. The dancers sometimes look like two wild animals locked in the early stages of a fight to the death; perhaps for this reason they tend to hiss to themselves.

Another *taverna* dance is the

Hasapiko (Butchers' Dance), which involves three dancers, arms on each other's shoulders, eyes on the ground, moving solemnly to the *bouzouki* music, in isolation from the rest of the company. Their slow and purposeful movements are communicated by the central dancers' hands. The *Syrtaki* is similar, but is often danced by five. It is the mood which differs from the *Hasapiko*: where that dance is tight and introverted, the *Syrtaki* is extrovert and loose, the spectators shouting their approval.

The National Dance

The Greek national dance is the *Kalamatiano* (originating from near Kalamata in the Peloponnese): this is the one you are most likely to be asked to join in with at a *taverna* or a Greek wedding party. You join hands with your neighbours, forming a W-pattern by bending the elbows and holding the hands at shoulder level. You move in a line by side-stepping slowly, following the movements of the leader. Early Greek vase-paintings depict men and women moving in this manner.

The *Tsamiko* or "handkerchief dance" is a more spectacular version of the same basic line dance, with the two front dancers joined by a handkerchief. The mountain warriors of Epirus used to dance it during the Wars of Independence, and it involves a military stance and movements. Some way into the dance, the leader performs acrobatic

The soulful bouzouki.

turns around the handkerchief, he firmly by the second dancer.

Women join in these primari masculine dances, but they also hav their own dances such as the *Tsiphte Te* in which the body performs a sensuo display of sinuous hip, arm and shou der movements. Men join in by copyir the female motions, though there never any sense of ridicule or loss pride in the parody.

Musical Instruments

Greek folk musical instruments are n dissimilar to those used by the ancien The lyre has been replaced by th *bouzouki*, which looks like a large ma

An evening of classical Greek drama can be a magical experience.

lin, and which has quite recently be-
me popular in western European folk
usic, particularly Irish.

The violin as in Ireland, is also a
vourite folk instrument: interestingly,
e Cretan version is also called a lyre.
u may be surprised to also see clari-
ts, but again, the basic sound is reed-
oduced, like the ancient *aulos*. Vari-
s types of drum or clapper provide the
at, and there are quite a variety of less
mmon instruments to provide melody,
cluding a goatskin bagpipe called the
ida.

Modern Music

e most fashionable folk music at the
oment is undoubtedly that called
etika, which has been described as a
d of Greek Blues music. It has its
gins in the rural Greek past, but this
ntury has seen it rooted and trans-
med in the porest urban fringe districts and sea-ports.

The lyrics reflect the life-style of the poorer Greeks in all its aspects: from opium dens to worry beads, from hatred to love. *Rebetika* can also be heard outside of Greece wherever the poorer Greek communities are found; "Life in a strange land is making me old before my time and eating me to death, and I can't stand it any more", begins a well-known *rebetic* song called *xenitia* (homesickness).

Rebetika is shunned by more "respectable" urban Greeks, but its influence can be clearly seen in the high cultural music of Greek 20th-century composers such as Mikis Theodorakis, as are many other influences including the haunting single melodic line of Byzantine church music. Music and dance reflects the real Greek character and cultural values, perhaps better than any other cultural manifestation: in it you will hear the pathos and the tragedy of the darker Greek past, the deeply felt love of the present sun-lit moment, and the herioc hopes and struggles for a brighter future.

Greek Museums

Discus thrower.

Bronze charioteer.

Museums can be pretty forbidding places to most of us. Wherever they are in the world, large or small, they tend to have the intimidating atmosphere of a sacred Church, where outspoken discussion about the surrounding objects is tacitly forbidden.

It is all too easy to step through the doors of the local museum, look at a few cases of either badly-labelled or even unlabelled antiquities and then head for the door out of boredom. I have found, however, that with a little bit of patience and forethought, visiting museums in Greece can enrich your understanding of wherever you happen to be. They have the additional attractions of being a cool retreat on a hot day in town, and many of them offer toilet and refreshment facilities.

Understanding a Museum

Greek Museums fall into three main categories: Archaeological Museums which display anti- uities from the prehistoric and Classical pas Byzantine Museums which contain painted ico and architectural fragments from the mediev Christian period; and Folk Museums which di play a wide variety of traditional Greek co tumes, cooking equipment and all sorts of od and ends which do not really fit in elsewher

The Archaeological Museum is usually a ranged chronologically, so that you begin in th prehistoric rooms and move through the A chaic (c 650-500 BC), Classical (c 500-300 B and Hellenistic (c 300-30 BC) periods and in the Roman era (c 30 BC to AD 300).

In most museums you will find that potte vessels fill a majority of the display cases; this simply because terracotta survives better th any other material. These are the everyday well as the ritual objects of the ancient cultur from which they poured their water and wine banquets or which they filled with perfumed and offered at the tombs of dead relatives.

Cherubs on metope.

Look at the painted decoration; the earlier ots tend to have abstract designs of geometric ıapes or of animals or sea-creatures. Archaic ıd Classical pots are more often painted with ɡure-scenes from mythology or everyday life: ıe earlier examples are black-figure (black silɔuette figures on the red clay background), hilst later ones are in red-figure (the background is painted black, whilst the figures are served in the clay, and details are carefully ainted in). You are also likely to see bronze, ver or gold objects and finely crafted jewelry; these were the most valuable materials in l periods and because of looting, little of it has ırvived. Finally there are usually a few marble atues and architectural fragments from the earby sites.

Power of the Imagination

ıe whole Greek Museum experience feeds the imagination so that you can mentally reconstruct the ruined sites with living people, their houses and temples; public spaces can be filled with beautiful statues and finely crafted vases, Greece can be truly imagined in the era of its greatness. Folk Museums give you just a glimpse of the life of ordinary Greeks through the centuries, and the significant loss of a colourful culture which took place when the Greeks moved (relatively recently) from the countryside to the towns.

The Goddess Dianne and below, statue of Zeus.

Art, Architecture & Crafts

Lovers of art and architecture have plenty to entrance them in Greece. It is not, however, a country for people whose interests tend towards Renaissance and modern art. Greece has no international art gallery, nor has it contributed much to the history of art since the fall of the Byzantine culture. However, this break in the production of high art and architecture, created by the centuries of Turkish occupation, has been filled to a certain extent by the continuing tradition of folk art in the villages, islands and back streets of Athens and other towns.

Fine example of Byzantine architecture.

Architectural Diversity

Many people go to Athens expecting to spend their time looking at Classical art and architecture of the fifth and fourth centuries BC. Certainly the most impressive surviving temples, such as the three main temples on the Acropolis, and the Temple of Hephaistus overlooking the Agora date from that period. But there are fine examples from the earlier and later ages of the

The Odeon of Herodes Atticus in Athens.

Greco-Roman period which are always a source of unexpected delight to less blinkered viewers.

Byzantine material, produced during the sovereignity of the Eastern Church at Constantinople, before it fell in 1453 to the Turks, is also plentiful. Byzantine church architecture is especially well represented throughout Greece, and there is a splendid collection of sculpture, painted icons and church-fittings in the Byzantine Museum in Athens.

Not much remains intact from the Turkish period apart from a few ruined mosques which have been converted into secular Greek buildings since independence. However you can see good post-Byzantine examples of Frankish castles in the hills and Venetian fortif cations on the coastline, whilst thes western late medieval cultures impose their religious styles by adding Gothi elements to the earlier Byzantin churches.

Lost by Time

No monumental painting survives fror the prehistoric and classical periods i Greece. We know from ancient writer that the art of painting flourished alonc side sculpture in the fifth and fourt centuries BC. The great classical sculp tors are now better known than the contemporary painters, simply becaus some of their work has survived, albe

Frescoes of the life of Christ, Patmos.

ıly in inferior copies made in later ·riods; good painters plastered their nvas before painting which led to the lours fading. Literary sources how- 'er remain to give us some idea of what ese painters achieved.During the fifth ntury BC, Polygnotos of Thasos pro- ıced a series of paintings to adorn me of the Acropolis' walls. These paint- gs comprised of violent battle scenes ›m the Trojan wars, juxtaposed with a ore romantic image of the hero lysseus encountering the beautiful incess Nausicaa on the beach.

In the early fourth century BC, we ar of a painter named Zeuxis who veloped the technique of *chiaroscuro* – ing gradations of light and shade to 'e an illusion of three-dimensional form. He once painted a boy holding a bunch of grapes, which were so realistic that birds flew up to eat them. But Zeuxis was unhappy with the painting: "I have painted the grapes better than the boy", he exclaimed, "for if I had depicted him properly, the birds would have been afraid to touch the grapes".

Apelles of Kos

In the late fourth century, Apelles of Kos painted *Aphrodite Rising from the Sea* – the well-known and more recent Renaissance version by Botticelli was a deliberate attempt to "reconstruct" Apelles' lost image – Apelles is said to have fallen in love with the model, who was

Byzantine Churches

Between the fifth and ninth centuries BC there were few building projects in the western Mediterranean and Europe owing to the chaos created by the barbarian invasions. During this period, the greatest architectural activity was concentrated in the creation of hundreds of churches by the Byzantine rulers, with the dual purpose of propagating their prestige and their religion.

Byzantine architecture reflected its geographical position by combining the old imperial Roman styles with those of the middle east. Roman features included the use of brickwork and concrete for the walls; the east contributed the ability to place a dome over square, rectangular and circular spaces.

This combination enabled the Byzantine architects to create complex plans and daring new buildings. Brickwork was covered with colourful (and expensive) materials such as mosaic. The main attraction of the Byzantine church is this combination of powerful structure with the richness of the decorative detail of carved columns and mosaics.

Architectural Style

The earliest Byzantine churches were built soon after the edict of Theodosius II in AD 435, which shut down the pagan shrines. Only traces of these very early buildings remain and many the new churches were simply conversions earlier temples. The early churches followed th western basilica plan of a central nave raise above the side aisles and a semi-circular apse the east end. The floors were covered in marb and mosaics decorated the walls.

This type of church continued until th Middle Byzantine Period (ninth to twelfth ce turies) when gradually the new, more easter domed churches began to replace the weste basilicas: Flattened domes began to appe supported by four columns or piers; four barr vaulted spaces radiated out from beneath th dome. This central part of the church w approached from the *narthex* (vestibule) at th western end; to the east was the altar. This pl is called the "inscribed-cross domed type referring to its appearance as a Greek Cross: remains the basic plan of later Byzanti churches. In the more remote places and islan you will often find it in a small and simplifi version, with the north and south cross-ar reduced to shallow recesses.

In the later churches, brickwork often fram square stone blocks to create new exterior p terns. Likewise you will sometimes see cut bric forming Greek letters or decorative patterns the external facades, and in some places y will even see glazed bowls set in the mortar create a beautiful decorative effect.

one of Alexander's concubines. Alexander awarded the woman to Apelles as a token of his respect. The Romans looted the painting and the Emperor Augustus had it placed in the shrine of the deified Julius Caesar. It had decayed by the late first century AD and Nero replaced it with a copy. Apelles's portrait of Alexander in the guise of Zeus was also admired for the way in which the thunderbolt appeared to project out of the picture.

Appreciating Architecture

Ancient Greek architects, unlike th contemporary painters and sculpto were always from the leisured wealt classes. They were expected to have broad education in all subjects fr music to astronomy, as well as to ha studied the writings of earlier architec Until the Hellenistic period, the tem was the main architectural form. D

Decorative Devices

roughout the Byzantine period interior deco-
ion consisted of mosaic and fresco. Biblical agery on the mosaics was purposefully used teach the illiterate stories from the bible and ir moral messages.

Standard decorative programmes were pre- ibed by the Church, therefore once you derstand the basic designs, you will be able read the visual narratives in any church; ncipally, the dome was seen as the heavenly here, whilst the lower walls were earthly. The presentations reflect this design with Christ *ntocrator* ("all-powerful") at the top of the me, surrounded by radiating angels, and low them on the walls of the drum are the ophets and Evangelists.

His mother Mary appears at prayer in the se, whilst on the wall below you will usually the Apostles and Bishops. The walls of the ve and aisles carry representations of the Life Christ, beginning with the Annunciation at east end and finishing on the west wall with Ascension and Pentecost.

Byzantine Churches are often neglected in our of the Classical remains; but they make a aceful, cool and colourful alternative when temple sites are hot and dusty, or the useums too crowded.

g later periods theatres and secular ildings began to be built using col- nns and other high architectural fea- res derived from the earlier temple adition.

Architectural style is usually referred as "order": there are three main or- rs of Greek architecture. Firstly the oric Order which developed in western d mainland Greece, consists of base- ss columns with fluted shafts topped saucer-like capitals; above the Doric column is a flat *architrave*, and above that is the Doric frieze, which consists of alternating vertical *triglyphs* (projecting member with vertical channels) and square *metopes* (panels), sometimes carved with sculptures. Above the frieze was the projecting cornice and then the sloping tiled roof. At each end of the roof was the pediment, which contained sculptures.

The Ionic Order was formed in eastern Greece and used more ornate columns with carved bases and scrolled capitals: the fluting of the columns also differed from the Doric order in being deeper and flat-edged; like the Doric the columns were tapered but those of the Ionic were slimmer. The Ionic *architrave* blocks are carved with three bands, whilst the Ionic frieze is either a continuous sculpture (like the Parthenon frieze) or is left plain, often with a projecting row of teeth-like *dentils* (projections) running along the top. Ionic pediments are generally unsculpted. The third Order was the Corinthian, this developed out of the Ionic order, and differed by having a circular column capital decorated with projecting acanthus leaves. This form was also popularized by the Romans, who synthesized the Ionic and Corinthian forms to produce a "composite" form.

The Romans & Byzantines

You will not see much art and architecture from the Roman period in Greece as

Greek Vase Painting

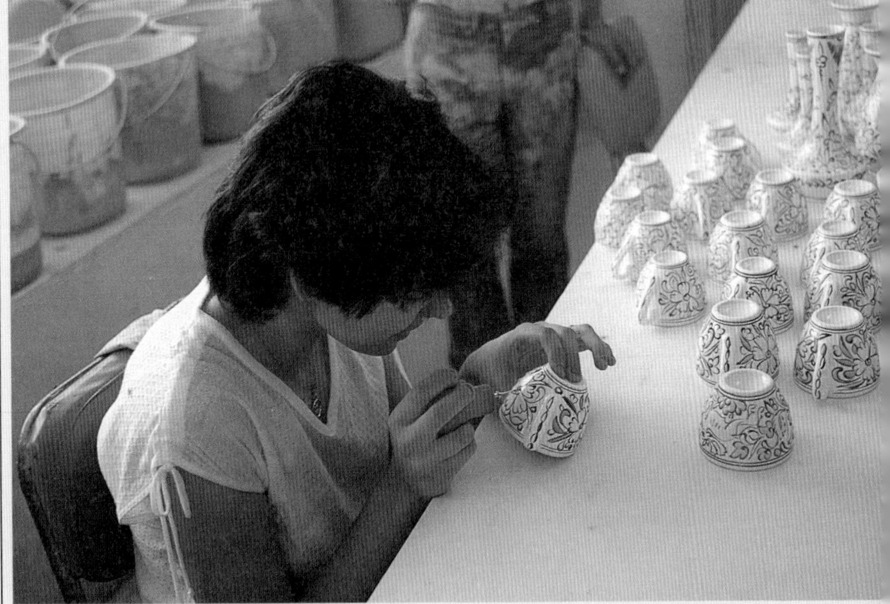

Perpetuating the tradition of Greek folk art.

The way Classical Greek vases were produced seems remarkable even today. The potters threw the vase on a wheel turned by the hand of an apprentice and the vase was left to dry in the open courtyard. In Black-Figure (black silhouette figures on a clay background), the painter incised the design and then painted an iron-rich clay and water mixture onto the figures. When dry, he incised drapery, hair and anatomical details with a sharp tool. White paint was often applied to female flesh (upper-class women stayed out of the sun!) and purple was appli to enrich drapery or sometimes male flesh. T vase was then fired in a kiln. Air-vents allow oxygen to produce iron oxides in both clay a paint (red in colour). The air supply was th stopped and the vase turned black as the c bon monoxide produced ferrous oxide.

The trick was to allow oxygen back into t kiln so that the normal clay background turned to red iron oxide, but the iron-rich pa remained black. The vase was then polished

modern Greek archaeologists tend to dig through the later Roman layers to highlight the Classical Greek past. Greek artistry was generally maintained with some modifications. In Athens the Odeon of Herodes Atticus is a marvellous example of a Roman theatre, bu in Greek style. Roman arches were us in the construction of the stage buil ing. The massive Corinthian style Ter ple of Olympian Zeus was completed the Emperor Hadrian, who built an e

oduce the black sheen which catches the eye this day.

Red-figure & White-ground

d-Figure (Black-Figure in reverse) reserved e figures in the normal red clay colour and inted the background, as well as the details of e figures. The more flexible brush and a riety of tones produced with different paint utions allowed perspective and foreshorten- g for the first time in the history of art, at last inters could give an illusion of three-dimen- nal figures on a flat surface.

There was also a third style of vase-painting led "white-ground". The style is much rarer, t you will see a few examples in the larger useums. The technique involved immersing e vase in a dilution of kaolin (a white clay). The coration was applied after the vase had been ed. Unlike the black and red-figure styles, ght figures were employed, which have some- nes faded since they were not fired onto the se. These vases give us some idea of what ntemporary easel painting must have looked e; panel paintings were also given a white ckground over which the figures were painted.

The Workshops

e Athenian potters and painters were lower ss citizens or *metics* (foreign workers). Slaves re also used in the workshops. The potters d their workshops in the area of the Temple Hephaistos (God of craftsmen) and the ramicus. Many potters and painters signed eir work as you will see from inscriptions, ich also identify mythological characters.

ance gate in the Classical style close . Roman portrait sculptures furthered e journey towards realism with indi- dual physical defects and idiosyncra- es highlighted rather than glossed over the Greek sculptors. With the growth of Christianity in Greece, the building of churches became the medium for the development of architectural forms and hundreds of Byzantine churches were built (see box story Page 136).

Frankish, Venetian & Ottoman Styles

The Frankish and Venetian culture, prior to the Ottoman Empire of 1453-1832, is most obvious in the stately fortresses, strategically placed on the tops of hills or spurs, overlooking the communication routes of the valleys and plains. The Venetians built a large number on the coast to control the sea-lanes of their empire. Church architecture took on narrower, more "Gothic" dimensions.

Under Turkish rule, there was a general decline in building and other cultural activities. There were exceptions in places which survived the Turkish invasion, for instance Crete, where new styles of fresco and icon painting were developed in the island churches by artists who had arrived as refugees from Constantinople. This "Cretan School" of artists later travelled to the monasteries of Meteora and Mount Athos. El Greco ("The Greek") was trained in the Cretan School before travelling to Venice and Spain. After the fall of Crete in the late 17th century, the artists moved to the Ionian Islands. The Venetians built baroque style churches on these islands, but few are still standing, except on Corfu.

Classical Greek Sculpture

The Greeks probably learnt the craft of stone-carving from the Egyptians: this can be seen in the Egyptian-like poses and proportions of the first human figures produced in the seventh century BC. Likewise, bronze-casting was learnt from the eastern Mediterranean, though large hollow bronzes do not appear until the late sixth century BC. The modern viewer can either enjoy the sculptures as they are – limbs and attributes such as weapons or musical instruments missing – or she can try to imagine them as they once were, originally often standing in the open sanctuaries and market-places, the marble painted with hair and facial details, the bronze polished to create a more naturalistic sun-tanned effect. Perhaps the originals would have been too gaudy for modern taste!

Journey Towards Realism

The early Archaic statues, conspicuous with their smiling faces, stand symmetrical, one foot in front of the other; the men naked, the women draped (the first nude female public sculpture – the famous Aphrodite of Praxiteles caused an uproar when it first appeared in the fourth century BC). These were employed as cult statues, grave-markers or votives to t gods. Relief sculptures decorated the temp and treasuries, whilst in-the-round sculptu were often used to fill the pediments.

By the Classical period the sculptors we producing much more naturalistic figur Classical gods, warriors and athletes ha now lost their "archaic smile" and stand w their weight on one leg and their d pery and anatomical features marv lously realistic. This new realism w made possible by the ability to c bronze, unfortunately most of t bronze originals have been lost, su that we have to make do with la Roman copies.

Sculpting Techniques

Marble sculptures were carved fro cubic blocks of stone on the sides which grid-patterns were drawn a framework for the figure's outline. T sculptor, using iron punches to move the excess marble, could o produce a symmetrical, four-sided f ure from the grid-patterns.

Final details were produced usi chisels and bow-drills. The figu was then painted and placed o base which held the names sculptor and patron and dedicatee. A sm metal "umbrella" was then attached (no have survived but you may notice the ir

Domestic Architecture

Various styles of domestic architecture can still be seen. Wooden Turkish houses with their projecting timber upper storeys survive in Pelion and Kastoria in northern Greece and Rethymnon in Crete. Grandiose and conspicuous town mansions built from the proceeds of se trade during the Turkish period inhab some of the islands: Rhodes, Lindo Patmos and Hydra have particular splendid examples. Perhaps the mo typically "Greek", and certainly the mo harmonious, forms of dwelling are th gleaming whitewashed cubic hous found in the Cycladic islands.

pport sometimes projecting from heads) to otect the statue from the weather and pi- ons!

To make a lifesize bronze, a clay archetype as first erected on a wooden armature. This as coated with wax, into which details such as ir and veins were incised. A layer of clay was en applied and attached with nails. Molten onze was poured through apertures and the ax ran out. When cool, the outer clay layer was moved and the figure was cleaned and pol- ied to a gleaming tawny finish (quite unlike e dull green/brown patina we see today). Lips d nipples were often coated in red copper d teeth with silver foil. Semi-precious stone as used for the eyes and hair-curls and other tributes were soldered on. Literary sources d surviving bases tell us that there were often ousands of these statues in one major site – e original effect must have been startling.

Early Cosmetics

e hear in literary sources of special craftsmen lled *cosetoi* (our word cosmetics is derived m this) whose job was to continually go ound public spaces and sanctuaries retouch- g marble statues which were losing their lour, and polishing the bronzes to stop them m developing a dull patina. The surviving tuary in the museums is therefore not only ually damaged by polishing, but has also lost original colouring, though traces of pigment n sometimes still be seen.

Folk Art

reek Folk Art involves objects of vari- s materials which combine aesthetics th practical functions. Painted plates, r example, are both used and decora- ely displayed on the walls of Greek ouses.

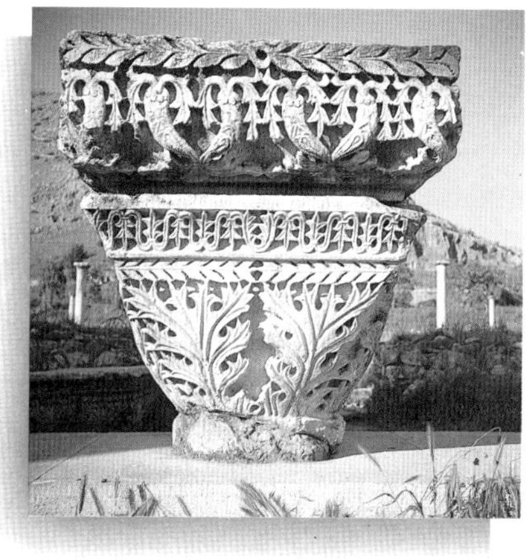

Corinthian column in Philippi.

Different regions offer their own specialities, but you will generally find an abundance of local painted pottery, woven and embroidered textiles, metal-work (jewellery, utensils), and wood-work. The shapes and decorative devices are often traditional, handed down from generation to generation. It is perhaps in these humbler arts that the real spirit of Greece has survived invasions and occupations by dominant alien cultures.

Whatever building or work of art or craft you find yourself looking at in Greece, remember that it has the power to tell you about the kind of culture which created it – militaristic or peace-loving; nature-lovers and politicians; people of different races and religions. Greek art, architecture and craftwork are the expression and embodiment of an evolving history and culture of one of the most ancient civilizations in the world.

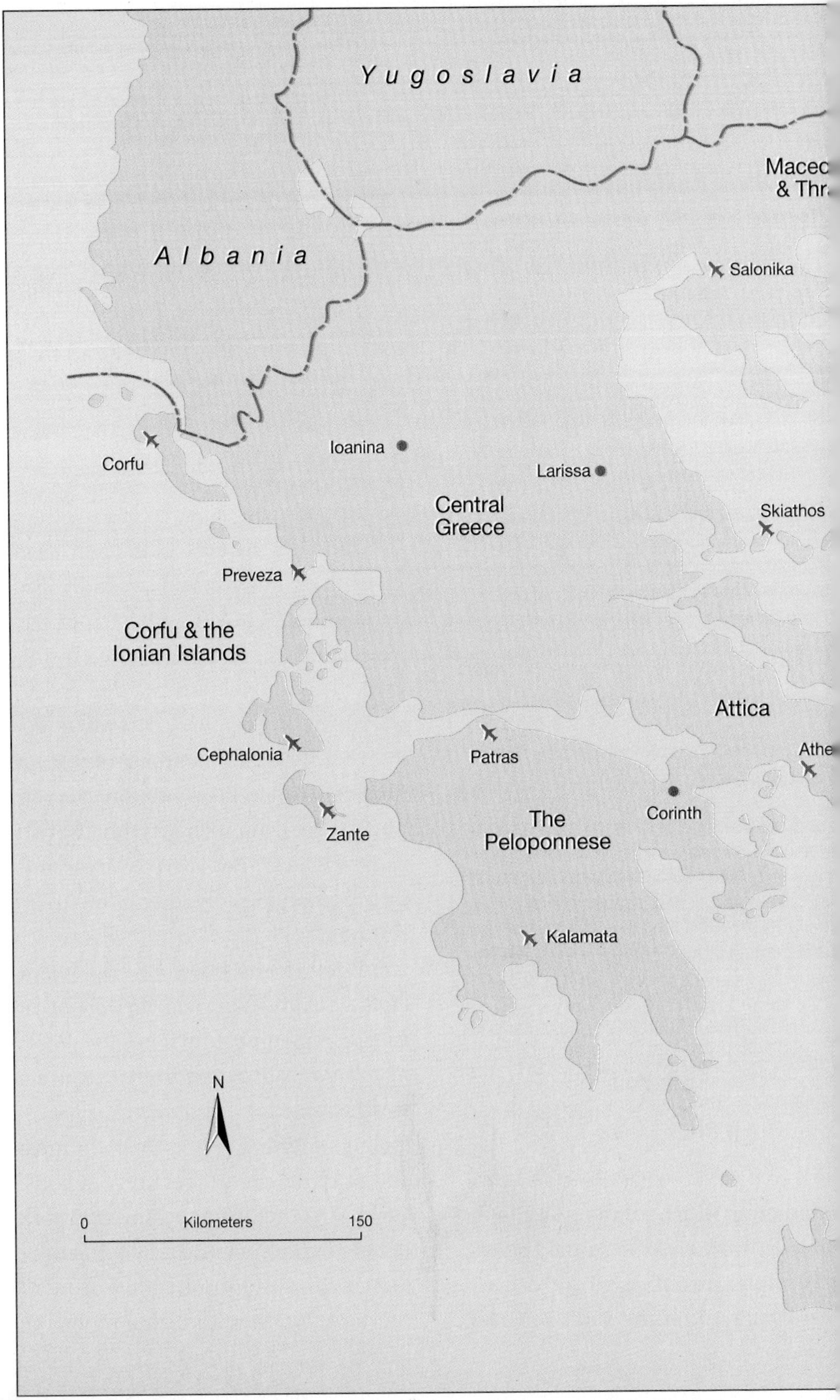

Yugoslavia
Macec
& Thr
Albania
Salonika
Corfu
Ioanina
Larissa
Central Greece
Skiathos
Preveza
Corfu & the Ionian Islands
Attica
Cephalonia
Patras
Athe
Corinth
Zante
The Peloponnese
Kalamata
N
0 Kilometers 150

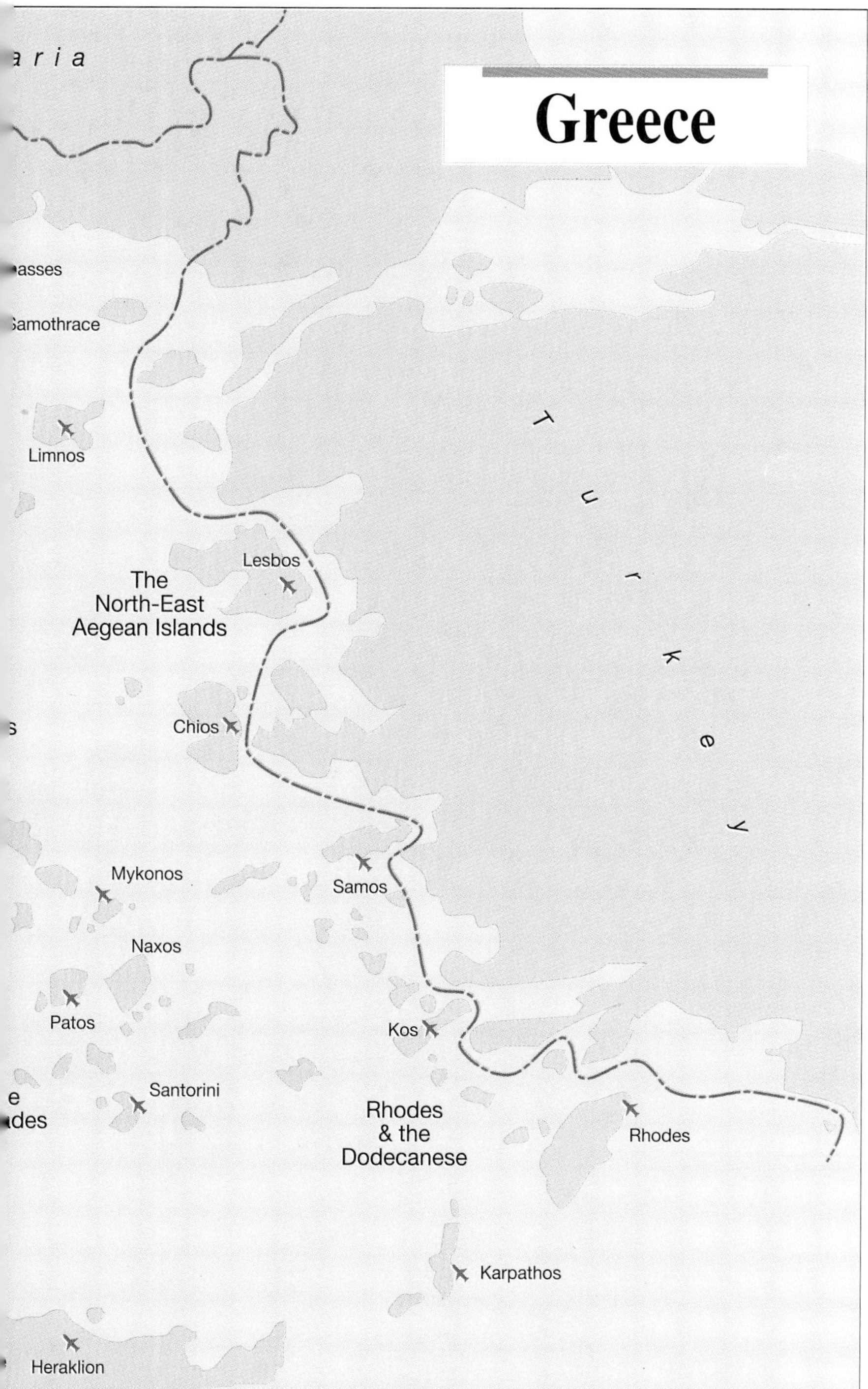
Greece
aria
asses
Samothrace
Limnos
Turkey
Lesbos
The North-East Aegean Islands
Chios
Mykonos
Samos
Naxos
Patos
Kos
Santorini
Rhodes & the Dodecanese
Rhodes
des
Karpathos
Heraklion

Athens

The first time I visited Athens, I found my expectations disappointed. In my dreams it existed as a gleaming white marble city, full of artists and philosophers discussing the latest ideas beneath shady colonnades. Instead I found a noisy modern metropolis which, with the exception of the Acropolis and its surroundings, lacked the grace and charm of say, the average Italian hill-town. Like Rome, Paris or any other major capital, the modern city can seem hot, crowded, dusty and full of traffic and petrol fumes, but once you get into the swing of it, you will soon learn to avoid the less desirable aspects, and to seek out and focus on the Classical dream city of Byron and his contemporaries.

Athens lives very much off its classical past – not surprising since most visitors are there for just that – and you will not find many indications of a progres-

...e Parthenon.

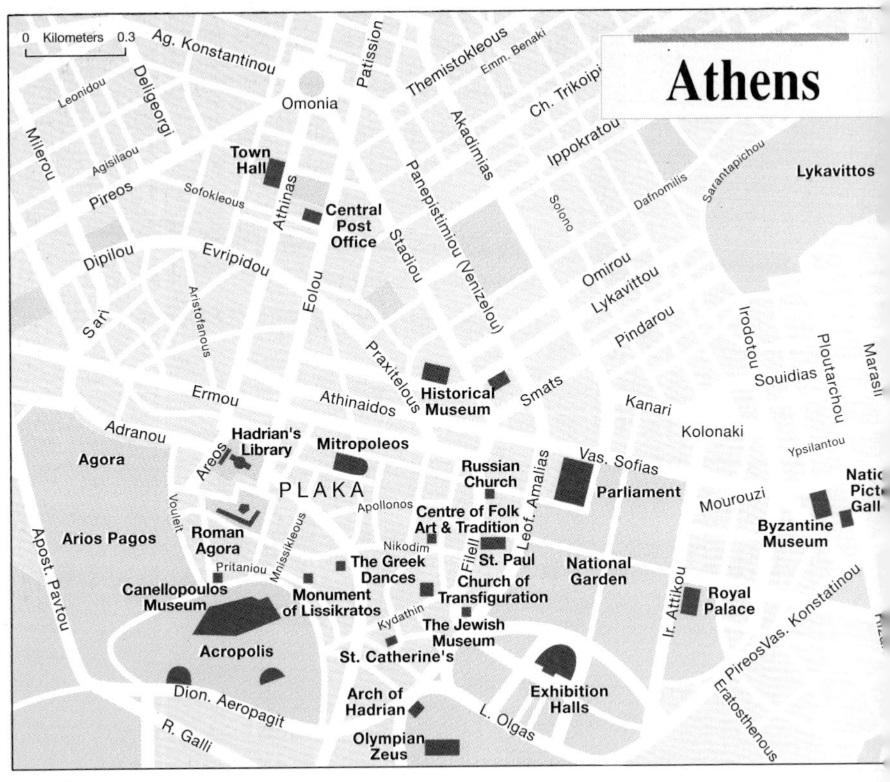

sive 20th century culture in its modern architecture. The neo-classical planning of the 19th century must have looked fine at the time, but the post-war high-rise buildings which line the rationally planned streets give a drab veneer to much of the modern city. The population has boomed since the war from 700,000 to over four million, and the city was never planned to cope with so many. Having said all this, I have found that Athens is a city that grows on you, if you relax and allow it to be what it is.

Getting Around

As in any city, you should not attempt to tour by car. Public transport is che and efficient, and though crowded, y will rarely be on it for very long Athens is quite compact. Armed wi the bus and metro route map (free fro the tourist office), you should be able get around without too much troub You will not use the metro that much there is only one line, running from t northern suburbs of Kifissia through t main squares of Omonia a Monastiraki, and out again to the sea Piraeus. Bus and metro tickets are standard price, but must be bought fro newspaper kiosks before you travel. Tic ets come in books of ten at 75dr p ticket and must be punched in the sp cial machine immediately on boardi

Wherever you are in Athens, the Acropolis beckons.

.e bus: it is often difficult to reach the achine on a crowded bus, but make ıre you succeed because there are heavy ot fines from inspectors if you fail to) this.

Taxis are a fast and comfortable ay to travel in Athens, especially if you e sharing the ride; you are likely to be 'er-charged (check that the meter is .nning and reset when you get in), but ıave found that the actual fares are ry cheap (rarely above 700dr) comıred to other European cities. Taxis are llow (beware of unofficial ones) and .n be flagged down – they can be hard find between 1:30 - 2:30 p.m and 6:3-3:30 p.m hours when Athenians are ıvelling about town. Your hotel will ıone for a taxi at any time, and it is often possible to negotiate a return fare and ask the driver to pick you up later if you are dining out.

The Acropolis

It is unlikely that you will want to start your tour of Athens anywhere other than the Acropolis, whose rocky summit, crowned with some of the most beautiful ancient architecture in the world, beckons to you from all over the city. My favourite approach is from the northwest: from this direction everything unfolds gradually, and your first close view of the Parthenon comes as a wonderful surprise as you enter the sanctuary itself. From Monastiraki Square

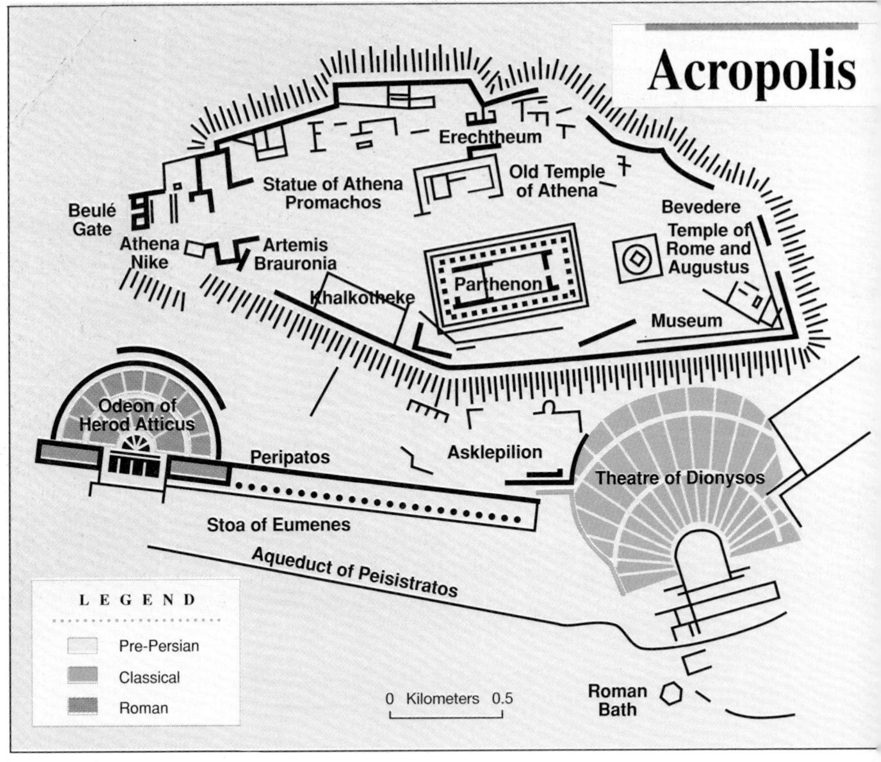

metro station, walk south down Areos, and continue with first the Library of Hadrian and then the Roman Agora (market) on your left. Follow Dioskouron as it climbs the lower slopes of the Acropolis past the small shops of the western edge of the Plaka. When you reach the very top of this road, turn right along Theorias and keep bearing left, this pedestrian route climbs towards the one and only entrance to the Acropolis.

The limestone outcrop of the **Acropolis** ("city height") dominates modern Athens as it once dominated the classical *polis* (city). One hundred and fifty six meters above sea-level, it rises some 90 meters above the surrounding city. The ancient, like t modern approach, was from the w meaning that the classical Atheni approached his temples from the re (all Greek temples faced the rising su

In prehistoric times there was Mycenean palace here: its "Cyclopea walls can still be seen in places. Most the wall you see today is fifth-centu BC and incorporates, on its north fa the broken column-drums of a Gre temple sacked by the Persians in 480 B This was an intentional reminder later generations of Athenians goi about their daily lives in the Ago below of the constant threat to "ci lized" Athens from oriental barbaria

Public transport is cheap and efficient.

The Propylia

'he western approach to the Acropolis 'asses a nine-meter high monument 'hich dates back to 178 BC when a 'ergamene king won a chariot victory 1 the Panathenaic Games: it was origi-ally crowned by a bronze chariot, which 'as replaced by statues of Antony and 'leopatra during their brief rule of the astern Mediterranean. Finally the Ro-nan consul Agrippa had his own chariot roup placed there. The sanctuary itself open Monday-Friday 8:30 a.m - 4:30 '.m, Saturday & Sunday 8:30 a.m - 2:30 'm hours; entrance 1500dr including nuseum) is entered through a magnifi-ent gateway of Pentelic marble called the **Propylaia** (437-432 BC). The exter-nal columns are in the sober Doric order whereas the columns framing the pas-sageway are in the oriental Greek Ionic style. This mixture of Doric and Ionic forms perhaps intentionally signified the Athenian Empire, which at the time of these buildings embraced both Dorian and Ionian cities.

Temple of Athena Nike

To the right of the Propylaia is the **Tem-ple of Athena Nike** (427-424 BC), an exquisite gem of a building in the orien-tal Ionic order. It was dedicated to Nike, the goddess of Victory, and its sculpted frieze depicted gods at the front east

The Changing Faces of the Acropolis

The Acropolis was once a royal citadel.

Acropolis means "high city", many ancient Greek cities were built around such a rocky height. It was an easily defended place to retreat to in times of military invasion, and it is not surprising therefore to find that during the Bronze Age many of the hills were the sites of Mycenaean settlements. The Acropolis at Athens was itself once a Mycenaean royal citadel, surrounded by similar "Cyclopean" walls to those found at Mycenae itself. These early walls ran along the changing contour of the edge of the summit, and some are visible to this day. Running water was available in the form of natural springs and there is evidence that Neolithic people were attracted to the Acropolis facilities some 7,00 years ago. It is probable that the main entranc to the summit has always been on the mo accessible western side. This caused some prob lems to the temple builders of the later perio since Greek temples are aligned eastwards to wards the rising sun, which means that th ancient, like the modern, pilgrim approache the temples from their back end.

Architectural Propaganda

There is little evidence of what happened to th

end, whilst on the sides were historical scenes of Greeks fighting Persians and other barbarian foes. Like all the other Acropolis buildings the marble is from Mount Pentelikon, a few miles to th north.

As you enter the sanctuary from th Propylaia, you will see two temples: o

:ropolis after the collapse of the Mycenaean lture (1200-1100 BC). Some of the earlier cred shrines survived and continued to be cuses of worship in the Classical period. The ectheion temple in particular seems to have corporated some of the more ancient ones – e worship of Erectheus, a legendary early king Athens persisted on this spot alongside other rly cults.

It is likely that the fifth-century temples you e standing today, were all built on some rlier shrine, though the worship of Athena ould appear to have been shifted from a major mple in the centre of the hill to the new mples to the south (Athena Parthenos) and rth (the main part of the Erectheion was also dicated the the patron deity of Athens).

When you visit the site you might not notice e ruined foundations of the Old Temple of hena, which were left intentionally by the :h-century Athenians after the building had en destroyed by the Persian invaders in 480 : – a visual warning to future Greek generans of the consequences of allowing barbars to successfully attack your city.

The Old temple was the center of a newly tified residence for the Peisistratid tyrants of e sixth century BC. Many of the sculptures ich decorated the various Peisistratid tem- s (now in the Acropolis Museum) depicted rakles performing his superhuman labours d being welcomed into Olympus by his fa- r Zeus. These were an ancient form of propanda – the Peisistratids traced their ancestry :k to Herakles.

Reigns & Restoration

510 BC, conveniently at the advent of de- cracy, the Oracle at Delphi ordained that the opolis was to be the home of the gods alone. After the Persian sack in 480 BC the site lay in ruins for some 30 years owing to an Athenian oath never to rebuild the desecrated spot. In the second half of the fifth century, the influential statesman and general Perikles argued that new temples should be built to reflect the wealth and culture of the powerful Athenian Empire. The buildings you see today are the results of his building programme, undertaken by his friend, the sculptor and architect Pheidias.

Christians & Turks

In the fifth century AD the temples were converted to Christian shrines and gradually the earlier Classical buildings became hidden behind later accretions. The Turks converted the Acropolis into a military headquarters, the Parthenon became a mosque, whilst the Erectheion served as a harem, its female priestess "caryatid" columns taking on a new role! The Turks demolished the little temple of Athena Nike, but luckily reused its stones in defences, which enabled archaeologists to reconstruct it.

After the War of Independence, the new Athenians tore away all the later additions to reveal the signifiers of their Classical Golden Age of Democracy. However, in spite of painstaking restorations, the monuments remain a subject of controversy.

Sulphur dioxide from car exhausts and industry has badly damaged the ancient Pentelic marble, and the surviving sculptures are now in the Museum, replaced with casts. The future perhaps depends more than anything on whether the law courts of the European Community decide that the marbles removed by Elgin in 1801 should be returned to their home – in the event it is highly unlikely that they would ever appear again in their original positions in the open air.

ur left, the Ionic **Erechtheion** (com- eted c 406 BC) and, on the peak of the ropolis to the right, the Doric **Parthe- n** (447-432 BC). In antiquity, the site was cluttered with additional shrines as well as bronze and marble statues dedicated to Athena as patron deity of the city. The modern viewer must also imagine that the upper parts of the temples were brightly painted to catch the eye. Today, only the four major fifth-century BC buildings remain standing, apart from the circular T**emple of Rome and Augustus** (first-century AD), deliberately positioned in front of the Parthenon to signify the power of Imperial Rome.

The Parthenon

The **Parthenon** (Temple of Athena *Parthenos* "the virgin") survived history by adaption, becoming first a Christian church and later a Turkish mosque. In 1687, it was being used by the Turks as an ammunition dump, and a direct hit from a Venetian mortar rocket split it in two, bringing down many of its columns and most of the inner *cella* (shrine-building). In 1801 the Turks permitted Lord Elgin "to remove some blocks of stone with inscriptions and figures": these are now in the British Museum, but have ever since been the object of Greek demands for their return to their original location.

The Parthenon building itself was a *tour de force* of classical architecture. The architect produced a number of optical "refinements", such as very subtly curving every apparently straight line. Place your hat on the corner of the top step and walk to the other corner: the hat will have disappeared as the step rises several certimeters at its center! Similarly the columns taper to counteract optical distortions.

Inside the *cella* was the 12-mete high gold and ivory statue of Athena b Pheidias (now lost). *Metope* sculpture filled the external frieze with illustrations of Greeks fighting Trojans, Amazons and Centaurs, whilst on the eastern front Gods fought giants: all wer symbolic of civilization defeating th barbarian. The west pediment sculptures showed the goddess Athena fighing Poseidon for control of the city; th east depicted the birth of the goddes from the head of father Zeus. The famous frieze (like most of the other sculptures now in the British Museum) ra around the *cella* (shrine building) wa behind the columns and showed th four-yearly Panathenaic Procession i which a newly-woven dress was presented to Athena. The procession ra alongside the viewer and culminated o the east end where the gods were sittin on Olympus.

The Erechtheion & Acropolis Museum

The architect of the **Erechtheion** produced the perfect response to the massive colonnades of the Parthenon: h omitted them, and instead produce the exquisite porch of the six priestesse of Athena (the originals are in th Acropolis Museum). Athena's revere archaic wooden statue was worshippe here, together with the early Athenia king Erechtheus. Athena's gift to Atl

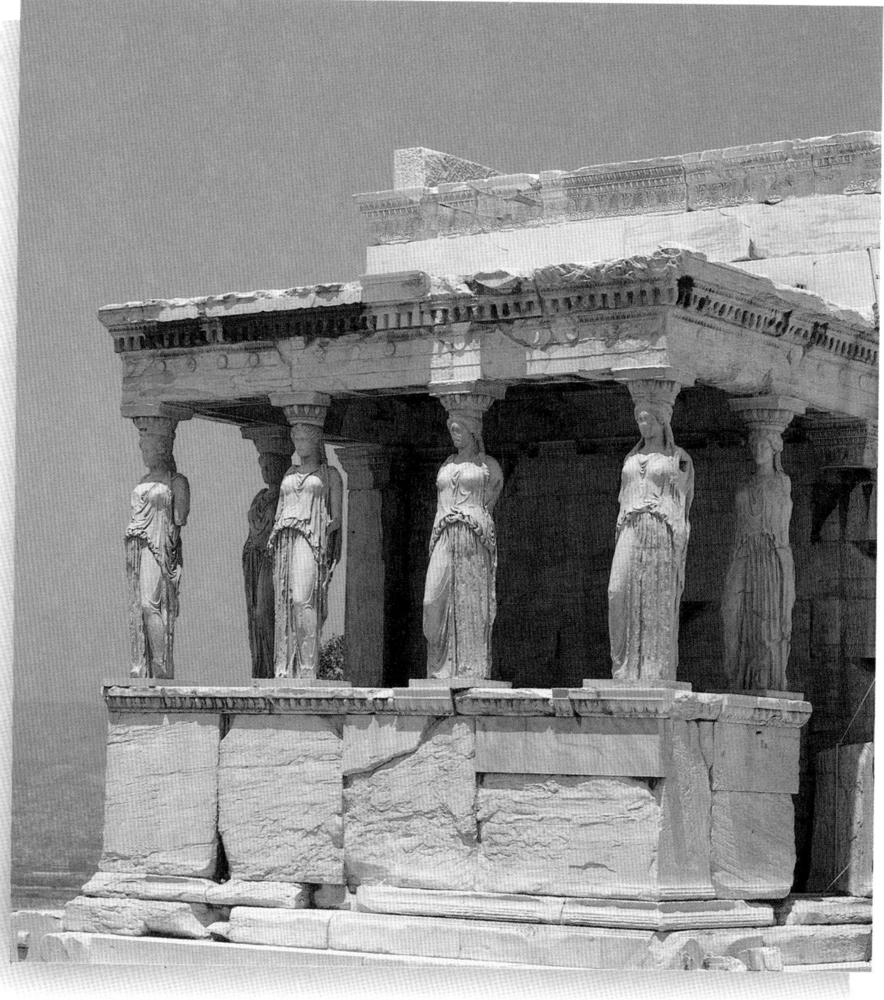

The Porch of the Caryatids, most celebrated feature of the Erechtheion.

ıs, the olive tree, has been replanted in ıe sacred space to the west. In antiq-ity, visitors were also shown marks in ıe rock under the north porch pro-ıced by Poseidon's trident in his con-st with Athena.

After visiting the **Acropolis Mu-um** (open Monday 10 a.m - 4:30 p.m, ıesday & Friday 8:30 a.m - 4:30 p.m, Saturday & Sunday 8:30 a.m - 2:30 pm) with its superb collection of sculptures discovered in excavations of the late nineteenth century, stop to admire the view through the Propylaia. The Athenians aligned the entrance in the direction of their navy in Piraeus harbour, whilst in the far distance lies the island of Salamis, scene of their great naval

Getting away from the crowds.

victory against the Persians in 480 BC.

The Areopagus & Surrounding Sites

To the west of the entrance to the Acropolis, you will see steps cut in the rock of a low, rocky hill called **The Areopagus.** This was where the ancient law court of the tyrants was situated, and where people continued to be tried for murder during the Classical period of democracy. Saint Paul preached here, winning a number of converts to the new religion.

Continuing southwards over the western flank of the Acropolis you will come to the **Odeon of Herodes Atticus** (c AD 161-74), paid for by the wealtl Roman patron after whom it was name The three-storeyed theatre building typically Roman in its design. It is on open for performances of the Athe Festival on summer evenings, seatir about 5,000 people on its marble sea set into the slope of the Acropolis. To tl east of the odeon are the remains of tl **Sanctuary of Asclepius** the Greco-R man god of medicine.

Further east is the **Theatre Dionysus** (open daily 8:30 a.m - 3 p.r closed Mondays; entrance 200dr) whe the tragedies of Aeschylus, Sophocl and Euripides and the comedies Aristophanes were first performed the fifth century during the annual fe tility festival in honour of Dionysu

adly, what you see today is mainly oman restoration. The original theae consisted of little more than wooden eats on the earth slopes of the Acropos, a wooden stage and a backdrop for ainted scenery. The orchestra – the pace between the audience and the age – was originally circular, this is here the chorus danced and sang whilst e actors performed on the low stage ehind them (the stage is now in the oman semi-circular form).

Seventeen thousand people could e accommodated, three times as many s in the later Roman Odeon of Herodes tticus. Twenty-five rows of stone seats urvive out of an original sixty-four. he most important magistrates and riests sat in the elaborately decorated arble thrones in the front row. The rst stone theatre was built in the fourth entury BC.

Philopappos Hill

aking your way back to the Odeon, oss the main road and follow any of e paths which wind their way up and nto **Philopappos Hill**, named after e Roman Consul whose commemorave marble monument (AD 114-116), epicting him in a triumphal chariot ocession, is reached after a tiring, but ercifully green and shaded, climb to e summit. From here there are excelnt views of the Acropolis to the north nd the Piraeus harbour to the southest. Make your way down the main track westwards to the exquisite Byzantine church of St Demetrius; nearby is a café, fashionable with the young Athenians, and above this is the **Pnyx Hill** where the Athenian democratic assembly met in the open-air arena on the northern summit. The space is now used for Sound-and-Light performances on summer evenings.

The Temple of Hephaistos

From Monastiraki metro station, walk one block south in the direction of the Acropolis and turn right along Adrianou. The entrance to the **Greek Agora** (open daily except Mondays8:30 a.m - 3 p.m; entrance 800dr) is clearly visible on the left. Inside the entrance, turn right and walk towards the **Temple of Hephaistos**, the well-preserved temple on a low hill (*Kolonos Agoraios*) in the near distance. The temple is indeed the best preserved classical temple in the world. The temple has been mistakingly named the "Theseion" for many years, because the various heroic exploits of the legendary Athenian King Theseus are sculpted on the north and south *metopes* and on the internal porch frieze of the east end of the temple. However it is now thought that this subject-matter was unconnected to the dedication of the temple to the god of craftsmen, Hephaistos, whose cult statue once stood inside the temple beside that of Athena, also an arts and crafts divinity. The area around the temple was inhabited by potters, blacksmiths and bronze-workers – some still exist in the vicinity today.

The temple was built in the second half of the fifth century BC, it is thought, by the same (anonymous) architect who designed the Temple of Poseidon at Cape Sounion. Both buildings were contemporary with the Parthenon, and bear certain stylistic similarities, such as the subtle tapering of the Doric columns and the employment of sculpture to represent great moments in the myth and history of Athens. In Classical proportions the number of columns on the short sides of the temple are doubled and one is added to give the number of columns for the long side – the Temple of Hephaisos accommodates this with six columns at the front and back and thirteen (corner columns counted) along the sides. On the *metopes* of the front east end you can still see sculptures (their heads defaced by later Christians) depicting nine of the Twelve Labours of Herakles, whose patron deity was Athena.

Eight of the Labours of Theseus are represented on the *metopes* on the north and south sides (the other *metopes* were left blank or possibly held painted scenes). In the *pronaos* (porch) Theseus' struggles against rival bidders for the throne of Athens are depicted. In the west rear porch, you can see Theseus involved again, this time fighting the uncivilized Centaurs. The pediments were also once sculpted, but these have not survived.

The Hephaisteion (as the Temple of Hephaistos is known) was preserved b its conversion in the seventh century A into a Christian basilica – the interi colonnade, which once helped suppc the roof, was replaced with a vault concrete roof.

In antiquity, the temple was flank by trees or shrubs, which would ha softened the rather harsh colonnad Various foreign travellers on the Gra Tour of antiquities in the 18th centu were buried inside the temple.

The Agora

The hill on which the Temple Hephaistos stands is a good vanta point from which to view the Gre Agora (open daily except Mondays 8: a.m - 3 p.m; entrance 800dr). Make yo way southwards along the western si of the hill to a modern belvedere, whi has a useful map of the *Agora*, whi can be compared to the confusing rui you see below. From here make yo way down the path to the southw corner of the ancient market, where y will see two ancient boundary stones 500 BC) with inscriptions stating "I a the limit of the Agora". The Agora w a sacred site and it was considered sa rilege to pass these stones in a state spiritual impurity.

The area of the Agora was defin by long colonnades called *stoas*, b only the foundations are now visib apart from the **Stoa of Attalos**, whi was restored by the Americans in t

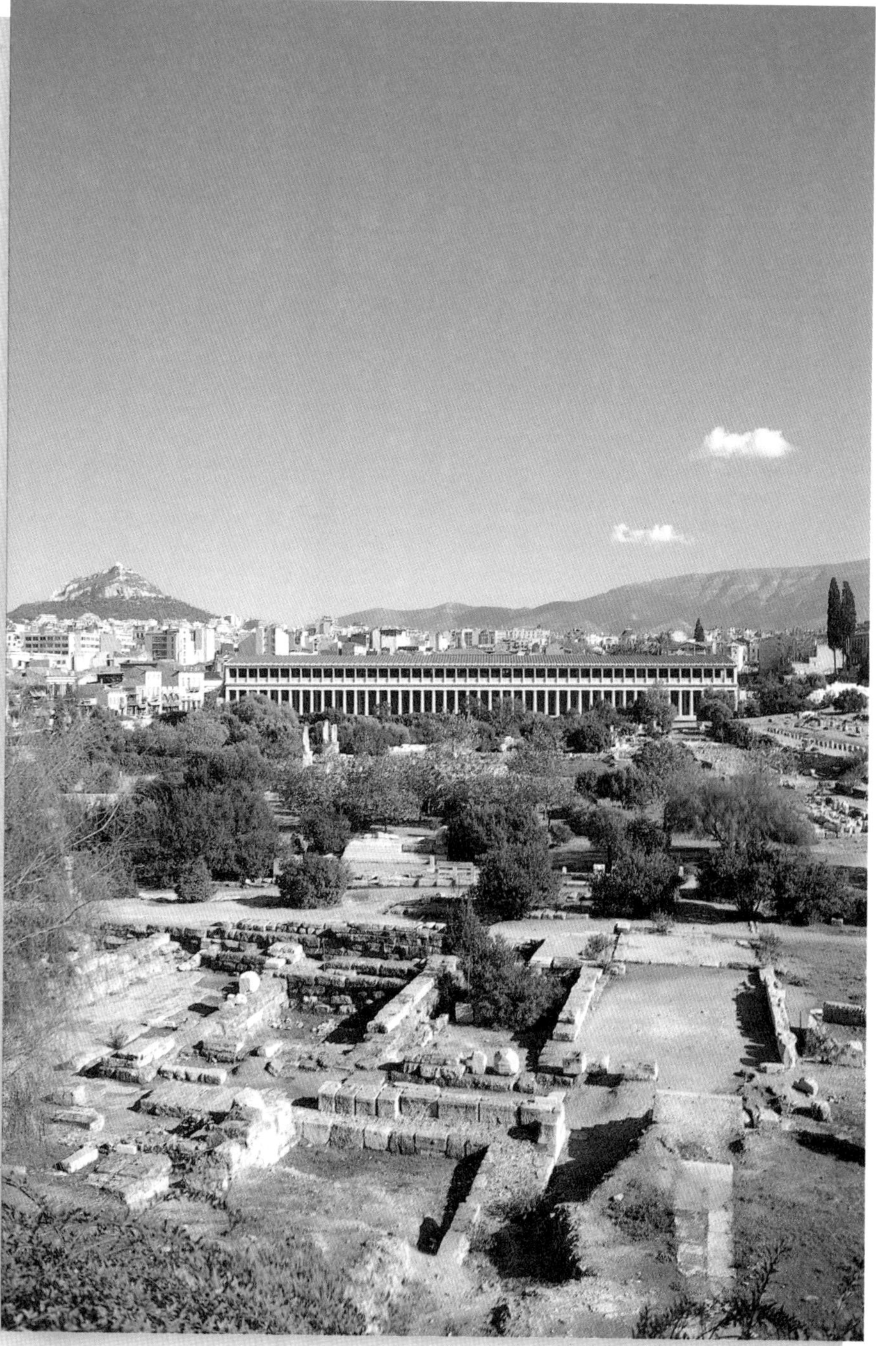

View of the Agora.

The Agora as a Political Center

In the fifth century BC, with the introduction of democracy, the Agora in Athens extended its function as a commercial and legal center to embrace politics. The Agora's development from then on ran hand-in-hand with the new political ideology. Statues, signifying the downfall of tyranny, were set up near the Panathenaic Way where it enters the Agora from the northwest. The statues were the "Tyrant-Slayers"; the two Athenians, Harmodios and Aristogeiton, who attempted to assassinate the brother tyrants Hippias and Hipparchus during the Panathenaic Festival, as they passed into the Agora. Hipparchus was slain, and the two rebels were killed – when Hippias was finally ousted, the two were seen as heroes who had lost their lifes in the struggle for democracy. The original bronzes were looted by the Persians, but were returned under Alexander the Great and stood alongside later replacements, where they were admired until AD 267, when they were destroyed along with many other famous Athenian monuments by the German barbarians, the Heruli. Only Roman marble copies survive, apart from an inscription from the statue-base: "A great light shone for the Athenians when Harmodios and Aristogeiton slew Hipparchus".

The Building of Democracy

New buildings were needed if the democracy was to function smoothly. The **Tholos a** **Bouleuterion** were situated in the south-w corner of the Agora. The Tholos was a circu building where a standing committee of fi citizens kept counsel day and night – for t reason a kitchen was attached. A set of standa weights and measures was excavated here (n in Agora Museum).

Only the foundations of the Tholos rem today (c 465 BC). The New Bouleuterion (l fifth century BC) stood to the north of t Tholos cut into the hillside. This was a rectang lar building for meetings of the **Boule** (C Council of 500 men). It was similar to a theat with a semi-circular seating area. This was wh some of the greatest political debates in At nian history took place.

One of the most fascinating finds of extensive Rockefeller-sponsored American cavations was that of the small building in angle of two streets at the south-west of square. Here archaeologists discovered hobn and bone eyelets for boots, all the signs of ancient cobbler's workshop.

They also found the broken base of a l fifth century wine-cup with the name "Simo scratched on it. Ancient writers refer to Sim the Shoemaker as a contemporary of Socrat who allowed the philosopher to discourse at workshop to students who were too young enter the sacred area of the Agora.

1950s. The original structure was paid for by King Attalos II of Pergamon (159-138 BC): the double-storeyed building had shops within a shaded walkway. Notice the different styles of column for upper and lower storeys. You should visit the **Museum**, located within the ancient shops, for plans of the Agora at different stages of its history, these will help you to make some sense of the site. There is also an excellent collection of finds from the excavations, which w allow you to picture some of the acti ties which took place here.

Roman Agora

Exiting the Greek Agora, turn right o side the entrance onto Adrianou, a continue straight; at the end of Adrian you will come to the Library of Hadri

AD 132). All that can be seen today is western enclosure wall, with its tem-e-like entrance approached by a flight steps and four Corinthian columns, nifying that you are entering a sa-d place of high culture and learning. ere was once a garden in the center of e rectangular enclosure behind this trance, with a water-pool at its center. e library-ilding itself s at the east-n end of the rden.

Following los Areos ithwards (to-rds the ropolis), you l see the Ro-an **Agora** (open ily 8:30 a.m - 3 p.m hours, closed ondays; entrance 400dr) to your left. is was originally connected to the eek Agora by a road, this Roman ora was already here, but is now led "Roman" because it was exten-ely rebuilt under the occupying power. e inscription on the monumental en-nce gate to your left tells us that the *w Agora* was dedicated in 10 BC hav- been built with money donated by ius Caesar and his adopted son gustus.

Walk to the opposite (eastern) end the Roman Agora by following the -zagging road to the left of the gate-y (there are several good *tavernas* on way). Continuing on you will pass a set of Roman latrines on your right and then you should turn right uphill to another cool place to have lunch and admire the ruins in peace, the *Ai Aerides* (Windy Ones) cafe, so-called because it looks out on the deservedly famous Roman public monument, the **Tower of the Winds**. This was built, like the Roman Agora itself, around the time of Julius Caesar. It is an octagonal Clock Tower, with a sculpted frieze around the top depicting the wind gods: originally there was a revolving bronze Triton on the top of the tower, which pointed in the direction of the wind. You can amuse yourself by trying to identify the colder and warmer winds according to the clothes each is wearing. The tower also functioned as a clock, with sundials on each of its faces, together with a water-clock for telling the time at night – the Romans thought of everything! The building survived the Turkish occupation by housing a monastic center for whirling dervishes.

The Arch of Hadrian & The Temple of Olympian Zeus

From the Tower of the Winds, walk downhill a little and turn right, veering left until you reach Odos Adrianou, where

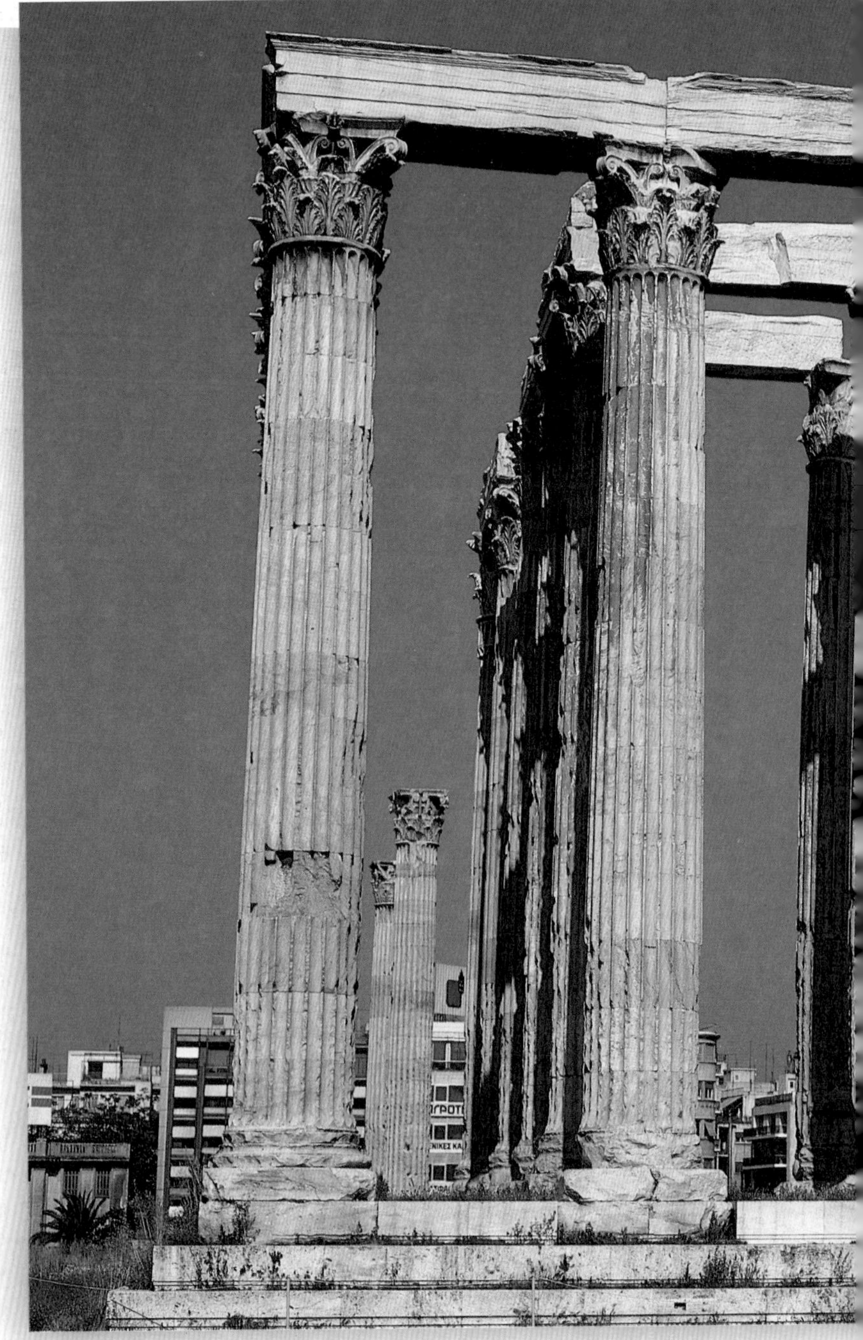

The Temple of Olympian Zeus with the Acropolis in the background.

The Plaka by Day & Night

If you are in Athens for more than a lightning visit, you are bound to get to know the area on the northern slopes of the Acropolis, known as Plaka, well. If your itineraries have not yet allowed you time for a stroll through this picturesque townscape, then you should make time for one. The early evening is a good time to wander in Plaka, perhaps stopping for an *ouzo* at one of its cafes, where you can sit and watch the world go by for a change, rather than chasing after it.

Plaka Possibilities

There is a timeless quality about Plaka; although obviously a place catering today mainly for tourists, it remains at its heart untouched by the 20th century, its pretty neo-Classical townhouses maturing with age into another slice of Greek history. Look upwards as often as you safely can: you will be delighted by terraco tile-ends with mythical images of gorgons, gri ning archaic faces and palmette desigr wrought-iron balconies are so varied and exq site that you can easily use up a film, trying capture them.

The houses were poor and bohemian earl this century, but many have more recen become gentrified, but not spoilt. They va from a simple lane of whitewashed stone hous with tiny gardens, to pretentious "classic mansions with grand classical pilasters frami doors and windows.

Plaka is also one of the most likely places find somewhere lively to eat, with the chance music and dance thrown in. The more touri *tavernas* are best avoided – anywhere w brightly lit photographs of dancers and mu cians tend to be rather soulless – listen out music that is not being thrust at you on t street, then you will often find some gems.

A stroll through the Plaka.

Brief History

storically Plaka's most important contribu- n to Athens' past was to keep the city alive d well during its long medieval period. After e Herulian sack of Athens in AD 267 the ople built a new wall, which diminished the e of the Classical city and enclosed the area ich came to be known as Plaka. Here Athe- n life continued for the next 14 centuries. ly in the 18th century was a new wall con- ucted by the Turks, with a perimeter of some km. The mixture of medieval and Turkish eet-plans – winding alleys and flights of steps ing you from one level to the next, is in total ntrast to the angular town-planning of the th century city to the north. Happily today, rs have been banned from most of Plaka's eets, making it a relaxing place to investigate the daytime.

Museums

ere are a number of interesting little muse- s in Plaka. The **Museum of Greek Popular t** (open daily 10 a.m - 2 p.ms, closed Mon- ys; entrance 200dr) is at 17 Kydathinaion eet, and makes an excellent introduction to e various local costumes of the islands and mountain districts; there are also art and craft objects and a room of wonderful paintings by the "primitive" Greek artist Theophilus Hadzimichail (1870-1934) of Lesbos. The Kanelopoulos M**useum** (open daily 8:30 a.m - 3 p.m, closed Mondays; entrance 400dr), housed in one of the finer neo-classical mansions at the top of Panos Street, covers the entire history of Athens from the third millennium BC to the 19th century.

Turkish Evidence

The area of Plaka between Monastiraki Square and the Tower of the Winds was the Turkish quarter during the centuries of Ottoman rule. There was a Wheat Bazaar of stalls and shops on the site of the Roman Agora, and the Tower of the Winds was itself a dervish center, its inner walls once covered with Islamic scripts. Other Turkish monuments are visible around the Roman Agora: to the north you can see the inscribed entrance gate of the "**Medrese**", a Turkish Theological School, which in the 19th century became a notorious prison, firstly for Greeks in the War of Independence, and later for political dissidents. There is also the **Fethiye Djami mosque** (closed), the oldest Turkish monument in Athens, built in 1456, just two years after Athens fell to the Turks.

u turn right and follow the street und until bearing left along Odos sikratous. Here, in a small square rrounded by pleasant cafes, you will e the well-preserved M**onument of sicrates** (335 BC), built to commemo- te the dramatic victory of the *choregos* heatrical producer) Lysicrates. Six rinthian columns support a conical arble roof, which is surrounded by a eze relating the myth of Dionysus and e Pirates: The god of wine and theatre turned them into dolphins when they tried to kidnap him. In the early 19th century Byron stayed here as a guest of the monastery which once surrounded the square, the Monument was then used as a reading-room. Continuing along Odos Lysikratous you will come to the busy junction of Leoforos Amalias, cross carefully to the **Arch of Hadrian**, built by the Roman Emperor and benefactor of Athens in AD 131 - 132. The inscription on the side towards the

Bell tower of church of St George at Mount Lykabettos.

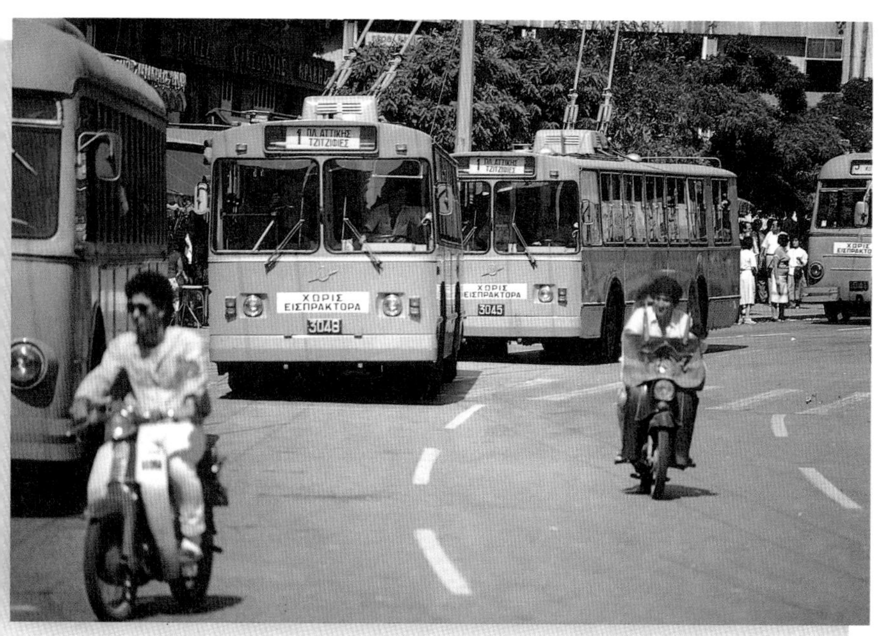

The streets of Athens.

cropolis reads "This is Athens, the rmer city of Theseus"; the other side ads: "This is the city of Hadrian, and ot of Theseus". Behind the arch rise the assive Corinthian columns of the **Tem-le of Olympian Zeus** (open daily 8:30 .m - 3 p.m, closed Mondays; entrance)0dr) which was begun in the sixth ntury by the Athenian tyrants, the eisistratids, but not completed until ne time of Hadrian himself, who was resent to see the colossal chryselephan-ne statue of Zeus unveiled to mark the edication of the building.

Mount Lykabettos

ount Lykabettos is, after the Acropolis, the most prominent landmark in Athens, and is well worth the climb (or you can cheat and take the funicular) to its summit, which enjoys fine views, particularly at sunset, across to the Acropolis and the distant sea. There is a little Byzantine **Church of St George** at the top, as well as a welcome cafe and restaurant (reasonably priced) – a lovely place to dine on a summer's evening, looking out over the lights of the nocturnal city.

Legend tells how the hill was formed when the goddess Athena was bringing it as a defensive outpost for the early city. The god Hephaistos tried to molest her as she flew into Athens with the hill in her hands; he was unsuccessful, but she dropped the hill where it now rests.

Attica

Stand on any of the hills of Athens and look to the horizon. On a clear day you will understand why ancient Athens became a naval power. To the south is the wine-dark sea of the Saronic Gulf and Piraeus, the ancient and modern port of Athens. In all other directions are mountains, protecting the city from its neighbours but also making communication and trade by land routes impractical. To the west is Mount Aigaleos; to the north, Mount Parnes; to the northwest, Mount Pendeli (Pentelikon, the source of the fine white marble used for the Acropolis temples); and to the east, Mount Hymettos.

Wildflowers on Mount Hymettos.

All of these mountains can be reached within an hour's bus journey from Athens. **Mount Hymettos** is the most accessible and rewards the walker with an increasingly breathtaking panorama of the Athenian plain. Choose a cloudless day, take a picnic and leave the bustle and fumes of modern Athens behind for a few hours.

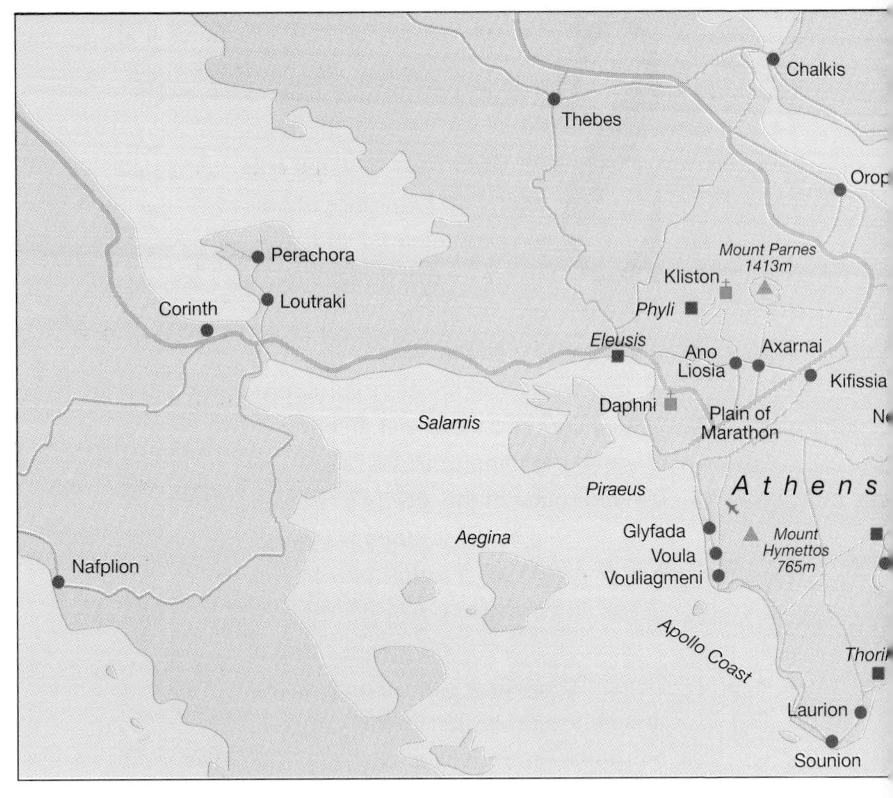

Mount Hymettos & its Monasteries

Take either bus 224 or 234, from the terminal beside the University (Akadimias St) which takes you to the suburb of Kaisariani – if you are driving, exit from Athens via the Alexander Boulevard to Kaisariani. From here the **Monastery of Kaisariani** (341m from Athens) is five and a half kilometeRs along the same road – walking it will take you almost an hour. It is well worth the trek along the road; the passing traffic becomes less frequent the higher you climb; the flowers and wild herbs exude aromas which attract be to produce the famous Hymettos hone

Nestled in a glen, the monaste was founded near the source of the Iliss in the 11th century. Athenian mothe still follow a pagan tradition of drinkir from what they believe to be the sacr spring, or bathing their sick children its waters. Outside the entrance is lovely rural spot for a picnic and a dr of wine, shaded by olive and cypres pine and plane trees. After a well d served break, you can visit the monast buildings, which include a bath-hous mill and bakery, hinting at the ever day activities of the former monks. Th church of brick and stone has a don

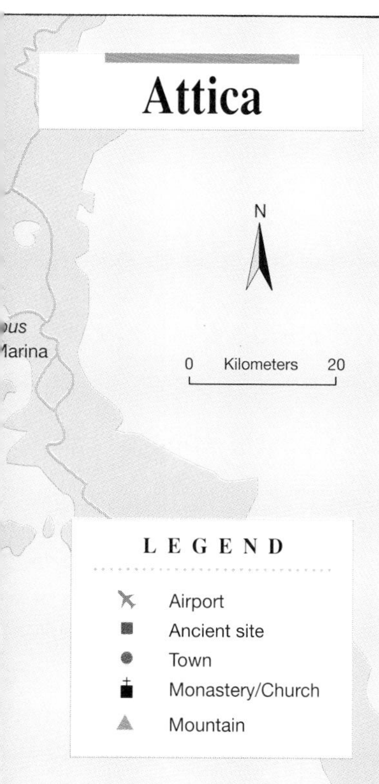

ꞏsting on ancient Roman columns; its yzantine-style frescos are mostly 17th entury. Literary sources tell us that uring the Turkish occupation the mon-stery housed a famous classical library nd became an oasis of Greek learning nd culture.

The road passes the **Monastery of** **.steriou** and one and a half kilometeRs ff track, the **Ayios Ioannis Theologou** efore eventually reaching the summit f Hymettos (1,027m high). Unfortu-ately, the summit itself is inaccessible wing to a telecommunications station, ut the magnificent views just before ıe prohibited area (3 km from the sum-ıit) take in the plain of Marathon to the northeast, with Salamis and the Pelo-ponnese to the southwest.

Mount Pendeli

Of the other mountains, **Mount Pendeli** is accessible from the fashionable Athens suburb of Kifissia and the whole trip forms an interesting contrast to the Hymettos walk. Kifissia, about 14½ km from central Athens,can be easily reached in twenty minutes by taking the *elektrikos* (underground train) from Omonia Square, or by car, following the Kifissia Boulevard north.

The ancient Romans recognized the cleaner air and elevated position of

Fresh produce from the coast.

Kifissia and built their villas here. Stop and have a drink in one of the many outdoor cafés on Kefalari Square (follow signs from the station) and you will notice the more Roman style of the rich Athenians, compared to the busy cafés of downtown Athens.

If you do not fancy the nine-kilometer walk along the road to Mount Pendeli, why not hire a *phaetoni* (horse-drawn carriage) in the park behind the modern church. The intrepid will make their way up Pendeli. Five hundred meters after a small chapel on the left, a bridge crosses the River Kephissos on its way down to Athens.

On the left, a path leads to the summit via goat-tracks. On the right you will see the ancient Pentelic marble quarries, and you can imagine the half-finished columns of the Parthenon being transported down-hill to Athens.

Like Hymettos, the summit is a prohibited zone, but the crag beside it allows views in clear weather of Lycabettos and the Acropolis: keen eyes might even make out the Parthenon columns! Beyond can be seen the beckoning mountains of the Cycladic islands.

Mount Parnes

Mount Parnes is the wildest of the mountains and although it too has a radar station, most of the summit area has been declared a national park. Here you will need a good map and compass in order to find a safe passage through the maze of trails which criss-cross the mou tain. Some tourist maps of Athens cov the area, but better maps can be four at the National Statistical Service Greece, 14, Likourgou, near Omon Square. Take bus 724 from the corner Stournari and Aharnon streets and a for the suburb of Thrakomakedhon which gives access to mountain path

The Coastal Road to Sounio

It is well worth spending a day or tv travelling southeast along the beautif coast of Attica to Cape Sounion a then northwards along the east At coast to Marathon. From here you c either return the way you came, or ta the direct inland route back to Athens you want to follow in the footsteps Byron and other Romantic travelle try to time your journey so that y reach Sounion at sunset. If time dicta a choice between Marathon a Sounion, the latter provides the bet scenery.

To reach Sounion from Athens, ta the hourly bus from the square Pattision Street, two blocks north of t Archaeological Museum. The route either inland or coastal: go out one w and return the other for scenic variety you prefer, there are half-day comm cial coach tours, but the much cheap bus journey provides a chance to wat the locals. The coast road takes y through a number of seaside reso you might be tempted to break yo

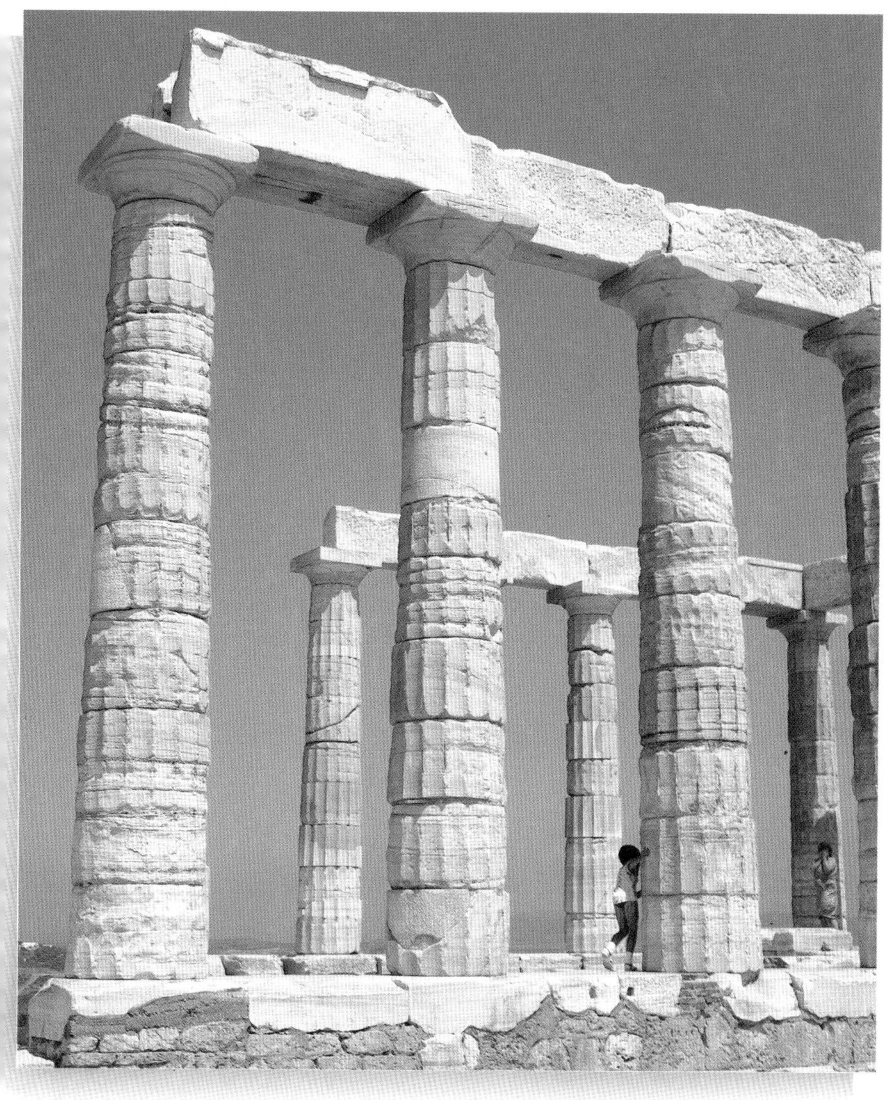

The Temple of Poseidon on the promontory of Cape Sounion was a landmark for sailors rounding the Attic peninsula.

urney for a swim and grilled fish. wenty five km from Athens, **ouliagmeni** is *the* fashionable spot for ndy beaches and fish-restaurants.

The road after Vouliagmeni be-mes a spectacular winding corniche, ıfolding views across the sea to the next headland at every turn. The southernmost tip of Attica is eventually reached at **Cape Sounion** (70km from Athens). Here you can take a drink at the restaurant beside the entrance to the **Temple of Poseidon**, thinking of Byron's response to "Sunium's (Sounions')

Lord Byron & Romantic Visions of Greece

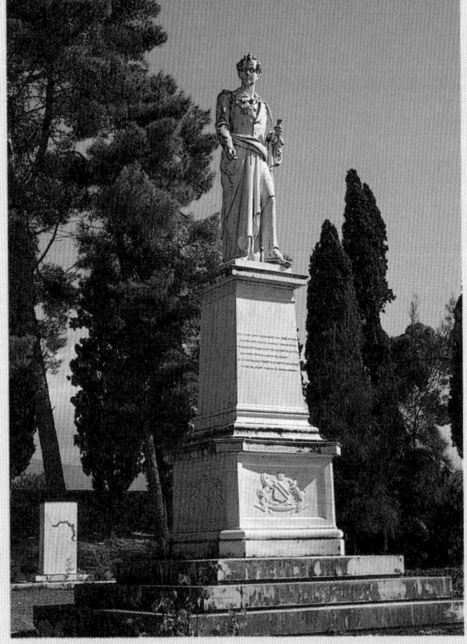

Lord Byron, who perished out of love for Greece.

Romantic European attitudes towards Greece, played a major part in raising public and governmental awareness of the plight of Greece, under the Turkish occupation. Lord George Gordon Byron (1788-1824), was one of the active *Philhellenes* (Greek-lovers) involved in this early 19th-century movement. Like his upper-class contemporaries, Byron had a classical education which introduced him at an early age to the "glory that was Greece". After studying Cambridge, he did the fashionable thing a set off on a Grand Tour of the Mediterranean. the autumn of 1809 he landed at Preveza on t west coast of mainland Greece and proceed to Ioannina, where he began to write ***Chi Harold's Pilgrimage***, a poetic response to Grand Tour experiences, which includes mous romantic verses on Greece:

"Ancient of days! august Athena! where,
Where are thy men of might? thy grand soul?
Gone – glimmering through the dream things that were..."

Byron & Lord Elgin

It was verses like these which encouraged m ancholy attitudes to Greece's past, and hope freedom in the future. At the same time, Eu peans were beginning to realize what Gree had to offer in the way of romantic ruins a antiquities. Byron's contemporary, Lord Elg brought the famous marbles of the Athen Acropolis back to London, leading to Byro scathing attack in ***The Curse of Minerva***:

"Oh, loath'd in life, nor pardon'd in the du
May hate pursue his sacriligious lust!

Byron was at the harbour seeing off friend Hobhouse, who was travelling on ship *Hydra*, which, by coincidence was tra porting the Elgin marbles back to Britain 1811. As they were being loaded on the ship,

marbled steep, Where nothing save the waves and I may hear our mutual murmurs sweep...".

The temple stands within a fortified acropolis which overlooks a bay once notorious as a haunt for pirates. The temple was almost certainly designed around 440 BC by the architect of the Temple of Hephaistos in Athens: li that building, it had a sculpted frie around the four sides of its porch. Doric columns originally number 6x13, but only 15 of the flank colum now remain standing. Little of the scu tural decoration has survived, but t massive nude archaic male statues we

ld Greek said to Byron's companion Hobhouse: Guard them well, for one day we shall ask for hem back again".

Undertaking the Greek Cause

yron stayed on in Athens by himself, taking oms in the Capuchin monastery in the Plaka, here he often studied in the ancient monu-ent of Lysikrates. During these months, Byron ll in love with the Greek people and began to ream of a free Greece. He swam often on the ttic coast and visited romantic Cape Sounion, here visitors can still see his signature scratched the white marble of the Temple of Poseidon. yron left his signature on other ancient monu-ents, making his attacks on Elgin's "vandal-m" appear slightly hypocritical to our modern raffiti-covered world.

Byron returned to London in 1811, and did ot journey to his "land of the sun" again, until 323. His reasons for visiting were no longer for e antiquities alone – he had been appointed gent by the London Greek committee, to assist e Greeks in their preparations for the War of dependence. He managed to get money and pplies to the various Greek rebel factions, and oked as if he might have died heroically, ghting with them.

This was not to be; on April 19th, 1824, he ed of a fever at Missalonghi. But his rather romantic death nevertheless inspired both ropeans and Greeks to fight for the cause of eek freedom, which Byron had so passion-ely espoused.

xcavated in the precinct: these were edicated to the god Poseidon around 00 BC (now in the Athens Archaeologi-l Museum). Byron carved his name ongside others on the square pillar to e right of the east entrance. Clamber own the west slope towards the sea, for xcellent views back towards the temple; the best Sounion experience is of the glorious sunset across the Saronic gulf.

En Route to Marathon

Taking the coast road northwards, you will pass through the now ugly industrial town of **Lavrion.** In fact it has always been industrial, being the site of the classical Athenian silver mines which financed their navy, and subsidized the Acropolis building programme. If you are interested in mining history, you can visit the best-preserved site, travelling by car to Kamariza, five kilometers west of Lavrion. Here you can see over 2,000 shafts that have been discovered, which were originally worked by slave labour.

A few kilometers further north, to the east of the road, is the conical acropolis (with Mycenean fortress) of ancient **Thorikos**. The classical ruins lie to the south of the hill and are worth visiting for the surviving defensive wall and tower. There is also an unusual theatre, its auditorium and orchestra a curious and unorthodox rectangular shape to accommodate the contours of the slope. A small temple dedicated to Dionysos, worshipped as at Athens during the dramatic festivals, stands to the west of the orchestra, the altar is still intact.

The road turns away from the coast through the small towns of Keratea and Markopoulo. Here you can stay on the bus back to Athens, or return northwards on the Marathon coast bus. Six kilometres further on is **Vravrona**, with the classical remains of **Brauron.** In the **Temple of Artemis**, young Athenian girls dressed as bears and danced to Artemis, both hunter and protector of wild animals. A museum houses some fine marbles and jewellery from the site.

Marathon – The Place & the Event

The village of **Marathon** is 42km from Athens. If you are on the bus, you will have to ask the driver to drop you off five kilometers before the village, in order to see the famous burial mound of the Athenians. There is a café here if you are thirsty.

The tomb is 10m high and around 180m in circumference. Excavations revealed the ashes and bones of the "192" young Athenians who died fighting off a huge number of invading Persians, in 490 BC. They were cremated and buried in this mass grave on the site of the battlefield. A recent theory suggests that the riders on the Parthenon frieze originally numbered 192 and they therefore represented the Marathon dead.

The *soros* (tomb) is now the starting point for the Athens marathon whi commemorates a certain Pheidippide who ran all the way to Athens to a nounce the great victory: not surpr ingly, as he was not as well nourished our modern athletes, he died of exhau tion upon arrival.

The Great Port of Piraeus

Piraeus, now as in classical times, t largest Mediterranean port east of Ita is just 10km from Athens. The easie way to get there is by *elektrikos* (unde ground train). During the day you mig wish to visit the **Archaeological M seum** in Filellinon Street. The museu houses finds from the classical port whi was connected to Athens' defence sy tem by the "Long Walls".

When the Romans conquered mai land Greece in 146 BC they looted Gre works of art and loaded them onto shi in the Piraeus harbour for transport tion back to Italy. Not all arrived safel and several got no further than t bottom of the harbour.

The most famous of these reclaim treasures is the splendid bronze *Pirae Apollo*, which dates to around 520 B and is the oldest surviving large-sca

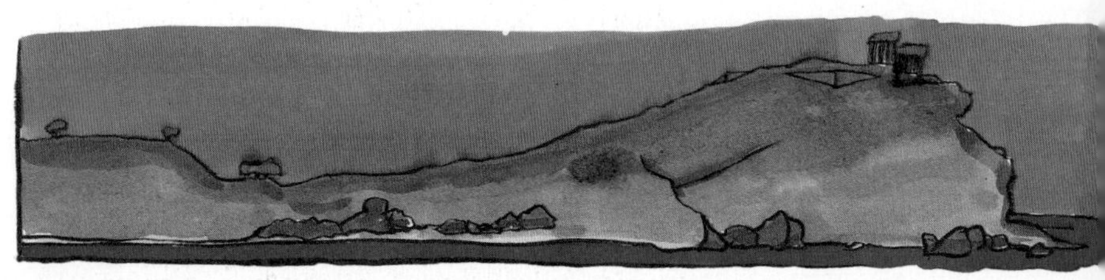

The largest Mediterranean port east of Italy, Piraeus is surprisingly serene.

ollow-cast bronze.

It stands in a stiff archaic pose, but e sculptor has explored the potential the bronze by giving the figure lifelike ojecting forearms which once held a w and a bowl. In their pristine condi- on these bronzes were polished to a wny gold.

Piraeus is also renowned for its fish- staurants, which are ranged along the rbour-side. It is particularly pleasant spend an evening here as the sea- eeze provides a cool alternative to hens.

The Offshore Islands

om Piraeus, ferries can be taken to the islands. Some of these are fairly close to the mainland and can be visited in a day trip. It is possible to book a commercial tour which takes you to Aegina, Poros and Hydra: the trouble is that it does not give you much time to explore the islands. It is perhaps more satisfying to visit just one of the islands. Whichever way you do it, the boat should be taken in preference to the hydrofoil: part of the island-hopping experience is to lie on the sundeck with a good book or tape, lapping up the deep blues of the Aegean sea and sky. Tickets can be bought by the gangplanks opposite the Piraeus metro exit.

Never too late for school!

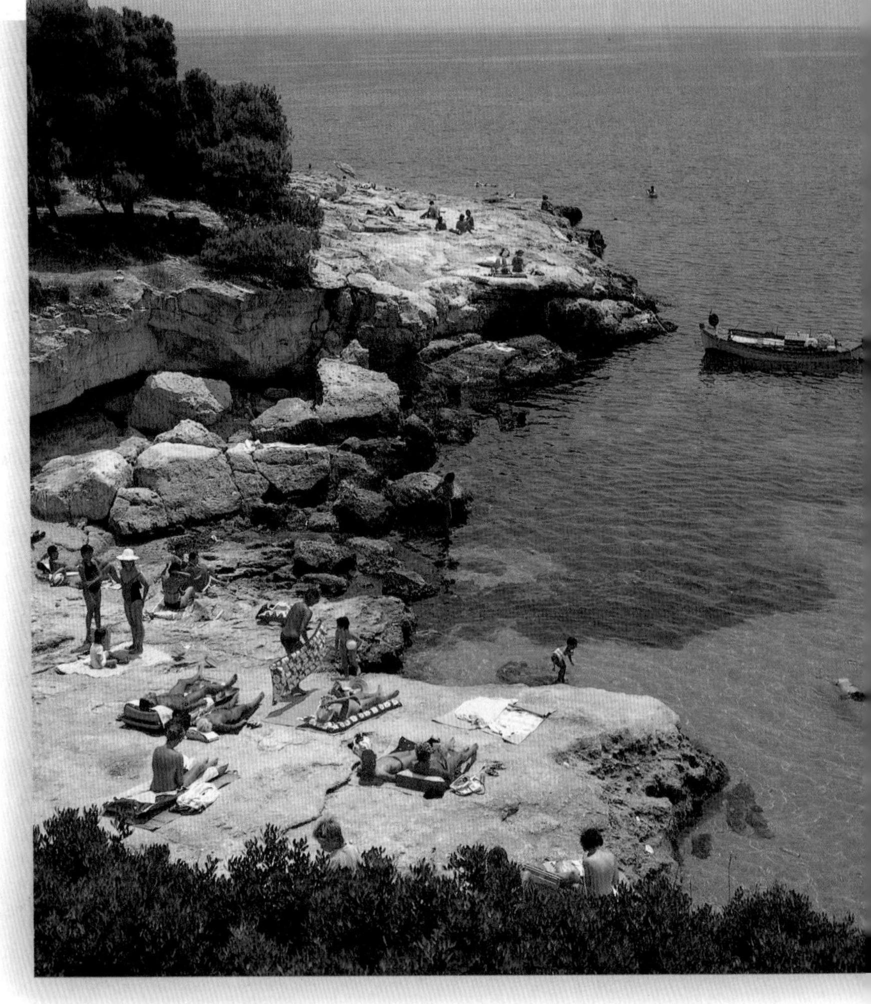

Aegina has its share of hidden coves and sandy beaches.

Aegina

Aegina can be reached swiftly by hydrofoil (35 mins) or in a more leisurely manner by boat ($1^1/_2$ hrs). The island is at the center of the Saronic Gulf and is therefore rich in history. Close to its harbour are fish-restaurants and cafés, as well as sandy beaches.

A bus will take you into the mountains to the **Temple of Aphaia**, remote situated (though there is a welcome ca across the road) on high ground wi views of southern Attica and on a cle day, of Athens and the Acropolis. T temple was constructed of local lim stone, now a silver-golden colour, b ginally coated in white plaster and ɔulded to emulate the finer marble of ɲens.

In 1911 archaeologists excavated pediment sculptures for the eccen- King Ludwig of Bavaria: they are w in Munich and represent the Tro- wars, with Athena (the goddess haia was a local version of her) stand- tall in the middle.

The temple was built around 500 and consisted of 6x12 Doric col- ɪns: most of the columns are mono- ɪs (single blocks) unlike the Acropolis ɲples and you can see how the double ernal colonnade once held the pitched f. Note the U-shaped grooves at the ls of the rectangular blocks: these ilitated lifting with rope pulleys.

Before returning to the main har- ɪr, take the bus a little further down **Ayia Marina**, where there are more ɪdy beaches. It is a busy resort, but at st you will get a seat on the return bus rney. Watch out for the angry tou- s waiting by the temple as you speed st them in the over-crowded bus!

Poros & Hydra

island of **Poros** is the next stop. It is of those happy places that manages absorb the tourists without ruining place. Henry Miller described the ival by sea in ***The Colossus of roussi,*** as like entering "the neck of womb" or of sailing through the ets of Venice. This alludes to the narrow entrance to the harbour. Above the busy waterfront, the white cubes of houses tumble as if scattered from the lemon groves above. Lawrence Durrell described the effect: "a child's box of bricks that has been rapidly and fluently set up against a small shoulder of headland". If you are staying longer than the hour allowed ashore by the ferryman, you will find peaceful walks to ruined temples and monasteries – such as that of **Zoodohou Pigi** (Virgin of the Life-giving Spring) – up behind the town.

Finally **Hydra**, a craggier, less lush island than Poros, but as with the latter, Persian King Xerxes was here in September 480 BC to defeat the Athenian navy with his massive fleet of 1,200 ships. The Athenians and their allies had a mere 378 ships, and the confident Xerxes set up a silver throne on the mainland at Perama to watch the Greek world fall into his hands. The kings' confidence was however to be shattered, when he was foiled by an Athenian trick. The Athenian commander Themistocles leaked false information that his ships were on their way to the Peloponnese. The Persian ships following this information moved into the narrow strait between island and mainland in pursuit of the Athenians, who suddenly turned and forced the less manoeuvrable Persian ships into the shallows where they were easily rammed and destroyed by the beaked triremes. It was a historic victory for the Greeks, hindering Persian expansion in the Aegean.

The Peloponnese

The Peloponnese means "the island of Pelops". Pelops was a mythical hero who won the hand of a local princess by defeating her father in a chariot race across the width of the Peloponnese from Olympia to Corinth. The "island" has been completely severed from northern Greece since 1893 when the Corinth canal cut through the isthmus which attached the area to the mainland. Rather sparsely populated (only one million people), it does have the feel of an island. This is a fine place to tour as it offers perhaps more variety than any other region of Greece. There are remote rocky coastlines with deserted sandy beaches, and mainly uncrowded resorts (not for those who love their nightlife).

he mountainous mainland.

The interior, like the mainland, is mountainous, but there are good roads along the whole coastline, which allow easy touring of the main modern towns and ancient sites. There are also routes from Corinth in the

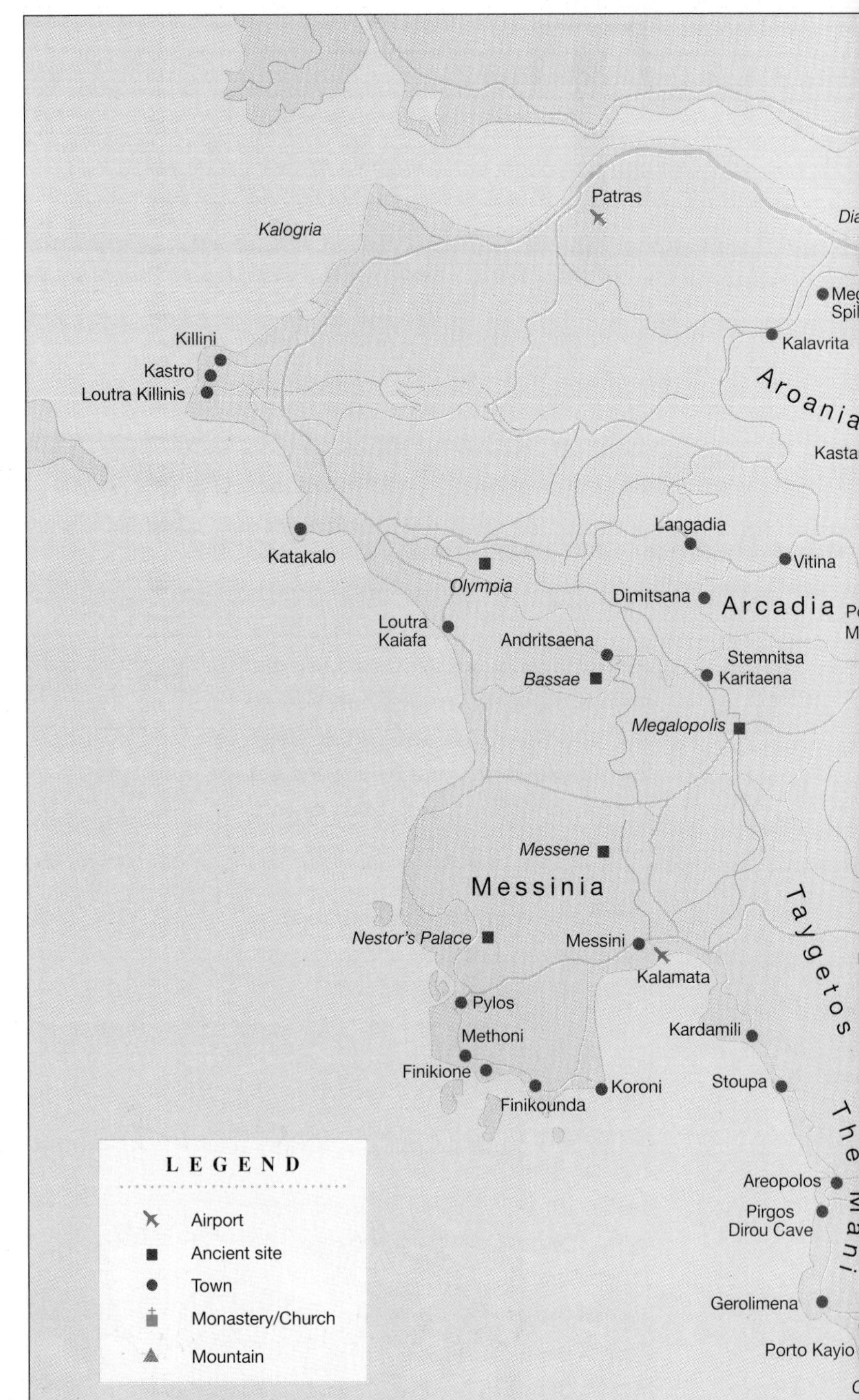

Patras
Kalogria
Kalavrita
Aroania
Killini
Kastro
Loutra Killinis
Katakalo
Langadia
Vitina
Olympia
Dimitsana
Arcadia
Loutra
Kaiafa
Andritsaena
Stemnitsa
Bassae
Karitaena
Megalopolis
Messene
Messinia
Taygetos
Nestor's Palace
Messini
Kalamata
Pylos
Kardamili
Methoni
Finikione
Koroni
Stoupa
Finikounda
The Mani
Areopolos
Pirgos
Dirou Cave
Gerolimena
Porto Kayio
LEGEND
Airport
Ancient site
Town
Monastery/Church
Mountain

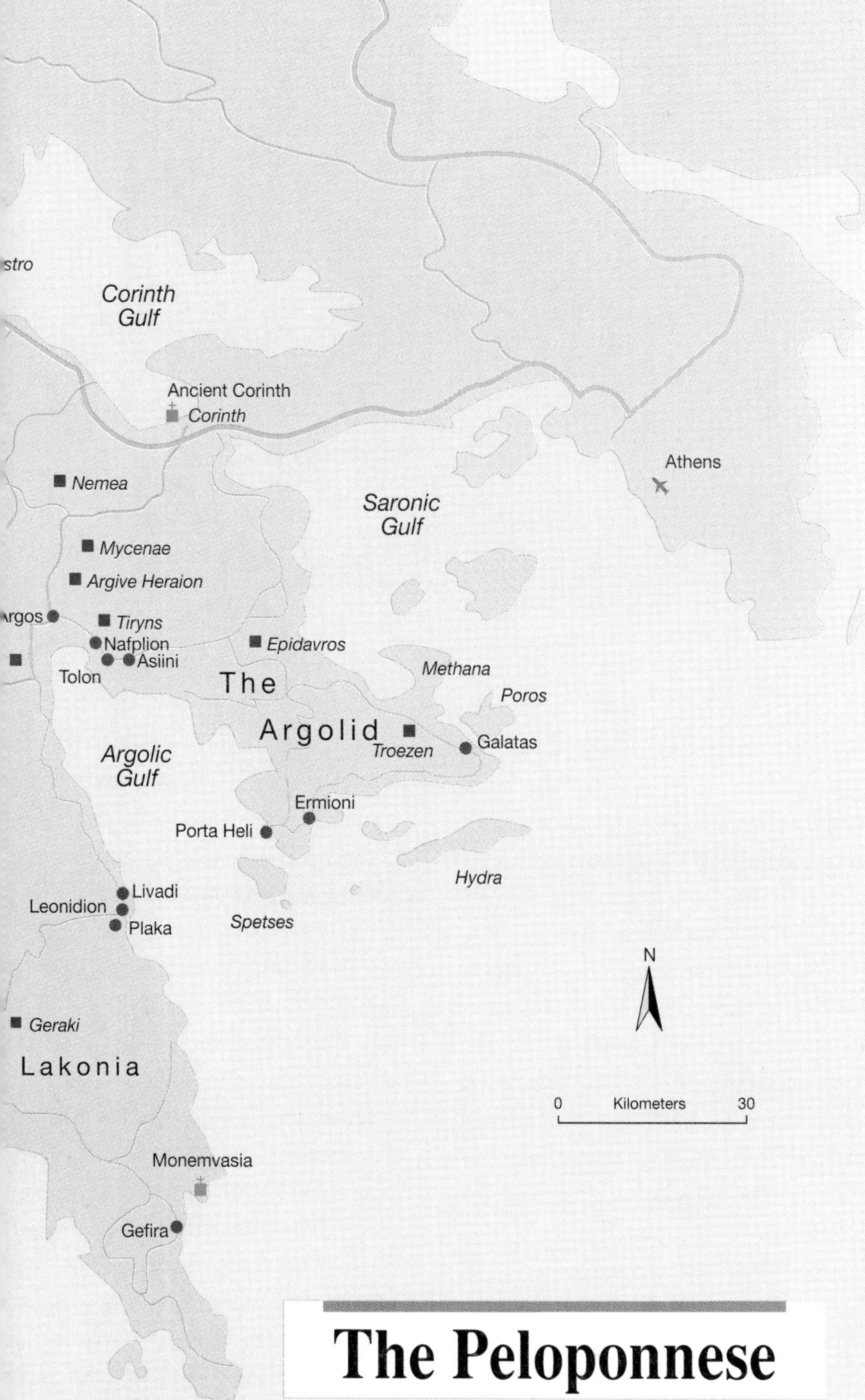

The Peloponnese

The Peloponnese has good roads.

north to Kalamata in the south via Tripolis, and, also via Tripolis, from Nafplion in the east to Olympia in the west. Therefore it is possible to work out various road routes depending on what you would like to do and see.

Three to four days is a reasonable time span, though this can easily be extended to a more leisurely week. The route used below travels anti-clockwise (against the normal tourist coach tour direction – it can become monotonous to keep seeing the same groups in the hotels and on the sites!).

The Corinth Canal & Corinth

The **Corinth Canal** is the final outcome of a number of brave attempts to cut th isthmus since antiquity, when the R man Emperor Nero went at it with golden pick-axe and several thousan Jewish prisoners-of-war. The attempt w halted at his death, and it was not unt the 1890s that French engineers cut th present canal, thus making an impo tant short cut for shipping, which woul otherwise have to circumnavigate th Peloponnese: however, the larger me chant traders are now too large to neg tiate its four-mile length – it is a me seven meters deep and 21 meters wid

The modern town of **Corinth** (popu lation: 23,000) is only worth visiting f a quick lunch. **Ancient Corinth** (ope daily 8 a.m - 6 p.m; 1000dr includin Museum) was far more important, an

Travelling the narrow passageway of the Corinth Canal.

ankfully now stands nine km away. ne ruins are now mostly Roman, since orinth became the capital of the Greek ovince in the Roman period. The **Foun- in of Peirene** was remodelled in mar- e with money provided by Herodes ticus in the second century AD. Its itural spring now provides the local llagers with water.

The main surviving Greek structure the **Temple of Apollo**, which dates ick to the sixth century predating any- ing standing in Athens by about a indred years. Its columns are mono- hs and taper, unlike the later Classcial nples, in a straight line. The surviving lumns (originally 6x15) are pictur- quely situated with the citadel of **rocorinth** (open daily 8:30 a.m - 6 p.m, closed Mondays; entrance 400dr) rising behind. You can share a taxi to make the four-km climb to the summit, where there is a welcome cafe-restaurant.

Here you can wander around the ruins of successive cultures from the Greeks to the Turks. On the topmost summit are the foundations of the famous **Temple of Aphrodite** which once housed a thousand sacred courtesans who worked in honour of the goddess of physical love.

From Patras to Olympia

Taking the scenic coastal motorway you arrive at the lively port of **Patras** (popu-

The Ancient Olympic Games

The Olympic Games as we know them today differ in certain fundamental ways from those held in ancient Olympia. Today women compete as well as men; we do not offer sacrifices to Zeus, nor do we observe a global truce for the duration of the Games. We do still follow the ancient tradition of the Games being held every four years, but whereas the modern Olympic Games are always held at a different location, the ancient were always held at Olympia, for the simple reason that the most important temple to Zeus was situated here.

The Sports

According to tradition, the Games were first held in 776BC, and a list has survived stating that the names and the cities of the winners from that date through to AD 217, when the Games were still being held under the Romans. The Christian Emperor Theodosius I finally banned them for being pagan in AD 393. The earliest games lasted just one day and events were limited to wrestling and running. In the seventh century BC the Festival of Zeus, as it was known, was reorganized to last longer and to include a variety of events – we know that in 472 BC they lasted for a full five days. The ma addition to the games then was the horse, signifier of wealth and power in antiquity: chari races, as well as single horse races were intr duced. There was once a *hippodrome* (hos racing track) to the south of the stadium, whi has been washed away by the River Alphei Ancient writers speak of an ingenious startin gate, the equivalent of the stalls in mode racing.

The Glory of Victory & the Price of Defeat

The main event was the foot-race, consisting a length of the stadium. For the first few Oly pics the victors tended to come from Spar but as the games gained in prestige, mc competitors entered from Greek colonies as away as Italy and Sicily, and they began to sha the honours. There was no honour for comi second or third, as there is today: to lose wa social disgrace, and we hear of losers slinki away down back-alleys never to be heard again. To win was everything: your city w entitled to set up a bronze statue in the *A* (sacred grove of Zeus), and the statues oft

lation 142,000). This is the largest town in the Peloponnese and overlies the important ancient Greek and Roman city. A pleasant area to head for to escape the crowds is the upper town around the Venetian ***kastro*** (castle) which stands on the ancient Acropolis. There are rock concerts and classical plays performed in the Roman Ode from July to September, and a big car val parade in ea March.

Oylmpia reached by continui down to Pyrgos wh you turn left: the sm village of **Olympia** h grown up to cater tourists visiting the c cient site (open Mond Friday 8 a.m - 7 p. Saturday & Sunday

epicted the naked athlete placing the victory
own on his head. If the victor was wealthy
nough, he might commission a hymn of praise
om one of the best poets, to be sung at the
ening feast.

Games Schedule

e know the daily schedule of the games from e fifth century BC onwards. They took place in igust or September at the time of the second l moon after the summer solstice. On the first y, the competitors and judges took oaths of r-play, and sacrifices were made to the Altar Zeus, before his temple. At dawn on the cond day heralds proclaimed the names of e competitors to the applause (or boos) of the sembled crowds: the day was spent in chariot d horse racing, and there was a tough pen- thlon event. The third day was devoted to y's events. On the fourth day came the men's ot-races, boxing, wrestling and long jump- g, and the final event of the Games was a race men in full hoplite armour. Also held on the rd day was the *Pankration*, a violent no-hold- rred fight in honour of the victor, who wore d olive wreaths sacred to Zeus.

m - 3 p.m; entrance 1500dr). This was nere the first Olympic Games were ld, traditionally in 776 BC (see box ory Page 184).

The great **Temple of Zeus** (470-456 C) suffered earthquakes and now all u can see are the temple platform and llen column drums, but its excellent ulptures are in the museum. The gold d ivory statue of the god which was ce enthroned within was sculpted by eidias, whose workshop has been cavated – the statue was one of the ven wonders of the world.

Beside the temple of Zeus stands the older **Temple of Hera**, inside which once stood the sculptor Praxiteles' Hermes (now in the museum). These two temples are within the sacred *altis* (sanctuary of Zeus); but you should also visit the **stadium** with its 200-meter running-track and earthen banks for spectators.

Elsewhere on this peaceful site are other buildings which are connected with the ancient Olympic Games, including the rectangular colonnade of the **Gymnasium**.

The wonderful **Archaeological Museum** (same hours as site, but 12 p/m - 5 p.m Mondays hours; entrance 1000dr) is essential for filling in the missing details of the earth -quake-damaged site. Here you will see the **Hermes of Praxiteles** (fourth century BC) who teases the infant Dionysus with a bunch of grapes.

Praxiteles was most famous for creating the first ever public naked female statue, the Aphrodite of Knidos, this has not survived, and the sinuous pose of the naked Hermes tantalizes us with what we are missing.

The sculptures from the Temple of Zeus depict the Battle of Centaurs and Lapiths, with Apollo placed centrally (west pediment), and the Chariot Race of Pelops, with Zeus himself in the center (east pediment). Also displayed are the 12 *metopes* depicting the founder of the Games, Herakles, performing his 12 Labours, under the watchful eyes of his patron deity, Athena.

History in the making – archaeological excavations at Olympia.

Mani, Sparta & Mystras

From Pyrgos, you can continue along the coast road via Kalamata and down to the Mani Peninsula. **Kalamata** (population: 42,000) suffered a devastating earthquake in 1986, which ruined its reputation as one of the finest resorts on the Peloponnese, it is still in the process of trying to pick up the pieces and is at present best avoided.

Continuing southwards to the west of the Taygetos mountains (the summit at 2,407m is the highest in the Peloponnese), you will reach The **Mani Peninsula**, which in spite of classic books written in praise of its wild and desolate beauty, remains an unspoilt region of rocky coast and mountains. The capi is the elegant little fishing-village **Gythion**, but most visitors head for t tiny village of **Areopolis**, where there access to the famous **Dyrou a Alepotripa caves**, seven km away: th are fascinating subterranean rivers a lakes, which are accessible in sm boats.

From Mani, the northbound ro takes you inland to **Sparta**. The mode city (population: 12,000) is rather la ing in charm, but has plenty of hote and is the perfect base for visiting bo Ancient Sparta and Byzantine Mistr **Ancient Sparta**, lies, unfortunately, neath the modern town, and all you c see today are a theatre and Acropolis the north of the town – a visit to th

The Spartans

rmed statue from the Roman period, Corinth Museum.

e Spartans, or Lacedaimonians as they were nerally called in antiquity, lived in their small y-state on the west bank of the River Eurotas the Peloponnes. The state's infamous totaliian political regime developed as a result of seventh century BC conquests of the neighuring Messenians (to the west of the Taygetus ɔuntain range).

The Spartan population was small, and to ep control of its new territories, which proled them with most of their agricultural proce, they turned the defeated into *helots* (serfs) d maintained control by means of their wellined army. There was no turning back once s system had been developed, and in the fifth ntury BC Sparta's entire educational proımme was geared to the production of fight- men. The women, unlike traditional Greek men who were trained in domestic tasks, re educated to be as tough as the boys, in order that their male children would become great soldiers.

Spartan Commandos

Sparta was at the height of its power from the eighth to the fourth centuries BC. During this period it remained a small city-state which, like its great rival Athens, grew increasingly powerful over its neighbouring states. It was ruled by two kings and an oligarchic assembly which was a political system diametrically opposed to Athenian democracy.

There was also the *gerousia* (assembly of elders) composed of men over 60 who prepared legislation for the younger men of the assembly to vote on. Each Spartan citizen was allotted land and a number of slaves to work it – this allowed the Spartan male to devote all his energies to the army.

When a child was born, the *gerousia* had the power to have it exposed on the slopes of Mount Taygetos, if they considered it to be too weak or deformed. The surviving children remined with their mothers until they were seven years old. They were then taken and placed in state barracks, where soldiers enforced a highly disciplined lifestyle, in which theft was encouraged (to become crafty and survive in times of war) but harshly punished if discovered: an ancient story tells of how a boy stuffed a fox down his tunic for fear of being caught – it ate his bowels. After a period in the secret police, who spied on the *helots* and arrested any troublemakers, the Spartan youth entered the army at the age of 20. Spartan girls were famed for both their beauty and their toughness – Helen of Troy was Spartan – and they received a similar education to the boys before they were married.

During the fifth century BC the Peloponnesian War was fought between Sparta and Athens and their respective allies. After thirty years of fighting the Spartans won the war with their highly disciplined army, but failed to consolidate their gains and the Macedonians managed to conquer the whole of Greece by the end of the fourth century BC.

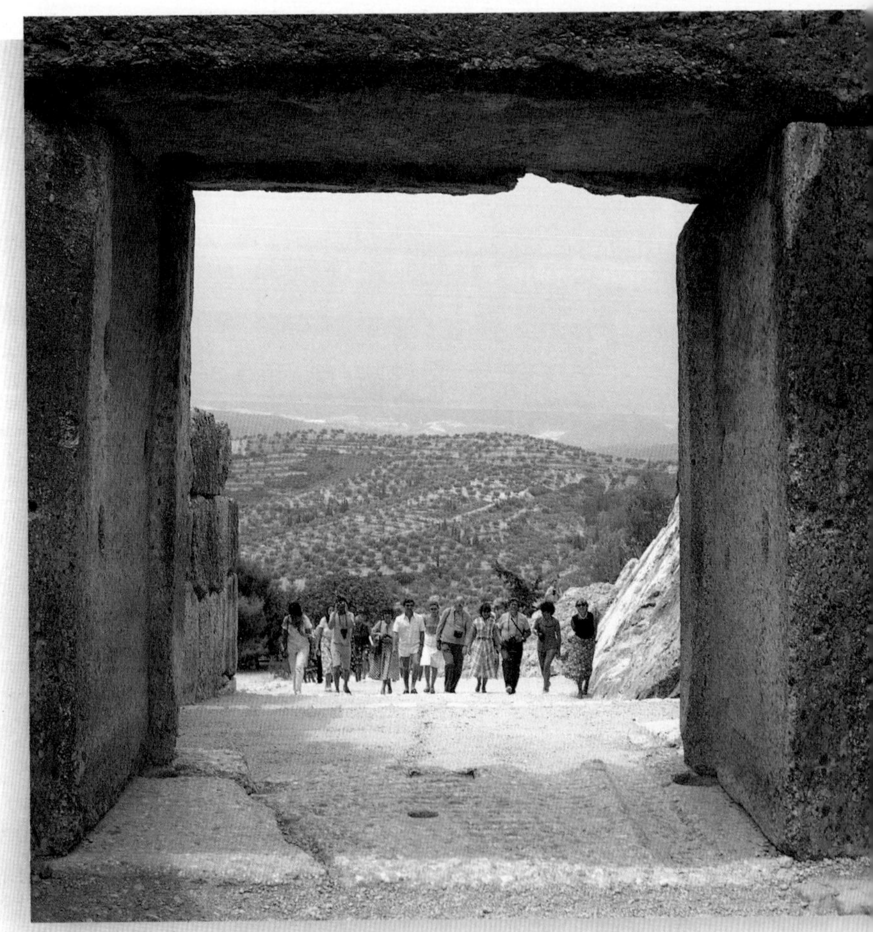

The imposing entrance at Lion's Gate, Mycenae.

unenclosed sites makes a nice evening stroll. To see the **Sanctuary of Artemis Orthia**, take the Tripolis road for 500m and follow a path down to the site – all that is visible today is a Roman grandstand used to watch the ritual spectacles which took place before the temple.

Mistras (open daily 8:30 a.m - 3 p.m; entrance 1000dr; museum closed Mondays), on the other hand, is well worth the five km trip westwards from Sparta. Magnificently positioned on th lower slopes of Mount Taygetos, it is o of the best preserved and evocative By antine sites anywhere in the world. Yo can wander in peace for hours aroun its sacred churches and monasteries, well as its secular palaces and fortress The ambience is that of Byzantine Gree when Christian Church culture was its zenith on the eve of the Turki invasion.

Medieval Mistra

istra, like Pompeii, is a city where a past age has
en almost perfectly preserved. It is a complete
edieval city, enclosed like a time-capsule within
original walls. Standing dramatically on a
othill of Mount Taiyetos at the mouth of the
orge of Mistra, the city was first called *mezythra*
cause it resembles a cone-shaped Greek cheese
that name.

Following the capture of Constantinople by
e Crusaders in 1204, the Franks consolidated
eir power in the Peloponnese by building
rtresses at various strategic points; the castle at
ezythra was built by Guillaume de Villardouin
1249 to protect the town from the Slavs – who
velt in the Eurotas valley – and the mountain
besmen; this was when the town's name was
rrupted to "Mistra", French slang for "mis-
ss".

The castle was Guillaume's favourite resi-
nce, and you can understand the attraction
en you stand on its ramparts, 564 meters
ove sea level, and look down onto the fertile
ain enclosed by purple mountains. However,
illaume's rule did not last; less than a decade
er he had completed the castle he was killed
a battle against the Byzantines who impris-
ed him until he agreed to hand over the his
ntrol of Mistra, along with his other castles at
onemvasia and Maina.

The triangle of land encompassed by the
ee fortresses thus passed into the hands of the
zantine Greeks and in 1349 became the
spotate of Mistra, governed by a son or
other of the emperor whose title was Despot.

Byzantine Mystra

The Greeks fortified the town beneath the castle which then became a refuge for the inhabitants of medieval Sparta (Lakedaimonia) in times of invasion. There followed two centuries of Byzantine rule when Mistra flourished into a center of political and cultural supremacy. Churches were built and decorated with wonderful frescoes, many of which have survived; houses were constructed for both rich and poor and there was a glorious palace for the Despots. Though in various states of preservation, all of these still omit a unique and powerful atmosphere, which makes you feel that you have been transported back to a former age and helps you to understand the Byzantine layers of modern inhabited Greek towns.

The penultimate Despot, Constantine Dragatses (1443-48), became the last Emperor of Byzantium, and was crowned in the cathedral of Mistra. Mistra fell to the Turks in 1460, some ten years after the fall of Constantinople, and continued to flourish during the centuries of the Turkish occupation, its population reaching 40,000: there was a brief interlude of Venetian rule from 1687-1715. In 1770 it was sacked by the Turkish sultan's Albanian troops, and again during the War of Independence, at which point Sparta was founded in 1834 and Mistra was abandoned, leaving a ghost town which never fails to come back to life for the modern visitor.

Unmissable Mycenae

om Sparta, the north-bound road takes
u via the town of **Tripolis** (popula-
n: 21,000) to **Nafplion** (population:
,600), a peaceful and pretty sea-side
wn, and a better place to break your
urney than Tripolis.

`It makes sense to use Nafplion as a base for visiting the archaeological sites of Mycenae and Epidavros, as you have to come back through Nafplion whichever of these sites (and both are a "must") you visit first. Four km along the road to Mycenae via Argos, it is worth stopping for a quick look at the Mycenaean citadel of **Tiryns**, which is far less visited than Mycenae itself, and gives you something to compare it with.

The oldest and best-preserved Greek theatre at Epidavrus.

Mycenae (open daily 8 a.m - 5 p.m, Sat & Sun 8:30 a.m - 3 p.m; entrance 1000dr) is 20km from Nafplion. You enter the citadel through the splendid **Lion Gate**, its two (now headless) lions standing aloof to guard the fortified palace. This was once ruled by King Agamemnon, who led the Greek troc against the Trojans to win back ▮ sister-in-law Helen of Sparta. Ag memnon spent ten years at Troy, only be murdered by his wife and her lov upon his return.

Inside the gate to the right you c

[se]e the royal burial ground, where the [1]9th-century German archaeologist [S]chliemann unearthed the famous [g]olden burial masks and bronze dag[g]ers, now in the National Archaeologi[ca]l Museum, Athens. It is a worthwhile [s]cramble up to the top of the citadel, [w]here you can make out the groundplan [o]f the palace itself, and admire the view down the fertile plain towards Argos and the sea.

On the way out, to the left of the approach track, it is worth investigating the **Beehive Tombs** (c 1600-1200). These royal tombs were looted in antiquity, but are still remarkable pieces of monumental architecture.

Epidavrus

The Sanctuary of Asklepios at **Epidavrus** (open Tuesday-Friday 8 a.m - 5 p.m, Sat & Sun 8:30 a.m - 3 p.m, Mondays 11 a.m - 5 p.m; entrance 1000dr) boasts the oldest and best-preserved Greek theatre (c 350 BC). The magnificent auditorium was placed in the natural hollow of the hill behind it, which was the Greek solution to their lack of cement technology.

Its 55 tiers of stone seats have a capacity of 16,000 and the theatre is still used for the Epidavrus Drama Festival in the summer. The architect produced a building of eternal visual appeal, its proportions are harmonious and its acoustics legendary.

The **archaeological site** and **museum** are also well worth visiting. The atrical events held here were in honour of the god of healing and medicine Asklepios. Elsewhere on the site you can see the foundations of his temple – where pilgrims stayed the night to be healed whilst dreaming of the god – as well as a well-preserved stadium. The road takes you along the coast back to Corinth.

Delphi

To the west of Athens, the highlight of the southern area of mainland Greece is the ancient site at **Delphi**. If you are travelling from Athens, there are a few other places along the way, but you would only have time for one of these if you are planning to return the same day. There are commercial coach tours to Delphi (sometimes also stopping at the **Monastery of Osios Loukas**), or you can take a public bus. There are about four of these departing daily, and the journey is a long one – three and a half hours. If you do use public transport, you will find it difficult to break your journey and should stick to just Delphi for the day. Buses leave Athens from the Liossion 260 terminal: to get there, take a metro from Omonia or Monastiraki to Ayios Nikolaos (St Nicholas' church), where if you walk under the line and turn left, you will see buses.

ne Temple of Athena was an spirational site for ancient pilgrims.

The Road to Delphi

In the 19th century, this area of Greece was called Sterea Elladhos (Greek Continent) – because territory further to

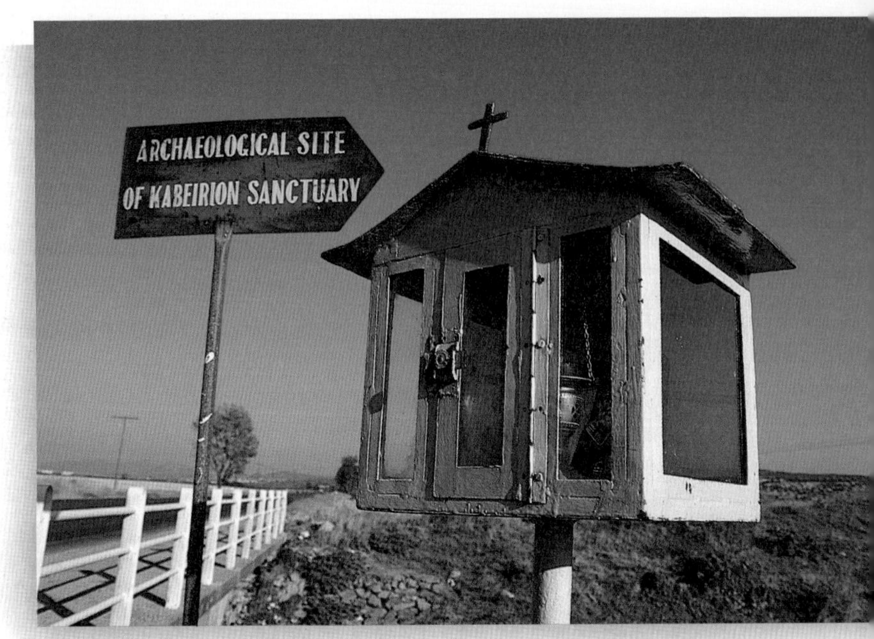

Wayside shrine on the road from Athens to Delphi.

the north was at that time outside of Greece. The 160 km journey from Athens to Delphi is accompanied by an increasingly dramatic mountainous landscape, which culminates in the awe-inspiring winding road to Delphi, perched as it is on the steep slopes of the Parnassos massif. The road from Athens takes you through ancient Boeotia, which lay between the island of Euboea on the east and the Gulf of Corinth to the south. You will pass **Mount Helicon** (1,750 m), the highest point in Boeotia, where 2,700 years ago the Muses inspired Hesiod to write some of the earliest Greek poetry. The region was always involved in Greek history, being fertile land and on the major communication routes from northern to southern Greece.

Today **Livadhia** is the administrati centre of the region, and along wi **Thebes** provides all the usual touri facilities. Accommodation can also found in the small modern town Delphi.

In the Footsteps of Oedipus

If time is not a problem, you should ta the "old road" from Athens to Theb (Thiva). This follows the course of t ancient **Sacred Way** which started the Acropolis and finished at Delp visiting the sanctuary of Demeter Eleusis (modern Elefsina) *en route*. Th was the road walked by Oedipus on h

The modern approach to Delphi.

ıy to consult the Oracle at Delphi. .ses 880, 853 and 862 leave for Elefsina •m Platia Eleftherias in Athens. The ɹrney takes about 45 minutes and, nning through the industrial outskirts Athens, is about as unsacred as any ban highway. Roughly halfway along is route is the **Monastery of Daphni** ɔen daily 8:30 a.m - 3 p.m), well ɔrth a stop if you are interested in rly Byzantine architecture: the 11th-ntury church and mosaics are among e finest in Greece.

Twenty-two kilometres from Ath-s, **Elefsina** (ancient Eleusis) was the e of the **Sanctuary of Demeter**, where itiates practiced secret rites and were ɔmised life after death. In the classi-l period some 30,000 pilgrims came here every spring: they gathered at the Acropolis in Athens, bathed in Phaleron Bay, and then walked here along the Sacred Way. The ruins (open Tuesday-Sunday, 8:30 a.m - 3 p.m) are sparse and difficult to interpret, but the museum's models give an excellent impression of the original layout.

The modern port of Elefsina is heavily industrialized and unattractive. You can escape along the Sacred Way into the hills towards Thebes (Thiva) by taking one of two daily buses. Thirty-three km along this road, the fourth century BC Athenian **Fort of Eleutherai**, becomes visible to the right of the road. The fort is the well-preserved and is complete with defensive towers. Twenty km further on is **Thebes** (Thiva). There

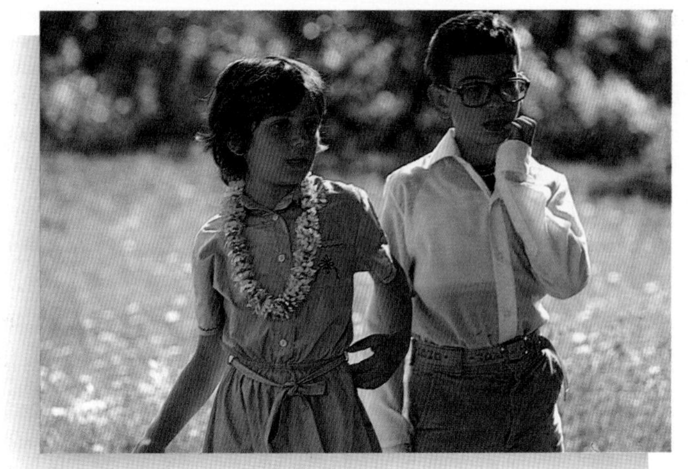

A couple of rather shy locals

is little to see of the famous ancient city, home or birthplace of such classical "greats" as Dionysus and Herakles, and the place where Oedipus married his mother Jocasta. The picturesque **Museum** (open Tuesday-Saturday 8:30 a.m - 3 p.m; Sunday 9:30 a.m - 2:30 p.m), is set in the grounds of a 13th-century Frankish castle and has a good representative collection from the Mycenaean to the Turkish period.

Monastery of Osios Loukas

Continuing on the road to Delphi 24 km beyond Levadhia (144 km from Athens) at the "Schist Crossroads", it is worth making a detour by turning left to the Byzantine **Monastery of Osios Loukas** – public transport involves an awkward change of bus at Dhistomo – otherwise continue straight on to Delphi

The Monastery of Osios Loukas (a local Saint Luke; open 8 a.m - 2 p.m and 4 p.m - 7 p.m) is worth a visit not just for its fine Byzanti architecture a (heavily restore wall and ceili mosaics, but al for its wonderful landscape setting. The is a tremendous feeling of space a clarity up here, with olives speckling t broad valley below behind which, to t east, rises Mount Helikon. To enter t precincts, you must be wearing a lo skirt or trousers, for this is a practisi monastery – ten monks still worsh here.

After refreshments in the cafe, y should visit the two main churches the other side of the courtyard. The 11 century **Katholikon** is similar to t Church at Daphni. Notice the splend variety of materials used on the ext rior: stone and brick walls, windo framed by different coloured marb columns – certain indicators of the cu tural and material wealth of the Chur in the post-Roman period. Within, y come first to the *narthex* (Byzanti porch), its vault covered in colourf mosaics on a gold background, depic ing the Apostles, the Crucifixion a Resurrection. *The Washing of the Apo tles' Feet by Christ* has typical Byzanti acial expressions, the Apostles looking naively shocked at this mundane and humbling service, performed by their master. In the domed nave, associated transepts and aisles are even more gold mosaics, as well as frescoes, many of them replacing earlier work destroyed by an earthquake of 1659. The gold mosaics glitter like a horde of treasure in the glimmering interplay of light and shadows produced by the many arches and windows.

The smaller church to the north is the **Theotikos** ("god-bearing" Virgin Mary). This is a little earlier in date, and is notable for its four granite Byzantine columns which support the dome. From outside, note the almost Islamic style decorated marble of the drum. A whole day could easily be spent at this beautiful and fascinating monastery.

The "Schist Crossroads"

Back at the "**Schist Crossroads**" and it is approximately another 20 km to Delphi, but first you must take stock of where you are. There has been a crossing of ways here since antiquity, and the ancient travel writer Pausanias tells us that it was here that Oedipus came when on his way back from Delphi, where the Oracle had told him that he would kill his father and marry his mother. His father, Laius, was travelling from his palace at Thebes with two servants; Oedipus, on foot but of royal birth, refused to get off the road, a fight thus developed and Oedipus killed all three. He then proceeded to Thebes, where by killing the local monster Sphinx, he won the prize of Laius' widow Jocasta and became King of Thebes. The original road was in the gorge below. Pausanias also went from here to Delphi; "the route becomes increasingly precipitous and is difficult for the fittest of men." In the modern car or coach, the uphill gradient allows you to contemplate the tremendous mountain landscapes on either side of the road. There is also a growing atmosphere of quiet excitement as passengers begin to look out for the ruins of Delphi.

Delphi

The Sanctuary of Apollo at **Delphi** was

In the footsteps of Oedipus.

excavated by the French in the late 19th century. If at all possible, try to visit the remains as early or as late in the day as possible, in order to avoid the crowds. There is plenty of climbing to do and you need to allow a good three hours for even a minimal visit. The site is now divided into three main sections: the **Precinct of Apollo** (the main site, open Monday-Friday 7:30 a.m - 6:30 p.m; Saturday & Sunday 8:30 a.m - 3 p.m); the **Sanctuary of Athena** (also known as "Marmaria" – open the same hours as the main site); and the **Museum** (open the same hours as the main site, except that it is closed on Mondays from 12 p.m - 6:30 p.m).

Delphi was the major center of worship of the god Apollo. The extremely unlikely location of the sanctuary – i barren territory, 600 m above sea-lev on the slopes of the Phaedriades ("shir ing rocks"), beneath the 2,500 m peak Mount Parnassus – is explained by a ancient story: the god Zeus sent tw eagles flying from each side of the worl and this was the spot that they met – th site was also known as "the navel of th world".

To the south extends a superb vie across a deep ravine towards anoth ridge. From the terrace of modern De phi the view extends westwards, ov the best olive-groves in Greece, towar the Gulf of Corinth, 10 km away.

Ancient tradition tells us that th original divine ruler of Delphi was th Earth Mother Gaia, and that the Orac elonged to her. A dragon called the ython guarded her Oracle, and one ay the new sky-god Apollo slew the ython and took control of the Oracle. very four years the Pythian Games ok place here in honour of Apollo's efeat of the Python.

On the site you will see evidence for ese games, which continued well into e Roman period. The stadium and mnasium are evidence of athletic competition, whilst the theatre reminds us at dramatic and poetic contests were so held here to honour Apollo as god High Culture. The site was most faous, however, for its Oracle (see box ory Page 200).

The Delphi Museum

e **Delphi Museum** can get crowded, t if you are patient you will find that e larger groups move rapidly from om to room. With a little imagination u can envisage the exhibits relocated the sacred, outdoor atmosphere of e site itself. Thus you will certainly get good idea of how important this reote sanctuary was to the Greeks. The ality of the sculptures which adorned e treasuries of the different Greek cityates, was of a very high standard. lphi was "panhellenic" (open to all eeks), and they vied with one another the display of their offerings to Apollo.

Highlights include: *Kleobis and Biton,* o marble male *kouroi* (statues of nad youths) in the symmetrical archaic

The Sphinx of the Naxians.

style of the sixth century BC. There is an ancient story that their mother wanted to borrow the family cart to visit the festival of Hera at Argos. Her husband required the oxen in the fields, so her sons, Kleobis and Biton, volunteered to pull the cart to Argus. When they arrived, the mother prayed to Hera to give her sons the best reward possible for mortals; the next morning she awoke to find them dead – presumably immortalised! The people of Argus set up these statues in Delphi, to commemorate the "miracle".

To the right of this room are the late Archaic sculptures from the **Siphnian Treasury**. The pediment shows Apollo and Herakles (Heracles) fighting over the sacred tripod of Delphi; the taller

The Oracle of Delphi

Thousands of pilgrims from all over the Greek world attended the Pythian Games, held every four years. Delphi was also visited for its renowned Oracle. To consult the Oracle in the Temple of Apollo, involved strict ritual procedures. Firstly, the pilgrims had to purify themselves in the sacred pool of the Castalian Spring, which is situated below the main sanctuary. For most, this simply entailed washing their hair, but murderers were obliged to immerse their whole bodies, otherwise they would defile the sanctuary with their blood-guilt. From the Spring, they would continue on foot along the Sacred Way. Just outside the sanctuary entrance, they could buy votive offerings of clay or, if they could afford it, metal: these would have to be placed on the temple steps before approaching the Oracle.

Entry Qualifications

At the top of the Sacred Way stood the Temple of Apollo. In front of its entrance on the east stood the Altar of the Chians. Here the poorer pilgrims offered a sacrifice of a sheep or a goat, whilst an ox or a boar was expected from wealthy citizens. The entrails of these animal victims were inspected by a seer: only if the auspices were considered favourable, was the pilgrim entitled to enter the temple and sta before the oracle. The priests then interrogat the pilgrim, asking whether he had perform any actions in his life which might render hi unsuitable for being present in the sanctua Women were not allowed to visit the Orac their questions had to be asked by their me The Oracle was originally only open for qu tions for one day in the year – on the annivers of the oracle's foundation. In the classical p riod, the Oracle was open every month, exce during three of the winter months when Apo was thought to have gone away to visit t southerly race of Hyperboreans. During t time his opposite, Dionysus, commanded t site in his absence.

Approaching the Oracle

The pilgrims then had to wait their turn standing in the *pronaos* (temple porch). O those who had special automatic rights to co sult the Oracle (often city-states which h dedicated major monuments at Delphi) gether with a few more chosen by lot, w admitted into the next room. Here they c tated their requests to a priest, who recorc the questions on wooden tablets.

The Pythian priestess (the "pythia") w spoke for Apollo, was selected from the lo

Zeus intervenes in the center. The frieze depicts Zeus and the other gods seated on Mount Olympus watching a battle between the Greeks and the Trojans, whilst the gods themselves battle with giants (all are dressed in contemporary armour). Originally the various figures were identified by painted inscriptions. The archaic *Sphinx of the Naxians* (c 560 BC) is another type of conspicuous monument designed to impress other Greek city-states.

In the main corridor you can see t *metope* sculptures from the **Treasury the Athenians** (c 490-480 BC). The At nians chose to depict their great dem cratic hero Theseus performing his bours alongside those of Herakles. N how the figures (slightly later than th from the Siphnian Treasury) are beco ing more naturalistic.

At the very end of this central co dor is the unmissable *Bronze Chariot* originally part of a group with a cha

ɔmen of Delphi. She had to be of mature age ɗ born in freedom: apart from these there ɜre no further stipulations, neither of wealth r virginity. However, once chosen, the new estess had to vow chastity and dwell in a :red room somewhere near the temple. Like ɜ enquirers, the Pythia had to bathe in the stalian Spring before consultations began.

Just before the consultation the Pythia ewed the leaves and inhaled the smoke from ɜ burning wood of laurel, sacred to Apollo. ated on Apollo's tripod in the inner chamber the temple, she uttered her replies, which ɜre then interpreted and passed on by the ests to the pilgrims. The pilgrim received a itten reply in verse (later in prose).

Sayings of the Oracle

e modern rationalistic view is obviously scep-al about the Oracle's reliability. The Oracle ded to play safe in its answers by making m deliberately ambivalent. A famous exam- of this was the reply given to King Croesus Lydia, when he asked whether he should ack the Persians: "If Croesus crosses the Halys, will destroy a mighty empire." Croesus took advice and was defeated, but the "mighty pire", according to the Oracle, was his own!

d horses (you can see the exquisite gments of their hooves and tails, in a e-case). The statue-group was set up commemorate the chariot-race vic-y in 478 or 474 BC of Polyzalus, a ant of Gela in Sicily.

The charioteer is of hollow-cast ɔnze and demonstrates how the new ıssical artistic style places great im-rtance on naturalism. The drapery ngs like real cloth; there are realistic s of white enamel with black stone

The Oracle's Seat.

pupils; the lips are coated in red copper and his headband is inlaid with silver and copper. These bronzes were originally kept polished and would have therefore been more of a reflective tawny colour in their pristine state. Before you leave the museum, have a look at the later Hellenistic and Roman sculptures, with their even more realistic approaches to art.

The Oracle's Seat

The **Precinct of Apollo** is approached through its ancient gateway via a small market area, where the ancient visitor would purchase terracotta or bronze votive offerings for Apollo. From here

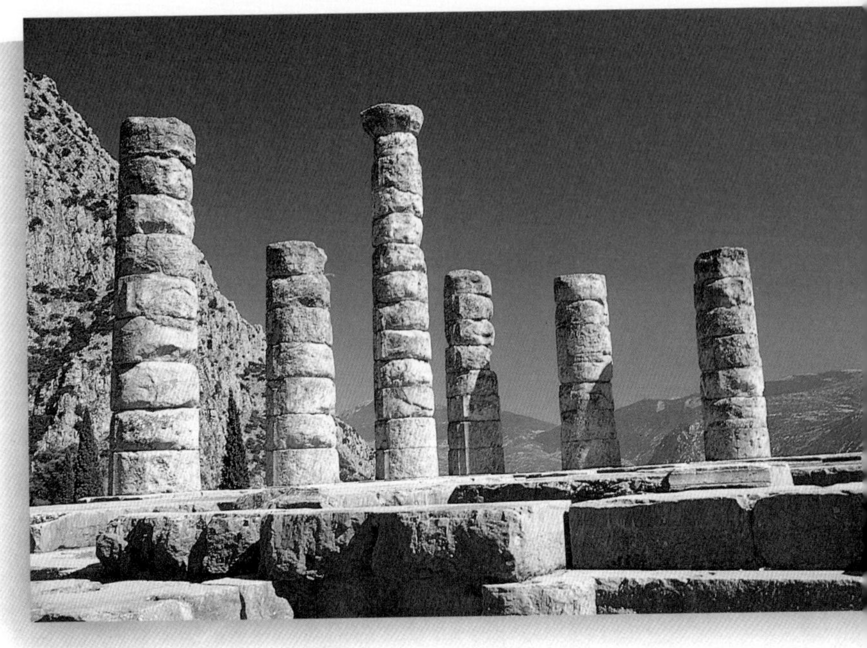

The Temple of Apollo.

you can follow the Sacred Way up to the **Temple of Apollo**, passing on either side, the foundations of treasuries and the inscribed bases of statues. Our knowledge of what these were is aided by Pausanias, who was here in the second century AD whilst many of the monuments were still standing.

We know, for example, that there were statue-groups of various gods and heroes set up by different Greek cities to signify their power, wealth and mythical traditions. On the left you can see the the foundations of the Siphnian Treasury, whose sculptures can be seen in the Delphi Museum.

As the way turns back on itself, the restored **Treasury of the Athenians** stands in a deliberately conspicuous position, overlooking the route. T sculpted *metopes* are again now in Delphi Museum, along with anci hymns to Apollo, complete with mu cal notation, which were inscribed the side walls during the Hellenistic riod.

Above the treasuries a fine poly nal retaining wall supports the pl form of the **Temple of Apollo**. The te ple is disappointingly ruined; only si its Doric columns (which originally around the building) have been erected. The first sixth century BC te ple which was destroyed by an ea quake, was replaced two hundred ye later.

Somewhere inside the temple the chasm over which the Pythian Pri

High-altitude refreshment.

s sat on the sacred tripod and uttered r Oracles: no evidence of this feature ıs survived, probably due to earth- ıakes. Ancient writers tell us that the ıilosophical maxims "Know Yourself" ıd "Nothing in Excess" were once in- ·ibed at the entrance to the temple.

Above the temple is the fourth cen- ıry BC **theatre** with a seating capacity 5,000, which gives some idea of the ıcient crowds present at the Pythian ımes.

Keep walking along a narrower and ·eper path uphill to reach the **Sta- um**. It is well worth the effort, as here u will see one of the best-preserved, d certainly finest situated, stadia in e Mediterranean.

The wealthy Roman patron Herodes ticus added the stone seats, to accom- ›date 7,000 people. As you enter from e of the short ends you can see the ›oved stone starting-line. The really ergetic should have a race – the eeks would generally run to the end d back!

Wash & Worship Places

Returning to the exit the way you came, turn left and walk down the main road; on your left you will see the **Castalian Spring**, where the ancient pilgrims had to wash themselves before entering Apollo's shrine. Byron immersed himself, believing that the god of poetry would inspire him. Unfortunately, this is no longer possible, since the area has been cordoned off, owing to rock-falls from the cliffs above.

Further along and to the right, you can visit the **Sanctuary of Athena**. Athena guarded the approach to the main sanctuary and was worshipped here. A beautifully proportioned *Tholos* (white marble circular temple) dominates the site – three of its columns survive.

To the northwest of the temple precinct is the **Gymnasium**, built like the *Tholos* in the fourth century BC. You can see an associated circular cold plunge bath, part of a complete set of baths, where the athletes could refresh themselves after training in the rectangular open courtyard.

PALEOKASTI

Northwest Greece

The western parts of the Greek mainland are undervisited and underrated – beach-loving tourists often stop briefly only at Athens before heading for the Peloponnesian coast or the islands. In so doing they are missing a remote and beautifully rugged part of Greece, with some of the country's prettiest and unspoilt valleys and villages. The Pindos Mountain range forms the heart of this region – this is mostly inaccessible territory, except perhaps to the intrepid walker. However, the visitor can make good use of recently constructed roads which allow a superb circular car tour around the mountain fringes. The following itinerary travels in a clockwise direction from Delphi. The main towns en route are also reachable by bus from Athens, but it really is worth making the effort to hire a car if you can drive.

ıe quiet coast of Northwest Greece is derrated and undervisited.

Delphi to Naupaktos

From Delphi, the motorist has a choice of routes westwards to Naupaktos; you can follow the

Old man from Metsovon, in the Pindus mountains.

old mountain road via the attractive little market town of Amphissa (22km northwest from Delphi), or a very new road will take you along the coast via the equally inviting fishing village of Galaxidhi.

Amphissa, medieval Salona, (population: 7,000) occupies two hills and is crowned by a ruined 13th-century Frankish castle of the same red stone which colours the dramatic cliffs around the town. The castle guarded the mountain pass and, if you have the energy to scramble up to it, you will still see signs of ancient defensive walls and towers; it fell to the Turks in 1394. The area is rich in olive groves, and Amphissa is reowned for its oil. Continuing westwards for 66km, you will reach the small, but growing, resort of **Navpaktos** – me eval *Lepanto*, (population: 9,000). The are hotels and some good beach nearby, as well as fish restaurants the edge of the medieval harbour, n bobbing with fashionable yachts rath than the fighting ships which conquer the Turks in the famous battle of Lepa in 1571. The curving harbour is fram by towers and overlooked by woods of which peeps a Venetian fortress. Th are two buses per day from Athens wh take four hours to reach the town.

Mesolongi & the War of Independence

Forty-eight km further west is **Mesolo** (or Missolonghi population: 11,0 which is only really worth stopping c you are a devotee of Byron or parti larly interested in the historical eve of the War of Independence. It is not attractive modern town and is positio by a broad lagoon which makes atmosphere humid and stuffy.

Byron, after several months sp here inspiring the Greeks to rebel aga Turkish rule, died of a fever on 1 April, 1824. The town remained western center of Greek resistance d ing the War of Independence and s fered three Turkish sieges. Some 8,(Greek men, women and children w massacred during the famous "Exod from the town in 1826 – this even commemorated annually in the "**G den of Heroes**" to the right of the

Ali Pasha "The Lion of Ioannina"

Pasha (1741-1822) was known to his con-
poraries as "The Lion of Ioannina". He be-
ne *pasha* (provincial Ottoman governor) of
nnina in northwest Greece in 1788, and
ceeded to expand his territory into Macedo-
and Thessaly to the east, and Albania in the
th. His rise to power was marked by rumours
nurder and political intrigue. Later historians
e labelled him "the most romantic monster
istory" and "the Mohammedan Bonaparte".
tor Hugo, writing in the early 19th century,
ed him a "colossus and man of genius wor-
to be compared with Napoleon." His
troversial life is remembered in Greek folk-
gs and ballads, and not surprisingly, he
acted the Romantic poet Byron to his infa-
us court. Byron immortalized him in ***Childe
rold's Pilgrimage***:

alk not of mercy, I talk not of fear,
neither must know who would serve the
er:
ce the days of our prophet the Crescent ne'er
,
nief ever glorious like Ali Pashaw."

A Crafty Conqueror

entry into Ioannina was typically dramatic.
city was in the 18th century the most
ortant city in Albania, if not in the whole of
ece. Its population numbered about 30,000,
consisted mainly of Greek traders. When Ali
nd himself in the vicinity early in his military
eer, the city was in a state of anarchy, with
ous local Ottoman factions fighting for su-
macy. Ali took this as his opportunity to gain
ver; he encouraged the local Greeks to dissension and to back him as a new leader – he already had a reputation for protecting Greeks from tyrannical Ottomans.

A battle fought outside the town ended in deadlock, but the ever-scheming Ali had secretly abducted the daughter of the most important family of Ioannina and sailing her across the lake, married her, thus securing his position in the town. His supporters then petitioned the Sultan at Constantinople to make Ali the new Pasha of Ioannina. But time was running out so he forged a decree and had it read out for him in the town; the bluff paid off and Ali occupied the citadel, A few days later, the genuine decree arrived!

Once in power Ali Pasha succeeded in turning Ioannina into a strongly fortified and well-organized town. Unlike his Ottoman predecessors, who turned their noses up at the local Greeks, Ali surrounded himself in his court with both wealthy Greeks and Albanians; he soon became popular. This power base allowed him to expand his domains, and soon he had conquered the rival town of Souli, and followed this up with further successful sieges in the surrounding provinces.

A Hero's Death

Ali died as he had lived, in the drama of battle. He was shot by fellow Ottomans vying for his power. His head was cut off and taken back to Constantinople where it was displayed to the public.

His epitaph can still be seen in Istanbul: "Here lies the head of Ali Pasha, former governor of Ionnina, who, for more than thirty years, made himself independent in Albania."

nce gate to the town. Here you will
a tumulus where the unnamed sol-
rs who stayed to defend the town
re buried.

Next to it is a **Statue of Byron**
81) under which his lungs are buried
ot, as the more romantic guides state, his heart). The rest of his body was taken back to his home at Newstead Abbey in spite of his poetic entreaty of "here let my bones moulder; lay me in the first corner without pomp or nonsense".

In the central town square of Plateia Botsari is the **Museum of the Revolu-**

Touring by car offers superb views of the mountains.

tion, which has a rather uninspiring collection of Byron memorabilia. From here take Odhos Trikoupis to Odhos Levidou at the end of which is a Byron memorial garden on the site of the house where the poet died – the house itself was bombed during World War II. There are nine buses a day to and from Athens, which make the journey in four hours.

Amfilokhia

Northwards towards Arta, you will come after some 80km to **Amfilokhia** (population: 4,000), at the head of the Karvasara Gulf. This is a good place to stop for lunch in one of the many restc rants which line its main street. T town was founded as a military outp in the 18th century by the notoric Turkish Ali Pasha of Ioannina (see b story Page 207). You are unlikely want to remain here for much lon than lunch: there is little to see, and inland gulf waters are a little stagn for swimming, though at night th exude an unusual phosphorescence

Arta

Arta (population: 18,000) is a hap little town, its streets radiating out fr the **Frourion**, a 13th-century castle co

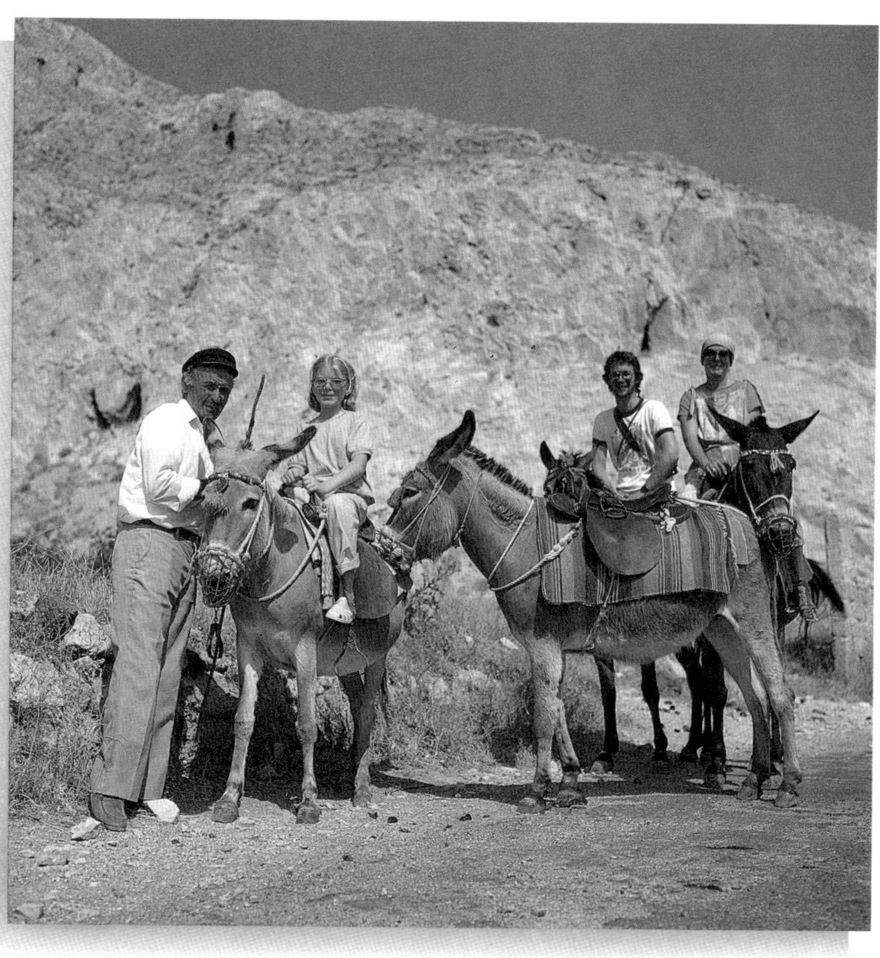

A ride in the hills.

ıanding views up and down the river rakhthos. There are several areas of :een orange groves, set amidst the reet-plan. It is a town with a visibly ontinuous history from its foundation c 625 BC as Ambracia, a colony of ncient Corinth, through periods of 'ankish, Venetian and Turkish rule – ıe older parts of the town still have the el of a medieval or even exotic, Turk- h market town. This is good place to stay the night – there are several hotels and some good value restaurants – spending an afternoon or morning exploring the shops and sites.

There is a famous legend of Arta, arising from the 17th-century Turkish arched bridge which runs parallel to a modern concrete one. The builder, it is said, was having problems keeping the bridge stable against the river currents and was advised by a bird to engage a human

The azure waters of Parga enticed many an ancient nymph.

spirit to guard over it. This led the builder to wall up his wife in one of the piers; legend has it that passers-by can still hear the unfortunate woman singing beneath the bridge.

Classical & Byzantine Arta

In classical times during the third century BC, Arta was the capital city of King Pyrrhus of Epirus, whose "Pyrrhic V tory" against the Romans in Italy h become the accepted term for victo with greater losses than the defeate Odhos Pirrou is named after the Kir and you can see the ruins of a fi century Temple of Apollo, and *bouleuterion* (council chamber) on yo left and right respectively as you wa down from the central square, Plate Kilkis, towards the **Frourion**, now s

Remains of Byzantine glories.

·unded by oranges in addition to its ·yzantine walls made from reused blocks ·om the Classical citadel.

The Byzantine Angelos dynasty ·led Arta from the 13th to the 15th ·ntury after they were expelled from ·onstantinople; during this time Arta ·mmanded the whole of Epirus, as in ·e days of Pyrrhus. Churches and mon·steries from this powerful period still ·rvive within and outside of the town.

The **Church of St Vassilios** (14th ·ntury) with its beautifully enriched ·ack and tile exterior stands opposite ·e market square at the Frourion end of ·dhos Pirrou. To the south is the **Church · St Theodora**, where Theodora, the ·nsort of Michael Angelos II, took the ·il and died. Her elegant marble tomb was excavated in 1873 and you can now see its reconstruction – the column capitals are thought to have been taken from ancient Nikopolis.

To the south of Plateia Kilkis is the larger square of Plateia Skoufas, overlooked by the cream and red bricks of the massive six-domed 13th-century **Church of Panayia Parigoritissa** (open Tuesday-Saturday 8:30 a.m - 3 p.m; entrance 400dr). This building reflects more than ever the prosperity of the Angelos dynasty, with its dark but majestic interior and central dome somehow supported cantilever-style by reused ancient columns. The *Pantocrator* and Prophet mosaics are from the original building, whilst the colourful frescoes are 16th century. All this Byzantine glory is well-balanced by the liveliness of the modern town.

Arta to Igoumenitsa

Take the Ioannina road northwards out of Arta, but branch left almost immediately on exiting the town for the coastal road to Igoumenitsa. You reach the coast above the Ambracian Gulf, on the north side of which is the sea town of **Preveza** (population: 12,000). Preveza offers a pleasant waterside promenade backed by some picturesque old houses, churches and a Venetian castle.

Seven km north of Preveza is **Nikopolis**, which means "city of victory". It was founded by Octavian, the future first Emperor of Rome, to commemorate his victory over Mark Antony and Cleopatra in the sea-battle of Actium in the Ambracian Gulf in 31 BC.

A visit to the **Roman ruins** (open Tuesday-Sunday 9 a.m - 3 p.m; entrance 200dr) make a nice afternoon compliment to an evening spent in one of Preveza's waterside fish restaurants, followed by drinking and music in one of its many bazaar *tavernas*. As you will see from the ruins, Nikopois continued to be occupied into the early Byzantine period, but was finally abandoned after various barbarian sackings and eartl quakes. If you are travelling to Prevez from Arta, you pass right through th middle of the site, with its impressiv theatre and stadium on your left, an public baths on your right. A little fu ther on you enter its well-preserved wal and reach the museum, which contai a motley collection of Roman sculptur and Byzantine mosaics.

I take about 4 minute to wa back up the theat abov which h on the hill the base of Octavian's mon ment to the victory of Actium. He archaeologists have recently unearth some of the ramming "beaks" of Anto and Cleopatra's warships, which we captured and displayed on the mon ment.

Parga & Igoumenitsa

Parga (population: 1,700) is 70km u the coast from Preveza *en route* f Igoumenitsa. This makes a good sto ping-place, though it gets crowded you should book in advance. You c swim from its sandy beaches in a b backed by woodland and a Veneti castle. You can take a boat to the Ioni Islands (Paxi is only 12 miles offshor

View of Parga.

you can drive to Mesopotamo and the ocative ruins of the **Necyomanteion Ephyra** (open daily 8 a.m - 3 p.m), here the dead gave advice to the living the Sanctuary of Hades and rsephone. Here you will find yourself andering in a marvellous labyrinth, ke a ghost-train, of enclosed rooms nd underground corridors. In antiqty this was believed to lead down to e River Styx, which could be crossed to visit the Underworld itself.

Igoumenitsa (population: 6,000), 48km further up the coast from Parga, is the main north-western port for boats to Corfu and Italy. As such it is hectic and charmless to stay in.

From Igoumenitsa you can either take the ferry to Corfu and visit the Ionian Islands, or continue westwards to Ioannina, for a tour of Central Greece and Thessaly.

Ionian Islands

The Ionian Islands are dominated by Corfu, the northern crown of the group of seven main islands known collectively as the "*Eptanisa*" (seven islands), which lie off the western coast of mainland Greece and the Peloponnese. South of Corfu, strung out in a taut but twisting line, lie Paxos – the smallest, Lefka, Ithaka, Cephalonia - the largest and highest; and Zakynthos. The southernmost of the group is Kithira, which is closer to Crete and the western Cycladic Islands than it is to its sister Ionians.

The Ionian Islands are quite different from the Aegean group. Their political and cultural history is tied up more with Italy and the west than with Athens; their winter climates are wetter and breezier, with twice as much rain falling annually on Corfu than on London; whilst the summer brings long lazy periods of calm and a hazy sun without the welcome, cooling Aegean winds.

Despite a marked increase in tourism, there are still many quiet, friendly harbours and villages to be found.

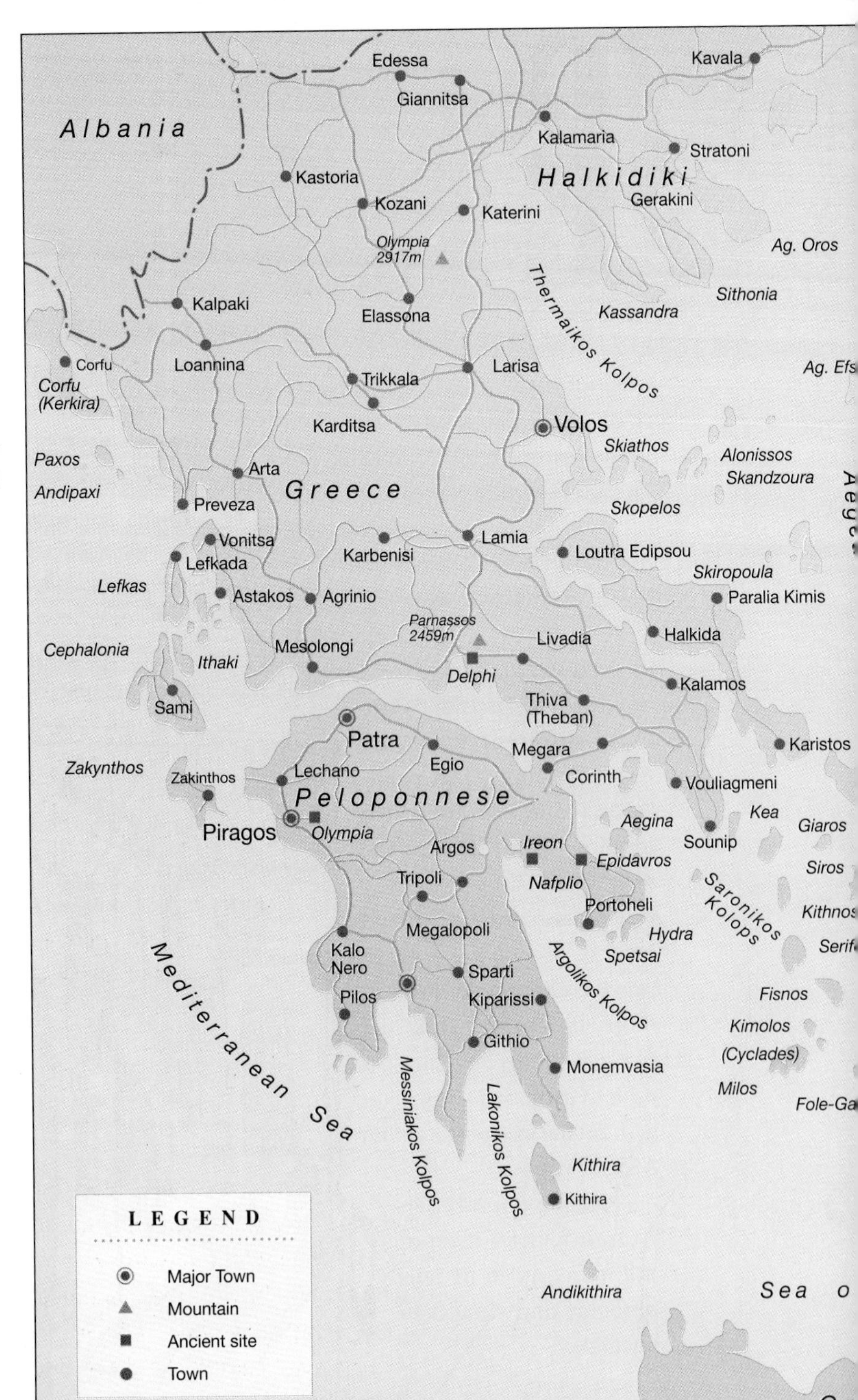
Albania
Edessa
Giannitsa
Kavala
Kalamaria
Stratoni
Halkidiki
Gerakini
Kastoria
Kozani
Katerini
Olympia
2917m
Ag. Oros
Sithonia
Thermaikos Kolpos
Kassandra
Kalpaki
Elassona
Corfu
Loannina
Larisa
Ag. Efs
Corfu
(Kerkira)
Trikkala
Karditsa
Volos
Skiathos
Alonissos
Skandzoura
Paxos
Andipaxi
Arta
Greece
Preveza
Skopelos
Vonitsa
Lefkada
Lamia
Karbenisi
Loutra Edipsou
Skiropoula
Lefkas
Astakos
Agrinio
Paralia Kimis
Parnassos
2459m
Livadia
Halkida
Cephalonia
Ithaki
Mesolongi
Delphi
Kalamos
Sami
Thiva
(Theban)
Patra
Karistos
Zakynthos
Zakinthos
Lechano
Egio
Megara
Corinth
Vouliagmeni
Peloponnese
Kea
Piragos
Olympia
Aegina
Giaros
Argos
Ireon
Epidavros
Sounip
Siros
Tripoli
Nafplio
Saronikos Kolops
Portoheli
Kithnos
Megalopoli
Hydra
Spetsai
Serif
Mediterranean Sea
Kalo
Nero
Sparti
Argolikos Kolpos
Pilos
Kiparissi
Fisnos
Kimolos
(Cyclades)
Githio
Messiniakos Kolpos
Monemvasia
Lakonikos Kolpos
Milos
Fole-Ga
Kithira
Kithira
LEGEND
Major Town
Mountain
Ancient site
Town
Andikithira
Sea o
Cr

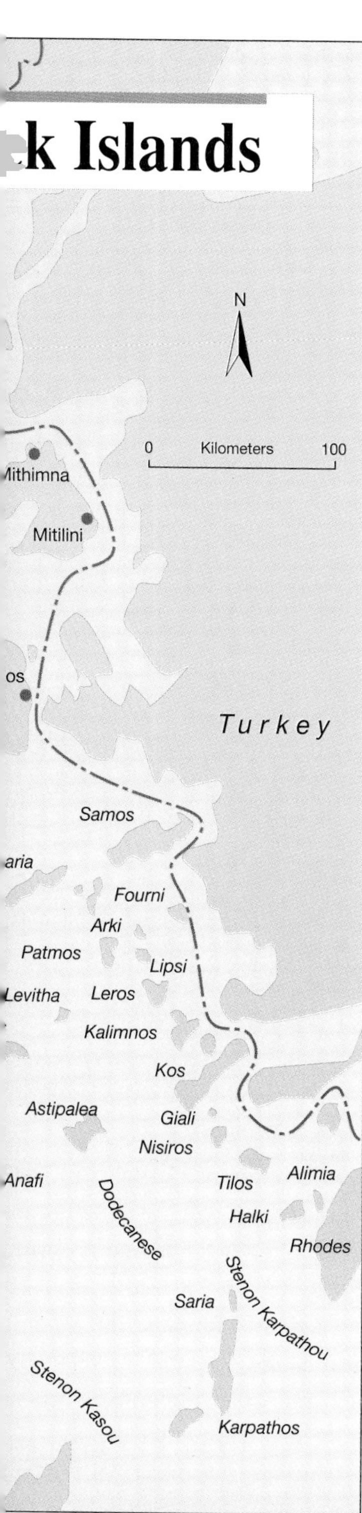

Literary Legacy

The Ionian islands are home to many a literary legend: Odysseus, featured in Homer's book ***The Odyssey***, had his palace on Ithaka. Corfu, is thought to be Prospero's Enchanted Isle in Shakespeare's The Tempest "full of noises, sounds and sweet airs that give delight and hurt not": though the music of the Corfu's resorts is now disco, the description still evokes the romantic mood of the less populated villages and luscious landscapes.

Corfu, in particular, has had its 20th-century devotees: Gerald and Lawrence Durrell have written their very different, but equally evocative, novels inspired by the Ionian land and seascapes. Henry Miller, under Prospero's spell, liked to lay for hours in the sun, "doing nothing, thinking of nothing".

This may sound like the artistic imagination talking, but it paints a pretty accurate of the Ionian summer, which is often too hot and becalmed to do anything but lounge around. The late Aristotle Onassis, who knew his Greek islands better than most, chose one of the islands to build his dream villa on.

The islands are a good place to head for if you have had your fill of action on the mainland, and want to relax for a few days. At the same time there is plenty of nightlife in the main resorts, as well as plenty of sight-seeing opportunities.

Brief History

The seven Ionian islands are linked throughout history from the prehistoric times of legendary King Odysseus, who in Homer's poems appears to have lived in a palace on Ithaka, from where he also ruled Cephalonia, Lefkas and Zante – Corfu and Paxoi were inhabited by the Phaeacians. Homer's poems are filled with flights of fancy, however, and you will be disappointed if you take ***The Odyssey*** as holiday reading, and expect it to offer accurate images of the ancient island landscape.

In the Classical period the islands took different sides: during the Peloponnesian War (431-404 BC) between Athens and Sparta, the islands Corfu, Cephalonia and Zante were Athenian allies, whilst Lefkas joined the Spartans.

The politics of the islands has always depended on their strategic positions for naval powers – Athens and Sparta needed them as much as the later empires of the Romans, Turks, Venetians and finally the British. Corfu fell to the Venetians in 1386, followed by the other six over the next three centuries.

The Venetians gained the long-term loyalty of the Ionians by forming ruling aristocracies out of the leading local families on each island. This allowed them to impose their own dominant culture: the official language became Italian, whilst the Orthodox Church was

replaced by Roman Catholicism. In 17
with the collapse of the Venetian ma
time empire, the French took over fo
year, before the Russians and Tu
moved in and founded the *Septinsu*
(seven-island) Republic of 1800 - 18
which has been remembered in lo
history as a reign of terror.

Between 1809 and 1815, the Ioni

Playground of the Gods.

ınds fell to the British, when they ·e given the status of independent ːes "protected" by the Lord High Com- ːsioner, whose base was on Corfu. ·pite the rather dictatorial style of the ːish (led by Sir Thomas Maitland), next 30 or 40 years saw a period of peace and economic growth in the islands, but the nationalist tide sweeping mainland Greece and the Aegean during the War of Independence soon inspired the islanders to espouse the Greek cause.

In 1864, the British rather reluc-

The Achilleion Palace in Corfu, built by Elizabeth of Austria in 1890.

tantly conceded Independence with the Treaty of London.

The modern islands are divided into four Ionian *nomes* (administrative regions), with a combined population of 183,000, but Kithira is now controlled by the *nome* of Piraeus.

Corfu

Corfu (*Kekira*; population: 37,000) is as large as Cephalonia, but it is b more populated and has always be more important strategically and po

Getting dressed for a ride.

lly owing to its proximity to the non-eek territories of Albania and Italy. It ust three km from the Albanian coast. e island is 64km long from north to ıth, and about half as wide. Both rth and south have their mountain aks, with Pantokrator in the north ıching 914m, whilst Ayioi Dheka to south stands at a modest 567m.

It is a green and fertile land, with ves in profusion (some four million), gether with vineyards, citrus orchards d figs. Everywhere are Mediterranean press trees and cacti. The local deli-cy is the *kum-kwat*, a tiny crystallised panese orange. The local wines in-de a sweet and heavy red and a her good white. The British colonial st is at its most evident in the buildings and customs of Kerkira Town, situated halfway down the east coast, which is also the most built-up and touristy part of the island. The four centuries of Venetian rule have also left their mark – Italian is still spoken with the Venetian lilt, and place-names continue to be given in Greek and in Italian. Ferries arrive from the mainland ports of Igoumenitsa and Patras, and there is an international airport. You can also take ferries to the other Ionian islands.

Kerkira Town

Kerkira Town (population: 36,000), the capital of Corfu, is, out of season, an elegant resort with an old quarter, the

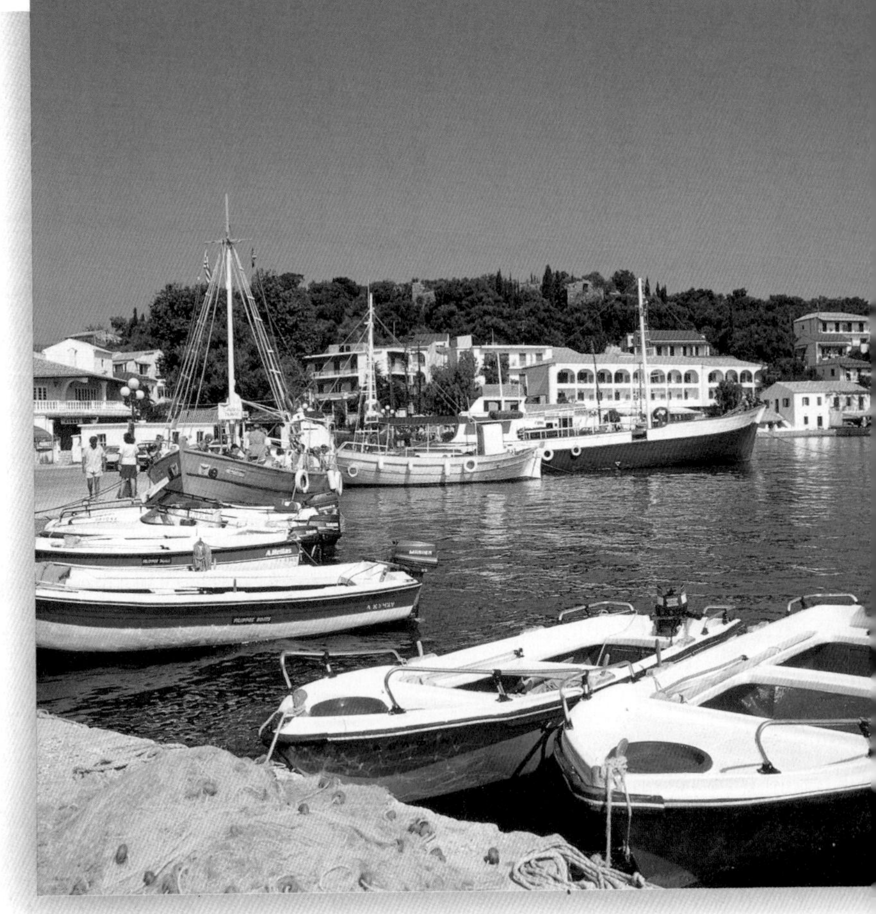

The harbour at Kassiopi.

Campiello (between the Palace of St Michael and St George and the old port), of tall houses and narrow winding streets. If you arrive by boat, you will disembark beneath the **Neon Frourion** (New Fort), built by the Venetians in 1577-88, and now used by the Greek Navy. Its older twin is the P**alaion Frourion** (Old Fort), (open 8 a.m - 7 p.m; entrance free), which dates back to the Byzantine period, and has on the south a conspicuous British colon **Church of St George** (1830) with a n classical Doric portico. Sound and li displays and Greek folk dancing t place here on summer evenings.

Behind the fort is the famo **Spianadha** – the esplanade which minded Evelyn Waugh of the Brigh equivalent. Here you should visit a c and watch the world go by with tra tional British ginger beer. In sumr

Corfu's Colonial Graces

e Turks never managed to occupy the Ionian nds, which have instead passed through the opean hands of the Venetians, French, Rusns and finally the British. Nowhere are these ous cultural layers better seen than in Corfu. e Venetians built the huge castle which still rlooks the harbour, whilst the tall narrow ses and tiny squares bring an Italian air to old **Campaniello quarter**.

The French brought a touch of Parisian ety to the **Esplanade** by building a replica of of the Rue de Rivoli, complete with arcades street-lamps to light the outdoor cafés on main square. The British imposed their own nd of colonialism onto the same square, n the grandiose **Regency Palace**.

The British "Protectorate"

er the demise of Napoleon, the British took trol of the island in 1814 at the request of local Count John Capodistra, who later ame President of independent Greece. oodistra wanted the British to protect the an Republic with their military strength, but surprisingly the Ionians found themselves erned by a series of autocratic High Comsioners who forcefully imposed their own ish cultural standards on the islanders.

One of these, Sir Thomas Maitland, soon ame known as "King Tom" because of his aordinary behaviour to what he saw as his ects. When local Greek dignitaries came to him he would suddenly drop his trousers to rid of them!

His domineering presence is still there in his dings; King Tom was a friend of the rened British architect Nash, whose influence can be seen in the Regency-style neo-classical buildings, which over-look the Esplanade.

Surviving British Customs

Not everything was bad under the British. Sir Frederick Adam built an aqueduct to bring water from the spring at Benitses into Corfu town. He also introduced local farmers to modern irrigation techniques, allowing them to improve the yield of their fruit orchards and field crops. The British also left their customs; Corfu apple chutney is still the main delicacy at Christmas, whilst *kek*, a type of rich fruit cake is eaten all year round and washed down with *tsintsinbeera* (ginger beer).

Cricket on the Esplanade continues to surprise and delight the summer visitor. Where else can you sit at a Parisian-style outdoor café and drink cold white wine whilst waiters interrupt play by wandering across the cricket pitch with their trays of drinks and ices? The British left Corfu in 1864, but the cricket remains.

Famous Appraisals

The lush beauty of the island's fertile landscape and the charm of its main town have attracted the praises of writers from Homer to the Durrells. Two and a half thousand years ago Homer observed that "pear follows pear, apple follows apple, figs are followed by more figs, and after the vintage come yet more grapes"; whilst more recently Lawrence Durrell referred to the town: "I doubt if there is any little town as elegantly beautiful in the whole of Greece".

might find a game of cricket being yed on the northern square or a brass d playing on the bandstand surnded by lawns to the south. There flower-gardens to stroll around in evening sun, with further reminders he British past in the Ionic rotunda commemorating Sir Thomas Maitland, the first Lord High Commissioner of the British Protectorate.

Meanwhile in the **Liston**, the tall arcaded houses on the west of the esplanade, the Rue de Rivoli in Paris is duplicated as a reminder of the brief French

The glories of Zant

by the Turks. The c ket is carried out a around the streets fc times a year, to c ebrate the saint's r

occupation of 1807-14.

To the north is the **Palace of St Michael and St George** (open Monday & Wednesday-Saturday 8:30 a.m - 3 p.m, Sunday 9:30 a.m - 2:30 p.m hours; entrance 400dr) with its Doric portico and triumphal arches. It was built in 1819 as the residence for the British Lord High Commissioner. The architecture is a blatant signifier of British Colonialism – an architectural style ironically inspired by Classical Greek temples.

Note the seven medallion reliefs on the facade depicting the Ionian islands. Within the state rooms is housed a curious mixture of objects from the island's Byzantine past, as well as some fine Japanese and Chinese porcelain and bronzes, donated by a former Greek ambassador to the Far East.

Among the other sights within the town is the **Church of St Spiridon** (1589-96), to the west of the Esplanade, which houses the bejewelled silver casket containing the corpse of the third-century Cypriot bishop Spiridon, whose body was carried here to escape desecration

raculous interventions during epide ics, sieges and famines. This religic event attracts Greek visitors, who oth wise tend to avoid Corfu, regarding it too "European".

The Archaeological Museum

To the south of the esplanade a through the city-walls along the wat front, you come to the **Archaeologi Museum** (open Monday & Wednesd Saturday 9 a.m - 3 p.m, Sunday 10 a - 3 p.m; entrance 200dr), which hou objects from the prehistoric, classi Greek and Roman past: its best kno exhibit is the pedimental sculpture fr an early Archaic Temple of Artemis 590 BC) which depicts a massive cent gorgon (winged snake-haired fem monster) flanked by panthers to sc off secular intruders. Twenty-five m utes walk further south around the b is the Mon Repos public beach wh you can swim and take a drink.

The Achilleion Palace

ıree km to the south of Kerkira Town, he **Achilleion** (1890-91), built for the ıpress Elizabeth of Austria by the Ital-ı architect Cardilo. This is a lavish ılianate palace with gardens (open ily) to match; at night it is now a sino. It is worth visiting for the view ·m the north terrace, which looks ross to the Albanian mountains. The ıpress' hero was Achilles, whose co-ısal statue domi-tes the ter-ce. The ıole place ›izarre and ulent, and actions ry – Henry iller ɔught it uld make excellent realist art ilery!

Away from the Crowds

:he crowded summer months you will ›bably not want to linger for too long the town. There are buses to other :ts of the island, or you can rent a car, ·ped or bicycle.

Once you are outside of the town d resorts, the renowned splendours of :fu and its countryside emerge. The

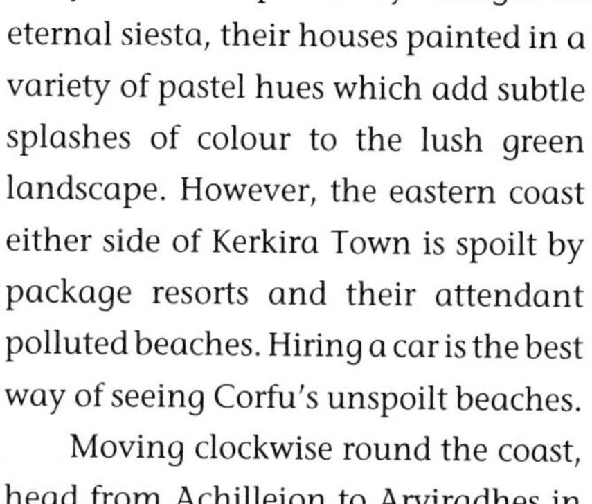

noisy beat is replaced by villages in eternal siesta, their houses painted in a variety of pastel hues which add subtle splashes of colour to the lush green landscape. However, the eastern coast either side of Kerkira Town is spoilt by package resorts and their attendant polluted beaches. Hiring a car is the best way of seeing Corfu's unspoilt beaches.

Moving clockwise round the coast, head from Achilleion to Aryiradhes in the south where branch roads take you eastwards to the small fishing village of **Boukari** or westwards to **Ayios Yiorgios**, which is an expanding resort with a relatively unspoilt sandy beach on its northern side. In the middle of the west coast is **Ayios Gordhis**, which still retains something of the beauty of old Corfu, with its pine-crowned vineyards stretching down to the sea, and a lengthy stretch of sandy beach, backed by just one large hotel: there is an enclosed American holiday complex here called the "Pink Palace", which has a good disco if you want to dance the night away.

Further north is the busy crossroads village of **Pelekas** with some good little tavernas, but it is best to avoid the

Siesta time in Corfu town.

crowded coast here and head instead for the unspoilt inland village of **Vatos** where you can find rooms and tavernas whose owners will direct you down a track in the cliffs to the rather incongruous pairing of a convent and nudist beach at **Mirtidhiotissa**. You can get here by taking a short bus ride fr Kerkira town.

Secluded Beaches

On the northwest coast is the fam

ırbour of **Palaiokastritsa**. This is pos-
›ly the best alternative if you want the
nenities of a resort without that pack-
e tourist feeling. This is thought to be
e spot where Homer's shipwrecked
lysseus was discovered by the beauti-
l princess Nausicaa, who then took
m to meet her father Alcinous, King of
e Phaeacians. You can explore the
ı-caves in the sheer cliffs which form
lramatic backdrop to three bays; you
n swim from the white pebble beaches,
take a *caique* (small fishing-boat)
le to a more secluded beach. In the
ıterside restaurant you can eat lob-
rs kept fresh in baskets hanging in
e sea.

The energetic will walk up the wind-
g road behind the beach to the lovely
raced gardens of the 13th century
eotokos Monastery (open daily 7
n - 1 p.m, 3 p.m - 10 p.m), where
›nks will show the modestly-dressed
eir collection of icon paintings and
e enormous bones of a local "sea-
›nster". Another trek is from the
arby village of Lakones up a mule-
ıck to the Byzantine fortress of
gelkastro where there are beautiful
ws across to the fortresses of Kerkira
wn. The less spoilt beach resorts on
north and north-east include the
ıestone-fringed bay of **Ayios Yiorgios**
the north of Palaiokastritsa, with its
ıdy beach, tavernas and discos; the
ıch smaller **Perouladhes**, with its
ctacular red sand backed by cliffs;
northern promontory of **Kassiopi**
h its Angevin fortress and pleasant village atmosphere, with some good nightlife thrown in. As you head south back towards Kerkira Town, you will find the resorts increase in size, though there are many secluded coves on this coast if you have a car.

Paxos

The island of **Paxos** (population: 2,000) can be reached in four hours by boat from Corfu. It is the smallest of the Ionian Islands (eight by three km). There are many day-trippers but peace returns in the evening to this lovely rural island, its low inland hills covered with magnificently old olives. The main harbour-town is **Gaio**, with a ruined Venetian fortress built on the islet called **Kastro** which fronts the harbour.

There is one sandy beach two km to the south at **Mogonisi**, a small island accessible by stepping-stones, or by a free boat in the evenings to and from Gaio. You can wine and dine on fresh lobster and swordfish in the taverna where you will find "Theo and Pan, probably the best Greek dancers in the world". Buses shuttle between Gaio and Lakka, but why not obtain the local walking and wild-flower guide, which points out the paths which criss-cross the island.

Lefkas

Lefkas (population: 22,000) is connected

A fine meal is worth waiting for.

to mainland Greece by a boat-drawbridge and a causeway. Ancient writers tell us that Corinthian colonists cut a canal in the seventh century BC, making it an island. The island is 32 km long by 13km at its broadest point; in the center is a white limestone mountain range (Lefkas means 'white'), with Mount Elati at its highest point (1,082m). The eastern coast has a series of wooded valleys leading down to the sea, and it is this mainland-facing side which is most populated.

The island has always been a strategic base and has therefore found itself involved in the main historical events of Greece. It provided Sparta with ships in the Peloponnesian War, and was consequently sacked by the Athenians. In 1479 it was captured by the Turk who vainly struggled to keep it from th Venetians, who in turn held it until th French took over in 1797. Finally th British captured the island in 1810, ar like the other Ionian Islands it remain a British Protectorate until unificatic with Greece in 1864.

Lefkas' Resorts

The main town of **Lefkadha** is on th northern tip of the island, overlooking lagoon. There have been a series of bc earthquakes here (most recently in 19 and 1953) and many of the old Venetic houses and churches have been rebui The town, like the rest of Lefkas, is n articularly attractive, but take one of e buses that criss-cross the island from ere and you can find reasonable aches on both the east and west coasts.

On the south-east coast is the broad y of **Vassiliki** which boasts that it is e of Europe's leading windsurfing nters. On the west coast, **Ai Nikitas** is small and unspoilt village, with a few oms and *tavernas*; from here a boat ll take you to the sand and shingle ach of **Milos**, which you can also alk to within an hour.

Cape Dukato on the southern tip the island is marked by a high white ff once surmounted by a Temple of ollo – in antiquity criminals could ove their innocence if they survived a ap into the sea some 75m below. This also the place where, according to gend, the sixth century BC lesbian etess Sappho, jumped to her death to re her unrequited love once and for . Byron sensed the romantic possibili- s of the spot – it was here that Childe rold "saw the evening star above ucadia's projecting rock of woe".

Ithaka

aka (population: 4,000) is the sec- d smallest of the Ionian Islands, be- just 27km long and six and a half at its widest point. It can be reached ferry from mainland Patras, or from islands of Corfu and Cephalonia. It three km across the sea from phalonia, and consists of a rugged mountainous landscape divided into two halves by a wasp-waist isthmus. It has relatively little cultivatable land, and as such has been ignored for most of its history. The island will however, be eternally remembered as the home of Odysseus, the hero of Homer's epic, ***The Odyssey***. Ithaka's rocky coastline peppered with tiny coves and creeks, is accurately described by Homer, as a pretty barren place, "good for goats", with occasional olive and almond groves in the valleys. There are also several vineyards, where the renowned Ithakan wine is produced – it washes down well with the local dish of roast hare.

Sites & Scenes

Ithaka's attractive main town of **Vathy** (or Ithaki Town) lies on the southern peninsula, with its single strip of white-washed houses curving round the horse-shoe-shaped (*vathy* means "horseshoe") bay. The local community was badly hit by the devastating 1953 earthquake. For wonderful pebble-and-sand beaches try the coves of **Cape Skinos** and **Saraniko Bay** on the south-east coast. The roads are not good and you can either travel around the coast in small boats from Vathy, or walk in search of secluded beaches and archaeological sites associated with Odysseus.

A mule-track out of Vathy leads (about an hour and a half) to Homer's **Fountain of Arethusa** – follow the signs *Krini Arethousas'* – where Odysseus met

Eumaios watering his pigs – swimming coves can be found by following the paths below the spring.

Another outing is one km south-westwards to the Grotto **of the Nymphs**, where Odysseus is supposed to have deposited his treasure on his return to the island. It is a large cavern with stalactites hanging from its roof.

The usual way to explore northern Ithaka is by moped – but take care on the rough terrain! There are rooms and *tavernas* at the unspoilt villages of Stavros, Frikes and Kioni, with swimming beaches accessible from them all. Sites include a Venetian fortress built on a Mycenaean citadel one km north of Stavros, which is possibly the location of Odysseus' palace.

Cephalonia

To the west of Ithaka lies the largest of the seven islands, **Cephalonia** (population: 28,000) is a slightly rougher version of Corfu, with fairly lush green foothills, scattered with olives and vines – the local dry, white wine *Rombola* is extremely good.

Along the spine of the island runs a high mountainous ridge which boasts the highest point of the Ionian Islands, the mountain slopes are covered with the indigenous Cephalonian Fir. Tourists – who include many Greeks – are attracted by the spacious bays with excellent beaches. Like Ithaka, it too was devastated by the 1953 earthquake, which levelled houses as well as Venetic fortresses. It has become more touris orientated with the building of an inte national airport, but with a car or mope (the bus system is not that good) yc can still, as on Corfu, find undevelope resorts. Ferries arrive from Patras, Pirae and even Italy, at the port of **Sami** – tl water here is very deep, reminding that the Ionian Islands are located the deepest part of the Mediterranea

Around the Island

A good base from which to explo Cephalonia is the capital town **Argostoli**, which was completely rebu after the 1953 earthquake.

The **Historical and Cultural M seum** (open Monday-Saturday 8:30 a. - 2:30 p.m; entrance 100dr) gives c excellent introduction to **Markopoul** where on August 15 the Assumption the Virgin is celebrated in a spectacul local festival which both the locals a travelling gypsies attend. Rituals invol clasping small and non-poisono snakes to your breast – legend has it th the snakes are drawn to churches c this day, by the icon of Our Lady, thou the priest keeps a few in stock, just case!

Five km west of Skala is **Potomak Beach** which has a nesting-ground f the local population of loggerhead s turtles, which are fast dying out owi to tourism. Volunteers from the Briti charity "Care for the Wild" is trying rotect them. They will show you the esting turtles, if you ask.

Zante

ante (population: 30,000) lies to the outh of the main Ionian group and can e reached by ferry from Cephalonia or om Killini on the Peloponnese. Here is e perfect mixture of fertile plain and ougher hill-walking territory, with cliffs nd beaches in profusion.

The volcanic island is barren on its ountainous western flank, but fertile n the foothills of the east. The island is articularly lush and renowned for its ild flowers as well as its gardens – the enetians nick-named it "Zante, flower the Levant".

Like its neighbours, Zante (the enetian name, Zakinthos is now freuently used) suffered badly in the 1953 arthquake, but tourism is developing pidly largely owing to the recent addion of an international airport.

You arrive by boat at **Zante Town**, hich as is usual for this area, has a enetian fortress (open daily 8 a.m - 10 ms; entrance 100dr) dominating the arbour, there is also an interesting **eo-Byzantine Museum** (open Tuesay-Sunday 8:30 a.m - 3 p.m; entrance 00dr), containing paintings of the Ioan School, produced in the 17th and 8th centuries by Cretan refugees fleeg the Turks.

Most of the island's churches were estroyed by the earthquake, but **St Dhionissios** on the south side of Zante town, remains standing and has lovely frescoes by Cozzari, a pupil of Tiepolo. Dhionissios is the island's saint and his festival is held on August 24th, when Zante Town becomes packed with Greek pilgrims. There are good beaches around **Vassiliko** to the south, whilst the mountainous west and north coasts are only worth visiting if you hire a car. Good cuisine is available on the island.

Kithira

Kithira (population: 4,000), situated off the southern coast of the Peloponnese, is somewhat remote from the other Ionian islands. Like the other islands, it has a rocky interior and fertile valleys and foothills, with olives and vineyards growing, but not in the profusion of the other islands, it is famous for its honey. You arrive by plane from Athens or by boat from Piraeus at **Ayia Pelayia** on the north-east coast. There are some good beaches just south of the town. A few kilometers inland is the large village of P**otamos**, which features a lively Sunday market.

The Byzantine ruins of P**alaiochora** is three km east of Potamos, and is a must. Smaller than Mistra, the town thrived in the middle ages, but was sacked by the Turkish admiral Barbarossa in 1537. The inhabitants were enslaved, the town sacked, never to be rebuilt; you can see the remains of a castle and several churches.

Thessaloniki

Although only half the size and population of Athens, Thessaloniki remains the second largest city in Greece, with a population of approximately 350,000. Tucked into the sheltered north-east corner of the Gulf of Thermaikos, it looks westwards towards the fertile coastal plains of the River Axios, which springs in Yugoslavia.

The Romans made the city the administrative center of the Roman province of Macedonia, when their legions conquered the area in 146 BC. Its central position within the roads network of the Empire (the Egnatian Way from Italy to Constantinople passed through the city) led to its development as a communications center and the city attracted more and more well-known figures: the Roman statesman Cicero lived here in exile and Pompey the Great took refuge from Julius Caesar here during one of Rome's many civil wars.

he Rotunda of St George, designed s a Roman Mausoleum.

The city took its name in 316 BC from one of Alexander the

Fresco of the Last Supper at the Church of St Nicholas Orphanos.

Great's step-sisters, Thessalonikeia. She was married to Kassandros, briefly King of Macedon after Alexander the Great's death. He made the city his capital and thinking that his wife's name would carry with it greater dynastic clout than his own, named it after her.

When the apostle Paul brought t gospel of Christianity to this pagan ci around AD 49, he met with mixed rec tions, but managed to establish a flou ishing church here. The city maintain its theological status for many cent ries, two important theological debat

ok place here; the Iconoclast Controsy in the eighth and ninth centuries d the Isihast Debate in the 14th cen-y.

Medieval Splendour

e city was at the height of its importance during the medieval period; from the sixth century it was known as the "second city" of the Byzantine Empire (Constantinople, later Istanbul, was the first).

The visitor to Thessaloniki can learn much about the art and architecture of this period. In fact Thessaloniki has the best representative sample of early Christian and Byzantine buildings and monumental art in Europe.

Building activity was often halted by invasion; the Goths had been repelled by Theodosius' new city-wall in the fourth century, but in AD 904 the Saracens sacked the city and some 22,000 Greeks were sold into slavery; in 1185 the Sicilian Norman invasion was accompanied by a brutal massacre of Thessalonians.

The following two centuries saw the city change hands many times: now Frankish, now Greek, now Turkish, until finally in 1430 it became the first Greek city to fall permanently under Turkish control. Turkish "ethnic cleansing" led to the death or enslavement of many Thessalonians, but during the 16th and 17th centuries some 20,000 Jews moved in from Spain and laid the foundations for the city's economic boom.

The Turks & Independence

The Turks left their architectural mark, as elsewhere in Greece, by converting churches into mosques. One of the last Turkish monuments is the birthplace of

A gang of locals.

Ataturk, one of a picturesque group of 19th-century houses near the eastern city walls. Thessaloniki played a major role during the Greek War of Independence: King George I was killed here in 1913. Allied troops were stationed in the city in both world wars, but 20th century destruction was caused by a accidental fire (1917) and an earthquake (1978).

The Modern City

The modern city streets still roughly follow the grid-plan of the ancient Hellenistic and Roman city and the city continues to be an important cultural as well as economic center.

Education is served by two conservatories, a university and teacher-traini college. The early Christian traditio of Thessaloniki are fostered at the the logical college, which is the first insti tion in the world to be dedicated to t academic study of literary texts of t Church Fathers. The city also has State-run theatre and symphony orch tra.

Exploring Thessaloniki

There are two main reference points an exploration of the city: the **Wh Tower** at the southern end of the ea ern city wall, overlooking the sea; anc the highest and most northerly poi the **Acropolis**, with its "castle of

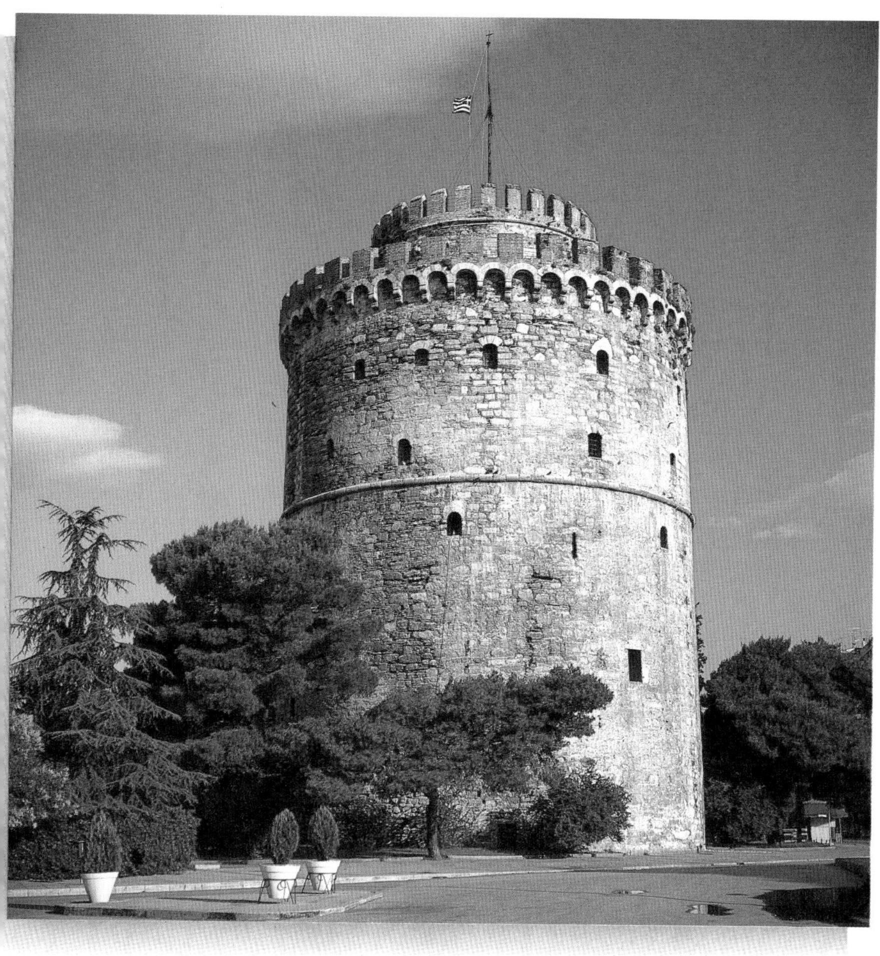

:xecutions performed in the White Tower in the 15th century has earned it the title of Tower of Blood.

en towers" (now a State prison).

The ancient city extended westwards ng the waterfront (originally a little :her inland) to what is now the mod- harbour. From here the wall ran th and then irregularly eastwards ng the ridge towards the Acropolis. : ancient city had been laid out on a ical grid-plan with streets running t-west and north-south, crossing at t-angles. The main thoroughfare was the Egnatian Way, which passed through the Arch of Galerius.

If you have two days, it is worth spending one of them concentrating on the Christian monuments, and the other on the Roman remains, together with the Archaeological Museum, which houses the Vergina Treasure. Binoculars are useful to view both the church decorations and the triumphal arch sculptures.

A Walk through the Medieval Christian City

The **White Tower** is situated in the southeast corner of the city in a park beside the sea. As part of the Turkish defenses it dates to the 15th century and stands 100m' high. The *Janissaries* (elite troops of the Sultan converted from Christianity) had their infamous prison here and it became known as "the bloody tower" when in 1826 the Sultan himself had the disloyal soldiers put to death. It now houses the **Medieval Museum**. On the ground floor are exhibits on the economy and organization of the medieval city.

The first floor displays evidence of early Christian life here, and includes a fragmentary wall-mosaic from the church of St Dimitrios. The second floor has a fine collection of early Christian burial offerings – colourful evidence of the continuation of the pagan custom of burying worldly goods with the dead. The third floor is occupied by a display of sculptures and paintings; look out in particular for the Byzantine hoard of 10th-century gold jewellery which includes a magnificent pair of gold and enamel armlets – it is easy to see why Thessaloniki was so often sacked.

The Christian City

There are far too many churches for a detailed visit to them all. The following are the most architecturally importa examples; you will find that the mainder conform more or less to the types.

The Rotunda of Saint George, w initially built in AD 306, probably a mausoleum for the Roman Empe Galerius. You can clearly see that it w part of an architectural complex inclu ing the triumphal arch, the palace a the hippodrome. Galerius was nev buried here (due to his Christi persecutions), and in the fifth centu an apse was attached to the east side produce a church. An extra wall w added to produce the circular aisle.

The interior must have been ma nificently rich with its Roman mu coloured marble walls and equally e catching mosaics added by the Chr tians. Note the two different mosaic signs: non-figurative decoration in t barrel-vaults, and figure scenes on t outer edge of the cupola – these dep 15 saints and martyrs placed within t framework of pagan Roman theatri scenery. The central figure was Chr but it has since been lost.

The **Church of St Sophia**, an ea example of the "cross-domed" style architecture, is considered by many be the most significant example church architecture in Greece and rival to the "Great Church" of St Sopl in Constantinople. It has undergo many alterations (including conversi to a mosque), but the underlying pl dates to the eighth century. As with many Byzantine churches, the exter

Philip's Tomb – Discovery and Preservation

e late Professor Manolis Andronicos devoted ɔst of his working life to locating and excavat- ʒ the Tomb of Philip II of Macedon, the father Alexander the Great. At 1500 hours on No- mber 8, 1977, the great Greek archaeologist ınd himself peering down into the darkness a newly uncovered royal tomb chamber at rgina. Many of the tombs on the site had en looted in antiquity; was he to be disap- inted once again?

Seventeen meters of earth had to be re- ɔved before the top of the barrel-vaulted nb chamber was reached. "Everything is act!" was the professor's exclamation as he tered the tomb down a ladder in the manner an ancient tomb robber. What Andronikos v as his eyes adjusted to the light was beyond wildest dreams: his torch revealed a square ımber with a marble door at its entrance; on floor beneath him he gazed on two groups objects – bronze weapons and vessels cov- d in green patina in one corner, glimmering er vessels in another. Scattered across the ɔr were the remains of wooden objects, with glint of gold shining amongst them.

Re-constructing a King

dronicos found no inscription to identify the nb's occupant but various clues pointed to being indeed the great fourth-century BC g's burial chamber. A collection of miniature y heads was found, one of which portrays xander the Great and another Philip himself. ɔ from the tomb came a golden diadem of type worn by Macedonian kings.

The objects, now on display in the **ssaloniki Archaeological Museum**, in- ded all the signifiers of royal monarchy. The nze objects were: a large circular shield er for an original ivory and gold ceremonial shield; a bronze lantern, perforated with ivy tendrils to allow the light to shine through; and bronze warrior greaves. One of the greaves was shorter than the other which supports the theory that this is Philip's tomb, since the king had a limp. A marble sarcophagus contained a golden casket inside which were the charred remains of a cremation – the bones had been wrapped in a purple and gold cloth, the colours signifying ancient royalty. The most exciting discovery was a skull which was sent for computer analy- sis. The computer allowed a three-dimensional reconstruction of the original face of the buried man. The result was very similar to portraits of Philip, and most convincing of all, one of the eyes had been badly wounded by a missile; ancient history tells us that Philip sustained just such an injury in one of his battles.

Queen Cleopatra

The antechamber of the tomb was found to contain a second marble sarcophagus with a similar cremation wrapped in gold and purple cloth; beside it was a golden diadem of inter- twined branches and flowers, perhaps the re- mains of Philip's wife Cleopatra. Elsewhere in the porch was a beautiful golden quiver finely decorated with scenes of warfare.

In an adjacent tomb Andronicos found that although it had been robbed long ago, the walls of the tomb had been beautifully painted with frescoes depicting royal hunters on horseback, with dogs and spears; another painting showed Persephone being raped by the god of the Underworld Pluto – a fitting subject for the funerary context.

Owing to the delicate nature of the monu- ments and their frescoes, the tombs remain closed to the public until a means of conserving them is eventually found.

npromisingly square and heavy, but t wait until you enter the central door n the *narthex* (Byzantine Porch): there ı breathtaking experience of space h a surprisingly high and broad nave broken only by the central dome.

The dull effect of the painted plas- ter (19th century) is misleading. Take a look at the richness of the original deco- rative details: the windswept acanthus

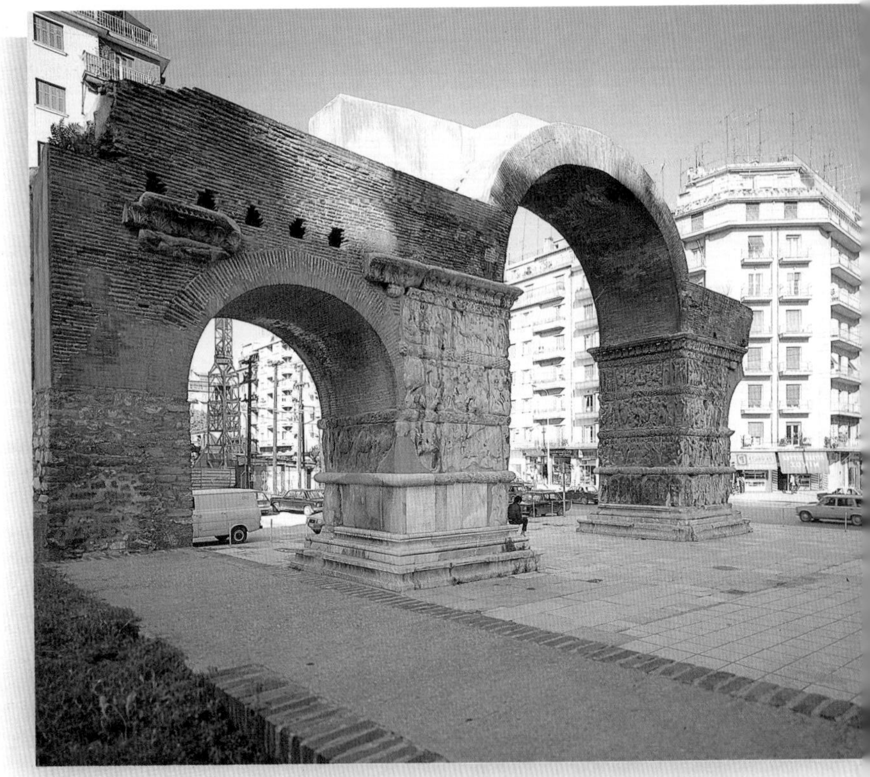

The Arch of Galerius bestrode the Roman Egnation Way.

leaf capitals of the northern arcade columns (reused from a Late Roman building) hark back to the pagan past, but the wall and vault mosaics are fine products of a Byzantine speciality craft.

In the apse, the enthroned Virgin sits in the conch, whilst the vault above displays a huge cross, with the monograms of the Emperor Constantine VI (AD 780-97) and his mother, Empress Irene (AD 790-802) and the inscribed name of the contemporary Thessalonian bishop Theophilos. These not only date the mosaics, but also tell us who paid for them.

The mosaics in the cupola we constructed a hundred years later, a their full beauty has recently been stored. The theme of the Ascension he is unusual for a dome: in most Byza tine domes you will see that of t *Pantocrator* (the Almighty Christ).

Basilica of the Akheiropoietos & Panagia Khalkeon

The **Basilica of the Akheiropoiet** was built (not "without hands" as t me translates!) in the fifth century. Its n differs from that of St Demetrios in ving three rather than five, aisles; wever, the original structure is better served than that of St Demetrios and es a superb impression of what it ıst have been like to worship in the ly Christian period. The clergy would ve occupied the nave and chancel, ilst the congregation stood in the les and gallery.

Note the simplicity of the design ich is complemented by the pale mar- columns which articulate the nave. apse would originally have been orated with the same colourful mo- cs as those which have survived.

Next to Dikastirion Square is the ırch of the **Panagia Khalkeon**'s ıurch of the Coppersmith's), whose jinal dedication is unknown, but the sent name, meaning "Our Lady of Coppersmiths", probably refers to proximity of the building to copper rkshops during the Turkish period, en it was converted into a mosque. the exterior, you will find that the cription above the west door gives us patron (a local court official) and date of its inception (1028).

Note the creative use of brickwork rrowed from Constantinople), with rnate courses of brick set back from main profile, and the intervening ce filled with mortar.

Turning to the interior, an inscribed s of middle Byzantine design with slender columns supports a broad ıe, creating a feeling of space. The original frescoes (now fragmentary or over-painted) were paid for by the patron and his wife.

The Holy Apostles & St Demetrios

The **Church of the Holy Apostles**, just off Paparigopolo street, dates to 1310-14 and is a very fine example of Late Byzantine church architecture. On the exterior, the marble inscription over the west door tells us that the patriarch Niphon I was the founder. Take a walk around the building to see how the brickwork avoids monotony by the use of different decorative schemes – on the east facade it is dazzlingly virtuoso. The remains of the attached monastery can also be seen.

The interior design is of an inscribed cross with four columns (from a fifth century building) supporting the central cupola. The decorative scheme of mosaics and frescoes depicting scenes from the life of Christ, was one of the richest in Greece: unfortunately, the Turks removed the gold *tesserae* (cubes used in the mosaic), but enough remains to point to a leading school of mosaicists, perhaps brought in from Constantinople itself. The best preserved are: the *Pantocrator* (Almighty Christ), in the cupola, with the Evangelists in the squinches below; the Nativity in the south vault, and the Transfiguration and Entry into Jerusalem, in the west vault.

The **Basilica of St Dimitrios**, on Ajiu Dimitriu street, dates back to the fifth century, but suffered in fires during 630 and 1917. The original form is preserved, but much of it has been modified by restoration. It is dedicated to the patron saint of Thessaloniki, who was martyred under the Romans in the fourth century, supposedly in a Roman bath in the crypt.

The five-aisled plan is a continuation of the pagan basilica, used for public and legal meetings. Not surprisingly the builders have reused Roman columns, carefully pairing up different designs. The mosaics date from many different periods: the earliest are rare examples of early Byzantine figurative art before iconoclasm.

St David's

The **Church of St David** – off Olympiados street, at the top of the hill – was originally dedicated to Christ the Saviour and dates to the fifth century. It was part of a monastery and had a Greek cross plan (the west section is destroyed). The Turks, whose Islamic faith prohibited icons, plastered over the mosaics, which were rediscovered in 1921.

The eye is drawn to the apse, with its rare sixth-century mosaics depicting the Vision of Ezekiel: note the young-looking, beardless Christ (early Christian representations usually show him like this). A circular glory surrour
him and the four rivers of paradise fl
beneath. Ezekiel the Old Testame
prophet, can be seen on the left, shie
ing his eyes from the glory of Christ: t
buildings of Jerusalem, in ruins as
foretold, are in the background. T
figure to the right of Christ has not be
identified. The rich contrast of colour
particularly beautiful, and the mosai
earlier than the m
famous examples
Ravenna in Italy.

Byzantine Bath & City Walls

The Byzantine Batl
not well-preserved, a
may still be under r
toration, but if y
can get in, y
will be
warded with an insight into everyc
life in the medieval city. Its date is
clear (approximately 1400) and its m
est size suggests that it was a privc
perhaps monastic, bath. The plan ha
back to the Roman baths, and lo
forward to the Turkish, with its h
tepid and cold rooms. The furnace
the north side heated water which
through clay pipes. You might like
visit the travel information bureau n
the sea front on Leotoros Vasil
Konstantinu Street, for further detai

The **city walls** were originally ab
eight kilometers in length and roug

Detail of the Arch of Galerius – commemorating victory over the Persians in AD 297.

f are still standing. The north-east ner of the city is the best place to see m. They probably include the early lenistic defences, but what you see ay is from the third to the sixth turies, with many later modifica- ıs (often recorded on the wall with criptions or monograms). The style l building techniques, are however, antine. The facing consists of un- ssed stone, with levelling courses of brick – sometimes arched for extra strength. There were square towers at irregular intervals. The acropolis wall encloses the "fortress of the seven towers" (15th century, now a state prison).

A Walk through the Roman City

Start at the White Tower and walk to the

Arch of Galerius at the end of Egnatia Street. The arch bestrode the Egnatian Way as it ran through the city from Constantinople to Italy. It was built in AD 303 to celebrate the victories of the Emperor over the Persians. Note how the brick-faced concrete was originally completely covered with marble. There was a large central opening for traffic and smaller side passages for pedestrians. The lower half displays four bands of relief sculptures depicting the battles as well as the triumphal procession, which would have passed this way 1700 years ago. The style is typically Late Roman; squat figures and irrational perspective, but with a great sense of vigour. You can see Galerius in armour, sacrificing to the gods for victory, beside his father Diocletian in civic dress.

Beneath this the artist showed the Thessalonians what a Persian town looked like, with war-elephants and other exotic oriental beasts depicted in the foreground, whilst behind, the Persians surrender to Galerius.

Palace of Galerius & the Forum

At right-angles to the arch a road ran southwards between the **Hippodrome** and the **Palace of Galerius**. In the Palace of Galerius, there are now just a few remains of what was once a splendid, marble-clad building.

The palace lies beneath **Navarinu Square**, where you can see the ruins of a hall, with well-preserved geomet floor-mosaics. The square also has r merous bars and cafés, for that mu needed break.

Northwards from the Arch, the c cient road led to the **Rotunda of George** (see "the Christian City" Pa 238); the circular form was normal Imperial tombs, such as those Augustus and Hadrian, in Rome.

To the west of the Basilica of t Akheiropoetos is the site of the **Rom Forum**: this was the market-place a civic center. It was a rectangular op space surrounded by double colonna on each side. Dating to the fourth c tury AD, it has recently been par excavated: columns, mosaics and *cryptoporticus* (underground passage) visible. To the east are the remains c small Roman theatre, built c AD 30

Archaeological Treasure Trove

From the White Tower, walk westwa for about 500 m to Khanth Square wh you will find The **Archaeological M seum**. You should allow half a day this renowned collection of objects fr northern Greece, dating from the p historic to the Late Roman period. T climax of the museum lies at the enc a corridor to the left of the door to ro 7 – finds from The Royal Tombs Vergina. The tombs are now known have been those of the Macedon royalty. The most spectacular finds we

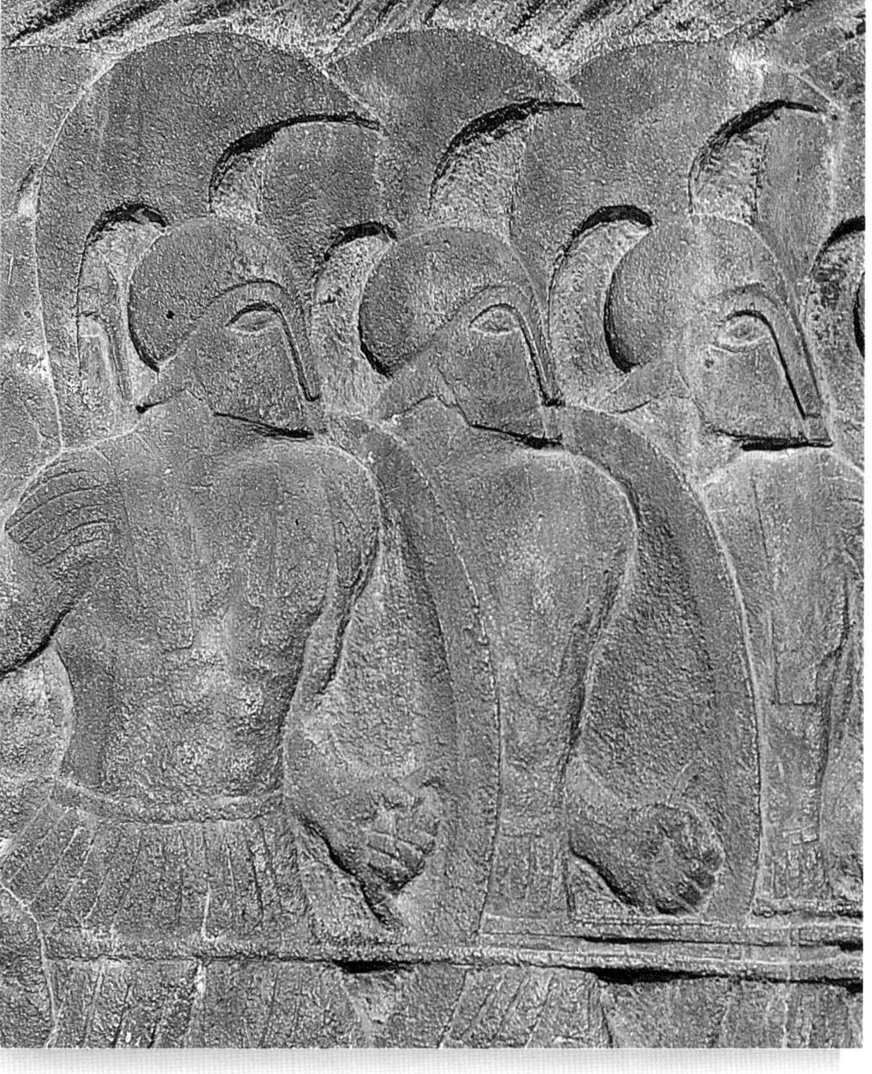

Frieze of ancient Greek soldiers.

ot surprisingly, from Philip II's tomb th century BC). His royal parapherna-a included: a beautifully crafted shield; gold wreath; a casket in which were ie remains of a cloak dyed with expen-ve purple from the murex shell-fish – a gnifier of royal/divine status; and a set of miniature ivory portraits of the royal family, including the youthful Alexander the Great. Room 7 also contains some luxury goods from other late Classical and Hellenistic sites, the most notable of which are from the **Dherveni Crater**.

Central Greece

The area of central Greece and Thessaly, is truly a delight. The region is one of great variety, capturing beauty, authentic and unspoilt. From the desolate landscape of Zagori to the fertile plain of Thessaly and the Pindus mountains, the landscape is one of rivers, mountains, woods and plains. There is a strong Turkish influence in the towns here; activities vary from haggling in the bazaars, to spending a day in the beautifully situated and historic monasteries of Meteora, or climbing the hillside with the local shepherd and his flock.

ɔectacular view from the Meteora
ɔnasteries.

You can start this itinerary from Igoumenitsa (at the end of the North-west itinerary) by taking the increasingly mountainous 100km road eastwards and inland to Ioannina the capital of Epirus. There are eight buses per day to and from Athens, which take seven and a half hours, as well as internal flights.

Ioannina

The great city of Ioannina (population:

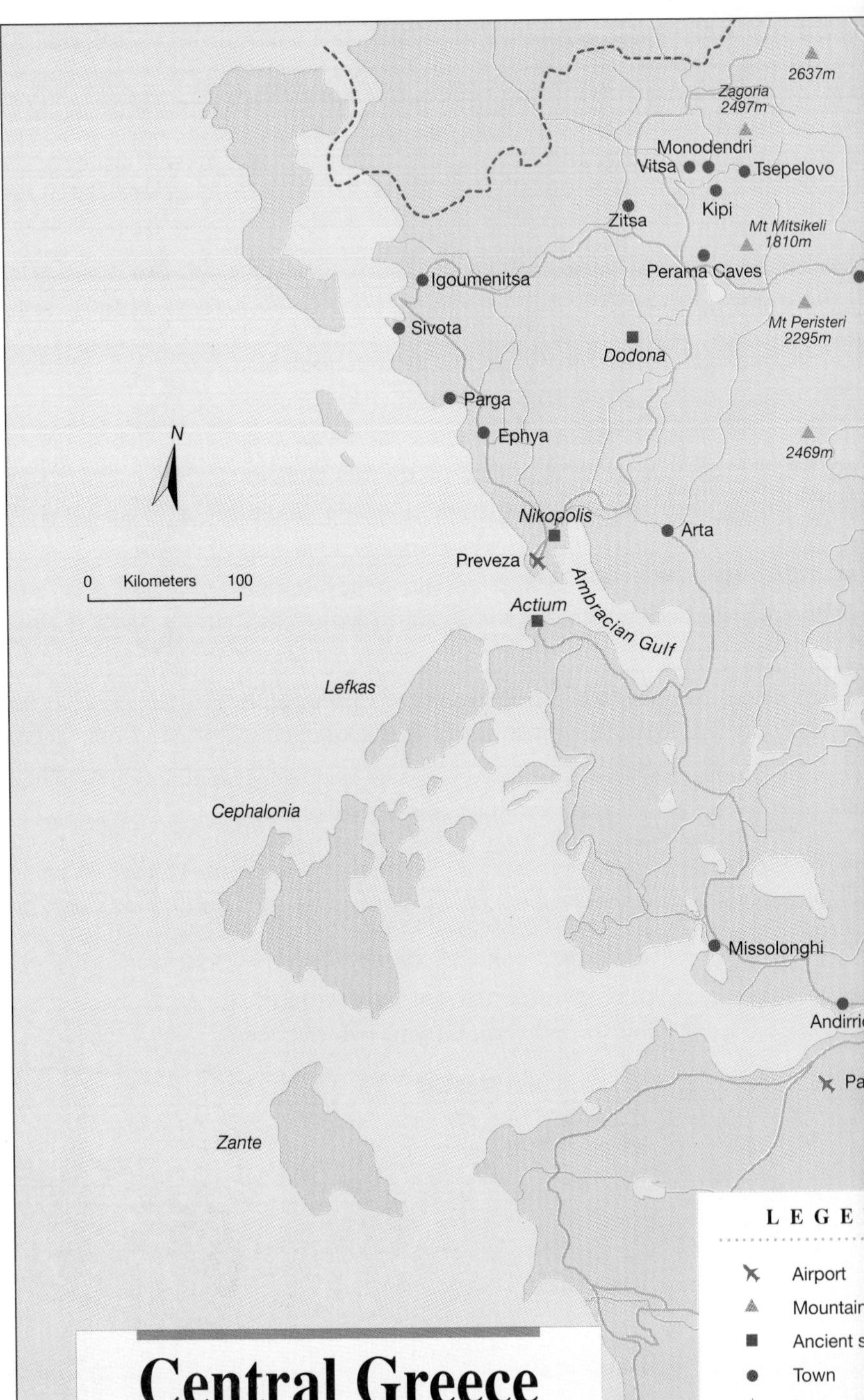

Central Greece

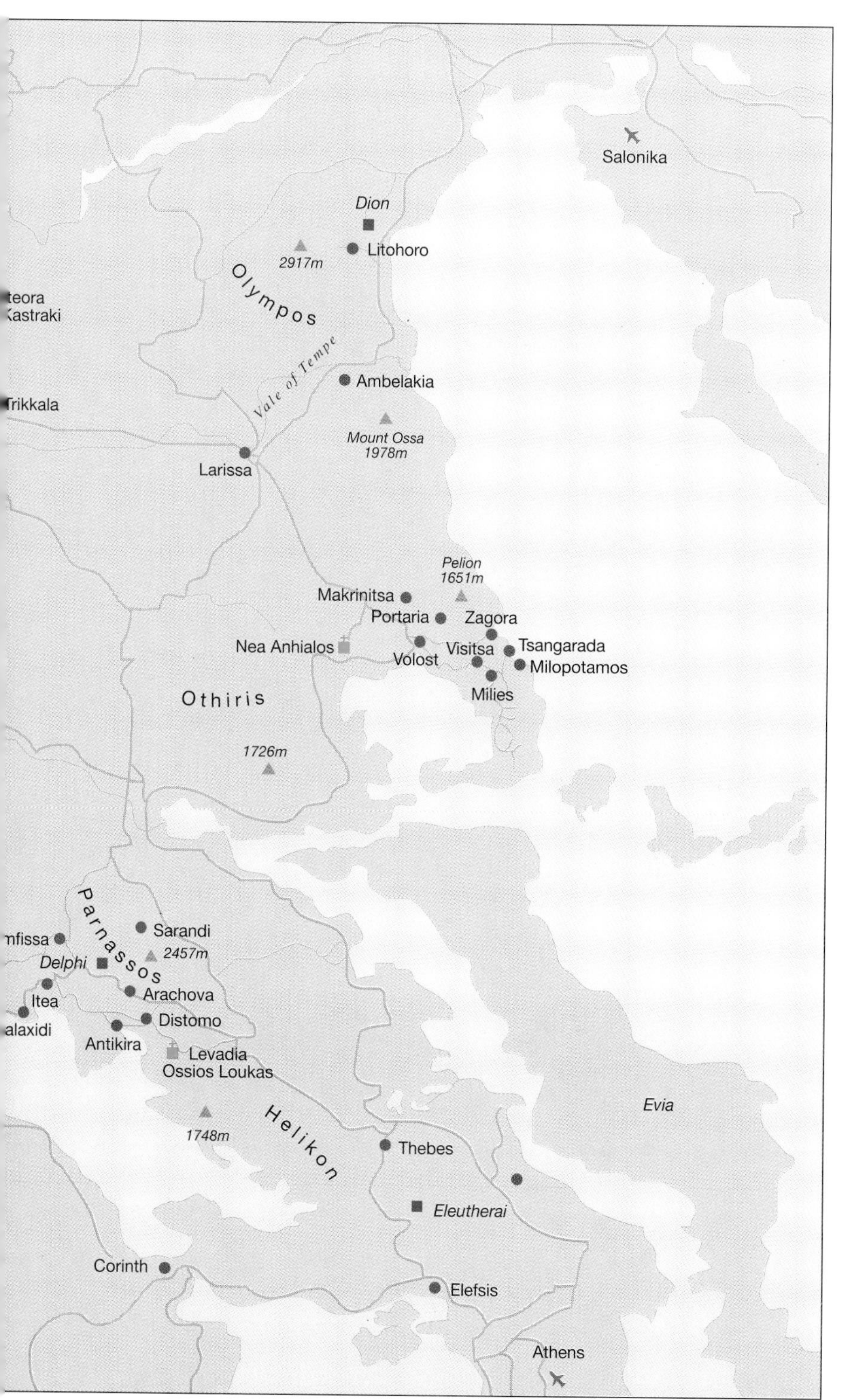

Salonika
Dion
Litohoro
2917m
Olympos
teora
Kastraki
Vale of Tempe
Ambelakia
Trikkala
Mount Ossa
1978m
Larissa
Pelion
1651m
Makrinitsa
Portaria
Zagora
Nea Anhialos
Tsangarada
Visitsa
Volost
Milopotamos
Milies
Othiris
1726m
Parnassos
Sarandi
mfissa
2457m
Delphi
Arachova
Itea
Distomo
alaxidi
Antikira
Levadia
Ossios Loukas
Evia
Helikon
1748m
Thebes
Eleutherai
Corinth
Elefsis
Athens

Untouched countryside.

45,000) lies under the highest peaks of the Pindus mountains. It was probably founded by the Byzantine Emperor Justinian in the sixth century AD, and by the 13th century had become an important center of Byzantine art and architecture (much of it was later destroyed by the Turks). Its most famous age, however, was the 18th century, when the Ali Pasha made Ioannina his capital, and tried to wrest Greek independence from the Ottoman Dynas His revolt was put down, his body w buried in Ioannina itself, whilst his he was taken to Constantinople.

There is plenty to do in Ioanni You can browse in the bazaars looki for locally-produced gold and silver f gree jewellery; you should also look for the traditional Epirus embroide Eating and drinking is a pleasure Ioannina, and you might try dining

.e fish restaurants of the island on the ljacent lake, where after visiting the onastery where Ali Pasha died fight-g (you are shown the bullet-holes in .e walls), you can choose your own out from a tank and have it cooked esh. The local wine is a delight too.

Though there has been much mod-n rebuilding there is still a good deal of ırkish atmosphere in the town; there e mosques, traditional Turkish houses, lakeside castle and a fine local mu-um.

The **Frourion** citadel has splendid ews over Lake Pambotis. It was remod-led by Ali Pasha and you should visit e **Cami of Aslan Pasha**, a rare open ample of a mosque in Greece, which ow houses the **Popular Art Museum** pen daily 8 a.m - 3 p.m; entrance 0dr), with its colourful collection of pirote traditional crafts and dress. Leg-d says that it was here that the 62-ar-old Ali Pasha raped his son's mis-ess, when she refused his lustful ad-nces; together with her seventeen ends, she was bound, gagged and rown into the lake after being tied th weights – a reminder of the cruel rannical side of Ali Pasha, who was herwise famed for his cultural stand-g. When Byron visited Ioannina he mmented that Ali Pasha had made e city "superior in wealth, refinement d learning to any town in Greece".

Below the walls of the Frourion you n take motor-boats (half-hourly) to e island of Nissi. The island village is ally beautiful, with tree-lined walks out to its five monasteries (11th-15th centuries), and plenty of waterside restaurants. Back in the city, head for the Old Bazaar in front of the citadel; if you get fed up with shopping, the **Archaeological Museum** (open Tuesday-Saturday 8:30 a.m - 3 p.m; entrance 300dr) is a little further on, and houses objects from the Nekyomanteion of Ephyra as well as material from the prehistoric period to the 20th century. For evening entertainment try the "studenty" *tavernas* and cinemas around Plateia Mavili, on the lakeside to the west of the citadel.

Zagori Villages

A bus leaves Ioannina in the morning and returns in the early evening for the remote **Zagori** villages to the north near the Albanian border. During the Turkish occupation, the 46 Zagori villages were given autonomy in return for tribute, they also became homes for refugees from the Ottoman empire: hence the Turkish influence. The wealthy Turkish-style houses were built in the last two centuries from money made abroad. You will notice that there is no fertile land in this desolate landscape.

Oracle of Dodona

Twenty-two km south of Ioannina is **Dodona** (open Monday-Friday 8 a.m - 5 p.m, Saturday & Sunday 8:30 a.m - 3

The Roman Heritage

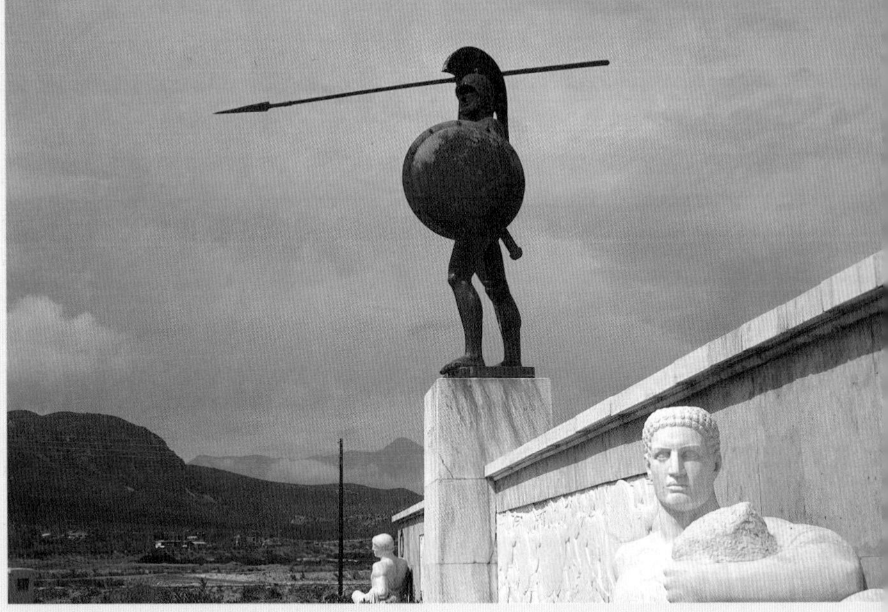

Monument to the Three Hundred Spartans, at the Pass of Thermopylae.

Nearly every archaeological site in Greece has evidence from the prehistoric cultures of the Minoans and Mycenaeans as well as the Classical Greeks. On most of these same sites you will also see the signs of later Roman occupation, as well as Byzantine churches in various states of preservation. The most common Roman architectural remains include huge bath buildings, temples and theatres, whilst large numbers mosaics and sculptures have survived from bo Roman houses and public buildings. This c become confusing since the Romans oft adapted or rebuilt earlier Greek theatres a temples. The **Theatre of Dionysus** at Athens f example now consists mainly of later Rom elements, and there is little of the origir

p.m; entrance 500dr) one of the most beautiful ancient sites in Greece, and home of the oldest oracle in Greece, predating even Delphi.

You enter the site alongside the ancient stadium, used for running races in the games, in honour of Zeus. To the left is the massive theatre, restored in the 19th century. This is still used durir the Summer Ioannina festival, but dat back to the time of Pyrrhus in the thi century BC. The Romans adapted th theatre for gladiatorial shows. The loc *Bouleuterion* (council building) is to th east, followed by the sacred area wi temples of Aphrodite and Zeus. A Chr

atre of Sophocles, Euripides and Aristophanes be seen.

Roman Remains

man remains, are often the most spectacular d best preserved. This is due to the Roman of concrete as a building material, which has ted longer than the classical Greek buildings, ose finely carved marble and limestone blocks re often removed and re-used to build medi- l churches and houses.

Concrete allowed the Romans to construct ssive vaulted public bath buildings, as well as endid and long-lasting theatres such as the **eon of Herodes Atticus** at Athens. This nument is also evidence for generous Ro- n patronage of the larger Greek cities; local althy Roman philhellenes often spent large ounts of money on public monuments, nes and shows, intended to keep the Greek oulace happy. The emperors also set up new nan temples to impress their authority on Greeks. There are a number of temples licated to the emperors themselves as gods, ich can now be seen standing rather incon- ously beside the earlier classical temples. can see this on the **Acropolis** at Athens, ere the Roman Emperor Augustus built a ular temple to "Rome and Augustus" in it of the Parthenon itself.

Roman Take-over

ece caught the eye of the expanding Mediterranean empire of the Romans when the Macedonians allied themselves with Rome's arch enemy in the west, Carthage, in the late third century BC. Rome defeated Carthage in 201 BC and the Hellenistic kingdoms of Rhodes and Pergamon (in modern Turkey) invited Rome to invade their mutual enemy, Macedonia. The Roman General Quinctius Flaminius defeated Philip V of Macedon and restored freedom to the Greeks, who then proceeded to fight one another, resulting in further military intervention by Rome.

In 146 BC Corinth was sacked as an example of how Rome would punish the Greeks if they failed to behave themselves. Northern Greece became the Roman province of Macedonia, whilst southern and central Greece became Achaea. Roman forms of government were imposed and Roman businessmen and traders moved in quickly to exploit the new territory; there was much money to be made in the sale of Greek slaves, who were often skilled craftsmen, doctors or teachers. Some 10,000 slaves were sold every day at the main slave-market on the island of Delos; you can still see evidence of Roman wealth on Delos by their surviving houses and fine mosaic decorations.

The Romans imposed their taxation system on the local Greeks, but otherwise preferred a policy of "live and let live", with local religious cults, for example, allowed to continue along with traditional festivals such as the Olympic and Pythian Games. Some Romans even took part in the games; the Emperor Nero entered the musical contests at Delphi and, though considered a mediocre performer, h emanaged to win everything!

n basilica was later built on the foun- ions of a temple of Hercules, son of is.

The Road to Kalambaka

e hundred and twenty km further east is Kalambaka, but you will probably want a break halfway at **Metsovo** (population: 3,000), a mountain village filled with traditional houses and people still wearing local costume – old men in flat black caps and pompommed shoes; women in blue tweed and head-scarves. This is traditionally the capital of the "Vlach" minority, and you will find their traditional crafts, especially the beautifully hand-woven rugs, for sale around the square. In winter Metsovo is transformed into a ski-resort.

Meteora Monasteries

Kalambaka (population: 6,000), is picturesquely situated at the foot of the Pindos mountains. This is the place to stay if you intend to visit **Meteora**, which is just two km outside of the town. Here six monasteries (there were once twenty-four) are perched on top of grey pinnacles of rock, from which the monks can safely watch the world go by and the Pinios River flow out of the Pindos mountains and into the Plain of Thessaly.

There were monastic retreats here as early as the 10th century, but it was only in the 14th century, with the rising wars between the Serbs and Byzantine Greeks, that they decided to build the substantial buildings of wood and stone which you can visit today. The stairs and ramps have been built for tourists – originally, the only way up was climbing a rope-ladder! Each monastery has basically the same plan: a courtyard surrounded by cells and refectory, with the *katholikon* (main church), in the center of the courtyard.

To visit all six monasteries in one day, you must leave Kalambaka early to visit St Nicholas, St Varlaam (closed Friday) and the Great Meteoron (closed Tuesday) between 9 a.m and 1 p.m. This

Astounding isolation on barren crags – Meteora's monasteries on pinnacles of grey rock.

The massive theater of Dodoni, used during summer for the Joannina Festival.

allows you the afternoon free to see Roussanou, Ayia Triadha (Holy Trinity) and St Stephanos (closed Mondays). Women must wear a skirt which covers the knees; men must wear long trousers and for both sexes, shoulders must be covered.

It costs 200dr to visit each monastery, and you can buy food and drink from stalls near the Great Meteoron. The day's walk from monastery to monastery covers some 20km from Kala baka and back, but you will hav unique experience, and the views mountains, rivers, woods and plains really breathtaking.

St Nicholas & the Great Meteoron

St Nicholas is opposite Roussanou c

ıs the most accomplished of the eteora frescoes by the 16th-century etan artist Theophanis, famed for his e-like portrayals of saints and biblical aracters.

The Great Meteoron is the oldest d tallest of the monasteries, with won-rful views and plenty of colourful and ry frescoes in the church. In the *narthex* yzantine porch), various particularly sty martyrdoms are depicted – notice e decapitated heads lying on the ound, haloes still attached! The rich lden setting of the inner church, illus-tes the former extent of the monas-y's wealth, standing in great contrast the simple cooking equipment in the onk's kitchen. The Meteora painters ve incorporated the local landscape o some of the frescoes – notice the ge rocky crags which frame the Bap-m scene.

Monasteries of Varlaam & Roussanou

rlaam is nearby, and repeats the ody martyrdom theme; the highlight re is the skinning alive of a saint nging by his ankles. The refectory is w a museum housing a collection of rtable icons, used for the protection of monks when they travelled abroad.

The smaller and less visited **Monas-y of Roussanou** is approached over a dge. Here the fresco highlight is an nost hallucinogenic Last Judgement h hard-hitting imagery – the souls of the departed are weighed in the center, the blessed fly away on clouds to a land of birds and flowers, meanwhile the damned are dispatched down a red slide to be devoured by voracious monsters! **Ayia Triadha** (Holy Trinity), is half-an-hour's walk from the main group, and is entered up a tunnel of 130 steps cut into the rock. The frescoes are black with soot and look forward to being cleaned, but you will note that the cloisters have been renovated and there is an interesting little folk museum.

St Stephanos stands on its own and is approached by a bridge which connects it to the solid mountain behind. From here there are magnificent views back to Kalambaka.

The Plain of Thessaly

Continuing eastwards you follow the course of the Pinios river which rises in the Pindos Mountains behind and drains the fertile expanses of the **Plain of Thessaly.** There are mountains on all sides, and the area can be sweltering in the summer months. The lower mountain slopes are covered in pine, oak and beeches and there are occasional sightings of bears and wolves, as well as wild boar.

The plain is one of the most fertile areas of Greece, producing crops of fruit, tobacco, corn and rice: lack of man-power, however, means that only parts of the plain are exploited. The people are a mixture of settled Greek, Vlach and Albanian farmers, whilst there is a roving population of shepherds who bring their flocks to the mountains, during summer.

Larissa

Following the Pinios, you might stop for a quick drink at the unremarkable market-town of Trikkala (population: 40,000) en route for **Larissa** (population: 102,000), the capital of Thessaly and at the center of its great plain. Most of the city is now modern, but evinces occasional glimpses of its Turkish past, when it was an important strategic post. The history of the town goes back to the prehistoric period, but it is unable to boast of any particularly remarkable happenings.

There is a castle above the town, still used by the military. At its center is the large city square of **Plateia Stratou**, where citrus trees provide shade for the cafes. Head north from here to Odhos Venizelou, which still has a few Turkish period houses. Following the road left towards the river, you will pass the **Clock Tower** and the unfinished modern **Cathedral**. A bridge then takes you across the river to the Alkazar Park, a place of retreat for the Larissans during the stifling hot summer months.

Lamia

From here the road heads south **Lamia** (population: 42,000), a mark town specializing in cotton and cere The most interesting feature is the pr ence of storks' nests on the roofs of houses and public buildings. British v tors might be interested to know tha is a sister town to Dover. It traces history back to the Classical period wh in the fourth cent BC, in the anarc following the de of Alexander Great, the "Lami War" between Ath and Macedonia fought, with Ath losing the battle.

The 14th cent ***Kastro*** (Catalan fortress) c be seen above the town and is still oc pied by the military. If you are stoppi head for **Plateia Elevtherias**, with cafes, cathedral and town-hall still sh ing the bullet-holes from riots dur the Rule of the Colonels. It is a liv small town, and if you are staying night, it is worth looking for *bouzo* music in the streets off the main squa

The Pass of Thermopylae

The historically-minded might like

low the road 10km south to see the ss of Thermopylae, where three hun-ed Spartans made their stand against e invading Persian army in 480 BC. ey all died (bar two to tell the story) – e Persian forces numbered 30,000 – t succeeded heroically in delaying the rsian advance.

Halfway along the pass you can see e **Loutra Thermopilion**, hot-springs ed since antiquity, as well as the grave ound of the dead heroes, and a mod-n memorial to their famous general onidas.

The Road to Volos

om Lamia, take the coast road in a rth-west direction for 111 km towards **los**; *en route* are beaches, *tavernas* and od coastal scenery. Fifteen km along e road, if you have not yet been npted by the beach-side *tavernas*, is **lis** where Maria Callas' grandfather, nself a renowned singer, once lived. ere is a beach and hotel here, but if u have a car, head for **Glifa**, a further km north, but another 10km off the ain road. It has the best beach on the ast and you can cross from here by ry to the island of Euboea.

Forty-five km further on the main ad to Volos, lovers of early Byzantine : and architecture should turn off to e village of **Nea Ankhialos**. Five large silicas have been excavated, dating m the fourth to the sixth centuries). There is a small site museum containing some of the more precious mosaics and building fragments.

Volos

The coast becomes prettier now, with secluded bays backed by olive groves framing your journey as you curve round the coast and catch your first glimpse of the sea-port of **Volos** (population: 71,000). This town dates back to antiquity and is the chief port of Thessaly, everything you have seen growing in the Thessalian Plain finds its way here to be exported.

It is mostly modern, concrete and industrial, but there is enough to do for an afternoon and evening (good night-life) if you are waiting to cross to the northern Sporades Islands or to tour Mount Pelion.

On the eastern waterfront is the **Archaeological Museum** (open Tuesday-Sunday 8:30 a.m - 3 p.m) with a splendid collection of *stelai* (Archaeological tombstones) painted with scenes of everyday life.

The **Mount Pelion Peninsula** is a wonderful region to drive through, with its cool summer breezes, its delightfully unspoilt villages and its constant panoramas of the sea. The hill-villages of **Makrinitsa** and **Zagora** to the east, and **Milies** and **Tsangaradha** to the south can all be reached by bus from Volos.

From Volos there are nine buses daily to Athens, which is a 5 hour journey.

Macedonia & Thrace

The hinterland of northern Greece, is made up of the extensive province of Macedonia, with the relatively tiny province of Thrace, to the east, near the Turkish border. Macedonia officially became part of Greece in 1912, followed shortly by Thrace in 1920. These provinces do however, still have a very distinct and colourful character of their own.

Macedonia was in classical times a kingdom in its own right, and at the time of Philip and his son Alexander the Great, it was the most powerful Greek-speaking state. In modern times, this rather ill-defined area has found itself divided between the southern parts of old Yugoslavia, Bulgaria and Greece itself. To the west it borders on Albania, and to the east with Thrace; whilst to the south it shares the Olympus massif with northern Thessaly.

ature unhibited.

There has always been a strong political movement in the region which would like to see Macedonia a separate nation: their demands are gathering momentum at the present time, with the Macedoni-

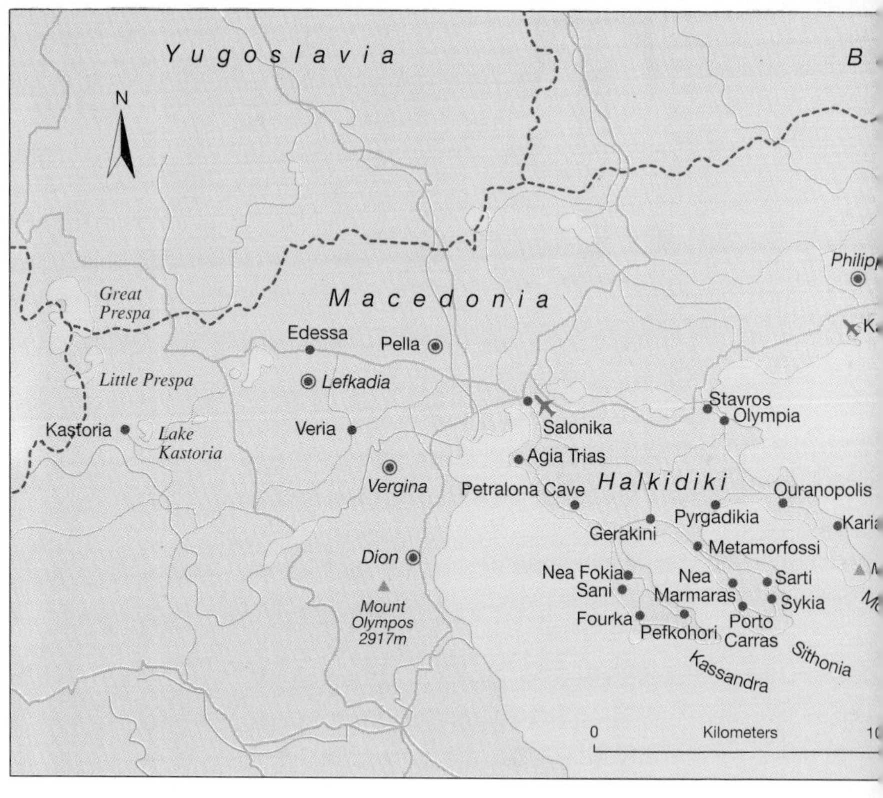

ans of broken Yugoslavia a particular threat now that their central government has collapsed. Macedonia has a population of over two million.

The region of Thrace is divided between Greece and Turkey, and the Greek part is often referred to as Western Thrace (population: 345,000). The area was ceded to Greece by the Treaty of Lausanne in 1923: a million Greeks then came into the area from Eastern Thrace as well as Asia Minor, whilst the Muslims already living in Western Thrace were allowed to stay. Out of a population of 360,000, roughly 30 per cent are Muslims of various ethnic backgrounds, which makes for an interesting cultural mix.

Northeast Greece

Thracian Greece is divided from Macedonia by the river Nestos and from Turkish Eastern Thrace by the river Evro Behind its coastline rise the Rhodop Mountains, whose main peaks are Bulgaria. The whole area of northea Greece has a Balkan feel to it. The c mate is more extreme than is usual f the Mediterranean; much colder in wi ter, and as hot in summer, with mo thunderstorms.

The rivers, rising in the Balkans, a

reduced to summer trickles as is mal in the Mediterranean, but re-in broad and swift-flowing through- the year. The landscape is rolling d tree-covered – quite different to oular idea of the typical barren and ggy Greek landscape.

The Khalkidhiki (Chalkidice) penin-a in Macedonia is the region's tourist ter, with hotels lining the coast of its stern and central prongs. This is the ce to go for crowded resorts with dern facilities and nightlife.

There is much else to see however: he west and south of Thessaloniki Greece's most spectacular moun-ns; the North Aegean coast is beautiful to travel along, with its backdrop of lush, well-watered hills and woodland; the modern cities are lively and cosmopolitan, whilst treasures of antiquity include the royal Macedonian sites of Pella and Vergina.

The monasteries of Mount Athos require permission to visit, but look just as wonderful from a boat off the shore. Shopping is varied and exciting, ranging from the modernity of Thessaloniki to the exotic silks of Soufli, on the Turkish border.

Katerini & Ancient Dion

Taking the coastal road south-west of Thessaloniki towards Litokhoron, you arrive at the market town of Katerini (population: 38,000), with its superb views of distant Mount Olympus. From here, a bus can be taken 16km south to the modern village of **Malathria** (also known as Dion): here there is a Museum (open the same hours as the ancient site), which contains various statues and small finds from archaeological excavations of the ancient site.

Ancient Dion (open Monday 12:30 p,m - 7 p.m, Tuesday-Friday 8 a.m - 7 p.m, Sat & Sun 8:30 a.m - 3 p.m; entrance 400dr), is just to the south of the village. The town was sacred to Zeus, who, as at Olympia, was worshipped here with athletic competitions held in a stadium. Alexander the Great sacrificed to Zeus here before setting out against the Persians. The Romans later

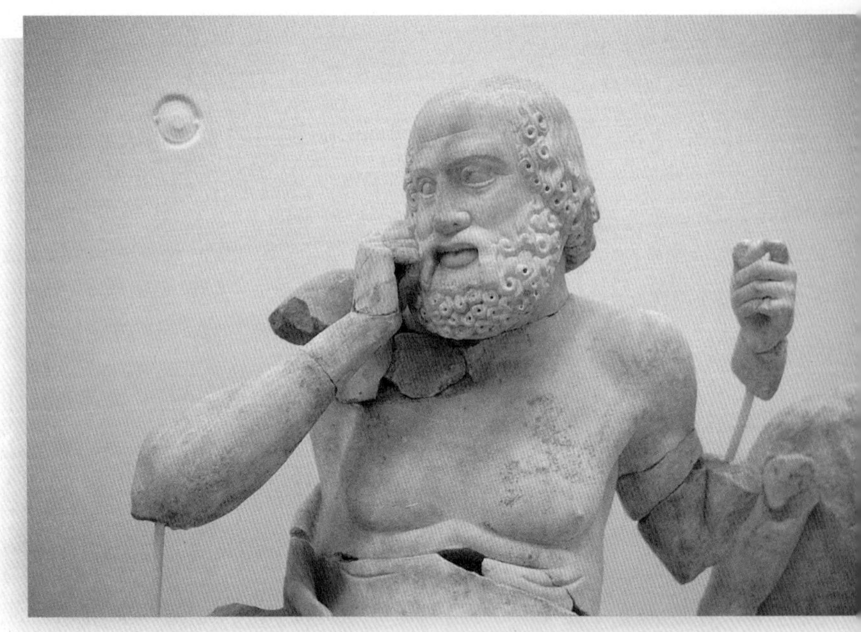

Zeus was worshipped at the ancient town of Dion.

turned Dion into a military colony of some 500 x 460m which gradually became a Christianized civilian town, before being sacked by Alaric in the late fourth century. Fifth-century earthquakes finally razed the town and covered it in mud, thus preserving its public buildings and mosaics.

Within the well-preserved eastern wall are the remains of a large second century AD Roman bath complex: statues of the god of healing Asklepios were found here (now located in the Museum).

Further into the site are the foundations of some private houses and an Early Christian basilica. Back outside the walls to the east, are the sanctuaries of Demeter and Isis.

The Regal Tombs of Vergina

West of Thessaloniki, the town of **Verc** (population: 37,000) is worth a visit the attractive streets of the old tow and a number of wattle and timb churches built surreptitiously during t Turkish occupation, when the town w used as a military base.

Journeying on 11km southwest, the modern village of **Vergina**, sig posts direct you to the royal Mace nian tombs of ancient Aigai. The s was excavated by Professor Manc Andronikos (died 1992). Aigai was t Macedonian capital before it was mov to Pella. The kings were traditionc

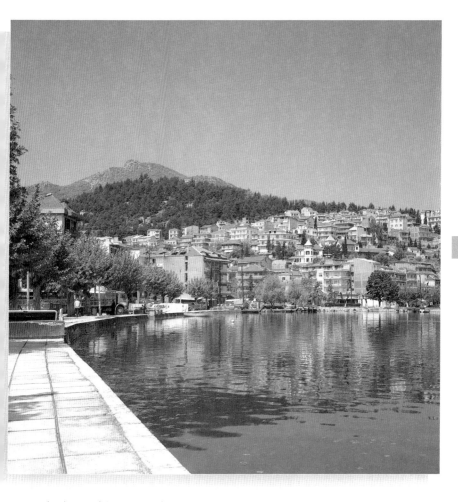

The beautiful setting of Kastoria, a town famous for its fur trade.

ried here and Andronikos has excavated the tomb of Philip II, father of exander: the wonderful gold finds are w in Thessaloniki Museum.

Nearby are the foundations of the called Pa**lace of Palatitsa** (open Tuesy-Sunday 0830-1500 hours; entrance 0dr), probably the summer residence the third century BC Macedonian ıgs. Any disappointment at how little ı are able to see, is more than made up for by the wonderful views over the surrounding landscape.

Pella & the Macedonia

Pella (open Tuesday-Saturday 8:30 a.m - 3 p.m, Sun 9:30 a,m - 2:30 p.m; entrance 400dr) can be reached by buses travelling from Thessaloniki to Edhessa, and is a much more rewarding ancient

Alexander the Great

Alexander was proclaimed king of Macedon after his father Philip was assassinated by a political rival. That was in 336 BC when Alexander was just 20 years old, and he inherited a kingdom which had already become a threat to the rest of Greece under the expansionist policies of Philip.

Alexander's life history is a mixture of fact and fantasy. He projected himself as a son of Zeus to be ranked alongside other sons of the king of gods; Herakles and Dionysos were seen as his brothers and coins of Alexander sometimes depict him wearing the lion-skin of Herakles or the elephant-scalp of Dionysos. His famous horse Bucephalus was also considered divine.

The reason Alexander created this divine image for himself would have been less surprising in the ancient world. The Athenians were still proud of their democracy, but they had lost their empire at the end of the previous century and the royal monarchy of Macedon was already gaining control of the rest of mainland Greece when Alexander came to power. Alexander had been sent to Athens for his education and was taught by the philosopher Aristotle.

This experience remained with him for the rest of his brief life, and his mission was to spread Greek civilization and culture to the rest of the world. Most of the powerful kingdoms of the eastern Mediterranean were more used to worshipping their rulers as divinities, and Alexander propagated the idea of his divinity by placing portrait statues everywhere he conquered and paying his troops, many of them mercenaries, with coins bearing his image.

Only the best contemporary Greek artists were allowed by him to sculpt or paint his portrait; these included the famous painter Apelles, who was greatly revered by Itali Renaissance artists (even though none of works have survived).

Persia & the Orient

Alexander took over his father's ambition conquering the age-old enemy of the Gree the Persians. He crossed the Dardanelles ir Asia Minor in 337 BC with about 40,000 m the Persians were there to meet him, but w convincingly defeated. Alexander celebrat his first victory over the barbarians sending 300 suits of Persian armour the goddess Athena, worshipped the Parthenon at Athens. Alexander continued to march ea wards, and was eventually n by the Persian King Darius at River Issos.

Alexander's brave vict meant that he now control the orient, and he continued far as the Indus valley, setting military colonies everywhere went, before finally turning b and conquering Egypt. Here founded the city of Alex dria as a trading post on Nile delta, and he was ev tually buried there – his to remains undiscovered neath the modern city.

Alexander's vision was Greco-Persian Empire and married the oriental princ Roxane to bind the two kingdo together. In 323 BC whilst holding cour Babylon, Alexander, just 33 years old, caug fever and died. His empire died with him; generals immediately set about fighting another, and eventually divided the newly c quered territories up into separate Helleni kingdoms. After his death Alexander achie mythical status, and was admired for m centuries by future generals for his brill military accomplishments and handsome roic image.

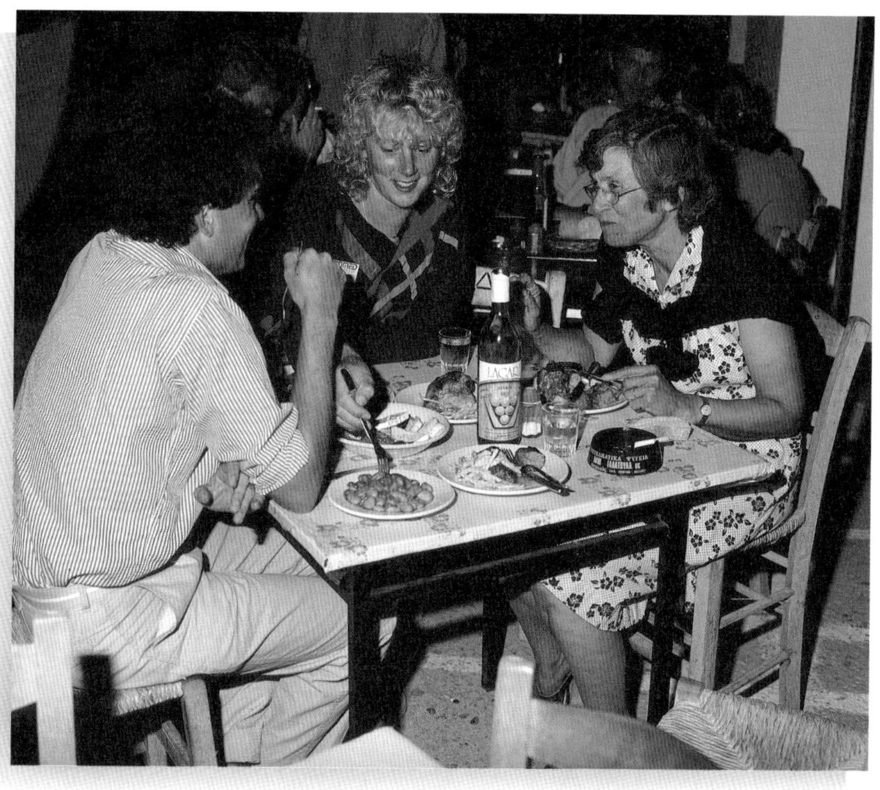

Time to wind down after a day at the ruins.

e than Vergina. It became the politi-l and cultural capital during Mac-onia's rise to power in the fourth ntury BC. Here you will see the foun-tions of the palace and fine pebble osaics from excavations carried out ice the site was first discovered in 57. The site **Museum** (open the same urs as the above; entrance 400dr) ntains most of the mosaics, which are extremely fine quality, made from verly selected natural pebbles.

Typically royal scenes are depicted ch as stag and lion hunts, as well as normal Greek mythological subjects of Dionysus on his panther, a Greek fighting an Amazon and the Rape of Helen.

A Refreshing Interlude

Fifty km further west is the summer resort town of **Edhessa**, refreshing place to stop on the way to the western borders. Here you must see the **waterfalls**, which fall in a 24m drop from cliffs covered with vines and fruit-trees.

Twenty-five km south the town of Naousa (population: 20,000), offers

Local man from the Turkish borderlands.

some of the best red and dry white wine in Greece. The town is also renowned for its peaches and its silk – stroll around the shops and wine and dine in the *tavernas,* for some excellent recreation. Back on track with the antiquities, four km to the north at **Levkadhia** are four more ancient (third century BC) Macedonian tombs (open Tuesday-Sunday 8:30 a.m - 3 p.m).

Kastoria & the Prespa Lakes

One hundred and twenty kilometers west of Edhessa (about four hours by bus), is Kastoria (population: 17,000) beautifully situated on a peninsula surrounded by a lake on its north and south sides. Fur is imported here from abroad, stitched together and sold; this business has been going on for several centuries

and accounts for the large 17th a 18th century town-houses.

Although modern developers hc spoilt the townscape with high-r blocks, there are still lovely walks alc the cobbled streets of the town as wel along the lakeside, where there are vi of the surrounding mountains. Th are also plenty of Byzantine and me

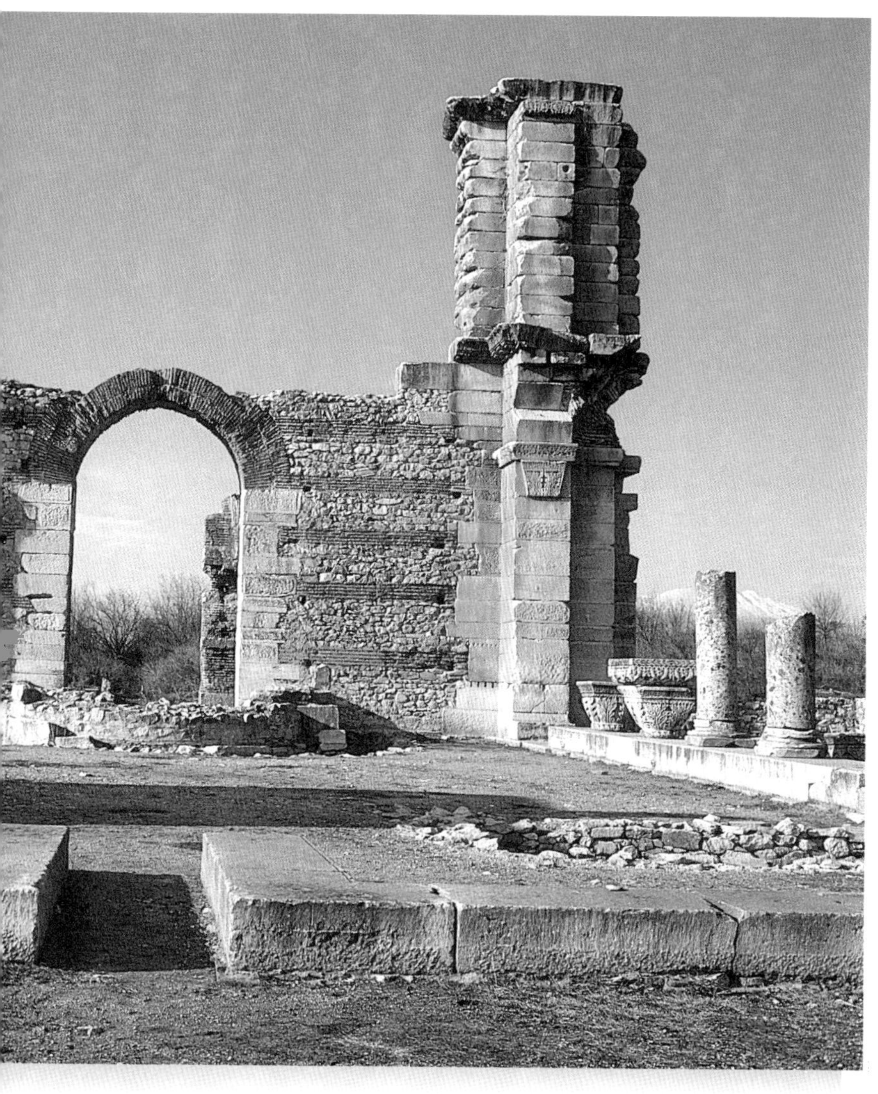

Basilica B was a 6th-century church left unfinished when its dome collapsed.

al churches to be seen (unfortunately
any are locked) as you wander round.
ty km north, straddling the borders of
oania and old Yugoslavia, are the two
espa Lakes, a national park since
71, which should attract bird-watch-
.

Khalkidhiki Peninsula

Little more than 50km southeast of Thessaloniki is the **Khalkidhiki** (Chalcidice) peninsula, which projects into the north Aegean Sea like a trident with its three lesser mountainous peninsulas. The easternmost peninsula is Athos, a Monk's Republic only open to male visitors over 21, with previously obtained permits.

The westernmost is **Kassandra**, which being the closest to Thessaloniki, is dotted with generally packed and characterless resorts. Kassandra has an extremely sad recent history – almost the entire population of farmers were massacred by the Turks as they tried to back out of the peninsula in 1821, during the Turkish occupation.

The central prong of Sithonia is a better proposition, being at once greener and rockier than Kassandra, with small sandy coves as opposed to vast hotel-backed beaches. There are pines on the hills and olive groves on the coast. Resorts vary from the massive holiday village of **Porto Carras** with its excellent watersport facilities and famous Carras wines, to the nearby long and sandy beach of **Toroni**, made lively by a few *tavernas*. The site of **Ancient Torone**, is still being excavated but it is an exciting destination with its walls and early Christian basilicas already visible.

Kavalla

Following the line of the Roman Egnatian Way from Thessaloniki towards Thrace, you come in 166km to Macedonia's second largest city **Kavalla** (population: 56,000). From here you can reach the island of Thasos and vi
the inland ancient site of Philip
Kavalla has always been the main p
of northern Greece and it was here th
St Paul landed on his way to Philip
(Kavalla was then called Neapolis). B
hind the town rises Mount Simvilc
this glorious setting makes Kavalla o
of Greece's prettier mainland sea-por

The old harbour and the streets c
full of character. The former citadel ov
looks the new city from a rocky promo
tory to the east, and it is to here that y
should head for an atmospheric str
around the old Turkish quarter, kno
as the **Panayia.** Here you will also fi
the liveliest *tavernas*.

Just above the harbour is the co
spicuous multi-domed **Imaret** whi
was built as an almshouse for Turki
theological students and is now a r
taurant. The Imaret's patron w
Mehmet Ali, born here in 1769. You c
visit his attractive wood-panelled hou
with its kitchen, stables and hare
North of the **Byzantine Citadel** (op
10 a.m. - 7 p.m) run the surviving spa
of a 16th-century **Turkish Aqueduc**

The city's **Archaeological Museu**
(open Tuesday-Sunday 8:30 a.m - 3 p.
entrance 400dr) is to the west of t
harbour and has some fine painted H
lenistic terracotta figurines, mosaics a
a reconstruction of a Macedonian to
chamber. Two blocks behind is the **F**
Art and Modern Art Museum (ope
a.m - 11 a.m and 6 p.m - 9 p.m) w
traditional Macedonian costumes as w
as some modern wood and stone scu

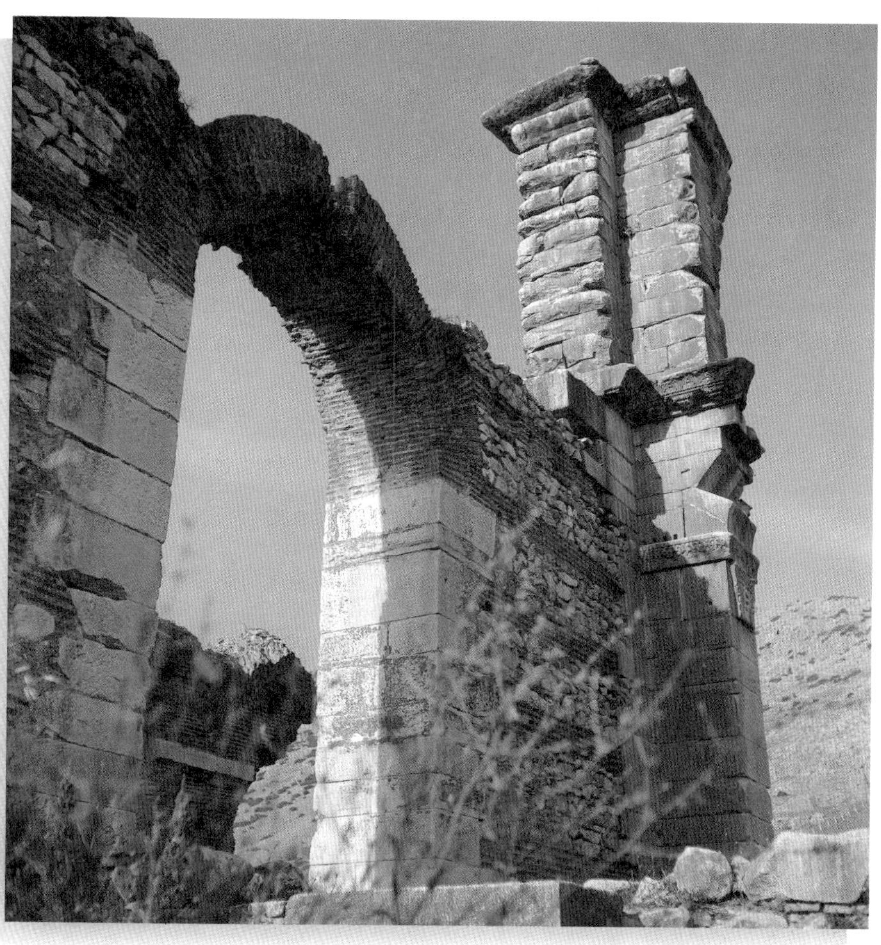

St. Paul passed through the town of Kavalla on his way to Philippi. These Byzantine ramparts stand as stoic reminders.

'es by Polignotis Vigis who was born Thasos, but emigrated to the United ıtes.

Philippi

:een km to the north of Kavalla (20- nutes by bus) is **Philippi** (open Tues- y-Sunday 8:30 a.m - 3 p.m; entrance)dr) through the center of which the Roman Egnatian Way once ran. This was the most important Roman city of eastern Europe, and has quite a history. Named after Philip II of Macedon, the surrounding plains were the site of the Battle of Philippi in 42 BC in which the Republican armies of the assassins of Julius Caesar, Brutus and Cassius were defeated by Caesar's nephew Octavian (the future emperor Augustus). Saint Paul made his first Greek converts here

Ruins of the Roman Forum.

in AD 49, and was imprisoned for his efforts.

The rectangular plan of the central Roman Forum is clear, though its surrounding buildings are ruined: the columns to the south are those of a sixth century Christian basilica, on which the architect attempted to place a dome. To its south-east are the well-preserved marble seats of an earlier Roman latrine.

On the north side of the road another basilica built on a terrace: the right of the stairway is a Rom crypt thought to be **St Paul's Prison**

A modern annual drama festiva held (weekends mid-July to early A gust) in the restored fourth century **Theatre**, cut into the hillside Gre fashion. The **Museum** (open Tuesd Sunday 8:30 a.m - 5 p.m; entrance 400 contains several representative fir

Excavated 4th-century theatre, where Roman gladiators fought.

m various stages of the city's history. the north you can climb to the medial towers of the **Acropolis**, from here view over the whole site is excellent.

Entering Thrace

irty km east of Kavalla you cross the stos river into Thrace. Fifty km from valla is the large town of Xanthi pulation: 32,000).

To the north of the main square is old quarter with narrow streets and nderful old houses – the homes of the althy 19th-century tobacco merants, and a bazaar. Travel 26km th, you'll come to ancient **Abdera**, ich was built on the coast in the 4th-century BC. There are well-preserved defensive walls, Hellenistic houses, Roman baths and early Christian basilicas.

Eastwards from Xanthi, the towns become increasingly Turkish in aspect. Forty-eight km further on from Abdera, is **Komotini** (population: 34,000), a garrison town 22km from the Bulgarian border.

In the main square of **Plateia Ireni** are functioning Turkish mosques, cafes and stalls selling interesting market wares (Tuesday is market day). The Archaeological Museum (open 9 a.m - 5 p.m) contains objects from all over Thrace, and provides an excellent introduction to the pre-history and history of the area, up to the Byzantine period.

Holy Mount Athos

You are not allowed to enter the easternmost peninsula of the **Mount Athos**, without a permit previously obtained from either the Foreign Ministry in Athens (Directorate of Churches, 3 Odos Akademias) or the Ministry of Northern Greece in Thessaloniki (Directorate of Civil Affairs, Plateia Dioikitiriou). You must also be male and over 18 and hold a letter of recommendation from your embassy or consulate in Athens or Thessaloniki. The embassy needs to be convinced that you wish to visit Athos for academic reasons – i.e. as a student of religion or art, or as a writer. If you are a clergyman, you require additional authorization from the Ecumenical Patriarchate of Constantinople. Only ten persons per day are allowed into the "Monk's Republic" and you therefore need to organize your visit months in advance. The permits allow you to stay for four days as a guest of the community.

The "Monks Republic" on Mount Athos, was set up by a Byzantine imperial edict in 1060. Though often described as "autonomous" it is actually part of the Greek state, but is allowed its own administration. It is therefore subject to Greek laws and there is a Greek civil administrator to keep it under state control.

The Community

The first monastery, **Lavra,** was founded by Saint Anathasios in AD 963. Today there are some 20 inhabited monasteries clinging to the slopes of the Holy Mountain, together with

The Monk's Republic.

about 700 related houses. At the height its activity, Athos had a population of 40,0 monks; 39,000 of them were sold into sl ery by the Crusaders. Apart from this dev tating intrusion, the community has mained virtually untouched by the outs world, and many of its former custo continue to differ from the rest of Gree Their own Orthodox calendar starts the y 17 days after ours, and their time zone is f hours later than the closest lay community Ouranopolis. In the census of 1981, Athos nu bered just 1,500 residents, with just 25 mo still living at each of the open monasteries.

Orthodox Traditions

The Athos monks follow the basic precepts the Orthodox religion, and the services similar to those you would hear elsewhere Greece, as well as in other Orthodox cent such as Moscow or Bucharest. The monks sp a number of languages and will gladly disc their beliefs with interested visitors.

Other attractions include one of the b collections of religious art in the world; there many beautiful Bibles, icons and frescoes for lovers. In the daytime, you can walk from m astery to monastery enjoying the unspoilt a luscious forests and flowers of the Athos mo tain range. You have to be inside the monast before sunset when the doors are locked.

The monks grow their own food, and spe their non-working hours at worship or religi study during the mornings, whilst they enj siesta in the afternoon. The evenings are sp dining and talking with any guests. Din generally consists of their home-grown veg bles: aubergines, olives, onions, cucumber a tomatoes; they also bake their own bread a there is the occasional fresh fish from the rounding sea. Home-produced wine and e *ouzo* are offered to the visitor.

St. Paul's Prison in Philippi.

Alexandroupolis & Soufli

ıally you reach Alexandroupolis ›pulation: 35,000) on the coast 355km ṣt of Thessaloniki. It was named in ↄ 1920s after the modern Greek King opposed to his ancient namesake. ere is a long sandy beach and the terfront is lively in the evenings, with ↄ locals promenading and drinking in the cafés around the lighthouse.

Thirty km up the Evros valley, **Soufli** (population: 5,000) on the Turkish border, is the place to shop for locally produced silk. The silkworm was brought here 300 years ago from Constantinople. You can return from Alexandroupolis to Athens, by train in about 8 hours, or, if the feeling takes you, make the 300km trip across the Turkish border to exotic Istanbul.

Sporades

The islands of the northern Aegean fall into two main groups. The Sporades Islands which lie to the north of the Cyclades, with the large island of Euboea, close to the Attic mainland. The north-eastern islands of Samos, Chios, Lesbos, Limnos, Samothrace and Thasos, do not have a collective name, but form a group lying to the north of the Dodecanese: all except Thasos are close to the coast of Turkey. These beautiful islands are less well known than the more southern groups, and therefore have a greater proportion of unspoiled beaches. The island of Skiathos has the famous Koukounaries beach, with its golden sands backed by the shady green of lofty pine trees.

…ne ruins of the kastro of Mytilene, …esbos reach out to deep blue seas.

To the east lies Skopelos, surrounded by reefs and pretty villages full of character. Skyros, rich in history and legend, is the largest of the Sporades and is renowned for its beautifully carved wooden furniture, decorated with traditional Byzantine designs.

The Islands of the North-East Aegean

The islands of Lesbos, Chios and Samos are accessible by boat from Piraeus (duration 12 hours), or by plane from Athens (about one hour). **Lesbos** (population: 89,000) is the northernmost and is the third largest Greek island after Crete and Euboea. It is a wonderful place, rich in cultural tradition and architectural legend, its famous native writers ranging from the sixth century BC poetess Sappho, to the modern poet Odysseus Elytis and novelist Stratis Myrivilis. It also gave birth to the Greek painter Theophilos, whose works can be seen in their own museum. The landscape of Lesbos is more variable than most, with large unattractive flat areas of cultivated land, alternating with barren, rocky regions; to counter this are green pine and oak woods, together with olive groves. The island's proximity to Turkey has left its mark on the architecture, with even the most remote villages often boasting a minaret.

Mytilene's Museums

The island is also known by the name of its main town and sea-port **Mytilene** (population: 24,000) which lies on the east coast facing the Turkish coast. Its 14th-century **Genoese *kastro*** (castle) sits on a promontory with the town to either side. Beneath it once lay the Temple of Demeter and Kore of the ancient cit The **Archaeological Museum** (ope Tuesday-Sunday 8:30 a.m - 3 p.m; en trance 400dr) lies behind the ferry bo quay and contains some excellent m saics from a Hellenistic house ar terracotta votive figurines offered Demeter and Kore at their temple (exc vated beneath the *kastro*).

The town also has a new **Byzantir Museum** (open Monday-Saturday 9 a. - 1 p.m; entrance 100dr) behind tl domed Italian Baroque-style 19th-ce tury **Church of St Therapon**, at tl back of the harbour. From here you cc cover the bazaar area by walking nort wards up Odhos Ermou, and wanderir off along the narrow streets towards tl *kastro*, where from mid-July to mid-Se tember, open-air musical concerts a held in the grounds.

For more culture, head along tl coast four kilometers south to **Vare** and then one-and-a-half km inland **Akrotiri** where there are two fascina ing and unexpected collections: tl **Theophilus Museum** (open Tuesda Sunday 9 a.m - 1 p.m and 4:30 p.m - p.m; entrance 100dr) houses work l the native Primitive painter Theophilc whilst the **Teriade Museum** (san hours) holds the collection of the nati modern art publisher Teriade and i cludes watercolours and engravings l Leger, Picasso, Miro and Shagall.

The east coast beaches are not th good, and you should head for **Moliv** on the north coast, for a more pictu esque harbour resort, with the best bea

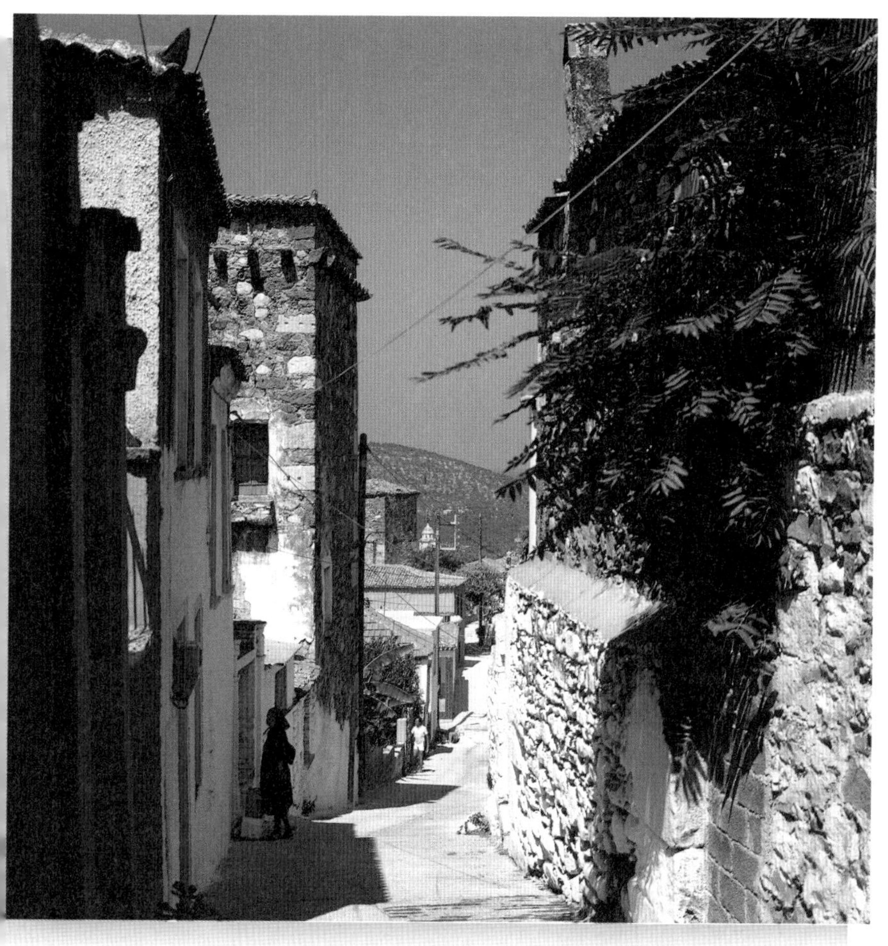

Domestic architecture in Lesbos.

e km south at **Petra**.

Chios

ios (population: 50,000) lies 50km ıth of Lesbos. It is popular with pack- tours, but its interior remains un- ilt and there are good beaches around island. **Chios Town** (also known as ora) lies in the east, opposite Turkey.

There was a bad earthquake in 1881 so most of the town today is modern and concrete, apart from the 14th century **Genoese *kastro*** (castle) and the **Old Mosque**. Chios town is a lively and attractive place, with good shopping in the **bazaar** and an atmospheric waterfront, particularly in the evenings.

The **Convent of Nea Moni** is worth a visit – a 14-km journey from Chios; there are a few buses, and a taxi can

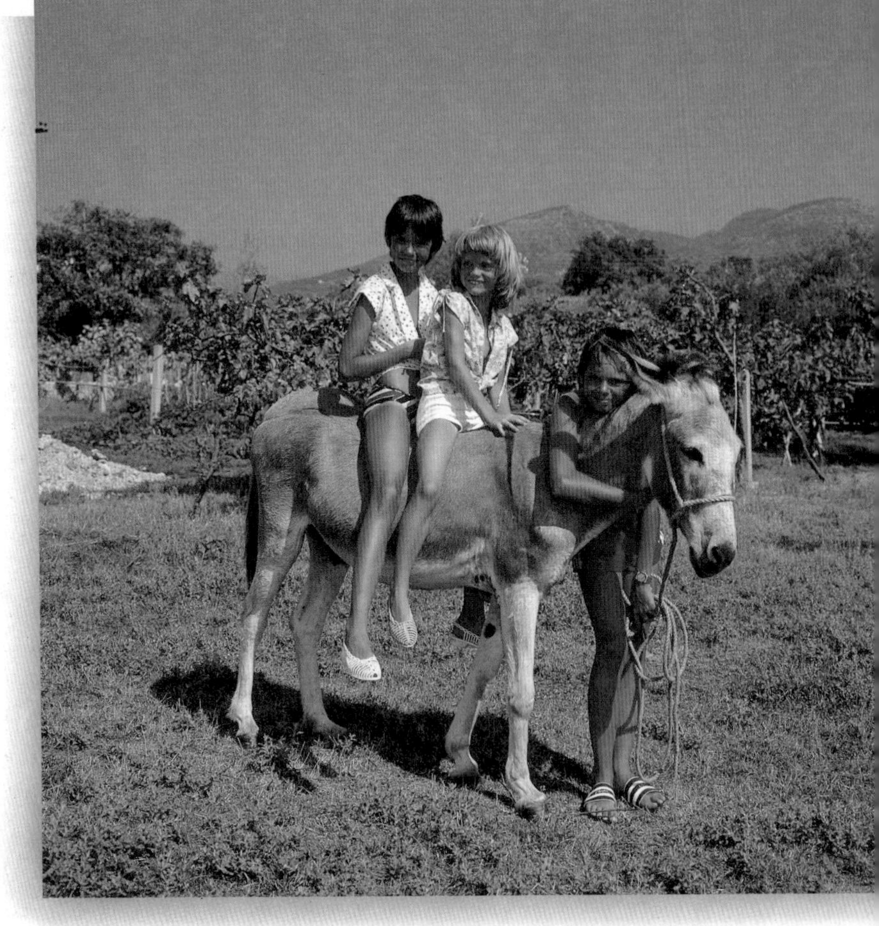

Angelic locals.

work out reasonably if you negociate the price before leaving town. The 11th-century church in a beautiful mountain setting, more than repays the cost of the outing. It was founded by the Byzantine Emperor Constantine IX on the spot where a peasant discovered a miraculous icon. The Byzantine mosaics are amongst the earliest still *in situ* in Greece, and include the only example in Greece of a *Deposition from the Cross*; others follow the lives of Christ and the Virg

Samos

Samos (population: 31,000), 70 km f ther south, lies only three km off Turkish coast and was connected in p historic times. The mountains wh cross the island from east to west ar continuation of the Turkish mainlo nge. The north of the island is rocky, hilst the south is flatter with some ood beaches. It is green and fertile, and as been renowned since antiquity for ; agricultural produce and sweet.

The island has a mixed history; in ntiquity it became an important and osperous place under the sixth cen-ry BC tyrant Polykrates, who com-anded a mini-empire with his power-l navy; it attracted famous writers and ilosophers including Aesop (of ***Fa-es*** fame) and Pythagoras who moved Italy to escape e tyranny. In e 15th century mos fell to rkish pirates, ho massacred e population. e island was populated with eeks a century later, t the Samians suffered during the ar of Independence; in spite of win-ng a naval victory in the strait, the stern powers ceded it to the Turks in 30, but it was re-united with Greece in 12. It remains a rather unsettled cul-re with few surviving folk traditions.

Vathy is the capital and port of mos, on the north-east of the island, it s founded in 1830 under Turkish rule d is relatively dull for a Greek sea-wn – there is nowhere clean to swim d the nightlife is moderate. There is wever an excellent **Archaeological useum** (open Tuesday-Sunday 8:30 n - 3 p.m; entrance 500 dr) contain-ing a colossal archaic early sixth century Greek *kouros* (male nude statue), dedicated to Hera in her sanctuary. There are also a number of Egyptian objects which reflect trade with the Nile, during the archaic period.

The eastern side of the island has been over-developed for package tours, but you can find remote spots elsewhere. It is possible to tour the island in a day in a hired car – the circular coastal road around the island is 85 km long – and this is the best way to get around as there are few buses. Fourteen km south of Vathy is the island's major resort **Pithagoria**, named after the ancient philosopher. The small harbour was the main ancient port of Samos, now a lively place with waterfront bars and bobbing boats.

There is occasional evidence of the ancient city, the exciting highlight being the **Tunnel of Eupalinos** bored under the mountain behind the town in the sixth century BC to provide water and an escape route in times of siege (Eupalinos was the architect). You can enter the tunnel with a torch for about a kilometer – it has collapsed in its center – and then scramble over the hill following the ancient city walls to see the tunnel opening at the other side. For swimming follow the pebble-and-sand

Pirates of Old

Pirates have operated successfully in the eastern Mediterranean from the time of the earliest ships of Greek prehistory through to the Barbary corsairs of the 18th century. It has always been a most lucrative profession, to chase and board richly-laden merchant ships or to land on foreign shores to make short, sharp raids on local communities.

Homer's Pirates

In the tales of Homer, it is the Viking-type sea-raider that usually carries out piracy. Odysseus himself tells an imaginative tale about a raid he made as a pirate on Egypt. His ships anchored at the mouth of the Nile and the men, driven by greed, plundered the land, killing the men and carrying off their women and children. The people of the nearest city heard what was happening and sent out boats and soldiers who caught up with Odysseus' men, killing or enslaving them.

Although Odysseus is fabricating, Homer's listeners must have been familiar with this kind of piracy. One of Odysseus' nurses had been the daughter of a wealthy Phoenician citizen but was kidnapped in a pirate raid and ended up on the slave market, which sold the older women as nurses, and the younger ones as prostitutes. The men were nearly always killed. Home most famous monster, the one-eyed Cyclc asks Odysseus and his companions, "Strange who are you? Are you here for trade? Or ha you wandered recklessly over the waves l pirates who go about risking their necks cause trouble to others?"

Pirating as a Profession

In the fifth century BC the historian Thucydic told how "in ancient times both Greeks a non-Greeks who lived along the coasts or on t islands, once they began to cross in ships each other's shores, turned to piracy...Th would fall upon and plunder the towns, whi were either unwalled or mere clusters of lages. Most of their livelihood came this way was a pursuit which was even thought to be honourable profession in its way...As a result the chronic piracy, cities long ago, both islands and along the coasts of the mainlar were built away from the sea." This agrees w what we see in Greece today – how often do arrive by sea on an island, only to find that t main town is several kilometres up a steep roa

Greek vase-paintings occasionally depi small low pirate ships chasing larger merch ships around the outsides of Athenian drinkir

beach to the west of the town.

If you wish to see the famous **Heraion** (open Tuesday-Sunday 8:30 a.m - 3 p.m; entrance 300dr) you must take a taxi eight km out of Pithagoria. This is the birthplace of the goddess Hera, and the remains include the foundations of the massive 8x20 Ionic-columned temple. The west of the island is beautifully rugged and has a number of unspoilt beaches which can be reached from the small port of **Karlovasi**, 51 km along the north coast from Vathy. Though a rather unattractive mode place, the people are friendly and w point you in the direction of the islan best beaches, but you will need a car reach them.

Euboea

Euboea is the second largest Greek land, but unlike Crete (the largest) does not really feel like an island, lyi as it does closely parallel to the mai

ps. These not only provide graphic images of e activity, but must have been of enough erest to rich Athenians, for them to be de- :ted at all. Presumably Athenian drinkers had perience of pirates or at least knew people o had.

Combating Piracy

acy has always affected trade; since antiquity, oneylenders and insurers have fixed their ces or invested in shipping according to the tential loss which could be brought about by acy.

The great Athenian naval empire even set up aval base to counteract pirate ships. Pirates st have been a constant worry to the people he islands: an inscription from Naxos records v pirates held 280 of its citizens to ransom, ilst the small nearby island of Amorgos had ne thirty of its women and girls carried away slavery.

Pirates could be useful however; they were en paid as mercenaries to fight against an emy navy. Philip of Macedon paid pirates n Crete to harass shipping travelling to and n Rhodes, whilst the 18th-century English y enlisted Barbary corsairs to help defeat the kish navy.

nd. Buses take just under two hours m Athens to the main town of **Khalkis** opulation: 45,000): no ferry is required a bridge straddles the narrow (70m at s point) "Euripos" strait. Ancient leg- d tells of Poseidon splitting Euboea m the mainland with his trident.

Khalkis makes an excellent base m which to explore Euboea since it is the center of the bus and road net- rk. The modern town lies over the er parts of the ancient city, with the liest remains still visible to the east. Most of the town is modern and indus- trial, but the Euripos bridge takes you into the more attractive **Kastro** area; the former Turkish quarter of the town, whose antique character immediately hits you as you pass the **mosque** and the **Church of St Paraskevi**, with its pointed Gothic arcades and re-used classical marble columns. There is also a **Turk- ish Aqueduct**.

South of **Khalkis** there is little to see until you reach **Eretria** (population: 2,500), built like Khalkis on an ancient predecessor, whose remains include well- preserved walls and house-foundations, together with a theatre. From the thea- tre walk up to the **Acropolis**, from where on a clear day you can see the mainland heights of Pentelikon and the Parnassos. Continuing south there are more classi- cal ruins (houses, walls and a Venetian fortress on the Acropolis) at **Dystos**.

One hundred and twenty seven km south of Khalkis stands the small and attractive sea-port of **Karistos** (popula- tion: 4,000), which has a beach and some good little *tavernas*. If you feel like doing some walking, take the road in- land three km to the village of **Mili**, and ask directions from the little square, to the red-stoned Venetian fort of **Castel Rosso**. You can also reach the summit of **Mount Okhi** (1,405m) in three hours from Mili: this is well worth the effort for the magnificent landscape and views.

For uncrowded sandy beaches on Euboea head for the town of **Kimi** on the central eastern coast of the island, but turn off at Avlonari to **Okhthonia**, where

A touch of the sun perhaps.

you can enjoy a swim and explore the hill-town with its pretty little church and Venetian tower. The roads to the northwest of the island are less travelled and in bad condition, but from Strofilia there is a road to the north-east which passes some good beaches: the resorts here are crowded with Greeks in the summer months.

Skyros – An Island of Legend

From Kimi on the central east coast of Euboea, a ferry to Skyros takes two and a half hours. **Skyros** (population: 3,000) is the largest and most easterly of the Sporadic group of islands. The island is full of legend: the ancient hero Achil was sent here dressed as a woman by h mother Thetis, in order to avoid t Trojan War where she knew he would killed; he stayed at the court of Ki Lykomedes until Odysseus found hi out and took him to Troy – and to h untimely death. The Athenian prin Theseus died here, some say he fell of cliff by accident, others that Ki Lykomedes killed his royal guest. T classical Athenians discovered Theseu bones in the fifth century BC and turned them to a special shrine in At ens. The island is an interesting pla where you will still see traditional cloth worn by the elders: the women we embroidered skirts and yellow hec scarves, the men wear clogs and bag

The ancient ruins of Moria.

·users.

The island is divided into two parts a low isthmus. To the north it is green d fertile, to the south rugged and rren. The main town is **Khora** (Skyros wn), which is an attractive place to y. From here you can reach good aches at the nearby villages of **ıgazia** and **Molos**. Khora itself stands the foot of a high rock, on top of ich is the ***kastro***, a ruined Venetian fort on classical and Byzantine foundations. It was from these rocks that Theseus either fell or was pushed.

Back in the town, you can see the **Memorial to Rupert Brooke**, who died here in 1915; he is buried in an olive grove on the south of the island. The poet of World War I is represented in Classical bronze, and the statue's nudity shocked the locals when it was set up. Nearby are the **Archaeological**

The generation gap.

Museum (open Tuesday-Saturday 9 a.m - 3 p.m, Sunday 9:30 a.m - 2:30 p.m; entrance free) and the **Faltaitz Museum** (open 10 a.m - 1 p.m and 5:30 p.m - 8 p.m): both have interesting little collections reflecting the island's cultural history.

Skopelos

Skopelos (population: 3,000) can reached by boat from Kimi (three an half hours journey), Volos (four hou or Ayios Konstandinos (five hours). I

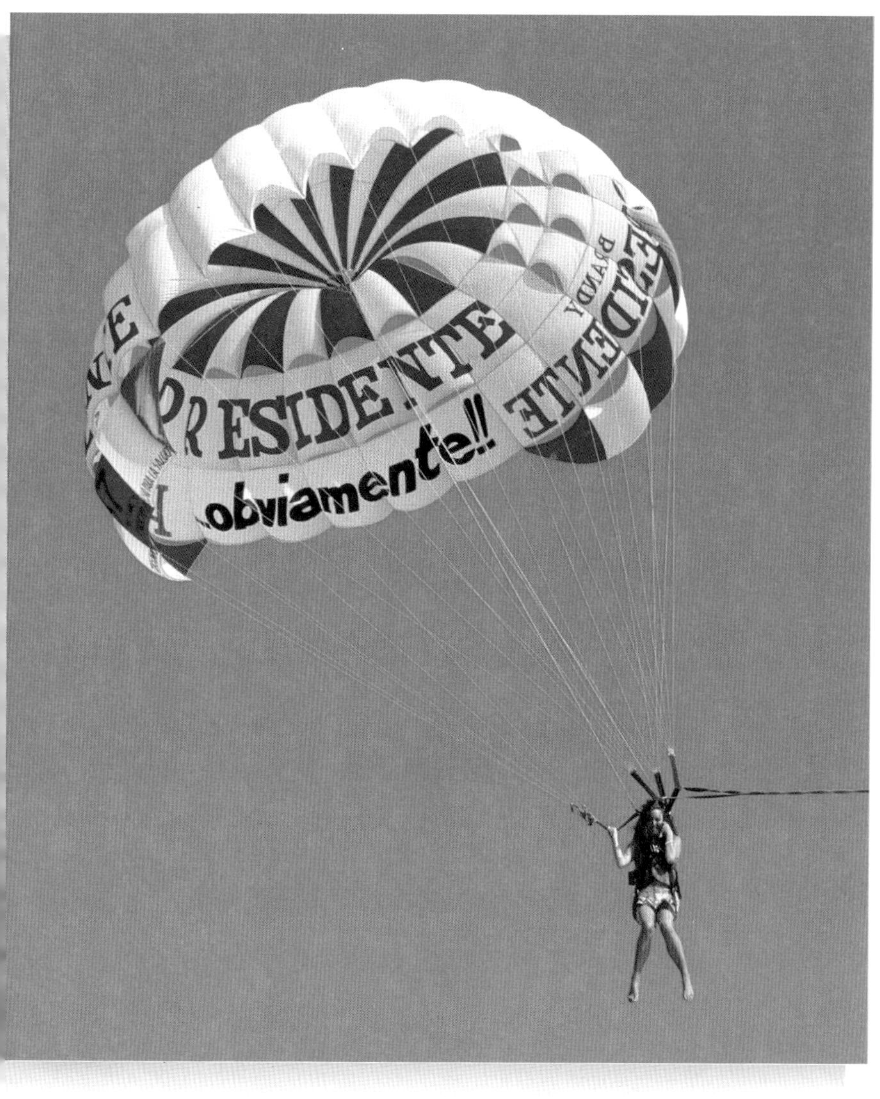

Getting highly-strung!

reen and cultivated island, with natu- pines on its rugged slopes, whilst the ver areas are covered with vineyards d olive-groves, along with fruits, in- ding almonds and pears.

The main center is **Khora** (Skopelos vn), which is set in the center of a broad, circular bay. It looks magnificent as you approach by sea, with its glowing whitewashed blue slate-roofed houses and 123 churches rising above the sea. It is a lively town with plenty of shops, though these tend to be touristy and pricey. The churches contain icons from the 17th and 18th centuries as well as beautifully carved altar-screens.

There are walks eastwards from the town to the picturesque convents of Ev**angelistria** and **Prodhromos**, and to the restored monastery of **Metamorphossi**. The nearest beach is at **Staphylos** four km away, and you can lunch there at a shady little *taverna*.

Skiathos

Skiathos (population: 4,000) can be reached by boat from Kimi (five and a half hours), Volos (three hours) or Ayios Konstandinos (three hours). There is also an airport with 45-minute flights from Athens. It has many sandy beaches which have attracted large numbers of package tourists and many find it overcommercialized. However, it is well worth a visit for its really excellent beaches, and as with all Greek islands, you can find beautiful, unspoilt landscapes, a short walk or bus-ride from the main resorts.

Skiathos Town is the port and main center, and some good nightlife is available at the *Kirki Bar* (Jazz/Blues); for disco try the *Banana Bar*. There is little in the way of culture here, but the atmosphere is fun if you do not mind the crowds. If you wish to sample some of the best **beaches** in Greece take the road west to K**oukounaries**, a glorious expanse of pine-fringed sand and clear water, where all water-sports are available. If you do not like the crowds, there are quieter beaches on the way there

Thasos

Thasos (population: 13,000) is the m northerly Greek island and is a popul resort for the northern mainland Gree There are boats from mainland Kava and Keramoti (one hour), which are ju 12km across the sea. It is an unusua circular island which reflects its v canic origins, it has a mountainous terior, with slopes covered with che nuts and pines. Lower down are oli groves, and the island is famous for beehives and honey. The island's lo history has been strongly influenced its gold and silver mines.

Thasos Town (Limen), is the ca tal on the north coast which lies on t site of the ancient centre. It is mos modern, but has an attractive watersi with a local fishing harbour and san beach.

From late July to mid-August drama festival is held in the **ancie theatre** above the town; above th you can climb up to the **Acropolis**, w its **Genoese Fort** and ruined classi temples of Apollo and Pan. Back in t town, the m**useum** and excavated a cient **Agora** should be visited (op Tuesday-Saturday 8:30 a.m - 3 p. Sunday 9:30 a.m - 2:30 p.m). From t town buses will take you on a circuit the whole island, passing throu **Limenaria**, the quieter second town the island, on the west coast.

Samothraki

amothraki (population: 3,000) is accessible by boat from **Alexandropoulis** 2km). It is a rugged island of high anite ridges and wild mountain goats. Homers' writings, Poseidon sat on the mmit of **Mount Fengari** (1,600m) to atch the Trojan War. The island was sited by ancient pilgrims who came to orship at the **Sanctuary of the Great ods**: this is still the main cultural attraction of the island. You arrive at **amariotissa** on the west coast, which as a fairly lively waterfront with *vernas* and discos. From here you can ke a bus, to the more picturesque land village of **Khora**, with its ruined zantine fort and whitewashed houses.

Northwards from here along a track r by road from Kamariotissa) is the llage of **Palaiopolis**, the Sanctuary of e Great Gods (open Tuesday-Sunday 30 a.m - 3 p.m; entrance 200dr) spectacularly situated in a ravine nearby, th torrents descending to the sea. The **useum** (same hours) provides an excellent introduction with its models of e original shrines and other buildgs. The site is well-labelled, and a axed wander round the ruins makes r a fascinating outing. From the museum a path leads through the remains the sanctuary. To the left is the **aaktoron**, a hall where ancient pilims were initiated into the Mysteries the Great Gods, who were pre-Greek ds of the Earth, including a Earth Mother and a Phallic male deity; later Greeks continued to appease these elemental forces. Beyond is the **Arsinoeon**, the largest surviving circular ancient Greek building; it dates back to the third century BC, when the Hellenistic Egyptian Queen Arsinoe dedicated it to the Great Gods.

Further on is the **Temenos**, an open rectangular courtyard which once contained a statue of Aphrodite and Pothos, the male and female gods of sexual desire. Beyond are more initiation halls and the outline of the **theatre**.

On the ridge above the theatre once stood the **Nike of Samothrace**, the winged statue of the Goddess of Victory, discovered by the French and taken to the Louvre in 1863. It formed part of a fountain monument commemorating a local naval victory.

Lemnos

Lemnos (population: 16,000) lies midway between Mount Athos and Turkey. Like Samothraki it has a volcanic origin. You can fly here from Athens (45 mins) or Thessaloniki (40 mins); there are ferry connections from various mainland ports, but it is not easy to get to by sea. Lemnos is not very attractive, with mediocre beaches, small resorts, and little in the way of sightseeing. The town of **Kastron** (or Myrina) has some old Turkish streets and well-preserved Turkish walls, following the lines of the classical town.

The Dodecanese

To the south and east of Athens are the islands of the southern Aegean, consisting of two main groups, the Cyclades to the west and the Dodecanese (including Samos and Rhodes) to the east, together with the great island of Crete forming a southern boundary to the Aegean Sea. The Dodecanese islands are the most remote of the Greek islands from Athens and the closest to Turkey. They have had a troubled history, most recently being the scenes of fierce fighting between British and German troops during the Second World War, after which they were finally united with Greece. The Italians occupied the islands between 1913 and 1943, and their grandiose fascist architecture can still be seen on most of the islands, alongside classical temples and medieval castles. Italian is still spoken by the older Greeks, who were forced to learn it by the fascist regime. The Dodecanese are great for island-hopping, with daily ferry connections between them, and fairly regular sailings to Piraeus, Athens (about 12

ew of Lindos town and beach.

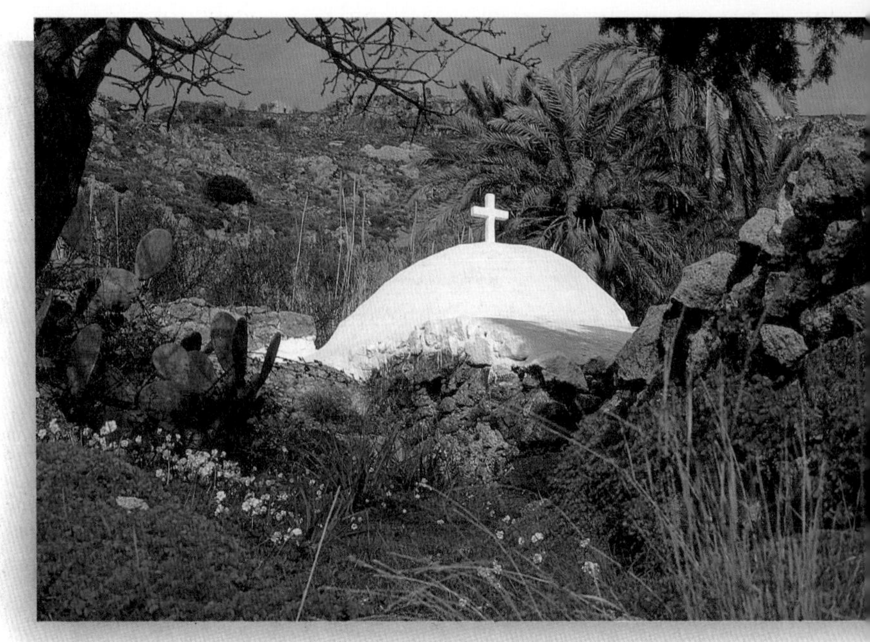

St. John's Chapel at Sikamia in Patmos.

hours). There are flights from Athens to Rhodes, Leros, Kassos, Kos and Karpathos.

Patmos

Working from north to south, and concentrating on the more important islands in the group, **Patmos** (population 2,500) is the most northerly – some 50km south of Samos. It is relatively small (39 sq km) but is a very beautiful island, its traditional character largely preserved by the monks of St John, whose monastery stands at the highest point of the island. In the Roman period, the island was reserved for exiled political prisoners, the most famous of these being St John the Divine, who was se here in AD 95 by the Emperor Domitia The island suffered during the mediev period from Saracen pirates. In 1088 Byzantine monastery was establish here in honour of St John, but t Venetians took the island in 1207, a it remained in Italian hands into t present century.

The main port of **Skala** has a live square which opens directly off the h bour; it is surrounded by Italian arcad which offer good places to eat. Or and-a-half km north is the excelle **Meloi Beach**.

Travelling uphill and inland fro Skala, by bus or by mule-track, you w reach Patmos Town (also known Khora) with its pretty alleys and 16

Waiting for the crowds.

'th century Italian houses built around e base of the **Monastery of St John** enerally open daily between 0800- :00 hours). This is a cool and shaded ace to visit on a hot day, with plenty of ırly medieval treasures to be seen.

Following the track back to Patmos u will pass the **Cave of St Anne** where John received a series of divine revela- ons, recorded in the New Testament ook of the Bible, ***Revelations***. The is- nd is excellent for walkers, and this is so the best way to find its many un- oilt beaches.

Leros

venty km southeast of Patmos (one hour by boat) lies **Leros** (population: approximately 7,000) which is best known in Greece for its prisons and lunatic asylum. That said, it is a relatively unspoilt island of a similar jigsaw-piece shape and size to Patmos, with an attractive modern Italian art-deco sea-port at **Lakki**, laid out with broad streets and piazzas.

The nearest beach is to the west at **Koulouki**, but you might prefer to stay in the island's capital of **Platanos** – situated on a ridge three km from Lakki – which has a fine Byzantine castle, rebuilt by the Knights of St John.

A short distance to the north and south respectively are the fishing villages of **Ayia Marina** and **Panteli**, with their good beaches. There are discos and

Kos was the birthplace of Hippocrates, the Father of Medicine.

lively bars and cafes, and you can take the bus (or walk) to other parts of the island, which consists of wooded hills and valleys cultivated with olives, vines, fruit and tobacco.

Kalymnos

Kalymnos (population: 15,000) is to the south of Leros (2 hours by boat) and slightly larger than both Patmos and Leros. The island is shaped like a seated dragon, its northern head turning back towards Leros, and it is for the most part rocky and barren. The valleys are however fertile enough to grow olives, fruit and crops. The history of the island is linked to that of Kos to the south, and it too has seen Venetian, Rhodian a Turkish rulers. During the more rece Italian occupation, the inhabitants fiantly painted the churches and hou in the blue and white colours of t Greek National flag.

The main port is on the south co at **Pothia**, a busy place, particularly autumn and winter when the spon divers are about. The sponge indus for which Kalymnos was once famo is however dying out owing to disea and every year there seem to be l boats involved. The waterfront has lively cafes and fish *tavernas* – octopu the scrumptious local speciality – w the typical Dodecanese mode Italianate architecture forming a gr diose backdrop.

Tradition is still very much preserved in the islands.

The former capital **Khorio** is three n along the fertile valley leading in- nd from Pothia. Here you should climb sunset to the ruined **Castle of the nights of St John** for fine views of the st coast. The west coast offers several nall resorts with moderate grey, vol- nic sand beaches. From Mirtees you n cross by small boat to the islet of **lendos**, here there are ruined Roman ths, an early Christian basilica, a edieval monastery and a castle – a fun y trip with a *taverna* lunch and swim own in.

Kos

s (population: 20,000) is 10 km south of Kalymnos (one hour by boat) and twice the size. It is shaped like a fish leaping out of the sea from west to east and is the second most popular Dodecanese island after Rhodes, the landscape and culture of which it is often compared to. The problem for the independent traveller is that it is heavily packaged as a tourist resort, and whereas the larger island of Rhodes absorbs the crowds, Kos is always filled to bursting point in the summer months.

The main town and port is **Kos Town**, set in the fish's eye on the northeast coast and again like Rhodes, it has a 15th-century Genoese **Castle of the Knights** (open Tuesday-Sunday 8:30 a.m - 3 p.m; entrance 400dr) dominating its harbour. It also has its share of

Rhodes: Island of the Sun

Today the island of Rhodes is one of the most satisfying Greek islands to visit. There are many excellent beaches as well as good facilities for tennis-players, golfers and windsurfers, together with plenty of nightlife, good food and wine. The historical aspects are also as rich as you will find in Greece.

Birth of an Island

In Greek mythology Zeus decided to apportion the islands of Greece to the other gods and goddesses. Rhodes was selected by the sun god Helios whilst it was still rising from the sea. Helios named it after his favourite sea-nymph, Rhodos, daughter of the Goddess of Love, Aphrodite, who then became his bride. No wonder this island of sun and romance is a favourite honeymoon resort!

Helios and Rhodos had seven sons, and the eldest three divided the island between them; the cities of Ialysos, Kameiros and Lindos were named after them. The Classical Rhodians remembered their patron Helios in an annual festival called Halieia, at the climax of which a four-horse chariot team was thrown into the sea.

The Hellenistic Rhodians honoured Helios with a huge statue, known as the Colossus of Rhodes, which stood almost as high as New York's Statue of Liberty, and became one of the Seven Wonders of the World.

It took 12 years to cast in its sections of hollow bronze and eventually stood beside the harbour, flaming torch in hand to guide the ships. Erected in 290 BC it was a short-lived wonder: in 225 BC it collapsed during an earthquake and lay in pieces for eight centuries before being sold as scrap metal to a Jewish merchant who took it away to Syria.

The Knights of St John

In the Roman period the Apostle Paul visited Rhodes around AD 42 and managed to convert a number of the islanders to Christianity. In 1306 the Knights of St John settled on the island after retreating from Jerusalem via Cyprus. Under their military protection the island enjoye
two centuries of prosperity and security. Th
Order of the Knights of St John was created
the 11th century by a family from Amalfi
Italy. They numbered about 600 members ar
were ruled by a French Grand Master. Th
knights purchased Rhodes from Genoese p
rates, but only controlled the whole island aft
a lengthy siege of the Byzantine fortress. Th
proceeded to build the high walls and the fo
of Rhodes Town which so impressed the mo
ern visitor; there was an additional network
castles all around the coastline, as well as on th
other Dodecanese islands.

Inside the walls of Rhodes Town the Knigh
built a hospital and eight inns, which repr
sented the eight tongues of the Order: En
land, France, Italy, Germany, Castile, Arago
Provence and Auverge – each "tongue" had
defend its own section of wall in the event
siege. By this method they managed to ke
the Turks at bay in the great sieges of 1444 a
1480. The end finally came when Suleiman t
Magnificent besieged the island for six mont
in 1522; Suleiman was enraged with Rhodi
attacks on Moslem pilgrim ships passing t
island. The Turks lost some 50,000 men in t
fighting but won the siege and the Knights f
to Malta.

Italian Style

The Italians governed Rhodes from 1912
1948. Although they were unpopular with t
local Greeks, suppressing the Orthodox Chu
as well as the Greek language, they suppl
the island with the basis to attract touris
Civic buildings were erected in the grandi
Italian style along with good roads, allow
the visitor easy access to all parts of this histo
island.

Today, the classical past can still be seen in
ancient cities of Rhodes, Lindos, Ialysos a
Kameiros, meanwhile the Knights of St Jo
continue to haunt the old town of Rhodes,
well as the castles of nearly every hilltop on
island.

odern Italian-style public buildings, gether with ancient Greek and Roan ruins, attractively peppered by ırkish minarets and palm trees.

To the south of the castle are the attered columns and broken sculpres of the **Ancient *Agora*** (market), ıd the massive Plane Tree of ppocrates, beneath which the "father medicine" Hippocrates (c460-377 BC) said to have taught: it is obviously not at old, but old enough nevertheless! earby is the picturesque 18th-century **osque of Gazi Hassan Pasha** its lower orey now a row of shops.

Forty-five minutes walk to the west the town is the **Asklepieion** (open esday-Sunday 8:30 a.m - 3 p.m; enance 600dr) where there are the Helıistic remains of the healing god kelpios' temple together with later man baths. The **beaches** at Kos are tremely packed, but the nightlife is as t as you would expect in a busy packe resort.

Tilos & Simi

ty km south (one boat a week) is the aller and much quieter island of Tilos pulation: 400) which the ancient ographer Strabo aptly described as ng, high and narrow". **Livadhia** is port on the northeast coast. This is e of those islands whose treasures are den – you can bathe and relax on aceful beaches, and walk into the y interior to discover the seven **Castles of St John**, and the inland village of Megalo **Khorio**. There are tracks from here down to **Eristos beach**, which is served by two *tavernas*.

Simi (population: 2,300) lies 40 km to the north-east of Tilos (one boat a week). It is hilly, with cliffs along much of its coast, occasionally broken by small coves. The island was once more wooded, but the people were renowned shipwrights and the timber supplies were used up during the War of Independence. The main towns on the north coast are the port of **Yialos** and above it **Khorio**, where most of the inhabitants have their homes.

The usual **Castle of St John**, houses remains of a classical **Temple of Athena** within its walls. The **beaches** are pebbly, but often deserted, and walkers can buy a map of footpaths which will take them across to the south coast in about two hours.

Simi's main cultural attraction is the 18th-century **Monastery of St Michael Panormitis** on the south coast, which is accessible by boat. The church has frescoes and offerings to the patron saint from Simians now living all over the world. A little museum attached to the monastery is filled with local curiosities which includes a collection of messages in bottles, washed up on the island.

Rhodes

Rhodes (population: 84,000) the largest

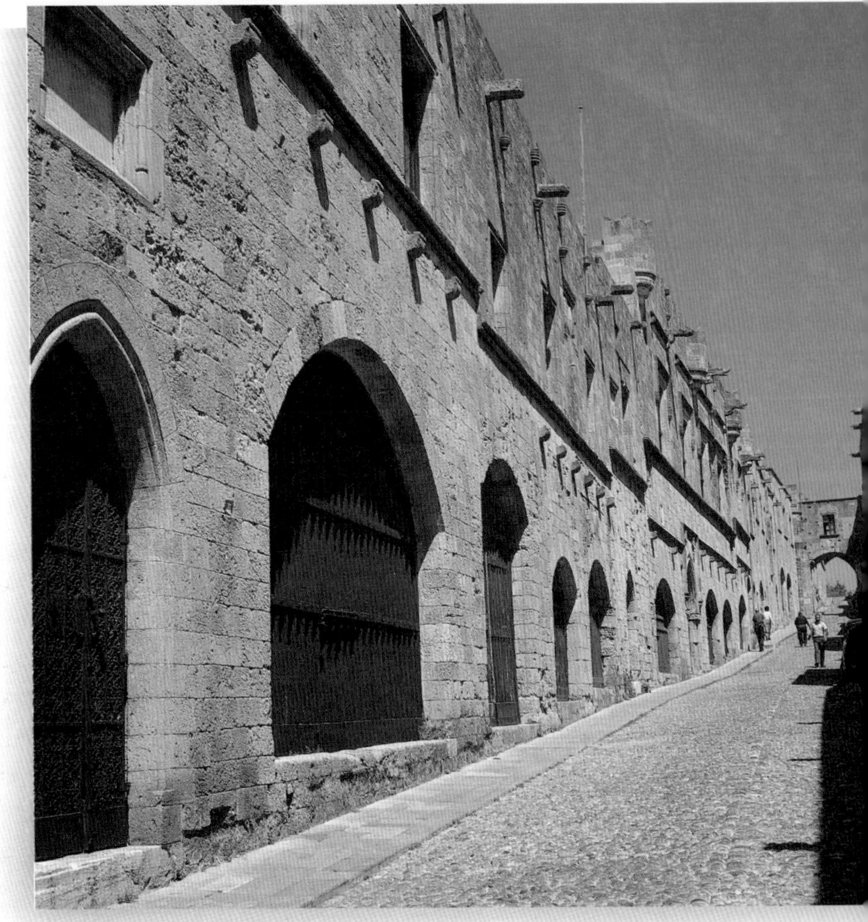

Street of The Knights of St. John in Rhodes.

of the Dodecanese islands, lies 24 km south of Simi, from where one boat crosses each day. There are boats from Rhodes to many other destinations and several daily flights from Athens. It is a popular place, but one which is large enough to absorb the crowds.

The island is particularly rich in natural and cultural beauty, and its capital, the **City of Rhodes** (population: 40,000) has preserved its medieval city to a remarkable degree. The city has to be said, does get very crowded the summer months, but there is much to see and do there that it does seem to matter.

The lively, modern part of the c lies behind **Mandraki harbour**, wh was once the site of the third century **Colossus of Rhodes**; a 27m-high bro statue of Helios, the sun-god, and on the Seven Wonders of the World. It

ıring an earthquake soon after its erec-
ɔn, but lay on the ground for several nturies before finally being melted wn by Saracen pirates. Mandraki is ɔw a yachting marina, its waterfront cked by modern Italian buildings. ere is a crowded beach to the north.

The island was the main base of the ights of St John between 1309 and 22 (when they moved to Malta to cape the Turkish invasion), and re-ains from that period can be seen in e **Old Town** to the south, surrounding e commercial harbour.

The medieval quarter of the Old wn is enclosed within a fine 15th-ntury defensive wall, and is a world to elf. Here you can get lost along the bbled alleyways, never quite know-g what you will find around the next ner.

The 14th-century Palace **of the and Masters** (open Tuesday-Sunday 30-1500 hours; entrance 400dr) was onstructed (after bomb damage) by Italians as a summer residence for ssolini. This was the main fortress of Knights, and its grandiosity reflects ir power and ambitions. The interior particularly richly decorated with ects brought in from elsewhere; there good selection of Hellenistic mosaics n Kos.

On Tuesday and Saturday after-ɔns there is a conducted tour of the dieval walls. The **Street of the ights** is lined with "inns" in which Knights actually dwelt: they are now inly government offices. The street has been tidily restored with coats of arms and other signifiers of the medieval age.

Just before you reach the harbour is the **Archaeological Museum** (open Tuesday-Sunday 8:30 a.m - 3 p.m; entrance 400dr), which was once the Knight's Hospital, and the **Byzantine Museum** (same hours and price), formerly the cathedral.

Both are worth visiting, for their original architecture as well as for their exhibits: the Archaeological collection's highlight is the third century marble *pudica* ("Modest Aphrodite"), so-called because of her strategically placed hands.

To the south of the Palace is the Turkish 16th-century **Mosque of Suleiman**, reconstructed in 1808; this whole area has a more Turkish flavour with its balconies and coffee-houses, though the former bazaar has become too touristy.

Rhodes' Resorts

Around the coast of Rhodes you will find tourist resorts such as **Lindos**, where the beaches tend to be crowded. The west coast is less accessible and rocky, but remains fairly touristy, though the ancient site at **Kameiros** (open 8:30 a.m - 4 p.m; entrance 400dr), is worth an outing (36km by bus from Rhodes). It is beautifully situated on a slope overlooking the sea, and you can see the remains of the *agora* (market-place) tem-

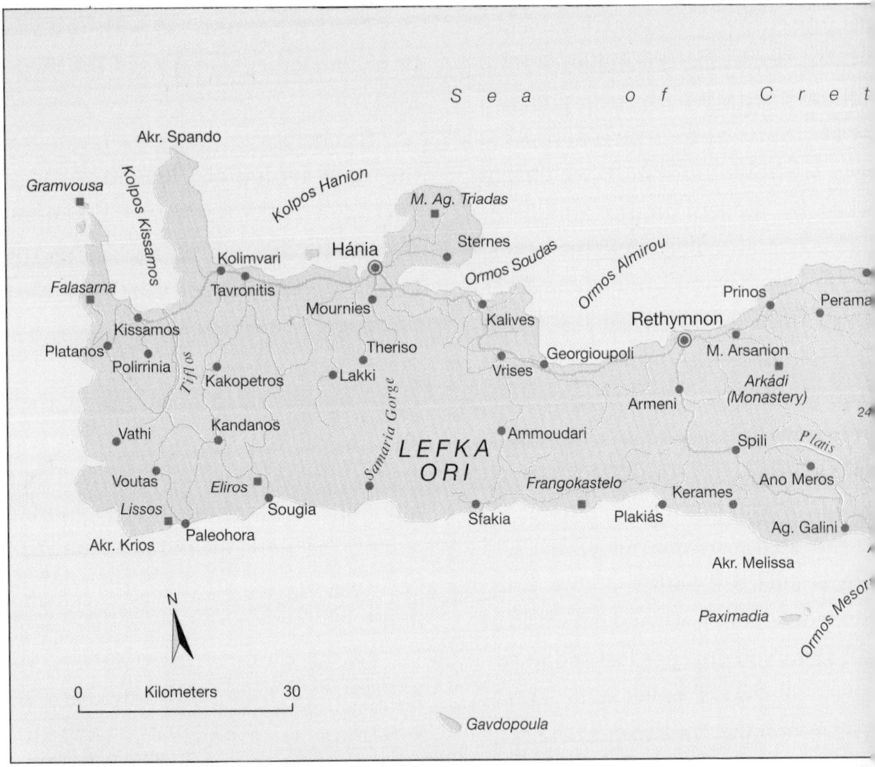

Sea of Crete
Akr. Spando
Gramvousa
Kolpos Kissamos
Kolpos Hanion
M. Ag. Triadas
Hánia
Sternes
Ormos Soudas
Ormos Almirou
Kolimvari
Tavronitis
Falasarna
Mournies
Kalives
Prinos
Perama
Rethymnon
Kissamos
Platanos
Polirrinia
Tiflos
Theriso
Georgioupoli
M. Arsanion
Kakopetros
Lakki
Vrises
Arkádi (Monastery)
Armeni
Samaria Gorge
Vathi
Kandanos
Ammoudari
Spili
Platis
LEFKA ORI
Voutas
Eliros
Frangokastelo
Ano Meros
Keramés
Lissos
Sougia
Sfakia
Plakiás
Ag. Galini
Akr. Krios
Paleohora
Akr. Melissa
N
Paximadia
Ormos Mesor
0 Kilometers 30
Gavdopoula

The King's Throne in the Palace of Knossos, Crete.

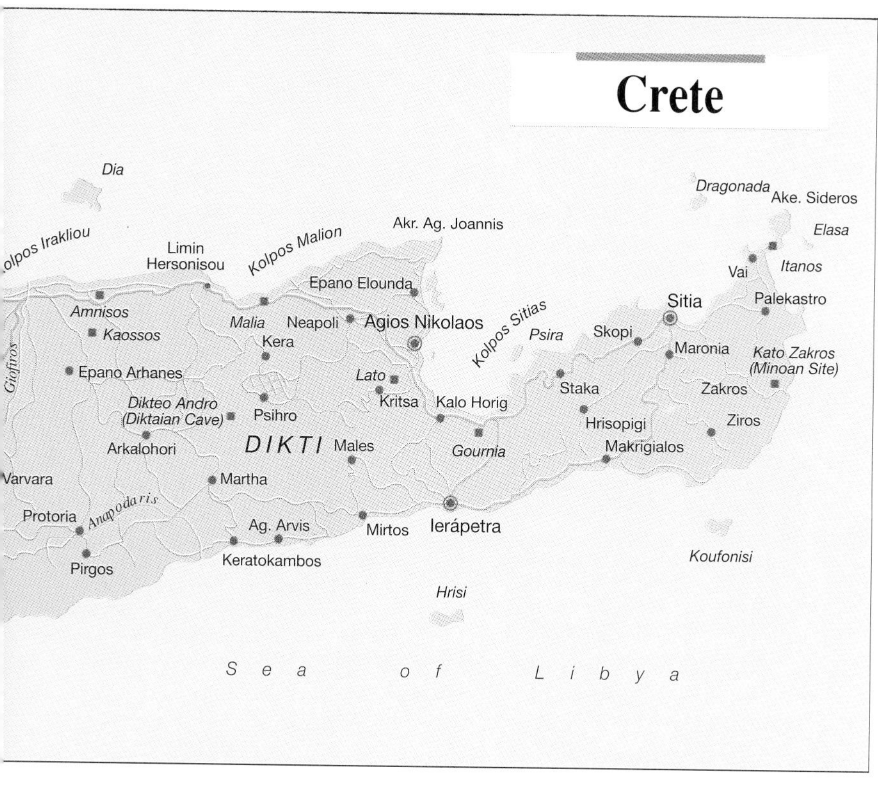

s and walls.

Afterwards you might eat and swim the beach below, before taking the ; back. The hilly and wooded interior Rhodes is well worth investigating in ired car; there are unspoilt villages, tles and chapels in abundance.

Crete

: largest Aegean island of **Crete** is nost a country in its own right. There o much to see and do that you need east a week before you have seen n the more important sites. There many daily connections by plane l boat with both Athens and the other islands. Like Rhodes (200km north-east), it is green and mountainous with a varied coastline, but unlike Rhodes, it is possible on the south coast in particular to find lovely uncrowded beaches and really charming villages.

The island's ancient and modern history is rich and cosmopolitan, with the prehistoric Minoan civilization having left its mark in several fascinating archaeological sites. Greeks, Romans, Saracens, Venetians and Turks have all been in control of Cretan affairs, and in the present century the Germans occupied it after a paratroop invasion.

You arrive by sea at Herak**lion**, now a noisy and unattractive port, with behind the waterfront, a modern, crowded

Crete: Minos & the Minotaur

The great god Zeus had many mortal lovers, but he could never appear on earth as himself, because his thunderbolts would destroy any person they touched. He appeared as a beautiful white bull to the princess Europa, as she played on the beach with her friends. She climbed on his back and he whisked her off to Crete, turning her into a cow and making love to her. Their offspring was King Minos of Crete, who grew up into a haughty and powerful ruler and womanizer, fully aware of his divine father. Minos married Pasiphae who was soon frustrated by his infidelity, and cast a spell on him that scorpions and serpents would enter his sperm, devouring his lovers.

The Birth of the Minotaur

One day, in order to prove to the Cretans that he was favoured by the gods, Minos prayed Poseidon to send him a bull from the se Poseidon granted the prayer, but demand that the bull be sacrificed to him in return. T bull remained the symbol of the Cretan ro line. Arrogant Minos refused to sacrifice handsome an animal, and substituted an in rior beast from his own herds. Poseidon, in anger, cast a spell on Pasiphae so that she felt unbearable lust for the bull. Every night s offered herself to the bull, who expressed interest in her approaches.

Pasiphae asked the island craftsman Daeda to help her by creating a hollow cow fr leather and wood which she could climb i and thus attract the bull. Poseidon's bull co not resist; animal and mortal mated and fr their union was born the Minotaur, a m strous hybrid with a bull's head and a ma body.

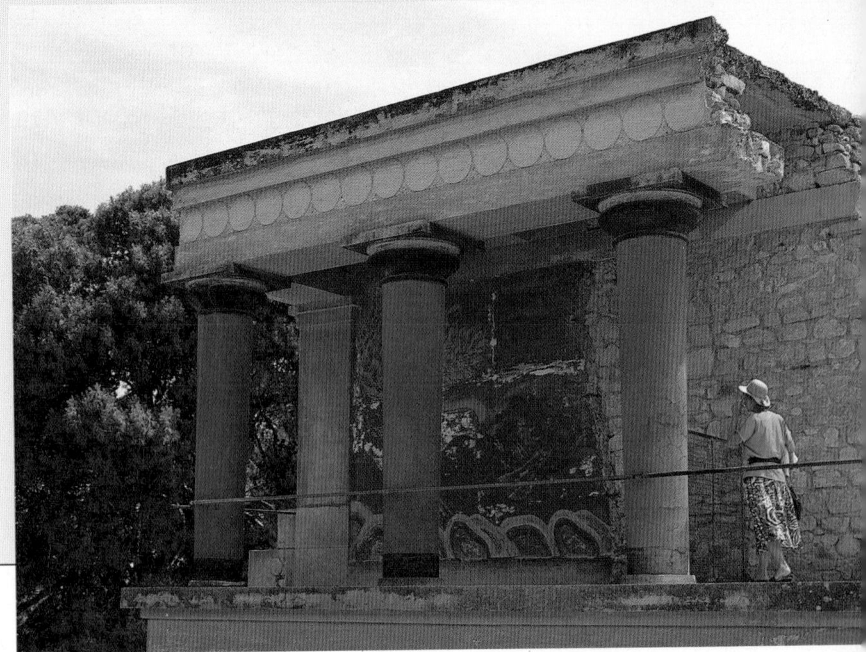

Palace of King Minos - son of Zeus' union with a mortal princess.

The Victory of Theseus

nos was so embarrassed by what he believed be his own offspring, that he ordered Daedalus construct a massive underground labyrinth, which the Minotaur could roam unseen. ery year King Minos had seven boys and ven girls sent as tribute from Athens, and he d them to the Minotaur. One year Theseus, prince of Athens, went in place of one of the ys and during the customary feast which eceded the human sacrifice to the Minotaur, in love with Minos' daughter Ariadne. That ght she begged him to take her back to hens in return for her advice on how to slay r half-brother and to escape the Labyrinth. e next day Theseus entered the maze with a l of wool which he unwound as he searched corridors for the monster. He found it and ed it in a gruelling hand-to-hand fight, and de his way back to Ariadne by following the ol. The two sailed back to Athens, but *en te* Theseus lost interest in Ariadne and abanned her on the island of Naxos. The wine-god onysus discovered her and made her his er.

Theseus meanwhile forgot to replace the ck sail of death with the white sail of victory, his father King Aegeus of Athens had reested: Aegeus saw the black sail and thinking son to be dead, leapt to his death off the opolis in to the Aegean Sea, which took its ne from him.

The bull continued to be a sacred beast on te. The people of Knossos had bull-leaping emonies in which young women and men formed daring athletic leaps over the horns harging bulls. Many think that the labyrinne plan of the palace at Knossos reflects the th of the Minotaur and his home.

vn enclosed by massive Venetian lls.

The **Archaeological Museum** en Tuesday-Saturday 8 a.m - 7 p.m ırs; Sunday 8 a.m - 6 p.m) contains a good deal of material from the many sites on the island. It can get very hot and crowded, so head upstairs for the **Hall of the Frescoes** where you will find the Knossos wall-decorations have been pieced together from surviving fragments.

Apart from this there is little else to detain you in Heraklion: there are better beaches elsewhere on Crete, as well as better nightlife and landscape.

The **Minoan Palace at Knossos** (open Monday-Friday 8 a.m - 5 p.m, Saturday & Sunday 8 a.m - 3 p.m; entrance 500dr) just five km from Heraklion and accessible by bus (No. 2 every 10 minutes), is a must. Controversially restored by the British archaeologist Arthur Evans, the ancient royal palace is literally a labyrinth of passages and courtyards, with stairways and drainage systems dating back some 4,000 years.

There are good roads along all four coasts of Crete, but if you do not have that much time and want to get to some less touristy areas, the northwest coast is superior to the northeast. It has better **beaches**, and plenty to see when you are tired of the sea: there are medieval castles at **Rethymnon** and **Frankocastello**; the picturesque Venetian port of **Chania** and the famous **Samaria Gorge** where you can walk through stunning scenery for 12 miles from the White Mountains to the Libyan Sea. Both Chania and **Rethymnon** have good beaches and nightlife on their waterfronts, whilst it is easy to find more remote beaches on either side of them.

Cyclades

Of all the Aegean islands, the **Cyclades** form the most compact and unified group for the island-hopper. They are all small enough to get to know well within a couple of days, and most of them share a harsh but beautiful rocky landscape, with wonderful whitewashed "cubistic" houses toppling down to pretty harbours. All the main islands have regular (at least once a day) boats from Piraeus (Athens) and from their neighbouring islands; several also have airports. The Cyclades are so called because they form a *cyclos* (circle) in the Aegean.

urch domes of Santorini.

Thira/Santorini

Sailing northwards from Crete you come to **Thira/Santorini** (population: approximately 2,500), flights and boat-trips arrive here each day from Athens). The ancient Minoans knew it as Thira, whilst the name "Santorini" was derived from the patron Saint Irene. It owes its crescent-

Volcanic eruptions and earthquakes have carved Santorini's landscape.

moon shape and black sand beaches to its volcanic origins; some 2,500 years ago there was a massive volcanic eruption here, which has left the imposing cliffs of the west side and the gentler volcanic slopes of the east. A famous local wine is produced along with tomatoes, pistachios and some wheat.

By boat you generally arrive at **Ormos Athinios** after the most spectacular island approach in the Mediterranean, with the vast cliffs gradually enfolding you in the island's arms. From there a bus or taxi takes you steeply up to the capital of **Fira**, in a wonderful setting, but sadly spoilt by tourism. There is a good **Archaeological Museum** (open Tuesday-Sunday 8:30 a.m - 3 p.m hours; entrance 400dr) which boasts a varied collection of archaic and clas cal statues and figurines – the preh toric wing is due to open soon.

On the southern horn of the isla is **Akrotiri** (open Tuesday-Saturday 8: a.m - 3 p.m; entrance 1000dr), "Minoan Pompeii", buried under v canic ash 2,500 years ago, during t great eruption. The sites' archaeolog Professor Marinatos, was killed by falling wall and buried on the site its You can see just three per cent of t entire city, which was larger than a other Minoan city outside of Crete. T pottery and frescoes are currently view in the Athens National Archa logical Museum, but it is hoped th they might soon be returned to the land museum.

Milos

Some 60 km to the north-west is anot volcanic island, **Milos** (populati 8,000), which has many fascinating r formations around its coast, but wh often bears the ugly scars of quarryi in its interior. The island was the sce of a horrific event in the history of "ci lized" classical Athens: the Melians 416 BC) refused to join the Atheni Empire and all the men were slau tered and the women enslaved. Me eval Milos was governed by the Fra and then by the Turks. The main po **Adhamas**, founded in 1912 by Cret fleeing the Turks.

Three km uphill from Adhama

e capital of **Plaka** with its Venetian *astro* (castle) and a couple of small useums: the **Archaeological Museum** pen Tuesday-Saturday, 8:30 a.m - 3 m, Sunday 9:30 a.m - 2:30 p.m; enance 200dr) has a sad plaster-cast of e *Venus de Milo,* which was removed om ancient Milos (below the *kastro* wards the sea) by the French in 1820. ear the **Roman Theatre** is a plaque arking the spot where the statue was earthed. There are not many good **aches** around the rocky coast, but if u want to swim, try **Plathiena** or **llonia** on the north coast.

Naxos

venty km to the north-east is **Naxos** opulation: 14,000); there are daily ghts and boat trips to Naxos from hens and from Naxos to the surroundg islands. It is the largest and one of e most beautiful of the Cycladed with iking mountain ridges and fertile vals supporting good vines, olives and rus fruits. Naxos is renowned for the ality of its honey.

The island has an interesting hisy, starting with the legend that eseus abandoned Princess Ariadne re on his way back to Athens from ete. The island was an important val base in antiquity and witnessed veral sea-battles.

In the 13th century it became the adquarters of the Italians during their riod of domination of the Cyclades, which lasted until the Turks arrived in 1566.

There are excellent sandy **beaches** on the southwest coast, whilst the north coast has an exciting and scenic winding coastal road. **Naxos Town** is where you arrive by sea, passing the islet of **Palatia** where the archaic columns of a sixth century BC **Temple of Apollo** are still standing.

The town is quite atmospheric with its narrow lanes behind the waterfront. Climbing up to the *Kastro* (castle) you will reach the 13th-century (restored) Italian Cathedral and the **Archaeological Museum** (open Tuesday-Sunday 0830-1500 hours; entrance 400dr), with its Cycladic figurines and pottery dating from prehistoric to Roman times. For the best beaches head south of the town on a bus or a motor-boat.

Paros & Andiparos

Just to the west of Naxos are the twin islands of **Paros** and **Andiparos** (total population: 9,000). Paros is much larger (population: 8,500) and is very inviting: not over-touristy, with a gentle landscape and plenty of nightlife, beaches, fishing-villages and old monasteries to explore. The Parian marble was famous in antiquity. What catches your eye will be the dazzingly white shops, archways, churches and houses and shutters painted blue and green.

In the middle ages it was controlled by the Italian Duchy of Naxos, and fell

Santorini & the Myth of Atlantis

Was this the ancient city of Atlantis?

The island of Thira/Santorini was originally one large circular volcano which erupted violently around 1500 BC in an explosion which has been compared to Krakatoa in 1889. This caused the central crater to disappear beneath the sea, leaving the crescent moon-shaped island of today. Since then there have been a series of further eruptions as well as devastating earthquakes, which keep changing the geography of the island; islets appear or disappear, new craters are formed and entire communities a destroyed and rebuilt. This century has w nessed a nine-month long eruption in 1925 in which the islets of Nea Kaimeni and Mi became one, as well as the earthquake of J 1956, when half of the buildings on the w coast collapsed.

Ancient Thira was known as *kalliste* ("t most beautiful") and was apparently well-pop lated by 2000 BC. The disaster of 1500 destroyed all its prehistoric settlements a many archaeologists and vulcanologists co sider that the force of the eruption would ha produced massive tidal waves and earth-tre ors powerful enough to destroy the Cret palaces (which also collapsed at this time), well as other Aegean island communities.

The Myth of Atlantis

The great eruption occurred before history a it is therefore not surprising that myths grew around the disaster. Some mythologists ha suggested that Thira was once the city of M tropolis, the capital of the sunken mythi continent of Atlantis. Our main literary sou for the myth of Atlantis is the ancient Athen philosopher Plato, whose ***Timaeus*** descrit the ancient civilization in detail. According this account, Atlantis was a massive island b yond the "Pillars of Hercules" (now the Strait Gibraltar), in other words in the Atlantic, wh derives its name from the lost continent. T location would argue against Thira being center of Atlantis, but mythology is rarely lo cal and there have been other versions givi differing locations for the island.

to the Turks in 1537. August 15th is the date to be here, there is a wonderful festival and firework display.

You arrive by sea at **Paroikia** (boats and aeroplanes make the journey from Athens daily), a busy harbour with the usual Cycladic backdrop of white cubist houses and Italianate church dom There is the usual local collection in t **Archaeological Museum** (open Tu day-Saturday 0830-1500; Sunday 090 1400 hours), but the architectural hig light is the **Panayia Ekatontapilia** (cathedral of "Our Lady of One Hu

Atlantis was bigger than Asia and North rica together, and was renowned for its wealth d military power. When Zeus divided up the rth among his fellow gods, Poseidon, god of e sea and earthquakes, received Atlantis where fell in love with the local princess Clito. He rned the island into an impregnable citadel by rrounding its central mountain with three gs of water and two of land. The land was rich d fertile and fountains of fresh hot and cold ater flowed continually. The children of seidon and Clito included Atlas, who gave his me to the island and surrounding sea.

Destruction of a People

e people of Atlantis were once peaceful and f-satisfied, but as time went by their divine alities faded and their human emotions took er, making them aggressive and jealous of her nations. The armies of Atlantis invaded orth Africa, Europe and Asia, but they were ally defeated by the Athenians. Immediately er the battle Zeus and the Olympians de-ded to punish the violent behaviour of the hole earth; there was a great earthquake and od which not only killed all the Athenian oops, but also submerged the entire island of lantis, together with its people.

Some believe that it was the great eruption 1500 BC and its tidal wave and earthquakes th their epicentre at Thira, which were re-embered in the myth of Atlantis. We shall ver know, but the myth itself tells us much out ancient Greek attitudes towards such tural disasters.

ed Doors" – open daily 9 a.m - 12 noon 4 p.m - 8 p.m). Dating back to the zantine sixth century, it has under-one many restorations and now con-sts of three side-by-side churches en-osed in an overall domed Greek cross sign.

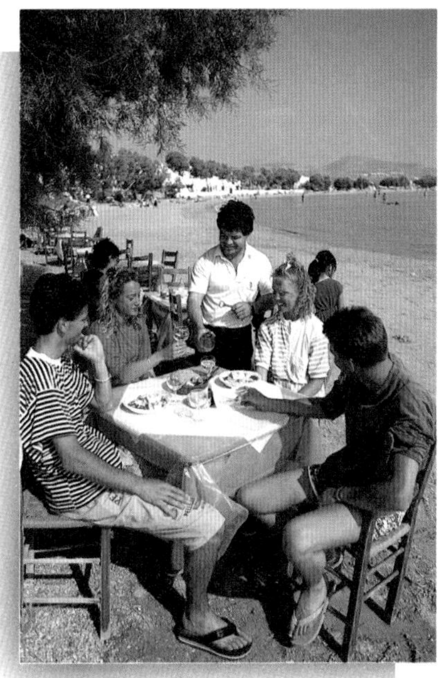

St. George's Beach is a stone's throw from Naxos town.

There are good beaches to both the north and the south of the town, as well as all around the island: the other major port is **Naoussa**, which has recently become more urbanized, but is worth a bus-ride for its nearby beaches. **Andiparos** was once joined to Paros, and is like a miniature version of it.

Syros

Twenty-five km to the north of Paros is **Syros** (population: 20,000) situated near Delos in the centre of the Cyclades. This island has retained its "Greekness" more than most, and is worth visiting for that reason alone. Homer called it "rich in herds and flocks, wine and corn" and

The Terrace of the Lions once guarded the Sacred Lake.

the workaday description still holds good.

The main town is at **Ermoupolis**, which is the Cyclades' largest port, founded during the War of Independence. The old parts are centered on two conical hills; the northern is the Orthodox quarter, the southern is topped by a Roman Catholic cathedral, reminding the visitor of the Italian past.

The town is lively during the evenings, which is a good time to take a stroll. The **Apollo Theatre**, modelled on La Scala in Milan stands in its own square close to the large main square of **Plateia Miaoulis**; there are good traditional music bars as well as discos nearby. For excellent **beaches**, take the bus across the island to **Kini** or **Galessas**.

Delos

Delos is the smallest of the Cyclade but in antiquity it was the most impo tant, being the site of a **Sanctuary c Apollo and Artemis**. You cannot sta on the island, and to visit it you mu take the boat from nearby Mykonos at a.m, returning at 1 p.m (fare: 900c return). This barely gives you time to se everything on the ancient site (entranc 500dr), so head for the highlights.

The Sanctuary of Apollo is th first, lying at the end of the Sacred Wa away from the harbour; the comple has three temples. Walking towards th Museum you will pass the **Sanctuary c Dionysos**, strikingly marked by larg

Mykonos has narrow winding lanes and alleys laid out in a labyrinth to confuse medieval pirates.

Gleaming white-washed chapels pepper the town of Mykonos.

marble phalli on columns. To the north of the sanctuary is the **Sacred Lake**, where Leto was made love to by Zeus in the guise of a swan, and gave birth to Apollo and Artemis.

Standing sentinel over the lake are the wonderful archaic seventh century BC **Naxian Lions**. Back towards the south of the Sanctuary of Apollo is a third century BC **theatre**, which or seated 5,500 people.

Nearby are many Hellenistic a Roman houses, some of which have f mosaic floors – notably, the **House the Masks**, where Dionysos can be se riding his Panther, and an exqui (signed) mosaic in the **House of Dolphins** where Cupids are portra ding on the dolphins' backs. If you ave time climb up to the modest heights .13km) of **Mount Kynthos** above.

Mykonos

ykonos (population: 5,000) is deserv-lly the most popular tourist island of e Cyclades. There are direct flights om Britain as well as from Athens. ke Rhodes it is worth putting up with e crowds for the delightful experience its main port, **Mykonos Town**. The ort boasts the best example of the fa-ous Cycladic domestic architecture, th gleaming white cuboid buildings emingly piled on top of each other, ppered with tiny chapels.

The island is well-known as a gay sort, and has one of the best ghtscenes in the Aegean. The rocky erior of the island is decorated with eek-style windmills, and (unusually Greece) scuba-diving is allowed off numerous beaches.

Get up early and get lost among the gar-cubes of Mykonos' narrow streets. parently the maze was intentionally oduced to fox 18th century pirates – u nearly always encounter other lost als asking you the way.

For the less crowded beaches take *kaik* (motor-boat) along the south ast to **Elia** or **Kalo Livadhi**, but be rned, nearly every beach on the is-d is nudist! A little further on from a is **Ayia Anna** where *Shirley Valen-* was filmed.

Tinos

Ten km northwest of Mykonos is **Tinos** (population: 5,000), which has an atmosphere almost totally opposite to that of Mykonos. Here you will find religion and tradition, rather than noise and nudity.

The religious motivation came in 1822 when a local nun was directed by a divine dream to unearth a miraculous icon of the Virgin Mary. A huge shrine called **Panayia Evanghelistria** (Our Lady of Good Tidings) was erected on the spot, and twice a year (March 26 – Annunciation, and August 15 – Assumption), the icon is paraded down to the harbour at **Tinos Town**, where it is displayed to the diseased, in the hope of a divine cure.

The harbour town is cheerful enough and you only have to follow the crowds to reach the white marble neo-classical church, which contains the shrine of the icon. The bus takes you round the islands **beaches** and some interesting and often beautifully unspoilt, villages.

In **Pirgos** there are quarries of green, black and white marble, which is still being skilfully carved by a local school of sculptors.

There are a number of other Cycladic islands, all of which have their own natural and cultural treasures, and all of which are a pleasure to explore, once you manage to escape the tourist resorts.

Sports & Recreation

Greece is the home of the ancient Olympic Games, which encouraged a high degree of physical fitness and athletic competition among wealthy young men. The modern Greeks do not at present excel in athletics, even though global attempts at a revival of the Olympic ideal began in Athens in 1896, when the ancient stadium, seating 60,000 in the Roman period, was reconstructed for the modern Olympics. The Greeks like most nations, do however find great enjoyment in a whole range of sports.

[M]ost resorts offer the thrills of water-[s]kiing.

Spectator Sports

The modern Greeks, like their classical ancestors, love spectacles, but athletics has been replaced by **soccer**, and the ancient Athenian Panathenaic athletic games are now remembered in the name of one of Athens' favourite soccer teams *Panathenaikos*. On a more local level you will see the game being played on

The Olympic stadium in Athens, home of the famous Games.

various surfaces in both towns and villages. The professional teams are heavily sponsored and the players have the status of local or national heroes. Notable teams include the Athenian *Panathenaikos*, *AEK* and *Olympiakos* (based in Piraeus), whilst Thessaloniki boasts *PAOK*; there are also major teams in Crete and Larissa.

Obviously you are unlikely to see a big match in the summer, but in *tavernas* and cafes, you will see signed team photographs and if you are a fan, it is easy to strike up conversation with Greeks, who will discuss their favourite European players well into the night. To give some idea of the relative size of the soccer scene, *Panathenaikos* play in a 25,000-seater stadium and there are daily football newspapers hanging fro
all the street kiosks.

The other national spectator spor
are **volleyball** and **basketball**, playe
locally as well as nationally, with th
Greek basketball team not so long ag
winning the European Championshi
to the delight of their fans.

Getting into Action

The Greeks cater well for the visit
interested in most types of physical a
tivity, from the water-sports of the coast
resorts to mountain-walking and th
increasingly popular winter-sport of sk
ing. **Tennis** is also popular, though gra
courts are rare because of the dry hea

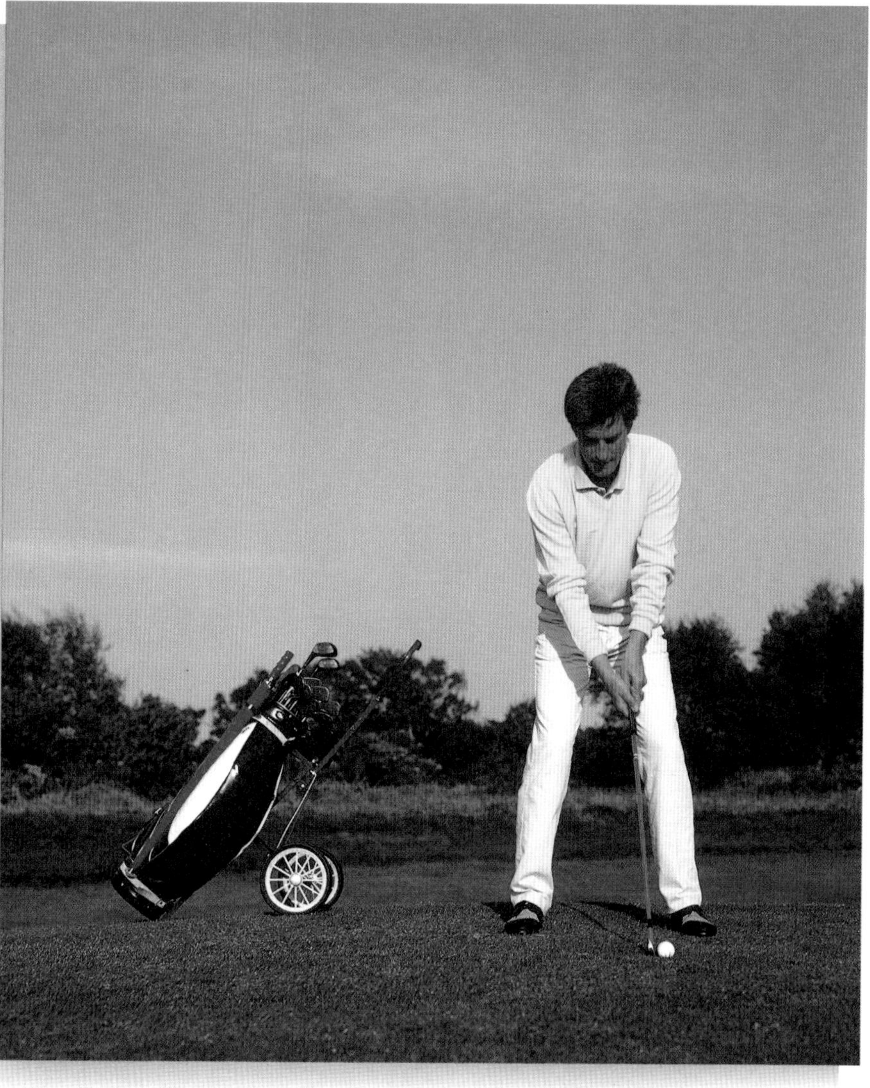

There are only four golf courses in the whole of Greece.

u will find hard courts attached to ıny hotels, as well as state-operated es behind some of the beaches; tennis ıbs are well-supported by Greeks and ıd to have long waiting-lists.

Golf is almost impossible for the ıtor, there are just four courses in the whole of Greece; Athens, Rhodes, Khalkidhiki and Corfu. If you are a really keen player, it would be worth writing to these clubs in advance of your visit, otherwise you will generally have to make do with the miniature courses connected to some hotels.

Snorkelling is ideal in Greece's pure-blue waters.

Fishing

Greece is not known for its freshwater **fishing**; there are few rivers and lakes to support fish in sizeable quantities. For sea-fishing you can negotiate with and seek advice from small-boat owners the harbours, but more popular w both Greeks and tourists is **underwa fishing**, though this has its restrictio It is prohibited at the more crowc beaches but permitted elsewhere; y must, however, be over 18 to use

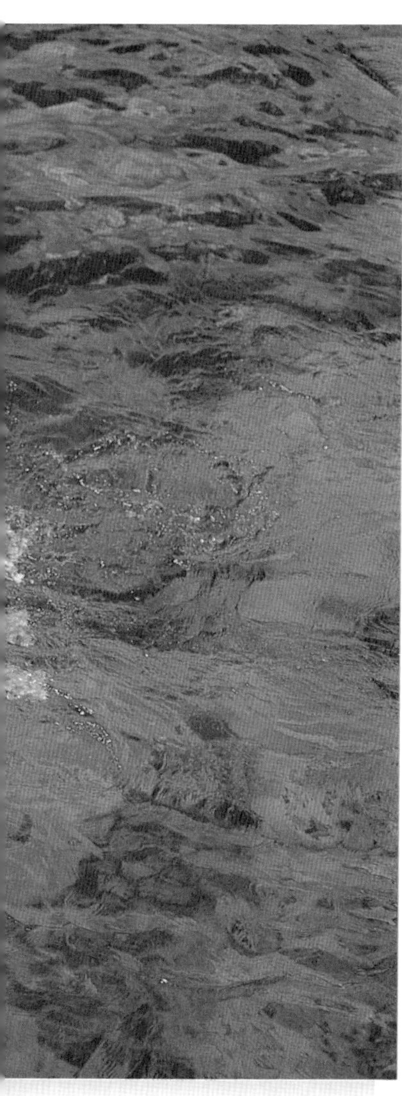

ırpoon, and you are not allowed to fire fish weighing less than 150g.

Water-sports

eathing apparatus, other than the orkel, is not allowed at most loca- ns, owing to the number of ancient wrecks which have yet to be excavated for their valuable treasures. **Scuba diving** is therefore restricted to those areas which the Department of Antiquities has already surveyed for possible wrecks: these include designated areas of the Khalkidhiki peninsula and certain islands including Corfu, Paxi, Rhodes and Mykonos. For further information obtain the leaflet "Sea Areas for Underwater Activities" from the Greek National Tourist Organisation.

On the beaches you will find varying degrees of water-sport provision. **Wind-surfing** and **water-skiing** are available in most resorts, with hire facilities as well as beginners' lessons. **Jetskis** and **paragliders** are becoming increasingly popular in the noisier resorts.

Sailboats and **catamarans** can also be hired from local naval clubs. The Greek National Tourist Organisation can provide information on all these sports, as well as lists of tour operators offering specialist water-sport holidays. Particularly good locations for experienced windsurfers and sailors are: Samos (Aegean); Levkas (Ionian); Kos and Rhodes (Dodecanese) and Crete.

On the Beach

There is no public **swimming** pool in Athens and they are not really necessary elsewhere, because of the profundity of beaches.

Nevertheless, many of the hotels

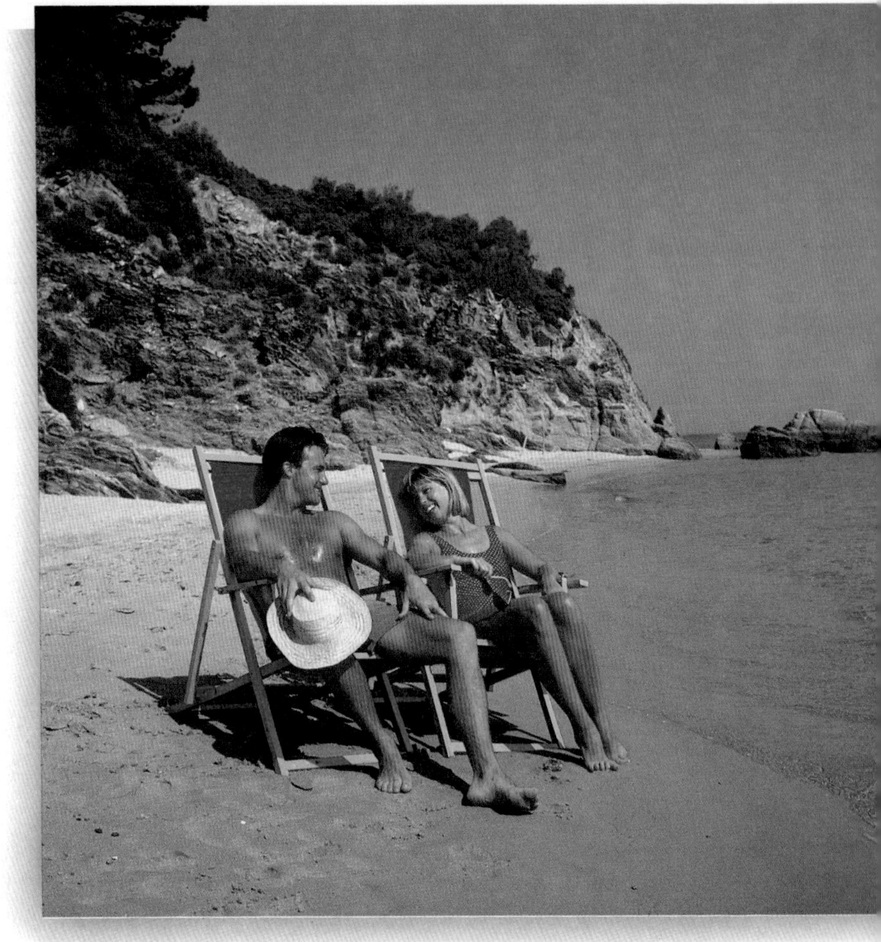

Relaxing on the beach.

have swimming pools. All types of beach locations are available with slowly-shelving beaches of every different colour of sand, from gold through silver to volcanic black; there is also the deeper water of the rocky coves with natural rock platforms allowing for diving into crystal-clear water as well as excellent snorkelling along coastal fringes. By avoiding areas near ports or major resorts you will find less pollution, but should be on the look out for jellyfish rockier locations.

Nude bathing is illegal on all bu few beaches (several on Mykono though you will often see people taki a chance in the more secluded coves at the far ends of the longer beach You should be careful not to offend lo feelings, and the same goes for fem topless-bathing which is nationally gal but some local councils continu

Yachting Around the Islands

Island-hopping is great fun when you travel on the public ferries; you can lounge on the sun-deck and watch the islands appear and disappear on the horizon, or chat to Greeks and other visitors over a drink in the bar. But the most stylish and independent way to travel the Aegean or Ionian Sea, is undoubtedly to hire your own yacht. The choice of destination is then your own: you can remain out at sea cruising in and out of the maze of islands, or you can find a little bay of your own choice to anchor in, inaccessible from the island roads; here you can dive straight into crystal-clear waters or enjoy a barbequed fish caught off the boat on a secluded beach. Alternatively you may prefer to moor at one of the hundreds of busy, picturesque harbours and dine and dance in town.

Yachts for Hire

There are now over 2,000 yachts available to the cruising yachtsman, these can be divided into three main groups; crewed yachts, bareboats and flotillas. Crewed yachts are longer than 15m and a full crew is included in the hire who will take you wherever you wish to go, as well as cook for you. Bareboats are under 15m long and can be chartered without a crew, as long as two of the charterers hold a skipper's licence. Flotillas consist of 8-12 boats of 4-6 berths sailing in ensemble and following a "lead boat": these are the most economical type of yachting holiday available.

Holiday Considerations

Supplies are easily obtained on the islands which are never very far away, but you do need to plan your itinerary at least roughly if you want to get the most out of a chartered yachting holiday. The Greek National Tourist Organization (GNTO), will provide you with all the information you require. The GNTO takes an active interest in promoting yachting by continuing to construct new marinas around the Greek coastline; they will also provide you with detailed charts and full-scale guide-books which are available in a number of languages. In the main yachting season (April to October) you do not need to worry about sudden bad weather since there are few parts of the Greek sea which are more than 30 miles from a sheltered haven.

The main cruise itineraries last for two to three weeks, but you can also charter a vessel for as little as three days. You can set off from any of Greece's 127 ports, including Piraeus (Athens), Sounion, Thessaloniki and Epidauros on the mainland or islands such as Mykonos, Paros, Rhodes and Corfu.

This allows for virtually any itinerary; you might for instance like to concentrate on an island group, or follow a theme, such as the Knights of St John or the Temples of Apollo. Everything and anything is possible for the adventurous yachtsman following in the wake of Odysseus and generations of other great Greek seamen.

-an" it with notice-boards. The ozone layer has been particularly thin over Greece in recent years, and you should always use good quality ultra-violet protection.

Roaming the Hills

Walking is a rewarding activity everywhere in Greece. In the cities it saves you having to board hot, crowded buses and this way you always discover much more on your way to intended destinations. The mountains are never far away wherever you are on the mainland or the islands, and you will usually find well-trodden mule paths to the ridges and summits.

The usual rules of mountain-walk-

An excellent way of touring the island.

ing apply in Greece, where the weather can change within the hour even in summer, when higher altitudes provide a welcome coolness.

You need a map showing the paths and a compass is essential as the maps are generally inaccurate. Walking-boots are also necessary as the tracks can become quite rocky and there is a danger of turning the ankle; on the lower hills (and for walking in towns), stout shoes suffice.

For really serious walkers I would recommend a stick for seeing off the wolf-like sheepdogs which roam the upper pastures. I have not personally encountered one but they are more than just a walker's myth – a British tourist was badly mauled in the Epirus Mountains several years ago.

In the islands you can often pick u a local walker's map and island-wal ing is by far the best way to make su that you see every deserted beach a cove, picturesque village, castle, shri or prehistoric ruin.

On the islands, beware of snak and bees, as well as village and fa dogs; remember that strangers are rare delicacy for them! One of the gre joys about walking in Greece is meeti with the locals, who are invariably cu ous in the friendliest sense of the wo and may well invite you for a glass bo at the farm or local *taverna*. Binocul are always useful for both bird-wat ing and dog-spotting, whilst a wild flov identification book is a must.

Another fun way to tour.

Touring the Islands

her good ways to get around and cover new beaches and monuments, rticularly on the islands, include hir-) a **car**, **motorbike/ ooter**, or least expen- 'ely, a **cycle**. e more m o t e ıds can full of t-holes, vear a helmet, however uncomfort- e it feels. Passports must be left as urity, and daily rates are reasonable:)-15 for a motorcycle (needs driving licence) or scooter; £2-5 for a bicycle. Cars are best rented through your travel agent before leaving for Greece; this is less expensive and you will get a better insurance deal. You could take your own bicycle, or buy one there: ferries, trains and buses usually allow them as free-of-charge baggage.

Skiing

Skiing is possible at several mountain centres between January and April, though Greece's snow fall figures are variable. **Parnassus** (above Delphi) is a good bet – it is the most developed of the resorts and if there is no action, you can always head for Athens and do some out-of-season sight-seeing – there are daily buses to and from the resort organised by Athenian tour operators. Other centers include Metsovo (Epirus), **Kalavrita** (Peloponnese), **Mount Pelion** (Thessaly); in Macedonia there are the beautifully wooded slopes of **Mount Vermion**. Equipment can be hired in all these resorts and beginners are made welcome everywhere. Whatever you fancy doing in Greece, be it skiing, sailing, climbing or horse-riding, the Greek National Tourist Organisation will give you useful information.

KEO
Ouzo
EXTRA FINE
650ml
CLAUSS
CAVINO

Cuisine

For the ancient as for the modern Greeks, dining was primarily a social occasion. In classical times the *symposium* (dinner party) was one of the most important social events. Political and arty friends would be invited to your house, where there was often a special room set aside for the party. Couches were placed around the walls so that everyone could see everyone else, and in front of each couch was a table to hold your food and wine. In the patriarchal ancient world, women (other than courtesans) were not allowed in the dining room, and witty conversation was expected from all present. Watch modern Greeks dining at the tables of the most expensive restaurants or the humblest *tavernas*, and you will witness the same animated discussions.

n invitation for some authentic Greek od.

The ancient menu consisted of a constant stream of different dishes, some small, some large. The fare was varied and often sophisticated. The classical Greek was highly

knowledgeable about his home-grown herbs, but also loved to import more exotic spices from the Orient. This cultural mixture of tasty foods from east and west is still very much present in Greek cuisine today, the eastern element having been boosted by centuries of Turkish occupation.

Foreign Influences & Exportation

When ancient Greece became part of the wider Roman Empire, it became fashionable for wealthy Romans to eat Greek food. Greek cooks were brought back as slaves to Roman households, and Greek recipes spread to the west and are still to be found today: the famous French bouillabaisse is thought to have come across the sea from Greece. There were also recipe books which demonstrate the classical heritage of Greek cuisine.

The second century AD cookery expert Athenaeus, wrote a book called ***Sophisticated Banqueting*** in which he describes how, as today, herbs were applied generously to fish and meat dishes; olive oil and vinegar dressings were on the table, and meatballs (modern *keftedes*) were popular. Ancient cuisine survived along with the old manuscripts in the medieval Orthodox monasteries; no surprise, since the Greek monks appear to have been gourmets in their eating habits! Modern Greek chefs of any pretensions still wear the erect white cap which was worn by monastic cooks. This continuity of Greek cooking habits is quite remarkable: invite Plato and Aristophanes to dinner in the Plaka today, and they will find few real novelties in the food offered.

Hard Liquor

The infamous Greek resinated white wine *retsina* may well have its origins in the ancient world. The classical Greeks often stored their wine in pine barrels, and the pine-resin therefore gave the wine its unique, and to some tastes, acrid flavour. *Retsina* is most refreshing served chilled to wash down the more spicy Greek dishes; whereas it tastes awful served with incongruous "international" cuisine such as steak and chips. There is a rose version called *kokineli*:: in both white and rose, pine resin is added during fermentation. Whatever you think of *retsina*, remember what foreigners think of some of your own favourite drinks back home!

Despite *retsina*'s fame, Greece's national drink is in fact *ouzo,* which is again an acquired taste. There are special drinking-bars called *ouzeris*, but you can buy it anywhere and it is a particularly good aperitif. The drink is accompanied by a glass of water, which you should tip into the *ouzo* until it turns milky. Traditionally, *ouzo* is served with *mezedes* (which in most places today have to be ordered), this is similar to Spanish *Tapas*, consisting of a small plate

Wine drinking in Greece goes back 2,000 years.

bbles – olives, fetta cheese, tomato, metimes octopus or fish. The *ouzeri* s the best variety of *mezedes* and, like Tapas Bar, can take the place of a ore conventional meal in a *taverna* or staurant. Greek brandies such as etaxas and Cambas are cheap and erior to French cognac, but mix well th water after dinner. *Raki* is a notori-s and highly alcoholic shnapps-like nk - not for the faint-hearted!

Wine Feasts

ne-drinking habits have changed ce antiquity; water was always mixed h wine in classical times. To drink re wine was considered barbaric and uncivilized, as was drinking without eating, and this is still true of modern Greeks whom you will rarely see with a glass but no plate. Drunkenness is still comparatively rare in Greece, though a striking exception is the Daphni Wine Festival. The festival takes place during the evenings of September and October, when the pine-woods and grounds of the early Byzantine Monastery echo with the good-natured rowdiness of tipsy Greeks. This event itself seems to be a continuation of the ancient festivals in honour of Dionysos, when the wine flowed as an integral part of the worship of the god.

To what extent the wines themselves are the same as those drunk two thousand years ago we shall never know. What we do know however, is that similar-sounding wines are still produced in many areas: the wine of Chios, for example, was famous in antiquity – it was the comic playwright Aristophanes who contrasted the Chians in a famous pun, with the sober Kean islanders.

Quality Wines

There are many (unresinated) national and local Greek wines, which do not tend to travel well because they are produced with the more spicy Greek foods in mind. A lot of wine production in Greece tends to be on a small scale, but with entry into the EEC, there is more pressure on Greece to produce controlled quality wines for the interna-

Tavernas

The Greeks love to go out to eat, which means that there are always plenty of places available to the visitor, and that they are competitively priced, so long as you eat where the Greeks themselves eat and avoid being tempted by touts and waiters standing on the street. *Tavernas* are the most common type of restaurant, and they come in all shapes and sizes. Some are fashionable with smart decor, well-presented waiters and courteous service; others are more rough and ready, and you will find that beach *tavernas* often consist of merely a wooden cabin with bamboo awnings providing shade. tend to be relaxed and informal, with th tables placed outside on the harbour-side, stre or even in the owner's back-garden.

Ordering Your Meal

Menus are nearly always in both Greek a English these days, though you will be mystifi and amused by some of the spellings; "ro lamp" appears on many menus! The Greeks a as friendly in their *tavernas* as el where, and they will always le you to the kitchen to point o various choices, if you prefer.

Horiatiki is the most expensive of Greek salads.

The range of choice var greatly from one *taverna* to a other. When eating in a *taver* remember that the idea of a ser of courses is unknown in Gre cooking today, as it was in ant uity. Instead you are brought yo chosen dishes in no particular der, and you should not compl when this occurs – the most a noying thing for the non-Gree to be served a "main course" wi out a salad or vegetables, wh thereupon arrive at the end of t meal! The best way to enjoy *taverna* is to go in a group and order a selection of starters, m dishes and salads, to be shared the Greeks themselves do.

tional market. "Own label" wines are produced by a number of commercial wine firms, and tend to blend wines from different regions. The best-known Greek wine companies are Achaia Clauss®, Boutari®, Cambas®, Carras® and Kourtakis®. They produce the popular and drinkable wines: *Blanc de Blancs, Demestica, Lac des Roches, Cambas Blanc, Rotonda, Cotes de Meliton* and *Hymettus.*

A second group of commercial win also produced by the main compani are those with an Appellation of Origi which have to be produced from grap grown in a defined area: there is go quality control of these wines and t label bears the words "appellation origin". The Appellation of Origin wi include *Mantinia*, which is from vi yards surrounding the ancient city

Salads

ɔriatiki ("Greek salad" or "village salad"), con-ıts of sliced tomatoes, cucumber, onion, green ɘpper, black olives and crumbled *feta* cheese, ith a generous coating of olive oil. This is the ost expensive of the salads, and you might efer to go for *domatosalata* (tomato salad) or *ıgourodomata* (tomato and cucumber salad). *arouli* (lettuce) is usually offered only in the nter.

Starters

arters include more exotic fare, though the shes are increasingly available in foreign su-ɪrmarkets. Tasty dips include *tzatziki* (a mix-re of yoghurt, garlic and cucumber), and *ɘlitzanosalata* (aubergine). Also good are; *lokithakia tiganita, melitzanes tiganites* (cour-ttes or aubergines fried in batter); *titopitakia, anakopites* (cheese and spinach pies) are ex-llent sources of protein for vegetarians, as are *ıandes* (butter beans in vinaigrette) or *saganaki* ied cheese). Fish-lovers may find octopus or uid as a starter.

Meats

ɘats include *souvlaki* (shish kebab) and *brizoles* ɔrk or veal chops); both of these are generally iable choices, though the *hirino* (pork) is the better quality if available. Lamb comes on kebabs as well as in *paidhakia* (small tasty cutlets); it also comes *arni psito* (roast). *Keftedhes* (meatballs) are very popular in *tavernas*, as are *loukanika* (spiced sausages) which are a good choice if you do not like olive oil.

Fish

Fish is often best avoided unless you are by the sea, when it is good and fresh. You will find inexpensive *kalamarakia* (fried baby squid) everywhere throughout the summer.

Expect to pay more for fish such as *barbounia* (red mullet) and *fangri* (sea bream). There are many types of fish depending on the catch, and I have found that you can generally trust the cook to provide it well-cooked and seasoned. Ask to be shown what is available in the fridge – this is perfectly acceptable in Greece.

Desserts

Desserts do not really exist as special courses in Greek *tavernas* or restaurants. You can usually get water-melon or grapes in season, but do not expect ice-cream etc. There is always a good choice of wines in *tavernas*, with the Cambas and Boutari Rotonda labels being a good bet for a reasonable and cheap wine. For a better taste try the Boutari *Naoussa*, or, if you like the idea, go for the local wines. *Retsina* tastes at its best from the barrel, and is often served in cans!

antinea in the Peloponnese. It is a dry ıite wine, with a light taste and a ntly aromatic bouquet. Another loponnesian favourite is *Nemea*, a ll-bodied red, grown south of ancient ɔrinth and referred to locally as "the ɔod of Hercules". Patras in the north-ɘst Peloponnese produces a light white ne, but is better known for its sweet ssert wines; the rich, red *Mavrodaphne* and the amber liqeur *Muscat of Patras*.

Up in western Macedonia is found *Naoussa*, perhaps the best of all the Appellation wines; the cooler, damper climate produces a light, clean, dry red wine which compares favourably with many Italian and French wines. Even further north on the Albanian border is found the white *Zitsa*, much praised by the poet Byron.

The islands produce wonderful wines whose flavours seem to be integrated into their individual landscapes. Rhodes produces the fine dry white *Rhodos*, whilst Crete is best known for its four full-bodied red liqueur wines; *Sitia, Daphnes, Archanes* and *Peza*. The volcanic soil of Santorini/Thira produces one of the strongest Greek wines, the 17 per cent strong *Santorini*, which is a sweet-white liqueur. Ionian Cephalonia has a light dry white called *The Robola of Cephalonia*, which is served chilled as a table wine.

Country Wines

Country Wines are those produced outside of the main companies and controls. Ironically they tend to be more "organic" and free of chemical preservatives, leaving you with a clearer head in the morning. Particularly renowned country wines are the dark reds of Paros, the whites of Euboea and the local wines of the Khalkidhiki peninsula.

The Eating Scene

The clichéd foreign view of Greek cuisine is that the food is always cold and unsophisticated, or that you are offered badly-presented cosmopolitan dishes. This is still true of packed resorts and the more touristy restaurants in Athens but travellers get what they deserve, and with patience and polite enquiry you

Enjoying a meal alfresco at one of the many restaurants.

The choicest cut.

can today sample wonderfully clean, fresh and well-presented traditional Greek cuisine in many places. If in Athens, you might play safe by starting at the Taverna Ta Nissia in the Athens Hilton, which produces a wide range of traditional island dishes. There are similar "cleaned-up" *tavernas* springing up in many hotels, which often serve surprisingly good traditional food, and they are a good education before going off in search of something more back-street and authentic.

Meat Dishes

Traditonally, Greeks have not been great meat-eaters since the climate and landscape nurtures goats and sheep rath than beef cattle – that is why the Eas Paschal Lamb is considered such a tre You will find separate meat dishes the international menus, but the tra tional recipes use spices and herbs flavour spit-roasted lamb or chops. *tavernas* lamb dishes include *paidha* (grilled cutlets with oregano) and *arn ladhorigani* (leg of lamb roasted in with oregano).

Vodhino (Beef) and *moshari* (ve are imported in increasingly large qu tities as they are seen as status symb of the prosperous western world. warned, the veal is often old enough be beef. In *tavernas* you will often f *brizoles mosharisies* (veal chops grille oil, with oregano and lemon) on

The choicest catch from the sea.

enu, but it is safest to translate this as eef chops". If you want to be really cadent, try the Greek version of the mburger, known as *biftekia*. Pork is eap in Greece and is generally cooked a similar manner to veal; you will d *brizoles* (pork chops) in most *ernas*.

Sufficient poultry is produced at me, and chicken will be found on ost Greek menus; it is often free-range d therefore quite tasty. Popular cken dishes include *kotopoulo me nies* (chicken casserole with okra), netimes tomato sauce replaces the a to become *kotopoulo kokinisto. opoulo sto fourno me patates* (roast cken with potatoes) is a favourite h with western tourists.

Succulent Seafood

Fish and seafood have always been an integral part of the Greek diet, and traditional fishermen, though their numbers have decreased, remain part of Greek culture. You can still watch them in the late evening chugging out to sea in their *kaikia* (broadbeamed caiques), whilst many Greeks supplement the family's shopping basket with fresh fish caught from their own small boats or by underwater fishing with harpoons. Always check that your fish is fresh; much is imported in a frozen state from the Atlantic deep-sea trawling companies. Large fish are the most expensive and are usually baked, whilst medium fish are grilled and the smallest are fried.

To be sure of good fish, head for a specialist fish *taverna*, known as *apsarotaverna*; if in Athens you will find that those in Piraeus are on the whole overrated, and it pays to head for the coastline at **Glyfadha** or to the small port of **Rafina** where the fish are really fresh and well-cooked. Good, cheap small fried fish include *gopa* (bogue) and *gavros* (anchovy) which are available throughout the year. For a larger, meatier fish try *sinagridha* (dentex) grilled and sprinkled with olive oil and lemon juice. *Barbouni* (Red Mullet) tends to be small and expensive in Greece, but if it is available, go for it fried for a very tasty fish.

Another more expensive fish is *fangri* (sea bream) the larger specimens of which are cut into steaks and grilled. *Glosa* (sole) is a delicacy in Greece, and often appears on the menu priced by weight: try them fried in breadcrumbs or baked with spinach. Seafood lovers will find *kalamari* (squid) everywhere, and they will be cooked as you want them – deep or shallow-fried. O*htapodhi* (octopus) and *astakos* (lobster) are now increasingly hard to find fresh, and should be snapped up.

Sweet Treats

Starters include the tasty dips of *tzatziki* (yogurt, garlic and cucumber) and *melitzanosalata* (aubergine dip). For des-

There is no lack of places to ea

sert, there are usually melons and grap but you might find fresh figs, aprico peaches and pomegranates in seas though I cannot resist Greek yogurt w *meli* (honey). Greek honey is the best the world, and includes *Attiki* produ on the hillslopes of the mountains s rounding Athens; there is also *Thimari* produced from thyme-fed bees.

Where & When to Eat

The Greeks love to eat and drink outs of their homes, and for the visitor means there is a good choice of place eat and that in general, eating times quite flexible. In addition to the tra tional Greek places, there are an easing number of cosmopolitan snack ıd burger joints in the more modern wns and resorts.

A good rule if you want to eat Greek od is to go where the Greeks themlves go, as well as when they go – the reeks tend to eat late – 9 a.m - 10 p.m. nly tourist restaurants will be serving od at nine in the evening, and this is cely to be international cuisine. You n always be unlucky but I have found at the less smart-looking places tend serve much tastier and more authen- food. So do not be put off by paper pkins and scratched dumpy glasses – ıat comes with them is often fit for a ıg! Try not to be drawn into a restaunt by insistent waiters standing outle, the food at such places tends to be ıuristy" both in price and in taste – t at all authentically Greek.

Greek waiters should be patiently erated. In the more Greek places they ely keep an accurate list of what you ve had, and tend to come round count- the plates and wine jugs left on the ıle! I am afraid that unless you want create a scene and go home with a d taste in your mouth, it is best to pass waiter's errors with a laugh. Do not ect too much and you will have a at time!

Estiatoria and ***tavernas*** are the two in types of restaurant. The *estiatorio* n urban place which tends to open lunch and have its tables indoors. *taverna* is the opposite: rural or all village in character and serving d to outside tables in the late summer evenings. The *estiatorio* serves more complex hot food; bakes such as moussaka, stews, oven-cooked meat and fish dishes. The problem is that the dishes are usually cooked in the morning, and rarely heated up properly for your meal; this is accepted in Greece and there is little point in complaining if your meal is lukewarm. There are few desserts apart form in-season fruit.

Snacks

Greek snacks which can be bought and taken away for picnics include some really tasty and practical pastries such as *tiropita* (cheese pie) and *koulouri* (ring-shaped bread covered with caraway seeds); there are other versions filled with spinach or other vegetables. *Souvlakia* (shish kebabs) are served on wooden skewers and are often sold on the street near to bus-stops or ferry boarding-points.

The *kafenia* is the traditional Greek coffee shop. You can buy beer, tea and *ouzo* here as well as coffee itself; *Kafe frape* is a refreshing iced coffee. Hot Greek coffee is served strong and in small cups (never ask for a Turkish coffee!) and comes with various amounts of sugar.

Ask for "nescafe" if you want a more western coffee. Finally, those with a sweet tooth will be attracted to the *zaharoplastia*, which sells all sorts of sweets, biscuits and cakes, including the rich honeyed Greco-Turkish *baklavas*.

370
370

Shopping

Wandering along the narrow bazaar areas of Greek sea-ports and cities, is one of the most pleasant ways of spending a morning or late afternoon when you have had enough of lazing in the sun or soaking up the culture.

Opening Hours

igh quality souvenirs - one of the best ys in Greece.

As with the archaeological sites and museums there is little rhyme or reason to opening hours, which vary from place to place and are constantly being altered. The hours reflect the climate, and like other Mediterranean countries, allowance is generally made for the early afternoon siesta, which is compensated for by opening in the cool of evening; the more cosmopolitan large towns and cities sometimes adopt the north European custom of opening all day.

On the whole shops start opening up from as early as 8 a.m in both summer and winter, though to be safe it is best not to set off on a spree before 9

It's worth browsing before buying.

a.m. Now for the complicated part: on Mondays, Wednesdays and Saturdays shops start to close for lunch/siesta any time from 2 p.m onwards; whereas on Tuesdays, Thursdays and Fridays they are closed a little earlier at 1:30 p.m, but re-open in the late afternoon at 5:30 p.m, to close at 8:30 p.m.

In winter the siesta is shorter and shops close an hour or so earlier in the evenings. If you need something important or are planning a serious shopping spree you can safely count on 9 a.m - 1 p.m, Mondays to Fridays. On public or local holidays it is best to seek advice from your hotel. Take note, however, that boutiques in resorts visited by big-spending cruisers will stay open till the last passenger boards.

Vital Shopping

Street kiosks are painted green and a lifesavers, being open some 18 hours the day and night. You can buy all sor of goodies from these seemingly tir booths: bus-tickets, films, sweets, stamp razors and other essential toiletries, well as newspapers (there are often En lish-language "What's On?" magazin as well as foreign newspapers at expc prices).

Chemists in the larger towns run 24-hour service between them. If yo find one closed it should have a noti stating where you can find one open. you are having problems, ask at yo hotel reception.

Bargains & Best Buys

Greece is not a place that people choo to visit for a shopping expedition in t way that they often do for London, N York or Hong Kong. If your sole purpo is to collect some bargains, the best b would be objects which become b gains when converted back into yo own currency: these might include coats (if your ethics allow) from Kasto in Macedonia and antiques, gold jew lery and silver objects from Athens a Thessaloniki.

Greece is best above all, for one the most varied assortments of go quality souvenirs in the world; th range from well-crafted pottery, wo ırving and metalwork, to colourful mbroidery, rugs and leather goods. here is always an interesting assortent of baubles, bangles and beads, gether with marble, alabaster and nyx bowls, or other objects beautifully orked in the classical tradition.

You will probably find as many mpting goods in the less obvious nonouvenir shops. You ould avoid buying anying imported into reece: it tends to be exensive because of transort costs and high conımer taxes. The excepon is Rhodes, where, beuse of special import spensations made after e Dodecanese was ited with Greece after World 'ar II, you can buy spirits less than duty-free ices. Throughout eece, bartering is excted in all the souver shops, but you should not e x - ct much more than 10 per cent off e marked price.

Shopping in Athens

ery town has its own special areas for fferent types of shops, and there are ually street markets on particular days. e larger towns and cities obviously ve the widest range. **Athens** often has od craft shops in its hotel lobbies, selling jewellery and reproduction antiquities such as ancient painted vases and bronze statuettes. You will find such reproductions all over Greece, but spend a little time browsing before you buy. It is not a bad idea to wait until you have seen original art objects in the museums, this will allow you to judge "authenticity" in the reproductions; some of them are completely insensitive to the original, others are very good copies and well worth buying. The main museums in Athens also sell top quality reproductions of antiquities.

For antiques and "oriental" style clothes and crafts, try the shops at the lower end of **Odhos Adrianou**. The Plaka area is also good for leather goods (very cheap sandals are not durable), modern jewellery, embroidered items and traditional Greek *flokates* (woollen rugs). In addition, Athens boasts a good number of **flea markets** active on different days of the week. The main one is on Sunday mornings in the streets surrounding **Monastiraki Square**: temporary stalls are set up beside permanent shops, and many simply lay their goods out on a rug. You can buy anything and everything here, from *bouzoukis* to boots and jewellery to junk.

The local scene.

Outside Athens

Many rank **Thessaloniki** superior to Athens as a modern shopping city, and before the recent troubles began, it used to attract many Yugoslav shoppers to its large department stores. The main shopping streets are those running parallel with the sea promenade: **Mitropoleos**, **Tsimiski**, **Ermou** and **Agiou Dimitriou**. Here you will find trendy boutiques rather than antique shops; for less flashy goods the bazaar area lies to the south of **Dhikastirion Square**.

Other good "serious" shopping centres include islands such as Mykonos and Rhodes which are stopping places for cruise ships. Mykonos has some very good clothes shops, selling high quali leather jackets and fashionable dress as well as traditional island woolle sweaters and leather sandals. In th smaller towns and islands, you will fir the more interesting shops are locat in the older parts where the communi bazaar is situated; just follow the crow and you will usually find it.

On the **islands** you can should lo in local hardware shops for Greek coo ing-wares such as coffee saucepans; yo should also buy your underwater ge locally, as snorkels, flippers and ha poons are much cheaper than if boug at home. **Corfu** is particularly good f olivewood objects such as salad bow remember to rub them with olive every time you wash them and they w

Pretty as a postcard.

st forever. Corfu and some other is-nds also offer local honey, which can easily taken home if you are careful. ıe Cycladic islands make hand-knit-d sweaters and fishermen's vests, both which sell well to visitors from colder mes.

Clothes

othes in Greece range from continen- fashion designs imported from Italy d sold in boutiques, through to flow- smocks, shirts, skirts and leggings ıich can be found hanging on the nts of market stalls or in the humbler ırist outlets. You should always ask urself whether the slightly exotic colours and designs will suit you as well back home! Department stores in **Athens** and **Thessaloniki** tend to import from foreign equivalents such as *Marks & Spencer®*.

Leather Goods

Leather goods such as jackets and coats are generally inferior to those you would find in Italy, France or Turkey. However, the sandals and slippers sold in the Plaka at Athens or in the bazaar areas of Rhodes, Corfu and other islands are well-made and comfortable to wear. High fringed "snake boots" are also a good buy. Many cobblers will measure your feet and make a pair according to

Rugs also make attractive wall-hangings.

our preferences, on the premises.

Gold & Silverware

old and silverware have received a oost since the 1960s with the increased narket for copies of ancient jewellery. ike the potters, the smiths have done neir research in local museums and ome out with high quality Minoan and Mycenaean, Classical and Hellenistic yles of bracelets, finger and earrings, s well as display objects such as metal ıps, bowls and plates.

Carpets & Rugs

ıgs are one of Greece's traditional best ıys. The problem for the visitor is their eight and bulk, and you should picre yourself struggling to the airport ith the rest of your luggage before ıying. Greek rugs, or *flokati* as they are illed (see box story on Textiles Page 4).

Woollen carpets are usually called *achovas* after the village you pass rough on the way to Delphi from thens. Arachova is the traditional cen- of carpet production, though factos have taken over their materials and signs.

If you do not have time to stop and ıy one at the village, you will see them ıck in Athens around **Monastiraki uare**. Like *flokati* they make attracre wall-hangings in bedrooms, or can be used to cover a sofa or chair.

Bags

Tagari bags are those bags which hang from the shoulder on a twisted cord. They come in all sorts of traditional designs as well as with logos for the tourist, and being very light and unbulky, make good gifts for younger friends and relatives. I have seen them used as cushion covers, with the carrying-cord removed!

Furs

Furs sell at competitive prices which surprise some and appal others, considering the warm Mediterranean climate enjoyed by the Greeks. The northern Greeks get very cold in winter, and the town of **Kastoria** imports fur from abroad and makes it up into long coats, jackets and hats; these are then shipped to Athens where they are sold in the **Mitropoleos-Ermou** districts.

Garments are made up of large numbers of scraps stitched together, making them heavier than their northern counterparts.

It is for the same reason they are also cheaper, and if you visit Athens in winter you will see a wider range of social classes wearing minks than in the north, though this is also due to a differing consciousness towards animal exploitation.

SHOPPING

Rugs & Textiles

Embroidery designs are handed down from past generations.

You will find local embroidered textiles in most parts of Greece, though more often in the south, as the colder northern climate demands more bulky woollen cloth to hang on the internal walls of houses for insulation as well as for clothing. In the warmer areas there is a folk tradition of the making of small and delicate items of clothing, such as headscarves, which are decorated with embroidered patterns. Co ours are often produced from local dyes, whil designs are handed down from one generatio to the next. These traditions result in truly loc and often very beautiful pieces, which the ma ers are proud to sell to visitors. You will notic that every island or district has its own particul favourite items, colours and designs, and yo should enjoy absorbing the variety before ma ing a final purchase.

Oriental Influences

On ancient Greek pots you will often see wome wearing long embroidered tunics and warri men wearing similarly decorated cloaks. Th decorative designs of sphinxes, lotus flowe and grazing animals were often imported fro the orient. This tradition of borrowing flo designs has continued, and the sensitive eye w be able to pick out what seems local from wh seems to be oriental. This is particularly true embroidery designs found in those islands whic have a tradition of both trade and invasion, su as Rhodes and Crete. On Crete for example, yo will see the double-headed eagle motif of t Byzantine empire, as well as stylized tulips fro Turkey; these motifs remind us of the islanc chequered history, and therefore make exc lent souvenirs.

Flokati Rugs

Embroidered textile weighs little and folds nic

Antiques

Antiques can be best buys in Greece, but you need to be aware of the export laws. Generally any object deemed to have been made before the start of the War of Independence (1821) is labelled "antiquity" and needs an export licence; without one the object will be confiscated customs and you could be prosecut because the Greeks are understandab sensitive about preserving their her age. Therefore deal only with outl which will provide the necessary exp documentation. Reputable antiq shops can be found in **Odh Voukourestiou** and **Leoforos Amali**

r travelling. The same can not be said for oollen rugs; but if weight and bulk is not a oblem, or if you can find a dealer who is lling to ship it home for you, a *flokati* rug can a good buy in Greece.

Traditionally these were an essential item in ery Greek woman's wedding dowry chest, til the dowry custom was banned earlier this ntury. I have been informed by excited rug alers that "this once hung in Helen of Troy's droom", and you also will be amazed by nilar stories if you but show an interest in a g. The best quality *flokati* rugs are still woven home: the women twist the wool on spindles produce a fluffy, cuddly textured yarn, which hen woven on hand-operated looms to proce a rug with a luscious surface of lengthy oollen strands. The underside remains matted stop it slipping on woollen floors. The rug is en placed under running water – traditionally nountain stream – for several days to produce e rug's unique softness as well as to shrink the ands to about 10cm.

You can buy *flokati* rugs either in their tural cream wool colour, or in the traditional y red colour with which they are often dyed nother Greek craft which survived the Turk- occupation, by being maintained in the re remote mountain villages of the north.

Cheaper and less bulky factory versions are available. You will find that they fit in ractively with most types of interior decor, are particularly cosy beside the bed or in nt of a real fire in winter time.

Athens as well as in the streets around **onastiraki Square**.

Pottery

ttery is a real Greek speciality and you l find confident modern designs of h pot and painted decorations, as well as very close copies of fine ancient designs. You find them in most of the craft and souvenir shops, whilst there are factories such as the **Ikaros center** on **Rhodes**, where you can watch the local girls painting their complex designs of mermaids, fish, trees and flowers on the sides of pots for sale in the display rooms. You might find it worthwhile to visit the **National Organization of Greek Handicrafts and Small Industries** at 9 Odos Mitropoleos in Athens: this has a permanent exhibition which demonstrates the range available all around Greece, and gives you ideas of what to buy and where to buy it.

Food & Wine

Greek foods and wines are also worth considering for yourself or as attractive gifts. Olives and olive oil are of international quality, whilst herbs, nuts and "Turkish Delight" (it is much more tactful to use the Greek *loukoumi*!) are easy to transport home, and are often gift-wrapped. You are allowed more duty-free from shops than from the airport (check your allowances), but should beware of taking *retsina* back as a gift to the uninitiated!

The golden rules for shopping in Greece are not to jump at the first thing you see, to imagine the object back home, and to buy Greek-made items only. Follow these and you will return home with interesting souvenirs, well worth any effort spent in chosing them.

CAFE
RESTAURANT
nefeli

Nightlife

If you are visiting Greece for beaches and wild cosmopolitan nightlife, the best destinations are the islands; Corfu, Kos, Mykonos, Paros, Crete, Thassos and Rhodes have particularly good disco scenes, where it is not unusual to find open-air "raves". These are also the popular destinations for nudist bathing and trendy beach activities in general.

Pubs

...e welcoming lights of Plaka tavernas.

If you want to talk over a drink, there are bars and pubs. You will find cosmopolitan bars in hotels and nightclubs; the traditional Greek bar is generally open only during shopping hours and is not associated with nightlife. Likewise, pubs are not indigenous to Greece and are usually located in those resorts popular with British tourists, often in complexes such as at **Benitses** in **Corfu**. Greek pubs typically have polished bars and low relaxed lighting with a smartly uniformed

Bouzouki clubs are one of the most authentically Greek nights out.

barman serving bottled beers and all sorts of spirits to customers seated on high barstools or reclining on soft and sunken leather couches in dark corners.

Music is usually piped but sometimes pianists add to the subdued atmosphere. On the islands the British tourist is often surprised to find a British or Irish barman with summer barmaids from back home. Greece has no licensing hours for the sale of alcohol, but entertainment venues are required by law to shut at 1 a.m, except on public holidays.

Music Scene

There is a wide range of musical entertainment in Greece, and this will b come apparent the moment you st into the *taverna* areas of any city, se port or village. Many eating-places ha their own resident bands, playing trad tional *bouzouki* music, sometimes wi dancers. You will find some of the be dancers and musicians on the islands the summer, moving back to Athens the winter. There are also native ja and rock bands, but the modern mu scene is small compared with Italy Spain, and virtually non-existent in t smaller islands.

Classical concerts have had a cent boost with the building of a n concert hall at **Leoforos Vassilisis Sofi** in Athens (next to the US Embass where there is now a winter programr

; well as the long-running Athens Fes- ʼal in the summer, when perform- ıces are also given outside in the Odeon Herodes Atticus. Discos can be found ʼerywhere, and in the touristy islands ʼe often up-to-date both musically and terms of lighting technology. At Ath- ıs, many of the disco clubs close dur- g the hot summer months, and the ene is shifted to the Attic coast where ere are huge purpose-built disco-halls r dancing the night away.

If you are in Athens, and ınt to sample some local zz or rock, you will find ısters on the walls and ıors of the trendier record ops such as *Melody ouse*, at 88 Odhos Mitro- ıleos, Monastiraki. ıring the Athens stival, you might find interna- ınal bands and performers playing at me of the larger venues – Peter Gabriel ıyed the Odeon of Herodes Atticus in 91.

Athens Festival

e **Athens Festival** runs from mid- ıe to late September, and its main ents are held in the **Odeon of Herodes ticus**. These include symphony con- ts, opera, ballet and sometimes jazz d rock. Remember that this is open- , and you might need a sweater for er in the evening. If you are at the ck, you will find the acoustics excellent, but will be some distance from the stage and might wish to take opera glasses. The tickets allocate you to a row rather than an individual seat, and you should therefore arrive early if you want a central view of the performers. The atmosphere can be really marvellous, with the ancient Roman proscenium stage before you, the floodlit Parthenon behind and the stars above as well as on the stage.

If the performer is a Greek you have never heard of, go – they are often a local hero/ heroine and you will see how emotionally-charged the Greeks can become. Your biggest problem will be getting tickets – the locals will queue all night when tickets go on sale for the big events. Although opera and ballet is not regularly performed in its own house, the new concert hall includes it in its winter programme alongside classical symphony concerts.

International Jazz & Blues Festival

If you are not able to obtain a ticket for the Odeon of Herodes Atticus, there are other open-air theatres in Athens. One of these is near the summit of **Mount Lycabettus**, which hosts the Athens **International Jazz and Blues Festival**

Athens Nightscene

A taverna is a great place to make new friends.

The Athenians love to go out at night. The city gets very hot and stuffy in summer, which encourages their out-of-door mentality, whilst energy is conserved by the afternoon siesta taken between 2 p.m and 5 pm. At 5 p.m or 6 p.m, the streets begin to fill for the evening promenade, and there is no better way to relax after an afternoon spent sight-seeing or on the beach than to sit at a pavement café and watch the siesta-refreshed Athenians meeting their friends.

When Athenians go out at night they do it in style and the evening lasts well into the night. If you are invited out with Greeks, do not expect to be back before 2 a.m, or even 5 a.mif you go dancing – this is the norm even on working weekdays as well as on Saturday nights! Sunday evenings are only slightly more relaxed, and during the summer months y can find the bright lights eve night. Take your dancing sho and have a good time.

Bouzouki Clubs

Athenian *bouzouki* clubs a noisy nightspots where the li band is loudly amplified, t wine flows freely, and cou geous non-Greeks join han with experienced locals in w dances. Plate-smashing banned nowadays, so do r expect it.

Modern Athenian *bouzouki* music is kno as *rebetika* and has its origins in the sleazy ba streets of Piraeus where a curious cocktail courtesans, drug-addicts and sailors broug about a form of Greek Blues, whose orient sounding music came from the Greek imr grants of Asia Minor, and whose song-lyr were drawn from the down-and-outs the selves. In **Plaka** you will find many clubs a *tavernas* playing this music, though in summ the more ambitious musicians head for t islands.

Discotheques

Discos tend not to have an entrance charge, b the price of the first drink pays for the enterta

in June, where you might catch Mikis Theodorakis or some reasonable jazz. Again, it is the setting which really counts. Another open-air venue is the theatre on the slopes of **Philopapp Hill**, opposite the Acropolis. Here Do Stratou found a summer evening ven for her Society of Greek Folk Danci

ent, whilst they become cheaper thereafter. ıey open from 9 p.m onwards and continue ell into the night. You should not go in skimpy ·sts and shorts – the Greeks dress casually but ell, with the men often wearing ties as well as ckets, whilst the women tend to dress in the ternational style of short black dresses, or in arkling stretch fabric in the trendier places. ıe best discos are to be found outside of hens, try the open-air **Aerodhromio** at 25 dos Pergamou, which is close to the airport as e name suggests, this remains open until 4 nwhereas city law closes the downtown dis-s at 2 a.m.

Cultural Activities

art from wining, dining and dancing, there e many different cultural events available in hens; performances by international as well famous Greek artists take place at the **Athens stival**, the **Lykabettos Jazz and Blues Festi-l**, the Sound-and-Light Show on the **Pnyx ll**, the **Dora Stratou Folk Dance Theatre** of ilopappos Hill...or you can watch movies in glish in the open air.

Romantic Retreats

the romantic, take a cab out of town into the rounding mountains, for superb views down to the lights of Athens from high altitude bars d restaurants – but you do not even need to that far; there is a wonderful restaurant ched on the summit of **Mount Lykabettos** Athens itself, which can be reached by cable-. Wander up through **Plaka** towards the **eopagus** on the northwest slopes of the opolis for an atmospheric evening with the rits of antiquity.

d Songs, which was formed to keep eek musical culture alive. Here you n see the whole range of Greek danc-g accompanied by a small orchestra with lute, violin and clarinet.

Theatre & Cinema

Theatre is very popular in Greece, but it is a winter activity, with some thirty to forty companies in repertoire at Athens from September to May.

Subjects of plays tend towards political satire or the classics and there is definitely a language barrier – you would probably become bored unless you were watching a musical.

Cinemas are very popular with the Greeks, who pack out the open-air venues in groups of friends or family. There are often small tables to sit at while waiters serve you snacks and drinks. The films are usually American or British and are not dubbed, and therefore there is no language problem, though you will often find difficulties in concentrating on the soundtrack – children chase one another round your table and there is a high level of chat throughout the film. To experience this in Athens try the **Agli Cinema** in the Zappeion. Indoor cinemas invariably screen pornographic films.

Night-time Illuminations

Sound and Light Shows can be found in Athens, Corfu, Crete and Rhodes. These are primarily intended for foreign tourists, and do not serve food. The subject-matter is a potted and romanticized

Entertainment at its best.

history of the city with coloured floodlights aimed at the local monuments, whilst a soundtrack fills in the visual display with battle-cries and heart-rending music. Your hotel or local tourist office will give details.

Tavernas & Nightclubs

The liveliest nightlife is found in *tavernas* and nightclubs. "Deluxe" *tavernas* have a live orchestra and are often open-air. The music, like the food, is aimed at an international audience, with native songs alternating with well-known songs of the European Song Contest variety – the aim is to get the Germans and Italians singing along with the British and Danes. There is variety with the floor show offering singers, *bouzouki* players and Greek folk-dancing in which you are strongly encouraged to participate. The evening will last from about 9 p.m - 1 a.m and can be fun, but is expensive and "organized" in feel.

Nightclubs are always indoors and tend to get going at around 2300 hours. Nightclub entertainment i more "adult" and cosmopoli tan in its content, with jug glers, acrobats and strip tease delivering a pretty un cultured display. Food an drinks are expensive at both delux *tavernas* and nightclubs, and you migh have a better time at the less "canned smaller *bouzouki tavernas*, which can b found in most areas of Greece. In thes the food and drink is reasonably price and you do not pay for the entertair ment, which consists of a small band c singers and instrumentalists sitting in line on a shallow stage. They are ofte amplified and can be very loud, bu there is generally a relaxed atmospher with the local men often providing ex tra entertainment when moved to spontaneous Greek dance.

Thessaloniki Nights

Thessaloniki also has its winter theat and concert programmes which tak place in the theatres by the White Tow along the waterfront. There is summ drama in the **Garden Theatre**, close the archaeological museum, as well among the pines of the ***Theatrou Kipc*** (Forest Theatre) above the city. A blo inland from the waterfront between th

Bulgarian cabaret troupe pays a visit.

'hite Tower and the Cathedral you will ıd plenty of nightclubs and bars. In ımmer, as at Athens, the livelier enter-.inment venues are found along the ɔast outside of the city, whilst locals so participate in the evening *volta* troll), which takes place between the ɔtunda and the waterfront along **Odos imitriou Gounari**.

Island Inspiration

ıe islands have dozens of cafes and staurants along their streets and in eir squares, and there is often music to company a meal or a drink. Agencies n organized tours advertised in the otels out to *tavernas,* plenty of food and wine as well as musical entertainment, are included in the price. In **Corfu** there is even the recreated traditional "Village" which is hard to avoid when you are touring the island – this has craft shops and a number of *tavernas*. The larger islands have their share of open-air cinemas. For more formal (and expensive) nocturnal entertainment there are casinos, the most famous being at the **Achilleion Palace** to the south of the town – this was used as the casino in the James Bond film *For Your Eyes Only* and you can see why – it is in a beautiful setting of formal gardens, with views down to the lights of Corfu town in the distance. There are no shortage of discos in both the large and small resorts of all the islands.

TRAVEL TIPS

CCOMMODATION

ou can always find somewhere to rest your head Greece. If the hotels are full there are always omfortable rooms available; on the more re- ote islands a child or an old woman will often pproach you, offering accommodation in their wn home. The DIRECTORY deliberately lists nly the higher category hotels, for the reason at from Grade C downwards you are very nlikely to have a restaurant and will have to go ut for meals – also there are many more of these ed & Breakfast type establishments, and it is erefore hard to single any out.

You will find even the higher grade hotels ery reasonably priced. As a rough guide to ices, expect to pay per double room per night: 30/US$45 upwards per double room in A and eluxe hotels; £20/US$30 upwards in B and the etter C hotels; the more basic hotels range etween £10-20/US$15-30 whilst it is possible find private rooms for as little as £6/US$9.

Tip: Take a plug-in electric mosquito-killer th you, together with plenty of poison tablets. summer you will be lucky to find Greek air- nditioning which really works, and thus you ll be sleeping with the windows open!

R TRAVEL

ympic Airways are the Greek national airline d their prices and services tend to be competi- e. Their contact numbers are listed in the RECTORY. Most flights into Greece land at hens, but it is also possible to take direct flights other destinations such as Thessaloniki or the ger islands. Scheduled flights offer the greatest xibility, but are obviously more expensive an charters, which your travel agent will give u details of. A good reason for using Olympic ways is that their international terminal in hens is in the same location as their domestic minal, therefore you do not have to change minals to another destination.

BANKING

Greek banks are open five days a week, from 7:40 a.m - 1:30 p.m. Exceptions can be found in cities and major tourist centers where banks often stay open in the evenings and at week-ends, for currency exchange only. Athens and Thessaloniki have international cash-card machines, which will give drachmas at the current exchange rate plus commission – in Athens try the machines on Syntagma Square.

The banks themselves require you to show a passport, and you will normally have to queue to have the exchange approved, and queue again to collect your cash. The banks charge commis- sion but their rates are better than hotel rates. However, unless you are changing a very large amount, the end results of an exchange are very similar in the hotel and the bank: coming off a little worse in the hotel should be weighed against having to queue for ages clutching your passport in an unfamiliar bank environment

Currency: The Greek unit of currency is the drachma; current exchange rates are approxi- mately 330dr to the £ST and 190dr to the US$. Notes are available in units of; 5,000, 1,000, 500 and 100; coins: 100, 50, 20, 10, 5, 2 and 1.

BUSINESS HOURS

Shopping hours vary a little depending on the type and the season. As a rule of thumb, you can usually count on them being open by 9 a.m and closed by 1:30 p.m. On Tuesdays, Thursdays and Fridays they re-open for three hours in the after- noon, between 5 p.m and 10 p.m. Newspaper kiosks can open whenever they chose and there are some in Athens which never close. Likewise souvenir and folk art shops are free of opening restrictions.

Pharmacies should have a sign on their doors directing you to the nearest one that is open. Mild medicines such as aspirin® can always be bought at kiosks. If you need to visit a government agency, 9 a.m - 12 noon would be the safest time to do so, and you should always allow for long delays.

CAR RENTAL & DRIVING

You can rent a car in nearly every large town or island – your hotel will usually supply recommendations. Greece is quite expensive for car hire; expect to pay around £200/US$300 per week for a modest vehicle. See the DIRECTORY for companies in Athens: they can give you lists of their agents elsewhere. You will be required to pay a cash deposit and to show an International Driver's Licence. Minimum age qualifications vary between 21 and 25.

Major credit cards are generally accepted for payment. Check the small print on your hire contract for insurance fees, tax etc. Some **advice for drivers**: drive on the right; vehicles coming from the right have priority; the accident rate is high, so drive with extra care. **Strange local custom**: in Athens, to combat pollution, cars with registration numbers ending in 1-5 are excluded one day and those from 6-0, the next.

CINEMAS

The only Greek indoor cinemas which stay open in the hot summer months are those showing pornography. Open-air cinemas have two shows per night, with the first starting as it gets dark, followed by the second two or three hours later. Expect to pay about 200dr entrance. Imported films are sub-titled in Greek, therefore going to the movies in Greece is a viable entertainment for the visitor. There is usually a 20-minute intermission for refreshments.

CLIMATE

April to June and September to October are traditionally the best months to visit Greece. Hotels begin to open in earnest from March, and you can often be lucky with a spell of fine weather in late March/early April. Early May is a good time if you are visiting archaeological sites – the sun is not too high, and the Spring flowers are at their best. July and August are the peak beach tourist season, and it can get very hot and crowded. The sea normally remains warm enough for swimming well into October, which is a particularly pleasant time to be in Greece.

Average temperatures: in Athens and southern Greece they range from 12°C/52°F in January/February to 33°C/92°F in July/August. Sunshine hours are not officially recorded, but yo will be unlucky not to see a good deal in th summer months. In Thessaloniki and norther Greece, summer temperatures are similar to th south, whilst the winters are a little colder.

Rainfall averages 406mm of rain annuall in Athens, 374mm of which falls from October t the end of May: only 32mm falls in the summe months, most of it as heavy thunderstorms. Thessaloniki, 452mm annually is the averag with 357mm falling between October and Ma and 95mm in the summer. Corfu is the wette (and greenest!) place in Greece, averagin 1,318mm per year, with 139mm falling in sum mer. For the visitor, more meaningful statisti are the average number of days it rains betwee May and September: Athens (14); Thessaloni (15); Corfu (17). These figures suggest that it rai harder, rather than significantly more often, Corfu.

Perhaps the worst foe for the summer visit is a stiff north-westerly wind known as th ***meltemi***. This hits the eastern mainland coast ar the Aegean islands almost every day from mi July until late August, commencing at about 08(hours and dying down as the sun sets. It reduc the humidity, but it is hot rather than cooling ar strong enough to blow any beach umbrella in outer space. Western Greece is not affected, b is consequently hot and sticky in these mont and you can be plagued by local flies and wasp

CLOTHING

Include a sweater in your luggage whatever t season, as the nights can be very chilly in t summer months. Remember to take stout shoe you are likely to do some walking, as the pat are generally hard and stony underfoot. A fold-u plastic mac is useful in many circumstances picnics as well as rain.

CREDIT CARDS

All major credit cards are accepted in hotels, t bigger shops and top restaurants.

CUSTOMS REGULATIONS

If you are a member of another EEC country, the are no customs restrictions. If arriving from no EEC countries you are allowed:

1. 200 cigarettes or 50 cigars or 100 cigaril or 250gr of tobacco (over-18s only).
2. One litre of alcoholic beverage or tw litres of wines, sparkling wines, lique

(over-18s only).
3. 50gr of perfume and 1/4 litre of eau de cologne.
4. 500gr of coffee or 200gr of coffee extract.
5. 100gr of tea or 40gr of tea extract.
6. Gift articles up to a total value of 45 Ecu or GDR 10,500 (for children under 15 years; 23 Ecu or GDR 5,500).

Prohibited: Plants with soil.

Money restrictions: You are allowed to ke 25,000 drs maximum into Greece, but may ıly export 10,000. There is no limit on foreign ırrencies.

ISABLED TRAVELLERS

reece is not an easy country for those with obility problems. City pavements can be as ızardous as archaeological sites, whilst the and towns and villages tend to have very ırrow thoroughfares. The National Tourist Or-nization of Greece is worth contacting prior to ıvel. They publish a standard questionnaire for sabled visitors to send in advance to hotels to eck for facilities.

As with other tourist destinations, you can ›w choose from a variety of tours specifically ned at the disabled. This is still probably the st way if you wish to tour the sites. In the more mote towns and villages attitudes towards the sabled can be old-fashioned, patronizing or en unkind. However, most Greeks are far too nerous to strangers for this to be the norm, and u will get a lot of assistance wherever you go.

ECTRICITY

reece uses a standard 220 volts A/C, so Euro-an appliances do not require transformers. owever, a plug adaptor is necessary to convert uare to round pins.

TRANCE FEES

ase note that the entrance fees to sites, muse-s etc, supplied in the text, were accurate at the e of writing but are subject to change.

UIPMENT

oculars are useful for visiting sites to look at tant architectural features or ceiling mosaics. ches can also prove surprisingly useful in ilar locations. Handbooks to flora and fauna uld be taken if you are interested in such ıgs at home. A compass can be a winner on n the most modest island walk, as well as when driving.

MEDICAL

No vaccinations are currently required before entering Greece. There are no endemic danger-ous diseases, insects or wildlife in Greece, but it is worth making sure that your tetanus injections are up-to-date. Hotels will call in doctors if necessary.

Health Tips: drink only bottled water; take care with soft cheeses and sea-food (start with a small quantity and build up gradually); salads are unavoidable, but I have never encountered a problem with them; peel and/or wash fruit.

Useful Medical Accessories: insect repellant and anti-mosquito devices; anti-diarrhoea and laxative tablets; anti-histamine for allergic reac-tions to sea-food or insect bites; an elastic band-age for twisted ankles on archaeological sites and cracked pavements; high-factor sun cream and after-sun; good UV protected sun-glasses.

NEWSPAPERS

The ***Athens News***, is the English-language Athe-nian daily; the newspaper summarizes world events and lists theatre, cinema, TV and Radio programmes. The ***Greek Weekly News*** provides similar listings of cultural events. ***The Athenian***, is a monthly magaziine which is sold in the resorts as well as the main cities; the paper includes interesting features on contemporary Greek politics and gossip, as well as good culture listings. Yesterday's foreign newspapers can be bought (at about 3-4 times the home price) from street kiosks.

POSTAL SERVICES

Post offices and collection centers work five days per week, closing at 1430 hours each day. The larger towns and cities have branches which stay open during the evenings and on Saturdays; ask at your hotel.

Greeks use post offices for all sorts of public bill payments, so expect long queues. If you have a letter under 20g, you can buy stamps at the kiosks. Letters are posted in the yellow boxes – take care to use the slot marked *exoteriko* (for-eign). Red boxes are for express letters.

PUBLIC HOLIDAYS

Museums and archaeological sites are generally closed on the main public holidays. Local feast days are too numerous to mention, and you should check locally for public holidays. The main national public holidays cover the major Christian Orthodox religious days, as well as a few national red-letter days:

January 1: Saint Vassilios' Day.
January 6: Epiphany.
March 25: Independence Day; Annunciation.
First Monday of Lent (1994 March 14; 1995 March 6; 1996 February 27).
Easter Weekend (Easter Sunday: 1994 May 1; 1995 April 23; 1996 April 17).
May 1: May Day.
Whit Monday (1994 June 20; 1995 June 12; 1996 June 3).
August 15: Assumption of the Virgin Mary.
October 28: *Ohi* Day
December 25 & 26: Christmas.

See Festivals chapter for further details.

RADIO & TELEVISION

There are two Greek TV channels, ERT I and II which are government-supervised. News bulletins can last up to two hours, punctuated by advertisements. Apart from news programmes, there are Greek serials and old films. You might pick up a foreign serial or film which, as with the cinema, is sub-titled and therefore watchable even if you are not Greek-speaking. Many hotels now carry satellite dishes, so you can pick up English language broadcasts. ERT Radio I has news in English and other languages between 7:40 a.m - 8 a.m every morning.

RELIGIOUS SERVICES

Whatever your religion no one will stop you from attending a Greek Orthodox service on a Sunday morning and there are many to chose from. Besides these, in Athens you will find five main non-Orthodox churches:

Anglican: St Pauls', 29 Philhellinon Street.
Roman Catholic: St Denis's, corner of Panepistimiou and Omirou Streets.
Protestant: St Andrew's (American Interdominational) and Christos Kirche (German evangelical) in Sina Street.

TELEPHONING HOME

If possible, avoid using hotel phones to make long-distance calls. OTE (Hellenic Telecommunications Organization) offices are far cheaper and can be found in most towns and resorts. **Telex** and **telegrams** can also be sent from OTE

TIME DIFFERENCES

Standard Greek time is two hours in advance of Greenwich Mean Time; from the last Sunday in March until the last Sunday in September it is three hours ahead. To work out the time in the United States and Canada, subtract seven hours (eastern standard), eight hours (central), nine hours (Mountain) and ten hours (Pacific).

Australia and New Zealand are in advance of the Greek clock. To calculate Australian time add eight hours (Melbourne and Sydney), seven hours (Brisbane, Canberra and Hobart), six and half hours (Adelaide and Darwin) and five and half hours (Perth). For the time in New Zealand add nine hours.

TIPPING

Restaurants/*tavernas*: Many bills will have the 15% service charge included, so be careful not to add more unless you are particularly happy with the service! The waiter expects his own tip on top of the service charge. The way to deal with this is to do what the Greeks do, and leave the loose change on the plate. Coins left on the table, as opposed to the plate, are for the lad who brings the bread basket.

Hotels: The bill will include services, but you should tip the barman a coin each time you drink, and tip the porter if he hails you a taxi; finally, leave a little something for the chamber maid. Greeks do not tip taxi drivers, though they appreciate keeping small change.

TRAVEL – Domestic Travel

Rail: within Greece the railways can be very picturesque, but are slow and often crowded. The journey on the "express" train from Athens to Thessaloniki, for example, takes 8 hours – the coach takes half-an-hour less and stops for meals and drinks.

Buses: a good way to travel around Greece, so long as you give yourself plenty of time to find the correct departure point and buy your ticket. All the coaches are non-smoking though few are air-conditioned. This is the cheapest and most popular way to travel in Greece, and you will therefore often find standing room only.

City buses: They require you to buy tickets in advance from kiosks: these must be punched when you board the bus, or you will be fined.

Taxi: Especially worthwhile if travelling

elatively short distance and in a group; prices hould be agreed with the driver before leaving nd many will be willing to take you to your estination, wait until you have seen it, and then rive you back, for a very reasonable rate. In the ig cities, taxis are the fastest way to get around, ut are often very hard to find empty because ney are so cheap.

Flying: The most expensive way to travel in ireece, but by far the fastest. If time is at a remium this is an exciting option. Olympic irways have a superb and regular network of nternal flights.

nternational Travel – Road & Sea

Rail: The most expensive option – besides ying – and is only to be recommended if you are avelling on a reduced price ticket (eg as a udent) or if you like that feeling of coming a long ay. Like long-haul coach travel to Greece, the ain can be really uncomfortable, and often gets ery crowded *en route*. It really is worth booking couchette well in advance. You should also be vare of the political situation in former Yugoslaa, since the train route runs through it.

Ferries: They operate from Italy to Greece; e route from Brindisi to Patras (20 hours) is rticularly satisfying, especially if you take the ght boat from Italy and watch the sun rising er the Ionian Islands.

Coach: This is the cheapest way of entering eece from the rest of Europe, be sure however at you have the stamina for a long and rather comfortable trip.

EIGHTS & MEASURES

eece has used the French metric system since 58 of meters, kilometers and liters.

DIRECTORY

AIRLINES

Domestic/International

Olympic Airways
GREECE: Tel:(01) 9666666 (60 lines)

AUSTRALIA: 84 William St, 3000 Victoria, Melbourne (Tel:03-602 5400)
44 Pitt St, NSW 2000, Sydney (Tel: 02-251 1047)

CANADA: 80 Bloor St West, Suite 502, Toronto, ON M5S 2V1 (Tel:416-920-2452)

GREAT BRITAIN: 164 Piccadilly, London W1V 9DE (Tel:071-493 3965)

USA: 647 Fifth Ave, New York, NY 10022 (Tel:212-838-3600)
168 N Michigan Ave, Chicago, IL 60601 (Tel:312-329-0400)
500 Grand St, Suite 1500, Los Angeles, CA 90014 (Tel:212-624-6441)

INTERNATIONAL

Air Canada
Tel:(01) 3223206

Air France
Tel:(01) 3238507-9

Alitalia
Tel:(01) 3229414-9

Americam Airlines
Tel:(01) 3230786-7

Britannia Airways
Tel:(01) 3605920

British Airways
Tel:(01) 3250601

Canadian Airlines International
Tel:(01) 3233825-6

Cathay Pacific
Tel:(01) 3240233

Cyprus Airways
Tel:(01) 3226413-4

Iberia
Tel:(01) 3234523-6

Japan Airlines
Tel:(01) 3248211-3

KLM-Royal Dutch Airlines
Tel:(01) 9380177

Lufthansa German Airlines
Tel:(01) 7716002

Qantas Airways
Tel:(01) 3239063-6

Singapore Airlines
Tel:(01) 3239111-5

Swissair
Tel:(01) 3237581-5

Trans World Airlines
Tel:(01) 3226451

United Airlines
Tel:(01) 9242645-9

Virgin Atlantic Airways
Tel:(01) 3250241

EMBASSIES & CONSULATES

Australia
37 D, Soutsou St,
115 21 Athens
Tel:(01) 6447303

Canada
4 I. Gennadiou St,
115 21 Athens
Tel:(01) 7239511

EEC
2 Vass,Sophias Ave,
106 74 Athens
Tel:(01) 7243982

Ireland
7 Vass. Konstantinou Ave,
106 74 Athens
Tel:(01) 7232771-2

South Africa
124 Kifissias & Iatridou Corr
115 10 Athens
Tel:(01) 6922125

Jnited Kingdom
Ploutarchou St,
06 75 Athens
el:(01) 7236211-9

Inited States of America
1 Vass, Sophias Ave,
15 21 Athens

IOTELS
ategories: Deluxe, A (top) to E
asic)
=swimming pool; b=bar;
=disco/night club; g=roof gar-
en; r=restaurant.

THENS

ristides (C,b)
) Sokratous St, 104 31 Athens
el:(01) 5223881

thenaeum Inter-Continental
)eluxe,*br)
)-93 Syngrou Ave,
7 45 Athens
el:(01) 9023666

thens Center Hotel (B,*brg)
Sofkleous & Klisthenous St,
)5 52 Athens
el:(01) 5248511

hens Hilton (Deluxe,*br)
Vass, Sophias Ave, 115 28
hens
l:(01) 7250201

talos (C,bg)
Athinas St, 105 54 Athens
l:(01) 3212801-3

st Western Athens Gate
brg)
Syngrou Ave, 11742 Athens
l:(01) 9238302-4

rian Inn (B,*brg)
-17 Pireos St, 105 52 Athens
:(01) 5239782

Golden Age (A,br)
57 Michalakopoulou St, 115 28
Athens
Tel:(01) 7240861

Grande Bretagne (Deluxe,br)
Syntagma Sq, 105 63 Athens
Tel:(01) 3230251

King Minos (A,br)
1 Pireos St, 105 52 Omonia Sq,
Athens
Tel:(01) 5231111-18

Nicola (C,bg)
14 Olenou St, 113 62 Athens
Tel:(01) 8837911-2

Novotel Mirayia Athenes
(A,*brg)
4-6 Michail Voda St, 104 39
Athens
Tel:(01) 8627133

Olympic Palace (A,br)
16 Filellinon St, 105 57 Athens
Tel:(01) 3237611

St George Lycabettus
(Deluxe,*brg)
2 Kleomenous St,
106 75 Athens
Tel:(01) 7290711-19

Stanley (B,*brg)
1 Odysseus St, 104 37 Athens
Tel:(01) 5240142-5

ATTICA

Marathon
Golden Coast Hotel (A,*brd-on
beach)
Tel:(0294) 57100

Mount Parnes

Mont Parnes Casino,(A,*brd)
Tel:(01) 2469111-15

Piraeus

Anemoni Hotel (C,b)
65-7 Evripidou & Karaoli
Demetriou Sts, 185 32 Piraeus
Tel:(01) 4130091

Mistral (B,br)
105 Vass, Pavlou Av, 185 33
Piraeus
Tel:(01) 4121425

Sounion
Cape Sounion Beach (A,*bdr-
on private beach)
Tel:(0292) 39391-4

Surf Beach Club (B,*r-on beach)
Tel:(0292) 25778

Vouliagmeni

Armonia & Paradise (A,*br-on
beach)
Tel:(01) 8960105

**Nafsika & Arion Astir Palace
Hotels** (Deluxe,*br-on beach)
Tel:(01) 8960211-9

ATTIC ISLANDS

Aegina
Apollo (B,*br-on beach)
Tel:(0297) 32271-4

Hydra
Miramare Beach (A)
Mandraki beach, 180 40
Tel:(0298) 52300-1

Poros
New Aegli (B,br-on private
beach)
Askeli beach, 18020
Tel:(0298) 22372

CENTRAL GREECE & THESSALY

Ioannina
Oresti's House (A,br-traditional
hostel)
454 53 Ano Pedina
Tel:(0653) 71202

Palladion (B,br)
1 Botsari & 28th October Sts, 454 44 Ioannina
Tel:(0651) 25856

Metsovo
Apollon (C,b)
Central Sq, 442 00
Tel:(0656) 41844

Kalambaka
Divani Kalambaka (A,*br)
Tel:(0432) 9219216

Xenos (B,*br)
Tel:(0432) 24445

Larissa
Divani Palace (A,br)
19 Alex, Papanastassiou St, 412 22
Tel:(041) 26243

Metropol (B,br)
8 Roodsevelt St,
Tel:(041) 229911-5

Lamia
Elena (C)
4 Thermopylon St, 351 00
Tel:(0231) 25025

Volos
Park (B,br)
Dimitriados & 2 Deligiorgi St, 382 21 Volos
Tel:(0421) 36511-5

CRETE

Chania
Panorama (A,*bdr)
5km from Chania,50m from sea
Tel:(0821) 96700-2

Vritomartis Hotel (B,*br)
Next to Samaria Gorge, Chora Sfakion 730 11
Tel:(0825) 91112

Heraklion
Galaxy (A,*bgr)
67 Demokratias Ave, 713 06
Tel:(081) 238812

Rethymnon
Mare Monte Beach (A,*bdr-on beach)
Georgioupolis (26km from Rethymnon) 741 00
Tel:(0825) 61390

Orion Hotel (B,*bgr-on beach)
6.5km from Rethymnon, 74100
Tel:(0831) 71471-4

CYCLADES

Milos
Venus Village (B,*br)
848 00
Tel:(0287) 22030

Mykonos
Cavo Tagoo (A,*br-on beach)
Mykonos Town 846 00
Tel:(0289) 23692-4

Santa Marina Villas (Deluxe,*br-private beach)
Ornos Beach (4km from Mykonos Town), 846 00
Tel:(0289) 23220

Naxos
Naxos Holidays (B,*br-100m from beach)
Ag Georgios, 843 00
Tel:(0285) 24350

Paros
Contaratos Beach Hotel (B,*br-on beach)
Naoussa, 844 01
Tel:(0284) 51693

Yria Hotel (A,*br-80m from beach)
Parikia, 844 00
Tel:(0284) 24154-8

Syros
Delagrazia (B,br-on beach)
Possidonia, 841 00
Tel:(0281) 42811

Dolphin Bay Hotel (A,*bdr-on beach)
Galissas, 841 00
Tel:(0281) 42924

Thira/Santorini
Mediterranean Beach Hote
(B,*br-on beach)
Monolithos, 847 00
Tel:(0286) 31167

Santorini Nine Muses Hote
(A,*br-beach 150m)
Perivolos, Emboriou, 847 00
Tel: (0286) 81781-9

Tinos
Alonia Hotel (B,*br)
500m from town, 842 00
Tel:(0283) 23541-3

Tinos Beach Hotel (A,*br-o beach)
Kionia, 842 00
Tel:(0283) 22626-8

DELPHI
Amalia (A,*br)
Tel:(0265) 82101-5

Vouzas (A,bgr)
Tel:(0265) 9823772

Zeus (B,br)
Tel:(0265) 82691-4

DODECANESE

Kalymnos
Hermes (B)
Mirtees 852 00
Tel:(0243) 47693

Kos
Alexandra (B,bgr)
25th March St
Tel:(0242) 28301-4

Caravia Beach (A,*bdr-beach)
Tel:(0242) 41291-4

eros
'aradise (A)
54 00
'el:(0247) 24718

atmos
atmos Paradise (B,*br)
ampos beach, 855 00
el:(0247) 32624
hodes
elvedere (A,*br)
)n beach, 851 00
el:(0241) 24471

lanousos (B,*br)
ear centre of Rhodes town, 851
0
el:(0241) 22741-5

liramare Beach (Deluxe,*bdr-
n beach)
ia, 851 01
el:(0241) 24251-4

mi
ireus (B,br)
56 00
el:(0241) 71386

ASTERN AEGEAN ISLANDS

nios
ios Chandris Hotel (B,*br)
n the port, 821 00
l:(0271) 25761-5

ytha Resort Hotel (A,*br)
rfas 821 00
l:(0272) 32311-6

sbos
siphae Hotel (B,*br)
lloni (300m from beach) 811

l:(0253)23212-3

mos
ryssa Bay Hotel (A,*br-on
ach)
5km from airport), 831 00
:(0273) 61390

Samos Bay (B,br)
Vathy, 831 00
Tel:(0273) 22101-3

IONIAN ISLANDS

Cephalonia
Cephalonia Palace Hotel (A,*br-on beach)
Tel:(0671) 92555

Corfu (Kerkyra)
Aeolos Beach (B,*bdr-on beach)
6 Mantzavou St, 490 84 Perama
Tel:(0661) 33132-4

Corfu Hilton International
(Deluxe,*br-on beach)
Tel:(0661) 332148

Elea Beach (A,*br-on beach)
490 83 Dassia
Tel:(0661) 93490-3

Ithaki
Mentor (B,bgr)
Tel:(0674) 32795

Lefkas
Lefkas (B,br)
Tel:(0645) 23916-8

Paxos
Paxos Beach (B,br)
Tel:(0662) 31211

Zakynthos (Zante)
Caravel Hotel (A,*br-on Alexandras beach)
Tel:(0695) 25261-5

Galaxy (B,br-private beach, Laganas)
Tel:(0695) 51171-3

MACEDONIA AND THRACE

Alexandroupolis
Alexander Beach Hotel (B)
Tel:(0551) 39290-5

Edhessa
Katarraktes (B,bgr)
4 Karanou St, 582 00
Tel:(0381) 22300-2

Kastoria
Tsamis (B,br)
Tel:(0467) 43334

Xenia du Lac (A,br)
Platia Dexamenis, 521 00
Tel: (0467) 22565

Katerini
Alkyon (B,br-on beach)
Tel:(0351) 61613

Kavalla
Oceanis (B,*bdgr)
32 Erythrou Stavrou Av, 654 03
Tel:(051) 221981-5

Tosca Beach (A,br)
Myrmigia (5km from Kavala), 655 00
Tel:(051) 244765-8

Komotini
Anatolia (B,br)
53 Anchialou St, 691 00
Tel:(0531) 36242-7

Naousa
Vermion (B,br)
Ag Nikolaos (2km from Naousa), 59200
Tel:(0332) 29311-4

Soufli
Orpheus (C)
68400
Tel:(0554) 22305

Veroia
Makedonia (B,bgr)
50 Kontogeorgaki St., 591 00
Tel:(0331) 66902

Xanthi
Nestos (B,bdr)
1 Kavalas Ave, 671 00
Tel:(0541) 27531-5

NORTHWEST GREECE

Amphissa
Amfissaeum (C)
Tel:(0265) 22161

Arta
Xenia (B,br)
Tel:(0681) 27413

Galaxidhi
Villa Olympia (A,*br)
Tel:(0265) 41174

Igoumenitsa
Mega Ammos (B,*br)
Tel:(0665) 93447-8

Mesolongi
Theoxenia (B,bgr-on beach)
Tel:(0631) 28098

Naupaktos
Amaryllis (B,br)
Tel:(0634) 27237

Xenia (B,br)
Tel: (0634) 22301-2

Parga
Lichnou Beach (B,br)
Tel:(0682) 31257

Parga Beach (B,br)
Tel:(0682) 31410

Preveza
Poseidon Beach Hotel (C,br-on beach)
Tel:(0682) 51291

Preveza Beach Hotel Club (B,*bdr-on beach)
Tel:(0682) 51261

Regina Mare (A,*bdr-beach)
Tel:(0665) 91118

PELOPONNESE

Corinth
Kalamaki Beach (A,bdr)
200 10 Paleo Kalamaki
Tel:(0741) 37331-4

Epidaurus
Xenia (B,br)
Tel:(0753) 22003-5

Kalamata
Elite Village (A,*bdr-on beach)
Tel:(0721) 22434

Filoxenia Hotel (B,*bdr-on beach)
Tel:(0721) 23166-8

Nafplion
Agamemnon (B,br)
Tel:(0752) 28021-2

Xenia (A,*bdr-beach)
Tel:(0752) 28981-5

Olympia
Andonios (A,*br)
Tel:(0624) 22348-9

Olympic Village (B,*bdr)
Tel:(0624) 22211-2

Patras
Astir Hotel (A,*br)
16 Ag Andreou St, 262 23 Patras
Tel:(061) 277502

Club Florida Hotel (B,*bdr)
Psathopyrgos, 265 00 Patras
Tel:(061) 931279

Sparta
Maniatis (C,br)
72 Con. Paleologou Ave & Lykourgou Ave
Tel:(0731) 22665

Menelaion (B,br)
91 K Paleologou St
Tel:(0731) 22161-5

SPORADES AND EUBOEA

Euboea (Evia)

Hilda (B,br)
Favierou & Goviou corner, 341 00 Khalkis
Tel:(0221) 28111

Karystos Beach (B,*bdr)
Bouros, 340 01 Karistos
Tel:(0224) 23141-4

Pelagos Hotel (A,*bdr-on beac
of St Minas)
Ag Minas, 34100 Khalkis
Tel:(0221) 98595

Lemnos (Limnos)
Akti Myrina (Deluxe,*br-o
beach)
Tel:(0254) 22681-5

Castro (B,br)
Mirina
Tel: (0254) 22772

Samothraki
Eolos Hotel (B,*bdr)
Kamariotissa, 680 02
Tel:(0551) 41595

Skiathos
Plaza (B,*bgr)
Kanapitsa, 370 02
Tel:(0427) 21971-4

Skiathos Palace (Deluxe,*bdr
Koukounaries Beach
Tel:(0427) 3242152

Skopelos
Dionyssos (B,*br)
370 03
Tel:(0424) 22243

Prince Stafylos (B,*br)
Livadi, 370 03
Tel:(0424) 22775

Skyros
Skiros Palace (A,*br-on beac
Girismata, 340 07
Tel:(0222) 91994

Thasos
Alexandra Beach (A,*bgr)
Potos 640 02
Tel:(0593) 523 91

Miramare (B,*br)
Potamia 640 04
Tel:(0593) 61040-3

THESSALONIKI

Capsis Hotel (B,*br)
18 Monastirou St, 546 29 Thessaloniki
Tel: (031) 521321-9

Makedonia Palace (Deluxe,br)
Meg Alexandrou St, 546 40 Thessaloniki
Tel:(031) 837520-9
Nepheli (A,bgr)
Komninon St, 552 36 Panorama
Tel: (031) 342024

RENT-A-CAR OFFICES

AI-ANSA RENT A CAR
3 Syngrou Ave,
1743 Athens
Tel:(01) 3248004

Elefteriou Venizelou St,
91 00 Corfu
Tel:(0661) 40390

9 Laskaratou St,
46 46 Thessaloniki
Tel:(031) 419109

AVIS
8 Amalias Ave,
05 58 Athens
Tel:(01) 3224951-5

HERTZ
76A Vouliagmenis Ave,
54 51 Argyrpoulis
Tel:(01) 9942850-9

INTERRENT-EUROPCAR
Syngrou Ave,
17 42 Athens
Tel:(01) 9215788-9

25th August St,
Heraklion, Crete
Tel:(081) 225291

28th October St,
Rhodes
Tel:(0241) 21958

TOURISM & TRAVEL ORGANIZATIONS

Greek National Tourist Organization (GNTO): Offices Abroad

Australia and New Zealand
GNTO, 51 Pitt St,
Sydney NSW 2000
Tel:(02) 2411663

Canada
GNTO,1300 Bay St,
Toronto, Ontario M5R 3K8
Tel:(416) 968 2220

United Kingdom & Ireland
GNTO,4 Conduit St,
London W1R ODJ
Tel:(071)7345997

United States of America

GNTO, 645 Fifth Ave,
New York NY 10022
Tel:(212) 4215777

GNTO,168 North Michigan Ave, Suite 600,
Chicago, Illinois 60601
Tel:(312) 7821084

GNTO,611 West Sixth St, Suite 2198,
Los Angeles, California 90017
Tel:(213) 6266696

Greek National Tourist Organization (GNTO): Offices in Greece

Athens
2 Kar, Servias St (inside National Bank)
Tel:(01) 3222545

1 Voukourestiou St
Tel:(01) 3234467

4 Stadiou St, Spyromiliou Arcade
Tel:(01) 3221459

1 Ermou St (inside General Bank)
Tel:(01) 3234130

East Hellenikon Airport
Tel:(01) 9702395

Corfu
15 Zavitsianou St
Tel:(0661) 37520

Heraklion (Crete)
1 Xanthoulidou St,
Tel:(081) 228225
Ioannina
2 Nap, Zerva St
Tel:(0651) 25086

Larissa
18 Koumoundourou St
Tel:(041) 250919

Patras
Iroon Polytechniou St, Glyfada
Tel:(061) 423866

Piraeus
Marina Zeas, NTOG Bldg
Tel:4135716

Rhodes
Archbishop Makarios & Papagou Streets
Tel:(0241) 23655

Samos
425th Martiou St,
Tel:(0273) 28582

Thessaloniki
34 Metropoleos St,
Tel:(031) 271888

Airport
Tel:(031) 471170

PHOTO CREDITS

Antiques of Orient : 19, 20
Bio Foto/Benny Gensbol : 75 (left top), 75 (left bottom)
Bio Foto/Lars Gejl : 75, 76
Randa Bishop : xi, 72, 82, 83, 85, 90, 92, 95, 98, 100, 101, 102, 105, 108, 109, 126, 128, 130 (right), 135, 178, 183, 186, 192, 202, 292, 294, 295, 332, 344, 348, 352
Maxine Cass : 28, 30/31, 104, 169, 199, 245
Greg Evans/K R Dovell : 138
Greg Evans/Greg Balfour Evans : xv, 11, 12, 48, 53, 54, 62, 86, 171, 196, 218/219, 221, 268, 287, 290, 300, 306, 308, 317, 318/319, 324, 333, 336, 353, Backcover (top, right), Backcover (bottom)
Greg Evans/John Flowerdew : x (bottom), 280, 314, 323, 328
Greg Evans/Sally Higgins : 56, 64/65
Greg Evans/Miwako Ikeda : 134, Backcover (top, left)
Greg Evans/A. Meadley : 312
Greg Evans/Colin Patterson : 4, 222, 320, 322
Greg Evans/Melvin Rutter : 10, 310
Greg Evans/Monica Wells : 3, 8, 74, 195, 204, 214, 220, 226, 228, 236, 330/331, 338, 341, x (top)
Photostock/S. Garnier : 106, 114, 131 (right top)
Carl Purcell : 32, 40, 46, 50/51, 119, 130 (left), 131 (left), 131 (Right bottom), 149, 154, 165, 166, 194, 198, 201, 203, 208, 286, 342
Spectrum : xii, xiii, xiv, xvi/xvii, 33, 38 (top), 38 (bottom), 39, 44, 52, 58/59, 66, 68, 69, 71, 78, 84/85, 91, 111, 129, 141, 144, 147, 150, 153, 157, 164, 172, 175 (top), 176, 206, 209, 210, 211, 213, 232, 234/235, 250, 252, 256, 260, 265, 267, 268/269, 271, 272, 273, 274, 275, 276, 279, 285, 298, 302, 309, 311, 316, 327, 346, 350, 354, Front endpaper, Back endpaper
Spectrum/David Askham : 14 (top), 14 (bottom), 23, 24, 187, 188, 237, 240, 243, 264
Spectrum/T. Boxall : xviii
Spectrum/M. Dubin :25
Spectrum/Dallas & John Heaton : 2, 16/17, 160/161, 254/255, 284, 304, 334
Spectrum/Rethimnon : 7
Spectrum/G. Sykes : 132
Bill Wassman : 116/117, 162, 175 (bottom), 182, 190, 224, 293, 340

INDEX